WILD MAJESTY

Wild Majesty

Encounters with Caribs from Columbus to the Present Day

AN ANTHOLOGY

Edited by Peter Hulme and Neil L. Whitehead

CLARENDON PRESS · OXFORD
1992

Oxford University Press, Walton Street, Oxford OX2 6DP

Oxford New York Toronto
Delhi Bombay Calcutta Madras Karachi
Petaling Jaya Singapore Hong Kong Tokyo
Nairobi Dar es Salaam Cape Town
Melbourne Auckland

and associated companies in
Berlin Ibadan

Oxford is a trade mark of Oxford University Press

Published in the United States
by Oxford University Press, New York

British Library Cataloguing in Publication Data
Data available

Library of Congress Cataloging in Publication Data
Wild Majesty: encounters with Caribs from Columbus to the present
day: an anthology / edited by Peter Hulme and Neil L. Whitehead.
Includes bibliographical references and index.
1. Black Carib Indians—History—Sources.   2. Carib Indians—
History—Sources.   3. Indians of the West Indies—History—Sources.
I. Hulme, Peter.   II. Whitehead, Neil L.
F2001.W58   1992
972.9'004984—dc20   91–39625

ISBN 0–19–811226–2 (hbk)
ISBN 0–19–812274–8 (pbk)

Typeset by Selwood Systems, Midsomer Norton, Avon

Printed in Great Britain by
Butler & Tanner Ltd
Frome and London

*To commemorate 500 years of
Carib survival on the islands of
Dominica and St Vincent*

Acknowledgements

Formal permissions to republish written material are acknowledged towards the end of this book. Here we would like to thank a number of people for their assistance with this project: members of the Carib Council in Dominica, especially Garnette Joseph; also in Dominica, Patrick Henderson, Lennox Honychurch, and Sister Irene Amirault—for access to various papers in the Bishop's House, Roseau, especially Father Raymond Proesman's manuscript history of Dominica; in Puerto Rico, Jalil Sued Badillo for transcripts of material from the Archivo General de Indias (Seville); in Paris, Donna Evleth, for transcription of material from the Archives Nationales, and Paul Milcent of the Archives Eudistes. We are also grateful to Elizabeth Weall for much of the typing, Phillip Morris and Michael Dudley for photography, Lesley Theophilus for compiling the index, and Andrew Lockett and Frances Whistler of Oxford University Press for their help and support.

A number of libraries were extremely helpful, especially the British Library, the Bodleian, and the libraries of the Royal Commonwealth Society, the Institute of Commonwealth Studies, Rhodes House, the Natural History Museum, and the British Film Institute.

For financial assistance Peter Hulme would like to thank the British Academy and the University of Essex Research Endowment Fund; Neil Whitehead would like to thank the H. F. Guggenheim Foundation.

Contents

List of Illustrations

Introduction

'Wilde Majesty' was a phrase used by the writer Samuel Purchas in the margin of his seventeenth-century compilation of English voyages. He was commenting on John Layfield's description of a native king on the island of Dominica, wild by nature, majestic in appearance.

In 1992 various European and American countries choose to celebrate the voyage made by Christopher Columbus, in the service of Castile, to the part of the world subsequently known as the continent of America. Columbus first set foot in what was for Europe a 'new world' in the islands of the Caribbean. Five hundred years later the few descendants of the then inhabitants of those islands—in common with native Americans throughout the continent—mourn rather than celebrate the quincentenary of Columbus's arrival. If anything is to be celebrated, it must surely be the survival of these native Caribbean groups, against all odds and against constant predictions of their imminent demise.

The history of the Caribbean over the last 500 years is one of extraordinary complexity, an intricate tapestry of events still far from fully understood. In the century and a half after 1492, many thousands of Caribbean islanders died, some savagely killed in the early years of Spanish occupation, many more succumbing to diseases against which they had no immunity. Some fled from the major islands of Spanish settlement—Española, Cuba, Puerto Rico, Jamaica—or into the remoter parts of these islands; others no doubt adapted themselves to life as 'Christian' peasants, soon inconspicuous amongst the ethnic diversity of European, Canarian, and African arrivals. The small flat islands to the north, known now as the Bahamas, were soon depopulated in the search for slaves. The mostly mountainous islands to the south and east (usually known in English as the Lesser Antilles) were never settled by the Spanish. England and France, amongst other European nations and groups, contested them from early in the seventeenth century, meeting stout resistance from the islanders referred to in English sources as 'the Caribs'. These islands were only finally 'pacified' at the end of the eighteenth century, when several thousand so-called Black Caribs were transported to the coast of Central

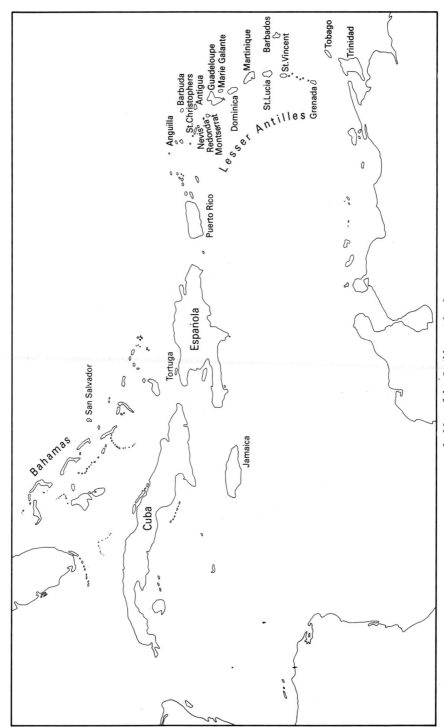

1. Map of the Caribbean islands.

America, from where their descendants spread both north and south. Left on the Caribbean islands were small groups of Caribs, principally on St Vincent (where they were referred to as 'Yellow' or 'Red' Caribs) and Dominica, where they still live.

This book is not a history of the Caribs or even of their contact with Europeans. Rather, these pages provide, in the form of an anthology, some of the materials with which such histories would have to contend, hewing from them and constructing with them some plausible account of a long and fraught relationship, which is not yet finished.

There are many difficult questions the book does not address, most notably the whole problem of the definition and use of the word 'Carib' in the fifteenth and subsequent centuries. For many years, indeed for many centuries, outsiders have imposed a cultural schema on the native Caribbean, separating the 'peaceful' Arawaks of the larger islands to the west and north from the 'fierce', in fact 'cannibalistic', Caribs of the south and east. 'Carib', or some variant such as 'Caniba', was taken as so clearly synonymous with the practice of man-eating that the word 'cannibalism' (and its cognates) replaced 'anthropophagy' in most European languages.

This schema has recently shown signs of collapsing under the weight of its own contradictions, not the least of which is that the language spoken by these 'Island Caribs' was—and in the case of the Central American Black Caribs still is—a language affiliated to Arawakan rather than Cariban linguistic stock; just as they show a greater cultural homology to Arawakan than to Cariban peoples. The old story of ferocious Caribs chasing timid Arawaks up the island chain from Venezuela, eating the men and possessing the women, is endlessly repeated in history primers and magazine articles, but fewer and fewer scholars will accept it. No new consensus has yet emerged, but recent work on the subtleties of cultural identity will ensure that any new version is more nuanced than the old, and less wedded to the stereotypes that served European colonialism so stalwartly.

Any full history or ethnography of the Caribs, however defined, would have to tackle such problematic issues. Our focus here allows them to stand to one side, although the materials in the anthology no doubt themselves suggest several possible lines of approach. Whatever may have been the situation in the fifteenth century, it is clear that by 1650 'Carib' had become as much a political category as a cultural one. Political alliances, cultural and social features, and a sense of ethnic identity were to an important degree the product of interaction with and resistance to European forces. This sense of a unique ethnic identity forged in contestation is strengthened by our retrospective angle of vision in focusing on accounts of contact with native islanders who might reasonably be thought of as ancestors of the surviving groups on Dominica and St Vincent. Two possible bodies of material are thereby excluded: those relating to the collateral branch of Black Caribs now in Central America—

theirs is, since 1797, a different and fascinating story; and those relating to Grenada, Trinidad, and South America, where groups referred to by the name 'Carib' (belonging to the Cariban language family and calling themselves Kariña) lived and in some cases continue to live. The nature of the interaction between the mainland Kariña and the 'Caribs' of the islands—including 'Island Carib' settlement on the mainland—is still a matter of dispute on which many ethnohistorical questions turn. Our backward-projecting parameters exclude accounts of European contact with these mainland groups, a massive body of written material in several languages.

One result of these exclusions is that the term 'Carib' is henceforth used in our text to refer to the indigenous inhabitants of the Lesser Antilles, a necessary simplification for a book of this kind, given the term's historical resonance, but one that should be recognized as covering a multitude of uncertainties. As a step towards such recognition we have chosen in the extracts that follow to give the word or words usually reproduced or translated as 'Carib' in a form as close as possible to the original transcription. In that way questions of ethnic and cultural identity and affiliation are left as open as possible.

Wild Majesty is not a history of the relations between Caribs and outsiders, but it does certainly provide the narratives which embodied, and continue to embody, a powerful series of Western ideologies *about* the Caribs. These narratives are the lenses through which outsiders have seen, and continue to see, the Caribs. In that sense the book is a history of Western perceptions of the Caribs. All the passages say something about Caribs; but they also speak, though less directly, of what the native people of the islands have meant to travellers of different kinds, soldiers, missionaries, government officials, anthropologists, sailors, writers, tourists, film-makers.

For Europe, the Caribs have always been special, though in different ways. For a long time they symbolized the most extreme form of savagery. Truculent by nature and eating human flesh by inclination, they stood opposed to all the tenets of Christian and civilized behaviour. The Enlightenment tended to draw back from this judgement. The lengthy and often idealizing accounts produced by French missionaries provided Jean-Jacques Rousseau with the ethnological support for his elucidation of the 'state of nature', an originary condition in which are apparent many primary human 'qualities'—to which Rousseau would attach no moral dimension. A third major phase has focused on the fate of this 'once powerful race' in its 'final home'. The 'last remnants' of the Caribs have been on their way out since the middle of the eighteenth century. The Carib 'Reserve' established on Dominica in 1903 has provided a physical focus which has enabled the recent cultural revival to take place, but has also provided a site to which travellers have come as elegists.

The division of our material reflects these phases as well as respecting the pattern of historical interaction. The five sections are roughly chronological, though with some overlap in places. The first section, though broad in years covered, deals with the early contacts made by the three major European

4

nations active in the Caribbean: the Spanish—to whom Columbus reported hearing of what he later took to be Caribs on the very first day of his arrival in America—and the English and French who, after initial contacts through watering and shipwreck and reconnaissance, both made their first concerted efforts at settlement on the islands in 1625.

The second section consists principally of the accounts written by (mainly Catholic) missionaries who often spent considerable amounts of time with the Caribs during the course of the seventeenth and early eighteenth centuries. These are often valuable proto-ethnographic descriptions, but they describe a culture already considerably altered from its state (if one can indeed truly speak of a *single* culture) in 1492.

From a British point of view the Caribs became a pressing problem after the Treaty of Paris in 1763 had put Tobago, Grenada, St Vincent, and Dominica into British hands. St Vincent, in particular, had potentially valuable land (for sugar-growing) which was controlled by the group referred to in British sources as the Black Caribs, a mixed group which resulted, so the story went, from the hospitality shown by Caribs to escaped or shipwrecked Africans. A 'Carib War' resulted in the 1770s, with an uneasy peace. War again broke out in the 1790s and, after massive infusions of arms and men from England had tipped the military balance, the Black Caribs were defeated, transported in large numbers to a concentration camp on the neighbouring island of Balliceaux, and finally shipped to Roatán, off the coast of Honduras. The third section consists of texts relating to these events and their aftermath.

Little interest was shown by Europeans in Caribs throughout most of the nineteenth century; a few Catholic priests are almost the only sources of information, and their letters and reports begin the fourth section, preceding the work of Frederick Ober, the US ornithologist who turned himself into the first modern travel-writer in the Caribbean. The other documents in this section relate to the establishment of the Carib Reserve (now called Carib Territory) on the north-east coast of Dominica in 1903 by the colonial Administrator of the island, Henry Hesketh Bell.

The final section begins in 1930 with extensive consideration of the most recent 'Carib War', an event that still has an important place in Carib perceptions of their relationships to a whole series of governments in London and Roseau, Dominica's capital. The post-war texts demonstrate a marked continuity in writers' concerns, while also briefly documenting Carib appearances in the visual media. A growing cultural awareness is witnessed during the most recent encounters.

Our principles of selection have been as follows. In all cases we have chosen eyewitness accounts, not out of a sense that these are necessarily more 'accurate', but because we are interested here in the implicit ethnography of the languages of travel and observation. All 'eyewitnesses' are in any case reliant on hearsay, 'common knowledge', and prior reading. Almost all our writers, however tentative their statements, become an 'authority' for someone else.

We have tried to represent all the writers generally recognized as 'major', at the same time as introducing lesser-known material from colonial archives and elsewhere. We have avoided thematic repetitions which would be tedious, while being alert to the ways in which certain stories and stereotypes have become established only through repetition.

In the one case where a near-contemporary English translation of a foreign-language source exists (John Davies's of Rochefort), we have used it. Elsewhere we have made our own translations, choosing literal meaning over stylistic grace wherever necessary. A few native Caribbean words have passed into English, others appear untranslated in italics; a note on some native Caribbean words can be found at the back of the anthology. With the older English texts we have reproduced from manuscript or original edition where possible, from standard editions of the time where not. In all cases we have remained as faithful as possible to the chosen transcription. Punctuation and spelling have not been modernized except where specifically noted. We have tried to respect the original texts by giving lengthy passages of continuous prose: our excisions are marked [...]. Occasional editorial inserts for clarification are also included in square brackets. Footnotes indicated by symbols belong to the original texts: marginal notes have become footnotes, we have silently suppressed those that seemed irrelevant to this anthology, and have changed numbers to symbols. We have deliberately avoided exegesis of the texts; our own numbered footnotes are limited to necessary clarification and elucidation. Historical and ethnological contextualization continues in the introductions to the five parts of the anthology; in our brief introductory passage to each text we have attempted to cover major matters of contention and to explain any especially problematic references. The only abbreviations used refer to major European archive collections: Archivo General de Indias (Seville) = AGI; Archives Nationales (Paris) = ANP; Calendar of State Papers (Colonial, America, and West Indies) = CSP.

PART I

The first part of the anthology includes materials relating to the earliest encounters between Caribs and Europeans. It begins with Columbus's first voyage to the Caribbean in 1492 and ends over a century later in 1607, on the eve of the first permanent French and English settlements in the region.

The Columbus material is relatively well known historically, as testimony concerning the early European conquest and settlement of the Caribbean, but it is less well understood anthropologically, as a source for the first evidence, however difficult to interpret, of native dispositions, terminologies, and social relationships. The *Letter* (No. 1), widely disseminated at the end of the fifteenth century, is included in its entirety in order to give Columbus's own summary account of his voyage. Extracts from the *Journal* (No. 2), not known until the nineteenth century, are intended to allow a more nuanced sense of Columbus's changing perceptions of the native peoples in the Caribbean. The *Report* (No. 3) of Chanca, a companion of Columbus on his second voyage, in turn represents a growing confidence, on the part of the European interlopers, as to their grasp of the ethnographic complexities of the native Caribbean. Here, the distinction between 'caribes' and other Amerindians begins to receive systematic expression.

Given the importance of evidence about native categories that such materials encapsulate, we have kept (and italicized) all the native words, though their precise referents are not always clear, in order to impose as little interpretation as possible; a practice that is not usually adhered to even in the most historiographically competent editions of the materials relating to Columbus. These procedures bring out the fluidity of forms used by Columbus and his contemporaries in their recording of native categories, though they have not been applied in the case of Spanish toponyms.

Although nearly 100 years passes between the *Report* of Chanca and the date of our next extract relating to the captivity of Luisa de Navarrete (No. 4), the information she gives in many ways represents a summary of those attitudes and relationships that had grown up between the colonizers and the Caribs during the intervening period. Thus her description has been selected as much on account of its notoriety as for its possible ethnographic value.

This hiatus in the Spanish-language accounts is partially offset by the variety of reports, from the 1560s onwards, that start emerging as a result of French and English penetration into the Americas (No. 5). While the early ethnographic schemas of the Spanish accounts have obviously been influential in structuring the perceptions of these early voyagers, new perspectives on the character of Carib society begin to emerge. However, as the accounts of English adventures on St Lucia at the turn of the seventeenth century show (No. 6), the Caribs, whatever their ethnographic curiosities, remained a potent source of resistance to unhindered European occupation of the region.

Further Reading

For a more extensive anthology of writings about this early period, see Tyler 1988. For general studies of the period, see Sauer 1966, Sued Badillo 1978*b*, and, specifically on Dominica, Boromé 1966. On native use of and commerce in gold-work, see Nagy 1982–3 and Whitehead 1990b. On the question of native cannibalism, Myers 1984, Whitehead 1984, Hulme 1986. On Luisa de Navarrete, Alegría 1980.

1. *The Letter of Columbus (1493)*

¶ *When Christopher Columbus (1451–1506) sailed west from Spain in the late summer of 1492 he expected to find Asia. Instead he ended up in that part of the world that eventually became known in English as the Caribbean. On his return voyage, Columbus wrote a letter to Luis de Santángel, clerk to the Catholic Kings, Ferdinand and Isabella, who had partly financed his voyage. For obvious reasons the* Letter *puts the best possible gloss on the events of those months. This* Letter *was published in Barcelona later in 1493 and, in Latin translation, became the principal means by which Columbus's news was disseminated throughout Europe, with nine editions before the end of 1494, in cities such as Antwerp, Basle, and Paris.*

According to Columbus, the first European contact with the Caribbean islanders was for the most part peaceful. Both sides were wary but curious, gifts were exchanged, hospitality offered and accepted. The emphasis in the Letter *is on the beauty of the islands and the variety of their natural resources, trees, plants, spices, and—most important of all—precious metals. The people are described as naked and timid, ignorant of weapons, but with a natural goodness which inclines them towards Christianity. Towards the end of the* Letter, *Columbus says that he has found no monsters, nor heard of any except on 'una isla que es Carib', an island which is* Carib, *and which becomes* Charis *or* Quaris *in the Latin editions. In fact, elsewhere in the* Letter *he mentions reports of people with tails and with no hair. However, pre-eminent amongst the repertory of medieval monsters were the Anthropophagi, man-eaters who had featured in classical writers such as Herodotus, and it is to this monstrosity alone that Columbus chooses to draw attention. The association between the name 'Carib' and the practice of eating human flesh has its beginning here, in this paragraph of Columbus's* Letter.

SIR:

Since I know that you will be pleased at the great victory with which Our Lord has crowned my voyage, I write this to you, from which you will learn how in thirty-three days I reached the Indies, with the fleet which the most illustrious King and Queen, our Sovereigns, gave to me. There I found very many islands, filled with people without number, and I have taken possession of them all for Their Highnesses, by proclamation and with the royal standard unfurled, and no objection was offered to me.

To the first island which I found I gave the name Sant Salvador, in remembrance of the Divine Majesty, who has marvellously bestowed all this; the indians call it *Guanahaní*. To the second, I gave the name Isla de Santa María de Concepción, to the third, Ferrandina, to the fourth Isabela, to the fifth La Isla Juana, and so each received a new name.

When I reached Juana, I followed its coast to the westward, and I found it to be so big that I thought that it must be the mainland, the province of Cathay. And since there were neither towns nor villages on the seashore, but small settlements only, with the people of which I could not have speech because they all fled immediately, I went forward on the same course, thinking that I could not fail to find great cities or towns; and at the end of many leagues, seeing that there was no change and that the coast was bearing me northwards, which was contrary to my will, since winter was already in the air, and I proposed to make to the south, and moreover, the wind was carrying me forward, I determined not to wait for a change in the weather and turned back as far as a notable harbour, from where I sent two men inland to learn if there were a king or great cities. They travelled three days' journey, and found an infinite number of small settlements and people without number, but nothing with organization, for which reason they returned.

I understood sufficiently from other Indians, whom I had already taken, that this land was nothing but an island, and I therefore followed its coast eastward for 107 leagues to the point where it ended; from which point I saw another island to the east, distant about eighteen leagues from the first, to the east, and to it I at once gave the name La Spañola; and I went there and followed its northern part, as I had followed that of Juana to the eastward for 188 great leagues in a straight line. This island and all the others are very fertile to an excessive degree, and this island is extremely so; in it there are many harbours on the coast of the sea, beyond comparison with others that I know in Christendom, and many rivers, good and large, which is marvellous; its lands are high; there are in it many sierras and very high mountains, beyond comparison with the island of Tenerife, all very beautiful, of a thousand shapes, and all accessible and filled with trees of a thousand kinds and tall, seeming to touch the sky; and I am told that they never lose their foliage, which I can believe, for I saw them as green and lovely as they are in Spain in May, and some of them were flowering, some bearing fruit, and some at another stage, according to their quality. The nightingale was singing and other little birds of a thousand kinds,

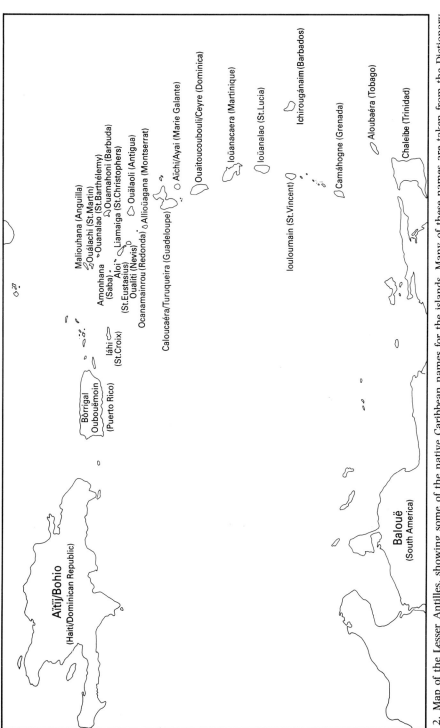

Maliouhana (Anguilla)
Ouálachi (St.Martin)
Ouanalao (St.Barthélemy)
Amonhana   Ouamahoni (Barbuda)
(Saba)   Liamaiga (St.Christophers)
Aloi
(St.Eustasius)   Ouálaoli (Antigua)
Oualiti (Nevis)
Ocanamainrou (Redonda) Allioüagana (Montserrat)

Caloucaéra/Turuqueira (Guadeloupe)
Aïchi/Ayai (Marie Galante)
Ouaitoucoubouli/Ceyre (Dominica)

Ioüanacaera (Martinique)

Ioüanalao (St.Lucia)

Ichirougánaim (Barbados)

Iouloumain (St.Vincent)

Camáhogne (Grenada)

Aloubaéra (Tobago)

Chaleibe (Trinidad)

Aïtïj/Bohio
(Haiti/Dominican Republic)

Bôrrigal
Oubouémoin
(Puerto Rico)

Iáhi
(St.Croix)

Baloüé
(South America)

2. Map of the Lesser Antilles, showing some of the native Caribbean names for the islands. Many of these names are taken from the Dictionary compiled in the seventeenth century by Raymond Breton (1665), but earlier material is also included.

in the month of November, there where I went. There are six or eight kinds of palm, which are a wonder to behold on account of their beautiful variety, but so are the other trees and fruits and plants. In it are marvellous pine groves, and there are very wide champaigns, and there is honey, and birds of many kinds and fruits of great variety. In the interior, there are mines of metals, and the population is without number.

La Spañola is a marvel. The sierras and the mountains and the plains and the champaigns and the lands [are] so lovely and so rich for planting and sowing, for breeding cattle of every kind, for building towns and villages. The harbours of the sea here would not be believed without being seen, and so with the rivers, many and great, and with good water, most of which bear gold. In the trees and fruits and plants, there are great differences from those of Juana: on this island, there are many spices and great mines of gold and of other metals.

The people of this island and of all the other islands which I have found and of which I have (or do not have) information, all go naked, men and women, just as their mothers bore them, although some of the women cover a single place with the leaf of a plant or with a net of cotton which they make for the purpose. They have no iron or steel or weapons, nor are they fitted to use them; not because they are not well built and of handsome stature, but because they are extraordinarily timorous. They have no other arms except arms made of canes, [cut] in seeding time, to the ends of which they fix a small sharp stick, and they do not dare to make use of them, for many times it has happened that I have sent ashore two or three men to some town to have speech with them, and countless people have come out to them, and as soon as they have seen them [my men] approaching, they have fled, a father not even waiting for his son. This is not because ill has been done to any one of them; on the contrary, at every place where I have been and have been able to have speech with them, I have given to them of everything that I had, such as cloth and many other things, receiving nothing in exchange; but this is how they are, incurably timid. It is true that, after they become reassured and lose this fear, they are so guileless and so generous with all that they possess, that no one would believe it who has not seen it. Of anything they have, if they are asked for it, they never say no, on the contrary they invite the person to share it and display as much love as if they would give their hearts and, whether it be of value or small price, they are immediately content with whatever trifle of whatever kind may be given to them. I forbade that they should be given things so worthless as pieces of broken crockery, and pieces of broken glass and ends of straps; although when they were able to get them, it seemed to them that they possessed the best jewel in the world; so it was found that for a strap a sailor received gold to the weight of $2\frac{1}{2}$ 'castellanos',[1] and others received much more for other things which were worth less. As for new 'blancas',[2] for them

---

[1] A gold coin.
[2] A copper coin of small value.

they would give everything they had, although it might be two or three 'castellanos' weight of gold, or an 'arroba'[3] or two of spun cotton. They took even the pieces of the broken hoops of the wine barrels and gave what they had, like animals, so that it seemed to me wrong and I forbade it. I gave them a thousand pleasing good things, which I had brought, in order that they might love us. And, more than that, they would become Christians and be inclined to the love and service of Their Highnesses and of the whole Castilian nation, and strive to collect and give us of the things which they have in abundance and which are necessary to us.

And they do not know any sect or idolatry, except that they all believe that power and good are in the sky, and believed very firmly that I, with these ships and men, came from the sky, and in this belief they everywhere received me after they had lost their fear. This belief does not result from their being ignorant, since they are of a very acute intelligence, men who navigate all those seas, so that it is marvellous how good an account they give of everything; but rather because they have never seen people clothed or ships of such a kind.

As soon as I arrived in the Indies, in the first island which I found, I took some of them by force, in order that they might learn and might give me information of whatever there was in those parts, and so it was that they soon understood us, and we them, either by speech or signs; and they have been very useful. At present, those I bring with me are still of the opinion that I come from the sky, despite all the conversation which they have had with me. And these were the first to announce this wherever I went, and the others went running from house to house, and to the neighbouring towns, with loud cries of, 'Come! Come! See the people from the sky!' So all came, men and women alike, as soon as they were confident about us, not one, small or great, remaining behind, and they all brought something to eat and drink, which they gave with extraordinary affection.

In all the islands, they have very many canoes, which are like rowing 'fustes',[4] some larger and some smaller, and some are greater than a 'fusta' with eighteen benches. They are not so broad, because they are made of a single log of wood, but a 'fusta' would not keep up with them in rowing, since their speed is incredible; and in these they navigate all those islands, which are innumerable, and carry their merchandise. I have seen some of these canoes with seventy or eighty men in it, each one with his paddle.

In all these islands, I saw no great diversity in the appearance of the people or in their manners or language; on the contrary, they all understand one another, which is a very curious thing, on account of which I hope that Their Highnesses will determine upon their conversion to our holy faith, towards which they are much inclined.

I have already said how I went 107 leagues in a straight line from west to east along the sea-coast of the island Juana. On account of that voyage I can

---

[3] One 'arroba' was the rough equivalent of 25 English pounds in weight or just over 10 kilos.
[4] A 'fusta' was a small longship, usually with oars.

say that this island is larger than England and Scotland together, for, beyond these 107 leagues, there remain to the westward two provinces to which I have not gone, one of which they call *Avan*, where people are born with tails. These provinces cannot have a length of less than fifty or sixty leagues, as could be understood from those Indians whom I have, and who know all the islands.

The other, Española, has a circumference greater than all Spain from Colunia[5] by the sea-coast to Fuenteravia in Vizcaya, for I went along one side for 188 great leagues in a straight line from west to east. This is a land to be desired and, once seen, never to be left. In it, although I have taken possession of all of them for Their Highnesses, and all are more richly endowed than I know how or am able to say, and I hold all for Their Highnesses, so that they may dispose of them as they do of the kingdoms of Castile and as absolutely; [so] in this Española, in the situation most convenient and in the best district for the mines of gold and for all trade as well with the mainland here as with that there, belonging to the Great Khan, where will be great trade and profit, I have taken possession of a large town, to which I gave the name Villa de Navidad, and in it I have made defences and a fort, which will now by this time be entirely completed, and in it I have left enough men for such a purpose with arms and artillery and provisions for more than a year, and a 'fusta', and a master of all seacraft to build others, and great friendship with the king of that land, so much so that he was proud to call me brother and to treat me as such. And even were he to change his attitude and offer offence to these people, he and his men do not know what weapons are, and they go naked, as I have already said. They are the most timorous people that there are in the world, so that the men who remain there alone would suffice to destroy all that land, and the island is without danger for their persons, if they know how to govern themselves.

In all these islands, it seems to me that all men are content with one woman, and to their chief or king they give as many as twenty. It appears to me that the women work more than the men. I have not been able to find out if they hold private property; it seemed true to me that all took a share in whatever any one had, especially of eatable things.

In these islands I have so far found no human monstrosities, as many expected, but on the contrary all the people are of fine appearance, nor are they negroes as in Guinea, but with flowing hair, and they are not born where there is too much force in the rays of the sun; it is true that the sun there has great power, although it is distant from the equinoctial line twenty-six degrees. In these islands, where there are high mountains, the cold was severe this winter, but they endure it, being used to it and with the help of meats [which] they eat with many and excessively hot spices. Thus I have found no monsters, nor report of any, except of an island which is *Carib*, which is the second at

---

[5] Probably Collioure, north of Barcelona.

the entrance into the Indies, which is inhabited by a people who are regarded in all the islands as very ferocious, [and] who eat human flesh. They have many canoes with which they range through all the islands of India, rob and take whatever they can. They are no more malformed than the others, except that they have the custom of wearing their hair long like women, and they use bows and arrows of the same cane stems, with a small piece of wood at the end, owing to their lack of iron which they do not possess. They are ferocious among these other people who are cowardly to an excessive degree, but I make no more account of them than of the rest. These are they who have intercourse with the women of Matinino, which is the first island found after leaving Spain for the Indies, in which there is not a man. These women engage in no feminine occupation, but use bows and arrows of cane, like those already mentioned, and they arm and protect themselves with plates of copper, of which they have much.

In another island, which they assure me is larger than Española, the people have no hair. In it there is incalculable gold, and from it and from the other islands I bring with me Indians as evidence.

In conclusion, to speak only of what has been accomplished on this voyage, which was so hasty, Their Highnesses can see that I will give them as much gold as they may need, if Their Highnesses will render me very slight assistance; presently, I will give them spices and cotton, as much as Their Highnesses shall command; and mastic, as much as they shall order shipped and which, up to now, has been found only in Greece, in the island of Chios, and the Seignory sells it for what it pleases; and aloe, as much as they shall order to be shipped; and slaves, as many as they shall order, and who will be from among the idolaters. I believe also that I have found rhubarb and cinnamon, and I shall find a thousand other things of value, which the people whom I have left there will have found, for I have not delayed anywhere, provided the wind allowed me to sail, except in the Villa de Navidad, so as to leave it secured and well established. And in truth I would have done much more if the ships had served me as justice demanded.

This is sufficient, and [illegible] the eternal God, Our Lord, who gives to all those who walk in His way victory over things which appear impossible. And this was notably one, for, although these lands have been talked or written of, all was conjectural, without getting sight of them, but amounted only to this, that those who heard for the most part listened and judged rather by hearsay than from anything else. So that, since Our Redeemer gave this victory to our most illustrious King and Queen, and to their renowned kingdoms, in so great a matter, for this all Christendom ought to feel delight and make great feasts and give solemn thanks to the Holy Trinity, with many solemn prayers for the great exaltation which they shall have in the turning of so many peoples to our holy faith, and afterwards for the temporal benefits, because not only Spain but all Christendom will here have refreshment and gain.

This is what has been done, though in brief.

15

Done in the caravel, off the Canary Islands, on the fifteenth day of February, in the year 1493.

At your orders.

THE ADMIRAL.

¶ [*Additional note which came inside the letter.*]

After having written this, and being in the sea of Castile, there came upon me so great a south and south-east wind that I was obliged to ease the ships, but I ran here today into this port of Lisbon, which was the greatest marvel in the world, whence I decided to write to Their Highnesses. In all the Indies, I have always found weather as in May. There I went in thirty-three days and I returned in twenty-eight, except that these storms have detained me for fourteen days, beating about in this sea. Here all the sailors say that never has there been so bad a winter nor so many ships lost.

Done on the fourteenth day of March.

2. The Journal of Columbus (1492–1493)

¶ *Columbus seems to have written up his journal most evenings of that first voyage. The journal was probably intended for the eyes of the King and Queen, to whom a copy was given, but does not appear to have been extensively rewritten: contradictions of fact and interpretation are certainly allowed to stand. However, both original version and copy were lost, and all that survives is an extended summary made by the Spanish historian Bartolomé de Las Casas, which refers to Columbus as 'the admiral'. Before its loss the journal was used extensively by historians like Las Casas and Peter Martyr, and by Columbus's brother and biographer Fernando. Las Casas's summary was itself mislaid and not published until the middle of the nineteenth century.*

Even in this form, the Journal *gives a much more detailed account of Columbus's voyage and of his changing ideas about the nature of the islands' inhabitants. Communication with those inhabitants was obviously limited, particularly in the early months, but Columbus was an enthusiastic interpreter of signs. To begin with, he was keen to find evidence of the Great Khan he had read about in Marco Polo. When the natives of the Bahamian islands where he first landed spoke about man-eating enemies to the south, called 'canibales', Columbus was sceptical, presuming that these were simply the soldiers of the Khan: 'canibal' sounds as if it might be related to the Spanish form of Khan, 'Can'.*

When no signs of Cathay and its cities were discovered, the idea that both man-eating savages and gold were to be found to the south and east took more of a hold on Columbus, and he eventually promised to destroy the 'caribes', enemies—or so he assumed—of the local chief in the area of Navidad, on Española, where Columbus built his first settlement after the loss of his flagship.

In January 1493, shortly before his return to Europe, Columbus landed at a beach on the north coast of Española and he writes about his first contact with natives he believed to be 'of the caribes who eat men', of whom he has heard, on account of their appearance and behaviour. The orthodox ethnographic picture of the native Caribbean, which posits a Carib invasion from the South American mainland, allows no 'caribes' on Española; so Columbus's attribution has been questioned. None the less, the stereotype had taken on its essential features, and in that respect the die was cast: Amerindians of this kind of appearance and behaviour were likely to be taken as 'caribes', with consequences usually detrimental to their freedom or health or both.

[Columbus has been in the Caribbean for nearly six weeks, and at this point is sailing along the north coast of Cuba.]

Friday 23 November [1492]

All day the admiral steered towards the land to the south, always with little wind, and the current never let him reach it; instead, today he was as far from it at sunset as in the morning. The wind was east-north-east and right for going south, although it was slight, and beyond this cape appeared another land or cape which also runs to the east, which those Indians he was carrying with him called *Bohío*, which they said was very large and that on it there were people who had one eye in their foreheads, and others that were called *canibales*, of whom they showed great fear. And when they saw that he was taking this course, he says that they could not speak, because these people would eat them, and are well armed. The admiral says that he well believes there was something in this, but that since they were armed they must be people with reason; and he believed that they must have captured some of them and because they did not return to their lands they would say that they ate them. They believed the same thing about the Christians and about the admiral the first time some of them saw them. [...]

Monday 26 November

At sunrise he raised anchor from the harbour at Santa Cathalina, where he was behind the flat island, and sailed along the coast with a slight south-westerly wind in the direction of the Cabo del Pico, which was to the south-east. He arrived late at the cape because the wind dropped, and having arrived he saw to the south-east by east another cape which was about 60 miles away; and from there he saw another cape that lay toward the south-east by south from the ship; which seemed to him about 20 miles away, to which he gave the name of Cabo de Campana, which he could not reach during the day because the wind again died down completely. In that whole day he sailed about 32 miles, which is eight leagues, within which he noted and marked nine distinct harbours, which all the sailors thought wonderful, and five large rivers, since he always sailed close to the land in order to see everything well. All of that land is made up of very high and beautiful mountains, not dry nor rocky, but all accessible and with very beautiful valleys. The valleys, like the mountains, were full of tail and leafy trees, delightful to look at; and it seemed that many of them were pine groves. And also, behind the said Cabo del Pico to the south-east, there are two islets, each of which is two leagues round, and behind them three wonderful harbours and two big rivers. On all of this coast he saw no settlements from the sea: it may be that there were some, and there were signs of this because, wherever they went ashore, they found signs of people and many fires. He judged that the land that he saw today on the south-east part of the Cabo de Campana was the island that the Indians called *Bohío*, and it seemed to be so because the said cape is separated from that land. All the people that he has found up to today, he says, are very frightened of those of *caniba*, or *canima*, and they say that they live on this island of *Bohío*, which must be very large, it seems to him; and he believes that they are going to take them to their lands and houses since they are very cowardly and know nothing about weapons. And because of this it appears to him that those Indians he was bringing with him do not usually settle on the coast because of being close to this land. He says that after they saw him take the route to this land they could not speak, fearing that they would have them to eat; and he could not take away their fear. And they say that they only have one eye and the face of a dog; and the admiral thought they were lying and felt that those who captured them must have been under the dominion of the Great Khan. [...]

Wednesday 5 December

All this night he beat about off Cabo Lindo where he spent the night in order to see the land, which ran to the east, and at sunrise he saw another cape $2\frac{1}{2}$ leagues to the east. Beyond that one, he saw that the coast turned to the south and trended south-west, and he soon saw a very beautiful and lofty cape in the same direction, seven leagues from the other one. He would have liked to go there, but because of his desire to go to the island of *Baneque*, which lay to the north-east according to what the Indians he had with him said, he did not; and he could not go to *Baneque* either, because the wind he had was north-east. Proceeding in this way, he looked to the south-east and saw land and it was a very big island, of which he says he had already received information from the Indians, [and] which they call *Bohío*, inhabited by people of whom, he says, those of Cuba, or Juana, and of all the other islands have great fear because, he says, they eat men. These Indians told him other very marvellous things by signs; but the admiral does not say that he believes them, only that the people of that island of *Bohío* must be shrewder and more intelligent than they to capture them, because these are very faint of heart. So, because the weather was from the north-east and shifting north, he decided to leave Cuba, or Juana, which until now he had taken for terra firma because of its size, since he had gone fully 120 leagues along one side. And he departed to the south-east by east since the land he had seen trended south-east. He took this precaution because the wind always went round from the north to the north-east and from there to the east and south-east. The wind blew hard and he carried all sails, the sea smooth and the current helping him, so that from morning until one hour after midday he made eight miles an hour, and this

19

was for six hours, although not quite, because he says that there the nights were nearly fifteen hours long.

Afterwards he went at ten miles an hour and thus up to sunset he made eighty-eight miles, which are twenty-two leagues, all to the south-east; and because night was approaching he ordered the caravel *Niña* to go ahead to look at the harbour in daylight, because she was fast. And when she reached the mouth of the harbour which was like the bay of Cadiz, and because it was night, she sent her boat, which carried a lantern, to sound the harbour; and before the admiral reached where the caravel was tacking back and forth and waiting for the boat to make signals that it should enter the harbour, the light on the boat went out. The caravel, when it saw no light, ran out to sea and showed a light to the admiral, and when they came up to her, told him what had happened. At this point those on the boat lit another light. The caravel went to it and the admiral could not, and passed all that night beating about.[...]

Tuesday 11 December

He did not leave because of the wind, which was still east and north-east. Facing that harbour, as has been said, is the island of Tortuga, and it appears to be a large island; and the coast of it runs almost like that of Española, and there can be from one to the other at most ten leagues; that is to say, from the cape of Cinquin to the head of Tortuga, which is to the north of Española. Further along, its coast runs south. He says that he wanted to see that passage between these two islands in order to see the island of Española, which is the most beautiful thing in the world; and because, as the Indians that he brought told him, this was the way one had to go to the island of *Baneque*. They told him that it was a very large island with big mountains and rivers and valleys, and they said that the island of *Bohío* was larger than Juana, which they call Cuba, and that it is not surrounded by water. And they seem to mean that it is the main land that is here beyond Española, which they call *caritaba*, and which is a thing of infinite size. And perhaps they are right, for they may be preyed on by cunning people, because all these islands live in great fear of those from *Caniba*. And so I say again what I have said on other occasions, he says, that *Caniba* is nothing else but the people of the Great Khan, who must be very near here. And they have ships and come to capture them, and since they do not return they believe that they have been eaten. Each day we understand these Indians better and they us, since many times they have understood one thing for another, says the admiral. He sent men ashore where they found much mastic, uncongealed. He says that the rains must cause this, and that in Chios they gather it around March and that in these lands they would collect it in January, since they are so temperate. They caught many fish like those of Castile: dace, salmon, hake, dory, pampano, mullet, corbina, shrimp; and they saw sardines. They found much aloe. [...]

Monday 17 December

That night the wind blew strongly from the east-north-east. The sea did not get very rough because the island of Tortuga, which is opposite and forms a shelter, protected and guarded it. So he remained there that day. He sent the sailors to fish with nets; the Indians relaxed with the Christians and brought them arrows of the kind from *caniba* or of the *canibales*; and they are made from spikes of cane, and they insert into them little sticks, fired and sharp, and they are very long. Two men showed them [the Christians] that pieces of flesh were missing from their bodies, and gave them to understand that the *canibales* had taken mouthfuls from them. The admiral did not believe it. He again sent some Christians to the town, and in exchange for small glass beads they secured some pieces of gold worked into thin leaf. They saw one man whom the admiral took for governor of that land or a province of it, called *cacique*, with a piece as large as a hand of that sheet of gold, and it seems that he wanted to trade it. He went off to his house and the others remained in the square; and he had small pieces of that sheet made and, bringing one piece at a time, traded for it. When none was left, he said by signs that he had sent for more and that the next day they would bring it. All these things, and the manner of them, and their customs and mildness and behaviour show them to be people more alert and intelligent than others they had found up to that time, the admiral says. In the afternoon a canoe came here from the island of Tortuga with fully forty men, and when it reached the beach all the people of the town who were there sat down together as a sign of peace, and some of those from the canoe, almost all of them, came ashore. The *cacique* alone got up and, with words that seemed threatening, made them return to the canoe, and threw water on them and took stones from the beach and threw them in the water, and after all of them very obediently got into the canoe and set off, he took a stone and put it in the hand of my bailiff for him to throw it. I had sent him and the clerk and others ashore to see if they would bring back anything advantageous. The bailiff did not want to throw the stone at them. There the *cacique* showed how much he favoured the admiral. The canoe soon went away and, after it had gone, they told the admiral that on Tortuga there was more gold than on Española because it was closer to *Baneque*. The admiral said that he did not believe that there were gold mines on Española or Tortuga, but that they brought it from *Baneque*, and that they brought little because the people had nothing to give for it. And that land is so rich that there is no need to work hard to get sustenance or clothing, since they go around naked. And the admiral believed that he was very near the source and that Our Lord would show him where the gold comes from. He had information that from there to *Baneque* would take four days, which would be thirty or forty leagues, so that they could get there in one day of good weather. [...]

¶ [*After the shipwreck of the* Santa María *Columbus is visited by the local* cacique *on the north coast of what is now Haiti.*]

Wednesday 26 December

Today at sunrise the king of that land, who was in that place, came to the caravel *Niña*, where the admiral was, and almost weeping said to him that he should not grieve, for he would give him all that he had, and that he had given the Christians who were on land two very large houses, and that he would give them more if they were needed, and as many canoes as could load and unload the ship and put on land as many people as he wanted, and that he had done so yesterday without a crumb of bread or any other thing at all being taken; so faithful are they (says the admiral), and without greed for what is another's and so, more than them all, was that virtuous king. While the admiral was talking to him, another canoe came from another place bringing certain pieces of gold which they wanted to give for a bell, because they desired nothing so much as bells, for the canoe was not yet alongside when they called and showed the pieces of gold, saying *chuq chuque* for bells, for they almost go mad for them. After having seen this, and the canoes from the other places leaving, they called to the admiral and asked him to order one bell kept until the next day, because they would bring four pieces of gold as large as a hand. The admiral rejoiced to hear this, and afterwards a sailor who came from ashore told the admiral it was marvellous to see the pieces of gold that the Christians who were on land haggled for a trifle. For a lace-end they gave pieces that would be more than two 'castellanos', and that was now nothing compared to what it would be after a month. The king rejoiced greatly to see the admiral happy, and understood that he wanted a lot of gold; and he told him by signs that he knew where there was very much, near there, in great quantities; and he should be of good heart, that he would give him as much gold as he wanted. And, about this, the admiral says that he gave him a report and, in particular, that there was gold in Çipango, which they call *Çybao*, in such quantity that they hold it as of no account and that he would bring it there, although also that in that island of Española, which they call *Bohío*, and in that province *Caribata*, there was much more of it. The king ate on the caravel with the admiral, and afterwards went ashore with him, where he did the admiral much honour and gave him refreshments of two or three kinds of yams with shrimp and game and other foods which they had and some of their bread, which they called *caçabi*. From there he took him to see some groves of trees near the houses, and a good thousand people, all naked, walked there with him. The lord was now wearing the shirt and gloves that the admiral had given him; and he was more delighted with the gloves than with anything else that he was given. In his way of eating, his honest manners, and attractive cleanliness, he showed himself certainly to be of some lineage. After having eaten, for he spent a long time at table, they brought certain herbs with which they rubbed their hands a great deal (the admiral thought they did it to soften them), and they gave him water for his hands. After they finished, he took the admiral to the beach, and the admiral sent for a Turkish bow and a handful of arrows; and he had one of the men of his company who knew how to, shoot it; and to the lord, since he did not know what weapons are, because they do not have and do not use them, it appeared a great thing, although he says that at the beginning there was talk about those of *Caniba*, whom they call *Caribes*, who come to take them and who carry bows and arrows without iron, for in all of those lands they have no knowledge of it or of steel or of any other metal except gold and copper, although of copper the admiral had seen but little. The admiral told him by signs that the sovereigns of Castile would order the *Caribes* destroyed, and they would order all of them to be brought with hands bound. The admiral ordered a lombard and a spingard to be fired, and seeing the effect that their force had, and how they penetrated, he was astonished. And when his people heard the shots they all fell to the ground. They brought the admiral a large mask that had large pieces of gold in the ears and eyes and on other parts, which the king gave him with other gold jewels that he himself had put on the admiral's head and round his neck; and to the other Christians who were with him he also gave many things. The admiral was greatly pleased and consoled by these things that he saw; and the anguish and sorrow that he had suffered and felt because of the loss of the ship were assuaged; and he recognized that Our Lord had caused the ship to run aground there so that he would found a settlement there. And to this end (he says) so many things came to hand that truly it was no disaster, but great fortune, because it is certain, he says, that if I had not gone aground I would have passed by without anchoring at this place, because it is situated here within a wide bay, and in it two or three sandbars; nor on this voyage would I have left people here; nor, even had I wished to leave them, could I have given them so many supplies or so many tools or so many provisions or materials for a fortress. And it is very true that many of the people who are here have begged me and have had others beg me to be willing to give them permission to stay. Now I have ordered built a tower and a fort, all of the best, and a big moat, not that I believe this necessary for these people, for it is obvious that with these men I have with me I would subdue all this island, which I believe is larger than Portugal and double or more in people: they are naked and without arms and very cowardly beyond remedy. But it is right that this tower be built and that it be as it should be, being so far from Their Highnesses, so that they get to know the skills of Their Highnesses' people and what they can do, so that they will obey them with love and fear. And so they have boards with which to build all the fortress, and provisions of bread and wine for more than a year, and seeds to sow, and the ship's boat, and a caulker and a carpenter and a gunner and a cooper; and many men among them who greatly desire to serve Their Highnesses and to please me by finding out about the mine where gold is collected. So everything has worked out just right for this beginning to be made, and above all that when the ship ran aground, it was so softly that it was almost not felt, nor was there wave nor wind. All this the admiral says. And he adds more to show that it was great good fortune and the particular will of God that the ship should run aground there so that he would leave people there; and he says that if it had not been for the treachery of the master and of the men, all or most of whom were from the same place as him, not wanting to cast the anchor astern in order to get the ship off, as the admiral ordered them, the ship would have been saved and so he would not have been able to find out about the country (he says) as he did in those days that he was there, and in future through those whom he resolved to leave, because he always went with the intention to explore and not to stop anywhere more than a day, save for lack of wind, because the ship (he says) was very slow and not suited for exploration; and in taking such a ship (he says) the men of Palos failed to fulfil their promise to the king and queen to provide suitable ships for that voyage, and they did not do it. The admiral ends by saying that of everything that was in the ship not even a lace-end was lost, neither plank nor nail, because she remained as sound as when she set out, except that she was cut and somewhat opened up to get out the water butts and all the merchandise, all of which they put on land and guarded well, as has been said. And he says that he trusts in God that on the return that he intended to make from Castile he would find a barrel of gold which those whom he had left would have obtained by barter, and that they would have found the gold mine and the spices, and those things in such quantity that the sovereigns, within three years, would undertake and prepare to go and conquer the Holy Sepulchre; for thus (he says) I urged Their Highnesses that all the profits of this my enterprise should be spent on the conquest of Jerusalem, and Their Highnesses laughed and said that it would please them and that even without this they had that desire. These are the words of the admiral. [. . .]

Saturday 12 January

At the dawn watch he steered east with a fresh wind and proceeded like this until daylight, and during this time made twenty miles and in the following two hours made twenty-four miles. From there he saw land to the south and went towards it; he was about forty-eight miles from it. He says that, keeping the ship a safe distance from shore, tonight he made twenty-eight miles to the north-north-east. When he saw land, he named a cape that he sighted the Cabo de Padre y Hijo because at its eastern point it has two headlands, one larger than the other. Later, two leagues to the east, he saw a large and very beautiful opening between two big mountains and he saw that it was an extremely large and good harbour with a very good entrance. But because it was very early in the morning, and so as not to lose distance, because most of the time in that part east winds blow, and at that time he had a north-north-westerly, he did not want to stop but continued his course to the east as far as a very high and very beautiful cape all of sheer rock to which he gave the name Cabo del Enamorado, which was thirty-two miles to the east of that harbour which he called Puerto Sacro. And when he reached it he discovered another cape much more beautiful and higher and rounded, all of rock, just like the Cabo de San Vicente in Portugal; and it was twelve miles to the east of the Enamorado. After getting to a position level with the Enamorado, he saw, between it and the other cape, that a large bay was formed, which had a width of three leagues and in the middle of it a tiny little islet. The depth is great at the entrance right the way up to the shore. He anchored there in twelve fathoms; he sent the boat ashore for water and to see if they could communicate; but the people all fled. He also anchored to see if all that land was continuous with Española or whether, as he suspected, what he had called a gulf might not form another island by itself. He remained amazed that the island of Española was so big.

Sunday 13 January

He did not leave this harbour, because there was no land breeze with which to leave; he would have liked to leave to go to another better harbour because that one was somewhat open, and because he wanted to observe how the conjunction of the moon with the sun that he expected on the seventeenth of this month would turn out, and its opposition with Jupiter and conjunction with Mercury, and the sun in opposition to Jupiter, which is the cause of great winds. He sent the boat ashore at a beautiful beach so they could take some yams to eat, and they found some men with bows and arrows with whom they stopped to talk, and they bought from them two bows and many arrows and they asked one of them to go to speak with the admiral in the caravel, and he came. The admiral says that he was very ill proportioned in appearance, more so than others that he had seen. He had his face all stained with charcoal, although everywhere they are accustomed to staining themselves with different colours. He wore all his hair very long, drawn back and tied behind, and then gathered in a small net of parrot feathers; and he was as naked as the others. The admiral judged that he must be of the *caribes* who eat men, and that the gulf that he had seen yesterday separated the land, and that it must be an island by itself. He asked him about the *caribes*, and he [the Indian] pointed to the east near there, which land the admiral says that he saw yesterday before entering that bay; and the Indian told him that over there was a great deal of gold, pointing to the poop of the caravel, which was quite large, that there were pieces that big. He called gold *tuob* and did not understand *caona*, as they call it in the first part of the island, nor *noçay* as they called it in San Salvador and in the other islands. In Española they call filigree, a base gold, *tuob*. Of the island of *Matinino* that Indian said that it was entirely peopled by women, without men, and that in it there is very much *tuob*, which is gold, or filigree, and that it is further to the east of *Carib*. He also spoke of the island of *Goanin* where there is much *tuob*. The admiral says that some days ago he received news of these islands from many people. The admiral also says that on the islands he passed they were greatly fearful of *Carib* and on some they called it *Caniba*, but on Española, *Carib*; and they must be a daring people since they travel through all these islands and eat the people they can take. He says that he understood some words, and through them he says he found out other things, and that the Indians he brought with him understood more, although they found differences between the languages, because of the great distance between the lands. He had the Indian given something to eat, and he gave him pieces of green and red cloth and glass beads, of which they are very fond, and sent him back ashore and told him to bring gold if he had it, which he believed he did, because of some little things that he was wearing. When the boat reached shore, behind the trees there were a good fifty-five naked men with very long hair, just like the women wear it in Castile. On the backs of their heads they wore plumes of parrot feathers and of other birds, and each one was carrying his bow. The Indian landed and made the others leave their bows and arrows and a piece of wood, that is like a very heavy [illegible] that they carry in place of a sword. Later they came to the boat and the men in the boat went ashore and began to buy from them the bows and arrows and other arms, because the admiral had so ordered. When two bows were sold they did not want to give any more; instead, they prepared to attack the Christians and capture them. They went running to pick up their bows and arrows where they had laid them aside and came back with ropes in their hands, in order, he says, to tie up the Christians. Seeing them come running toward them, the Christians, being prepared (because the admiral was always warning them about this) attacked them, and they gave one Indian a great slash across the buttocks and another they wounded in the chest with a crossbow shot. Having seen by this that they could achieve little, even though the Christians were seven and they fifty odd, they took flight so that none remained, one leaving his arrows here and another his bows there. He says that the Christians would have killed many of them if the pilot who went as their captain had not prevented it. The Christians then returned to the caravel with their boat; and when the admiral found out, he said that on the one hand he had been pleased and on the other not. Because they would fear the Christians, since without doubt (he says) the people there are evildoers and he believed they were those of *Carib* and that they would eat men. Because if the boat that he had left for the thirty-nine men in the fortress and town of Navidad came there, they would be frightened of doing them any harm. And if they are not of those *caribes*, at least they must be their neighbours and with the same customs and be men without fear, not like the others of the other islands, who are cowards and, beyond understanding, without weapons. All of this the admiral says, and that he would like to take some of them. He says they made many smoke signals, as was the custom in that island of Española.

Monday 14 January

He would have liked to send out this night in search of the houses of those Indians to capture some of them, believing that they were *caribes*, and because of the strong east and north-east wind and the high sea it caused [he could not do so]. But when day came they saw many Indians on the shore, because of which the admiral ordered the boat to go there with well-equipped men. The Indians quickly came up to the stern of the boat, and especially the Indian who, the day before, had come to the caravel and to whom the admiral had given the trinkets for barter. With him, he says, came a king who had given some beads to the said Indian to give to the men in the boat as a sign of security and peace. This king, with three of his men, entered the boat and came to the caravel. The admiral ordered them to be given biscuit and honey to eat, and he gave him [the king] a red cap and beads and a piece of red cloth; and to the others also pieces of cloth. The king said that tomorrow he would bring a gold mask, affirming that there was much gold there and in *Carib* and in *Matinino*. Afterwards he sent them ashore well contented. The admiral also says that the caravels were leaking heavily around the keel and complained greatly about the caulkers who caulked them very badly in Palos; and that when they saw that the admiral had realized the deficiency of their work and wanted to make them put it right, they fled. But despite the large amount of water the caravels were taking on, he trusted in Our Lord who brought him [here] to return him because of His piety and mercy, for His High Majesty well knew how much controversy he had at first before he was able to set out from Castile, and that no one else was in his favour except Him, because He knew his heart, and after God, Their Highnesses. And all the others had been against him without any reason at all. And he says more as follows: and they have been the cause that the royal crown of Your Highnesses does not have a revenue of a hundred millions more than it has, since I came to serve you, which is now seven years ago on 20 January this very month, and more that would be added from now onwards. But that powerful God will make all well. These are his words.

Tuesday 15 January

He says that he wants to leave because there is no benefit in staying, because of the difficulties with—he should say the outrage towards—the Indians. He also says that today he has found out that all the abundance of gold was in the region of Their Highnesses' town of Navidad, and that on the island of *Carib* there was much filigree, and in *Matinino* too, although it will be difficult in *carib* because those people, he says, eat human flesh, and that from there their island was visible, and he had resolved to go to it since it is on the way, and to that of *Matinino* which, he says, was entirely populated by women without men, to see both and to take, he says, some of them. The admiral sent the boat ashore and the king of that land had not come because, he says, the town was distant, but he sent his crown of gold as he had promised, and many other men came with cotton and with bread and yams, all with their bows and arrows. After they had bartered everything, he says that four young men came to the caravel, and they seemed to the admiral to give such a good account of all those islands to the east on the same route that the admiral had to follow, that he decided to take them to Castile with him. He says that they have no iron or other metal that has been seen, although in a few days not much can be learned about a country, owing to the difficulty of the language which the admiral did not understand, except through guesswork, and because they did not know in a few days what he was trying to do. The bows of that people, he says, were as big as those in France and England; the arrows are just like the spears of other people he had seen up to that time, which are made from shoots of canes when planted, which remain very straight for the length of $1\frac{1}{2}$ or two yards. And afterwards they put at the end a piece of sharp wood, a palm and a half long, and on top of this little stick some insert a fish tooth, and some, the most, put poison there. And they do not shoot as in other places, but in a certain way that cannot do much harm. There was very much cotton there, very fine and long, and there are many mastic trees, and it seemed to him that the bows were made of yew and that there is gold and copper. There is also much chilli, which is their pepper, of a sort worth more than pepper, and nobody eats without it because they find it very healthy. Fifty caravels can be loaded with it each year in that Española. He says that he found much weed in that bay, of the kind they found in the gulf when he came on the discovery, because of which he believes that there were islands to the east, even directly from where he began to find them, because he considers it certain that that weed grows in shallow water near land; and he says that if this is so, these Indies are very near the Canary Islands, and for this reason he believed that they were less than 400 leagues distant.

3. *The Report of Dr Chanca (1494)*

¶ *Diego Álvarez Chanca (d. ?1515), a native of Seville and doctor to the royal family, was appointed surgeon for Columbus's fleet on the second voyage to the Americas. The account he wrote for the municipality of Seville is recognized as the principal source for the events of this second voyage. Chanca soon returned to Seville, where he married twice and maintained financial connections to the new Spanish settlements. He formed part of an important intellectual movement in early sixteenth-century Seville, and wrote books on medicine and alchemy.*

Columbus's skill as a navigator enabled him to take up his exploration of the Caribbean islands just south of where he had been forced to leave it off earlier in 1493. His course to Dominica, the first island Chanca mentions, followed prevailing winds and currents, and would be repeated by many European ships throughout the age of sail.

Chanca describes Columbus's course northwards through the Lesser Antilles, probably as far as Nevis. Chanca, who had not been on the first voyage, had clearly been introduced to Columbus's expectations: human bones on Guadeloupe are immediately taken as evidence of 'people who eat human flesh' rather than, for example, of people who have certain mortuary practices that involve reducing a dead body to bones. However, a group of Spaniards got lost on the island and, as Chanca reports, turned up four days later without having been eaten— somewhat to Spanish surprise.

The distinction which Columbus had begun to draw during the first voyage between the peaceful Indians he met and the ferocious man-eaters he heard about is developed by Chanca and given the beginnings of an ethnographic basis in dress. Other topics make their first appearance, such as the castration of boys and the bestial nature of the Carib way of life. One of the key incidents described by Chanca is the unprovoked Spanish attack on four men and two women in a canoe. Being 'caribe'—or at least being taken as such—is already justification in itself for violence.

On the morning of the Sunday before mentioned, we saw an island ahead of the ships, and afterwards another came in sight on the right hand side. The first was a high and mountainous land on the side we saw; the other was flat and also covered with dense woods; and when it grew lighter, islands began to appear on one side and on the other, so that during that day six islands were seen in different directions, most of them very large. We steered directly to look at the one which we had first sighted[1] and reached the coast, going more than a league in search of a harbour in which to anchor, but which could not be found in all that distance. As much of the island as was in sight was very beautiful and very green mountains, right down to the water, which was a delight to see, since in our own country at that season there is scarcely any green. When we found no harbour there, the admiral decided that we should go back to the other island which appeared on the right hand, and which was four or five leagues' distance from the first. Meanwhile one ship remained off the first island, looking for a harbour all that day, for when it should be necessary to return to it, and she found there a good harbour, and houses and people were seen. And later that night she came back to join the fleet which had put into harbour at the other island,[2] where the admiral, with the royal standard in his hands, landed, and many men with him, and there took possession for Their Highnesses in form of law. On this island the trees were so dense that it was marvellous, and there were such varieties of trees, unknown to anyone, as was astonishing, some with fruit, some with flowers, so that everything was green. There we found a tree, the leaf of which had the finest scent of cloves that I have ever seen, and it resembled laurel, except that it was not so large; I think, however, that it was a species of laurel. There were wild fruits of different kinds, which some, not very wisely, tasted, and touching them only with their tongues, from the taste their faces swelled up and such great heat and pain came over them that they seemed to be going mad; they cured this with cold things. In this island we found no people, and no sign of any; we believed it to be uninhabited. We were there some two hours, for when we arrived there it was late evening.

Then on the next day, in the morning, we left for another island, which appeared beyond this and which was very large, being from this one about seven or eight leagues distant.[3] We reached it near the side of a large mountain which seemed to want to touch the sky, in the middle of which mountain was a peak higher than all the rest of the mountain, from which many waters flowed in different directions, especially towards the part where we were sailing. From three leagues away, there appeared a waterfall as broad as an ox, which hurled itself from such a height that it seemed to fall from the sky; it was visible from so far away that many wagers were

---

[1] Dominica.
[2] Marie Galante.
[3] Guadeloupe.

3. *Insulae canibalium* (The Islands of the Cannibals). An engraving in Honorius Philoponus, *Nova typis transacta navigatio novi orbis Indiae Occidentalis* (Venice, 1621), pl. 5. The Bodleian Library: VET. L2. d1. Honorius Philoponus was the pseudonym of the Austrian Benedictine monk Caspar Plautius. The text of this volume concerns the history of Benedictine evangelism in the New World from Brendan's legendary travels to Fray Juan Buyl's arrival in Española on Columbus's fleet.

4. A cannibal feast. An engraving in Honorius Philoponus, *Nova typis transacta navigatio novi orbis Indiae Occidentalis* (Venice, 1621), pl. 17. The Bodleian Library: VET. L2. d1. These kinds of illustrations were instrumental in promulgating the imagery of cannibalism which came to be intimately associated with the islands of the Caribbean during the sixteenth and seventeenth centuries.

laid on the ships, for some said that it was white rocks and others that it was water. When we came nearer to it, the truth was apparent, and it was the loveliest thing in the world to see from what a height it fell and from how small a space sprang out so great a waterfall. When we came near, the admiral ordered a light caravel to coast along looking for a harbour. It went ahead and having reached land, sighted some houses. The captain went ashore in the boat and reached the houses, in which he found their inhabitants. As soon as they saw them [our men] they took to flight, and he entered the houses and found the things that they had, for they had taken nothing away, and from there he took two parrots, very large and very different from all those seen before. He found much cotton, spun and ready for spinning, and articles of food; and he brought away a little of everything; especially he brought away four or five bones of the arms and legs of men. When we saw this, we suspected that the islands were those of *Caribe*, which are inhabited by people who eat human flesh. For the admiral, in accordance with the indications as to the situation of those islands which the Indians of the islands which they had previously discovered had given to him on the former voyage, had directed his course to discover them, because they were nearer to Spain and also because from there lay the direct route by which to come to Española, where he had left people before. To these islands, by the goodness of God and by the good judgement of the admiral, we came as directly as if we had been sailing on a known and well-followed route.

This island is very large and on this side it appeared that the coast was twenty-five leagues in length; we coasted along it for more than two leagues, looking for a harbour. In the direction towards which we were going, there were very high mountains; in the direction which we were leaving, wide plains appeared, and on the seashore there were some small settlements, and as soon as they saw the sails, they all ran away. Having gone two leagues, we found a harbour and that very late. That night the admiral decided that at daybreak some should go to speak with them and to find out what people they were, despite the suspicion felt and [the fact that] those who had already been seen running away were naked people like the others whom the admiral had already seen on the earlier voyage.

That morning certain captains set out; some returned at the hour of eating and brought a boy of about 14, as was afterwards learned, and he said that he was one of those whom these people held captive. The others divided up. Some took a small boy, whom a man was leading by the hand and deserted in order to flee. They then sent him with some of them; others remained and of these some took certain women, natives of the island, and other women who were amongst the prisoners, who came willingly. From this party, one captain, not knowing that there had been any communication, went off with six men, and got lost along with his companions, so that they never found the way back until, after four days, they reached the coast and, by following it, came back to the fleet again. We had already given them up for lost and eaten by those people who are called the *caribes*, for there was not sufficient reason for thinking that they were lost in any other way, since there were amongst them naval pilots, who by the star know how to go and come from Spain; and we thought that in so small a space they could not get lost.

On this first day that we landed there, many men and women walked along the shore next to the water looking at the fleet and marvelling at something so novel. And when a boat came to land to speak with them, saying to them *taino, taino*, which means 'good', they waited as long as they [the sailors] did not leave the water, staying near it, so that when they wished they could escape. The result was that none of the men could be taken by force nor willingly, except two who felt confident and who were afterwards taken by force. More than twenty women of the captives were taken, and other native women of the island came of their own accord and were captured and taken by force. Some boys, captives, came to us, fleeing from the natives of the island who held them captive.

We were in this harbour eight days, because of the loss of the above-mentioned captain, and we often went on land, going about their dwellings and villages which were on the coast, finding an infinite number of men's bones and skulls hung up about the houses like vessels to hold things. Not many men appeared here, the reason being, according to what the women told us, that ten canoes had gone with people to raid other islands. These people seemed to us more polished than those who live in the other islands which we have seen, although they all have dwellings of straw, but these have them much better made and better provided with supplies, and there seems to be in them more industry, both male and female. They had much cotton, spun and ready for spinning, and many cotton cloths, so well made that they lose nothing by comparison with those of our own country.

We asked the women who were captive on this island what these people were; they replied that they were *caribes*. After they understood that we hated those people for their evil custom of eating the flesh of men, they rejoiced greatly, and if after that they brought any woman or man of the *caribes*, they said secretly that they were *caribes*, for even here where all were in our power they went in fear of them, like subjugated people; and so we found out which of the women were *caribes* and which not, for the *caribe* women wear two rings made of cotton on each leg, one near the knee and the other near the ankle, so that the calves are made large and the places mentioned very constricted, and it seems to me that they regard this as something graceful; so, by this difference we know the ones from the others.

The way of life of these *caribe* people is bestial. There are three islands, this one is called *Turuqueira*, the other, which we saw first, is called *Ceyre*, and the third is called *Ayai*. They are all agreed, as if they were of one

33

lineage, doing no harm to each other. All together they make war on all the other neighbouring islands, going 150 leagues by sea to make raids in the many canoes which they have, which are small 'fustas' made of a single piece of wood. Their arms are arrows rather than iron weapons, because they do not possess any iron; they fix on points made of tortoise-shell, others from another island fix on fish bones which are jagged, being like that naturally, like very strong saws, a thing which, for an unarmed people, as they all are, can kill and do great injury, but for people of our nation are not arms greatly to be feared.

These people raid the other islands and carry off the women whom they can take, especially the young and beautiful ones, whom they keep to serve them and have them as concubines, and they carry off so many that in fifty houses nobody was found, and of the captives more than twenty were young girls. These women also say that they are treated with a cruelty which seems incredible, for sons whom they have from them are eaten and they only rear those whom they have from their native women. The men whom they are able to take, those who are alive they bring to their houses to butcher for meat, and those who are dead are eaten there and then. They say that men's flesh is so good that there is nothing like it in the world, and it certainly seems so for the bones which we found in these houses had been gnawed of everything they could gnaw, so that nothing was left on them except what was much too tough to be eaten. In one house there a man's neck was found cooking in a pot. They cut off the male member of the boys they take prisoner and make use of them until they are men, and then when they want to make a feast, they kill and eat them, for they say that the flesh of boys and of women is not good to eat. Of these boys, three came fleeing to us, and all three had had their members cut off.

And at the end of four days, the captain who had got lost came back. We were already in despair of his coming, for other groups had already gone to look for them on two occasions, and on that very day one group had come back without having found out any certain news of them. We rejoiced at their coming as if they had been newly found. This captain, besides those who went with him, brought in ten head, boys and women. Neither they nor the others who went to look for them ever found men, because they had fled or perhaps it was because in that region there were few men, since, as was learned from the women, ten canoes with people had gone to raid other islands. He and those who went with him came from the mountain so shattered that it was pitiful to see them. When they were asked how they had got lost, they said that the thickness of the trees was such that they could not see the sky, and that some of them, who were sailors, had climbed the trees to look for the star and had never been able to see it, and that if they had not come across the sea, it would have been impossible for them to return to the fleet.

We left this island eight days after we had arrived there, then, the next day at noon, we saw another island, not very large, which was about twelve leagues from the first, because most of the first day after leaving we had been becalmed. We went close to the coast of this island, and the Indian women whom we carried with us said that it was not inhabited, for those of *caribe* had depopulated it, and for this reason we did not stop there.[4] Then that afternoon we saw another;[5] that night, near this island, we found some shoals, for fear of which we anchored, as we did not dare go on until daylight. Then, in the morning, another very large island appeared.[6] We did not go to any of these the better to bring comfort to those who had been left in Española, and it did not please God, as will appear below.

On the next day, at the hour of eating, we reached another island and it seemed to us very good, for it seemed to be very populous, judging from the many signs of cultivation there were on it.[7] We went there and put into a harbour on the coast; the admiral then ordered a well-manned boat to put ashore in case communication could be had to find what people they were, and also because we needed to inform ourselves of the route, despite the fact that the admiral, although he had never followed that route, was very much on course, as eventually appeared. But because doubtful matters must always be examined with the greatest possible care, he wanted to have communication there. Some of the men from those who went in the boat jumped on shore and went by land to a village, from which the people had already gone into hiding. They took there five or six women and some boys, of whom most were from the captives, as on the other island, for these people were also of the *caribes*, as we already knew from the account of the women whom we brought with us.

When this boat was on the point of returning to the ships with the captures that had been made, below this place along the coast came a canoe in which were four men and two women and a boy, and as soon as they saw the fleet, they were so dumbfounded with amazement that for a full hour they were there without moving from a place about two lombard shots from the ships. In this time, they were seen by those who were in the boat and even by the whole fleet. Then those in the boat went towards them, so close to land that they, what with their fascination, wondering and thinking what thing this could be, never saw them until they were close to them, so that they could not do much to escape although they tried hard to do so; but our men closed so quickly that they could not get away. The *caribes* when they saw that flight was useless, with great daring took up their bows, the women as well as the men, and I say with great daring, because they were only four men and two women, and our men were more than twenty-five, of whom they wounded two, one they hit twice in the breast with

---

[4] Montserrat.
[5] Redonda.
[6] Antigua.
[7] Nevis.

35

arrows, and the other once in the side, and if it had not been that they [the sailors] carried oval shields and targets, and that they came near them with the boat and overturned their canoe, they would have wounded most of them with their arrows. And after their canoe was overturned, they stayed in the water swimming and sometimes standing, as there were some shallows there, and they had great difficulty in taking them, for they still shot as much as they could, and with all this, there was one whom they could not take until he was badly wounded with a spear thrust from which he died and whom they brought, thus wounded, to the ships.

The difference in dress between these and the other Indians is that those of *Caribe* wear their hair very long; the others have it cut irregularly and their heads marked in a hundred thousand different ways, with crosses and other drawings of different kinds, which are done with sharpened reeds, each as he pleases. All of them, those of *Caribe* and the others, are beardless, so you will very seldom find a man with one. These *caribes* whom they took there had their eyes and eyebrows stained, which I think they do for show, and in that way appear more frightening. One of them says that in one of their islands, called *Cayre*, which is the first that we saw and to which we did not go, there is much gold; that they go there with nails and tools to make their exchanges, and that they bring away as much gold as they like.

Later on that day, we left this island, where we could not have been more than six or seven hours, and went towards another land which came into sight and which was on the route that we had to follow. We approached it at night. Next day in the morning we went along its coast; there was very much land, although it was not very continuous, as there were more than forty odd islets.[8] The land was very high and most of it bare, which was not the case with any other, either those we had seen before or those which we have seen since. The land seemed of the sort that would have metals in it. We did not land here, except that a lateen-rigged caravel went to one of these islets, on which they found some fishermen's houses. The Indian women we brought with us said that they were not inhabited.

We went along this coast for most of this day, until on the following day in the afternoon we came in sight of another island, called Burequen,[9] the coast of which we ran for a whole day. It was judged that it extended down that side thirty leagues. This island is very beautiful and seems very fertile; those of *Caribe* come here to make conquests, and carry away many people. These people have no 'fustas' and do not know how to go by sea, but according to what these *carives* we have taken say, they use bows as they do, and if by chance they are able to capture those who come to raid them, they also eat them, just as those of *Caribe* do them. We were two days

---

[8] Virgin Islands.
[9] Puerto Rico.

in a harbour on this island, where many men went ashore, but we were never able to communicate because they all fled like people terrified of the *caribes*.

4. The Captivity of Luisa de Navarrete (1580)

¶ *From the inception of Spanish settlement in the Caribbean, and as was seen in the foregoing extracts from the era of Columbus, the Amerindians of the Lesser Antilles bore the reputation of being intractably warlike. Although the experiences of the non-Spanish colonizers were often very different, as will be seen in the next section, there can be little doubt that both local shipping and the isolated farms and plantations of the Spanish settlers were often attacked by 'caribes'. Although European adult males were often killed outright during such attacks, many other individuals were simply taken into captivity as wives, servants and perhaps future victims of ritual war-dances (areytos). In 1576 just such a raid on the island of Puerto Rico resulted in the capture of a Creole woman, Luisa de Navarrete.*

Despite the attention that was given to the captivity of Luisa de Navarrete, her plight was not that uncommon. Estimates of there being up to 300 European and African captives on Dominica, as well as the imprisonment of the son of Juan Ponce de León II, indicate that it was not only this aspect of the case which accounted for its interest to the Puerto Rican authorities. Rather a desire to widen the scope of slave-taking to include women and children, by demonstrating their full participation in raids on Spanish settlements, as Luisa's testimony illustrates, underlay the presentation of a number of petitions and depositions in this vein to the Spanish Crown in the latter half of the sixteenth century.

In this context the importance of the testimony of Luisa de Navarrete, taken in 1580 following her escape from Dominica, lay in her apparent probity as a witness, since she was married to a white rancher on the island, Luis Hernández; her testimony also later being used extensively by the Bishop of Puerto Rico. Furthermore she also mentioned that the Amerindians on Dominica had a store of gold and silver that they had collected from their raids, no doubt enhancing the prospects that the Spanish Crown would consent to more extensive counter-raids against the 'caribe' population. Interestingly, the existence of this treasure of gold and silver on Dominica is raised a century later in the case of 'Indian' Warner (No. 8). At the same time that Luisa's testimony was recorded the authorities also interrogated a 'caribe', called 'Pedro', a cacique *who had been captured by French corsairs on Dominica in 1567; clearly the inclusion of this native testimony augmented the authority of the petition and its claims as to the barbarity of the 'caribes'.*

The following extracts from the petition of Bernáldez de Quiroz, Procurator General of Puerto Rico, are not a verbatim transcript of Luisa de Navarrete's testimony or of that of the 'caribe' Pedro, but his rendition of their verbal testimonies under oath. Given the highly charged political background to those testimonies it cannot, therefore, be taken as a piece of direct ethnographic reportage concerning the Amerindians of Dominica but should be seen as descriptive of their relations with the colonial society that increasingly encroached upon them.

PROCEEDINGS AND TESTIMONY TAKEN IN THE ISLAND OF PUERTO RICO CONCERNING THE INJURIES AND WRONGS DONE BY THE INDIAN *CARIBES* OF THE ISLAND OF DOMINICA, 1558–1580

[. . .]—and as in all the rest of the content in my aforementioned petition, in order that it is clear to his Majesty I ask and supplicate your honour to examine by virtue of my aforementioned petition the [testimony] of Luysa Nabarrete who comes from the island of Dominica and fled from the *caribes*. Paulo Bernaldes de Quiros.

And following the above on the nineteenth day of the said month of October in the said year of 1580, the said Pablo Bernaldez de Quiroz, Procurator General, presents for this reason as a witness Luysa de Nabarrete, black skinned, a free ex-slave, and of good name and Spanish-speaking, and a resident of this city, from whom a sworn statement was taken and received according to the law under which obligation she promised to speak the truth, and being asked the meaning of the said questioning, replied as follows—

1.—to the first question she said that she knows the said Pablo Bernaldes de Quiros and understands that he is the Procurator-General in this said city and knows of the harm which the said *caribes* have done in this island, because this witness knows that in times past they had robbed the town of Guadianilla and Humacao and Maunabo and when the said *caribes* plundered Humacao and carried off this witness to where they held her, and being there she saw that they fitted out their armadas in order to come to this island and the said Indians used to bring their wives and sons, and this she knows about this question—[she] was asked about the general questions of the law. She said that she was 23 years of age, more or less, and that the general questions do not apply to her.

2.—To the second question, being asked by the said petition that was offered by the witness, she said that what is known is that, as has been said, the said Indian *caribes* in past times robbed the town of Guadianilla and Humacao and

39

Maunabo and other areas, and when they robbed Humacao they took away this witness and left her in Dominica as the captive of an Indian *casique* of the aforementioned Dominica, where it had been four or five years that they held her captive, and this witness has seen that in the time that this witness was in this island [Puerto Rico] and in the time that she was in Dominica, without giving offence to the *caribes* nor causing them any harm, they arm themselves every year and cross to this island of San Juan [Puerto Rico] and rob and destroy whatever they can and this witness has seen that the three times they have come to this island while this witness was captive, they have carried away a great quantity of negroes and left some in Dominica and distributed the rest amongst the Indians of these islands, which they take to their lands in order to serve them; and this witness saw that one of these times that they carried off a quantity of negroes that they had stolen, they took from Luysa [Loiza] a white boy, son of one Domingo Pinero, and another time that their armada came this witness saw that they took from this island two other negroes that this witness knew, and the aforementioned Indians said that they had carried off another to another island, and the said Indians always used to go boasting and making great fiestas saying that they had burnt and destroyed many farms in this island and killed many people, and this witness saw that in the Dominica passage a ship appeared that was passing by, making its voyage, and they attacked and overcame and burnt and robbed it of whatever was within, carried off and killed three or four of the principal Spaniards who were travelling in the ship, and captured six principal women and ten or twelve men, among whom this witness saw one called Doña Maria and another Doña Juana, who was her sister, and the mother of these two women was called Juana Dias, and she does not remember the names of the others. They held all these people captive, and many more from before this witness was captured; they held there the ones that serve them and treat them very roughly, making them work and go about naked by day and night, and they paint them like themselves, making them sleep on the ground, not allowing them to eat meat except lizards and rats and snakes and some fish, and they do not let them roast this nor cook this, but they are made to eat it raw, and they tell them to eat human flesh, and when they want to make wine they make the Christians chew cassava at night to make it, with which wine they get drunk, take the female captives and force them, knowing them carnally, making them do as they wish, and the wives of the said Indians, seeing this, shoot arrows at the other captive women in parts where they do not kill them, and when the said Indians want to eat others that they have captured they make their *areytos* [ritual songs] and call to and speak with the Devil, and there in their *areytos* they agree to kill one, and so they kill him and eat him, and when it is agreed that they kill some Christian of another nation, they kill him and throw him in the sea, and when some Indian who holds captives dies, they kill some of his captives and say that they kill them in order that they should go on serving him, and if it were not for this there would be many more captives than there

40

5. *Chef caraibe, d'après une ancienne peinture espagnole.*
Lith. Wl. Hegel. From Lucien de Rosny, *Les Antilles: Étude
d'ethnographie et d'archéologie americain*, ed. V. Devaux
(Société d'Ethnographie: Paris, 1859), opp. 118. The British
Library: Ac 6226/8 opp. 118. 9071296.

are, and among the captives that they have this witness saw that there is Don Garcia Troche, son of Juan Ponze de Leon, resident of this city, Governor and Captain General, who was in the island of Trinidad, whom, when this witness was taken prisoner, was already captive in the said island of Dominica for the said Indians had captured him when going to the conquest of Trinidad, and later the said Indians spread it around that they had killed him, and so the said *caribes* carried him away because they took him from the Indians of the said island of Trinidad in a war that they and those of the other island had between them, and this witness knows that the said Indians have much gold and worked and unworked silver, and Reales and silver collars and plates and much merchandise that they have taken from the ships, and this witness just now coming in an armada that the said Indians organized, they made port in this island and berthed in the mouth of the Maunabo river, where they were hidden with fifteen pirogues that came, and five of the aforementioned pirogues remained here in order to burn and destroy Guayama and another five remained on an island fronting the mouth of the river Abey, and another five pirogues passed on and went as far as the river Xacagua, and there jumped ashore; in which pirogues the witness was travelling and here they left her in a pirogue with a guard to stop her fleeing, and the said Indian *caribes* went upriver and attacked the farms that were there, and burnt and robbed and destroyed so that they left nothing for the residents that there were here, and next they came and embarked again and went to the island where they had left the other five pirogues with the chief *casique*, and so, when the five pirogues that they had left arrived, they rested here and the other five left for the town of Guadianilla, where this witness heard it said that they had taken a ship above San German, which was coming from Santo Domingo for the island of Margarita, which they said they robbed, and killed a Franciscan monk and six or seven old men, and the rest they say they took with them, and also this same witness has heard it said that they ate some Indians that came in the said ship, and then the five pirogues that waited at the said island, in which this witness came, went to the mouth of the Abey with the plan of robbing some farm or ranch if they could find one, entered the river, and when they moved upriver a bit, they leapt ashore and all the men went to see if there was anything to rob, and they left the witness in the guard of the women, and the said Indian women declared that they would catch crabs and went ashore and this witness with them, and walking about catching crabs this witness entered a marsh saying that here there were large crabs, and as she saw herself somewhat off the track, made her escape and hid herself from the said Indian women, who did not recapture her, and so brought herself to Coamo the next day in the morning, and this witness knows and saw in the said island of Dominica that there are two women and a man who were already as much *caribes* as the rest of them, and the women say that they no longer remember God, and the man neither more nor less so, and he eats human flesh and they do just as the Indians do, neither more nor less, and another man comes with these said Indians that has now become as *caribe* as them and likewise eats human flesh, and this witness and other Christians speaking with this man asked him why he did not remember the mother of God, since he was a Christian, and the said man replied that since the mother of God had not remembered to take him from here in forty years, neither did he wish to remember her, and this witness saw the same among the other Negroes who eat human flesh and do as the Indians do, and what she has spoken is the truth and what is known of the case under the oath she made and she did not sign because she said that she could not. This passed before me, Andres Goncales, public notary—[...]

—And following the above, on this day of 20 October in the said year 1580, the said Paulo Bernaldes de Quiros, in order to learn about the robberies that the said *caribes* have carried out, and where these Indians are located who have done these wrongs, and the treatment they give to the Christians, and if they eat human flesh, asked that the testimony be taken of Pedro, a *caribe*, who has been in this island about fifteen years and is already a Christian, and so his testimony was taken, and saying in this case that what he knows of this case is that this witness is from the island of Dominica, born and brought up there, and this witness being a boy heard it said by the said *caribes* of Dominica how they had come to this island and had taken a ship belonging to one Juan de Salas, and carried off the people who were in it, and burnt the said ship, and after this, the witness being now a man, they collected an armada on the said island of Dominica in which came six pirogues, and they came to this island and attacked in the valley of Guayama where they found a caravel that was in the port and was being loaded with cassava and maize, and when they reached it they burnt it and killed all the people who were on board except a Christian they called Guadalupe and another boy, and after the burning of the caravel they leapt ashore and went to Guayama and along the way killed a Negro, and then went to the huts and burnt them and robbed whatever they found, and they went from there and took their prisoner and went to an island next to Bieque [Vieques] from where the aforementioned Guadalupe fled from them, and they took with them the boy to the said island of Dominica, and afterwards being already in Dominica a ship of Pedro Melendes went aground there on the coast of the island of Guadalupe, and from here the said Indians of Dominica went to it and took all the Christians and killed one or two of the fattest and the rest they captured and carried off to the said island of Dominica, and this witness knows that the Indians of the said island of Dominica and others which are in Guanarao and Guariaquira and Yarumay and Camahuya, and in the surrounding areas are *caribes* and they eat human flesh and, in their drunkenness, he knows that the Indians kill the Christians for very little reason, and give them a hard life, and he knows that when they go to war the said Indians join together on the said island of Dominica and [illegible] and come in their armadas to this island and to other parts and this is as much as he knows, and he did not sign because he did not know how to. Andres Goncales, public notary—

5. *Early English and French Voyagers (1564–1596)*

¶ *This is not the place to retell the story of early English and French penetration into the Caribbean, but the Amerindians of the Lesser Antilles, especially those of Dominica, lay directly in the path of the favoured sea-route of the many European fleets that vied for control of this region. Accordingly, as Dominica became a regular site for ships to 'wood and water' following their Atlantic crossing, the nature and disposition of this tiny island population became a matter of considerable interest, and references to them, and recommendations as to how they should be treated, figure prominently in the accounts of these voyages, reflecting those pragmatic priorities.*

By the end of the century, as the proto-ethnographic description of the Amerindian king of Dominica by the Earl of Cumberland's chaplain makes clear, the Amerindians had incorporated many items of European culture; some, as Keymis relates, even deserting the islands for the mainland. Thus the more rounded accounts that appear in the seventeenth century relate to a situation already substantially changed from the 'traditional society' which they attempt to describe and it is for this reason that special interest attaches to this early material despite its fragmentary character.

Nevertheless, the ambiguity over the real identity of 'canybals' and 'caribes' that Columbus initiated remains, and descriptions totter uneasily between identifying some measure of nobility in the scarlet savagery of the islanders (Drake) or emphasizing the desperate character of these 'Canybal' warriors of the Indies (Hawkins). Undoubtedly neither of these characterizations was wholly misplaced, reflecting precisely the plurality of attitudes and actions on the part of both Europeans and native Americans, before the colonial enclaves stabilized.

The fragmented nature of the extracts themselves also reflects the intermittent nature of contact with the Amerindians. These descriptions are typically short yet cover a period of thirty-two years. Equally, the irregular nature of these encounters provided little scope for serious conflict between native and European and we find Lawrence Keymis reflecting on the importance of this to colonial trade and settlement generally. This 'honeymoon' period was soon to end, however, as the strategic

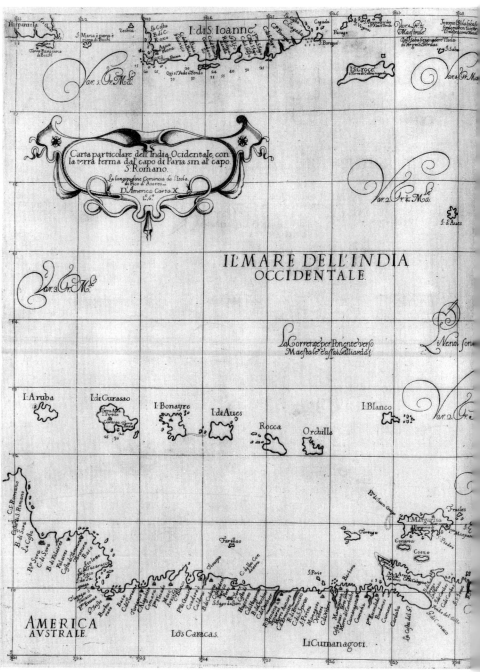

6. Map of the Caribbean. From Robert Dudley, *Dell' arcano del mare*, 5 vols. (Francesco Onofri, Florence: 1646–7). The Bodleian Library: Mason B.B. 183. Maps x. Although this work contains maps of many different regions of the world, Dudley was himself acquainted with this particular area by virtue of his voyage to Trinidad, Grenada, and Puerto Rico in 1594–5.

S. Martino

S. Bartolomeo

Barbada

Nioues   el Antigua

Rutunda

Monserato è
alta è piena di Boschi

Guadalupa è
Terra di Montagna   Carib

Los Sanctos

Qui si tocca per andare
a Porto Rico   Qui sono
Fondo

Marigalanto è Isola
piana piena di Boschi

I. dell' India Occidentale
ò di Caribes.

Li Ventifissi son Gre.
cali con buon tempo

La Descada è Isola senza
Alberi assimiglia una Galera di lontano.

L'OCEANO OCCIDENTALE

a qui tocca la Terra
è mi seno

Dominica à marea piena per la Parte
Maestrale mostra di lontano come fusse
due Isole.

Assimiglia C. Tuberon
del Hispaniola

Terra di Montagne
in mezo.

La Corrente è Gagliarda
Verso Maestrale

L'Aria è buona.

Il tempo è quasi sempre
buono & eguale.

La Corrente p. Ponente

Var. Gr. ½ Mae⅓

S. Lucia

S. Vincente, è poco
praticata da nauiganti.

Barbudas

Var. Gr. ½ Ma.

BeRia

Vogeleglande

Granadillos
pericolosi

I. Granada

I. Tabagua ò
di Tabacco.

I di S. Bernardo ò
Fonseca

Li Venti Fissi Sono
Grecali e Leuanti.

Var ò ½ Ma.

Flusso à H 3   B. del Drago   Fl. Verde

la Trinidada

B. di Ca
ribas

Lagua Bianchegia

S. Diouese M.

Blanqui
Salei

R. Arenas

R. di Ledo

Æ Lutini fec.

necessities of inter-colonial competition overrode the niceties of native diplomacy.

The following extracts are taken either from the 1927–8 reprint of Richard Hakluyt's famous collection, The Principal Navigations *(1599–1600), or from the 1905–6 reprint of that of his less able successor and rival, Samuel Purchas, who published much of the remaining Hakluyt manuscripts as* Hakluytus Posthumus or Purchas His Pilgrimes *in 1625. The second extract from the* Primrose Journal *of Francis Drake's 1585–6 voyage follows Mary Keeler's (1981) transcription.*

The first extracts relate to John Hawkins's (1532–95) second voyage of 1564–5, two others being made in 1562–3 and 1567–8. All three of these voyages were connected to the development of the Atlantic slave-trade in that the Spanish Crown, not having renewed the general German supply monopoly (asiento) in 1532, chose rather to offer specific contracts to various individual merchants, up until Philip II's occupation of Portugal in 1580. In this context, rather than being pure piracy, Hawkins's voyages were probably designed to win permission to participate in the American trade.

In any case he was keenly aware of the commercial possibilities of the African slave-trade and on his second voyage was hoping for better prices by dealing directly with the settlements on the mainland of South America. On his return voyage through the Florida Channel, having oversailed both Española and Jamaica, Hawkins still had an important part of his plans to accomplish; to evaluate the attempts of French Protestants to establish a strategic base in this region under René Laudonnière, whose own encounter with the Dominican natives is presented later in this chapter.

We join Hawkins as he leaves the coast of Africa.

The 29 of this same moneth [January] we departed with all our shippes from Sierra Leona, towardes the West Indies, and for the space of eighteene dayes, we were becalmed, having nowe and then contrary windes, and some Ternados, amongst the same calme, which happened to us very ill, beeing but reasonably watered, for so great a companie of Negros, and our selves, which pinched us all, and that which was worst, put us in such feare that many never thought to have reached the Indies, without great death of Negros, and of themselves: but the Almightie God, who never suffereth his elect to perish, sent us the sixteenth of Februarie, the ordinary Brise, which is the Northwest winde, which never left us, till wee came to an Island of the Canybals, called Dominica, where wee arrived the ninth of March, upon a Saturday: and because it was the most desolate place in all the Island, we could see no Canybals, but some of their houses where they dwelled, and as it should seeme forsooke the place for want of fresh water, for wee could finde none there but raine water, and such as fell from the hilles, and remained as a puddle in the dale, whereof wee filled for our Negros. The Canybals of that Island, and also others adjacent are the most desperate warriers that are in the Indies, by the Spaniardes report, who arc never able to conquer them, and they are molested by them not a little, when they are driven to water there in any of those Islands: of very late, not two moneths past, in the said Island, a Caravel being driven to water, was in the night sette upon by the inhabitants, who cutte their cable in the halser, whereby they were driven a shore, and so taken by them, and eaten. The greene Dragon of Newhaven, whereof was Captaine one Bontemps, in March also, came to one of those Islands, called Granada, and being driven to water, could not doe the same for the Canybals, who fought with him very desperatly two dayes. Four our part also, if we had not lighted upon the desertest place in all that Island, wee could not have missed, but should have bene greatly troubled by them, by all the Spaniards reports, who make them devils in respect of me. The tenth day at night [10 March], we departed from thence.

¶ [*After which Hawkins proceeded to Margarita off the Venezuelan coast and then west to Cumaná where he was able to trade with both the Spanish and the Amerindians. He left here on 28 March.*]

[. . .] the next day we passed between the maine land, and the island called Tortuga, a very lowe Island, in the yeere of our Lorde God one thousand five hundred sixty five aforesaide, and sayled along the coast untill the first of Aprill, at which time the Captaine sayled along in the Jesus pinnesse to discerne the coast, and saw many Caribes on shore, and some also in their Canoas, which made tokens unto him of friendship, and shewed him golde, meaning thereby that they would trafficke for wares. Whereupon he stayed to see the manners of them, and so for two or three trifles they gave such things as they had about them, and departed: but the Caribes were very importunate to have them come on shore, which if it had not bene for want of wares to trafficke with them, he would not have denyed them, because the Indians which he saw before were very gentle people, and such as do no man hurt. But as God would have it, hee wanted that thing, which if hee had had, would have bene his confusion: for these were no such kinde of people as wee tooke them to bee, but more devilish a thousand partes and are eaters and devourers of any man they can catch, as it was afterwards declared unto us at Burboroata, by a Caravel comming out of Spaine with certaine souldiers, and a Captaine generall sent by the king for those Eastward parts of the Indians, who sayling along in his pinnesse, as our Captaine did to descry the coast, was by the Caribes called a shoore with sundry tokens made to him of friendshippe, and golde shewed as though they desired trafficke, with the which the Spaniard being mooved, suspecting no deceite at all, went ashore amongst them: who was no sooner ashore, but with foure or five more was taken, the rest of his company being invaded by them, saved themselves by flight, but they that were taken, paied their ransome with their lives, and were presently eaten. And this is their

49

practise to toll with their golde the ignorant to their snares: they are blood-suckers both of Spaniards, Indians, and all that light in their laps, not sparing their owne countreymen if they can conveniently come by them. Their policie in fight with the Spaniards is marveilous: for they chuse for their refuge the mountaines and woodes where the Spaniards with their horses cannot follow them, and if they fortune to be met in the plaine where one horseman may overunne 100. of them, they have a devise of late practised by them to pitch stakes of wood in the ground, and also small iron spikes to mischiefe their horses, wherein they shew themselves politique warriers. They have more abundance of golde than all the Spaniards have, and live upon the mountaines where the Mines are in such number, that the Spaniards have much adoe to get any of them from them, and yet sometimes by assembling a great number of them, which happeneth once in two yeeres, they get a piece from them, which afterwards they keepe sure ynough.

Thus having escaped the danger of them, wee kept our course along the coast, and came the third of April to a Towne called Burboroata, where his ships came to ancker [. . .]

¶ [*Here they traded black slaves to the Spaniards, although they had no licence to do so, and had some difficulty in persuading the settlers to reach a fair price. During this time a French trader also appeared with news from the Guinea coast and the night before his departure on 4 May we are told that:*]

[. . .] the Caribes, whereof I have made mention before, being to the number of 200. came in their Canoas to Burboroata, intending by night to have burned the towne, and taken the Spaniards, who being more vigilant because of our being there, then their custome was, perceiving them comming, raised the towne, who in a moment being a horsebacke, by meanes their custome is for all doubts to keepe their horses ready sadled, in the night set upon them, & tooke one, but the rest making shift for themselves, escaped away. But this one, because he was their guide, and was the occasion that divers times they had made invasion upon them, had for his traveile a stake thrust through his fundament, and so out of his necke.

¶ [*Hawkins had no further encounters with the 'Caribes' and, following his failure to make landfall on either Española or Jamaica, came on 12 July to the Florida coast, where he met with the French colony led by Captain René Laudonnière.*

René Goulaine de Laudonnière had been sent out to Florida by the Admiral of France, the Huguenot Gaspar de Coligny. In the struggle with Catholic Spain the occupation of the Florida coast by fellow Protestants was of great interest to the English Crown, but at the same time the removal of this colony would certainly be a recommendation to the King of Spain in the quest for the elusive asiento. *In the event, although Hawkins found Laudonnière and his compatriots on the verge of starvation, they declined his offer to evacuate them and Hawkins arrived back in Padstow, Cornwall, on 20 September 1565.*]

The following account of Dominica, written by Laudonnière, and translated by Hakluyt himself, takes up the story of this colony before Hawkins's arrival and relates to the second voyage that Laudonnière made to Florida, the first having been in 1561–2. We join Laudonnière after he leaves France on 22 April 1564 and having taken on fresh water in Tenerife.]

[...] I continued my course towards the West, wherein the windes favoured me so well, that 15 dayes after our ships arrived safe and sound at the Antilles: and going on land at the Isle of Martinino, one of the first of them, the next day we arrived at Dominica, twelve leagues distant from the former.

Dominica is one of the fayrest Islands of the West, full of hilles, and of very good smell. Whose singularities desiring to know as we passed, and seeking also to refresh our selves with fresh water, I made the Mariners cast anker, after wee had sayled about halfe along the coast thereof. As soone as we had cast anker, two Indians (inhabitants of that place) sayled towards us in two Canoas full of a fruite of great excellencie which they call *Ananas*. As they approached unto our Barke, there was one of them which being in some misdoubt of us, went backe againe on land, and fled his way with as much speede as he could possibly. Which our men perceived and entred with diligence into the other Canoa, wherein they caught the poore Indian, & brought him unto me. But the poore fellow became so astonied in beholding us, that he knew not which way to behave himself, because that (as afterward I understood) he feared that he was fallen into Spanish hands, of whom he had bene taken once before, and which, as he shewed us, had cut of his stones [testicles]. At length this poore Indian was secure of us, and discoursed unto us of many things, whereof we received very small pleasure, because we understood not his minde but by his signes. Then he desired me to give him leave to depart, and promised me that he would bring me a thousand presents, whereunto I agreed on condition that he would have patience untill the next day, when I purposed to goe on land, where I suffered him to depart after I had given him a shirte, and certaine small trifles, wherewith he departed very well contented from us.

The place where we went on shore was hard by a very high Rocke, out of which there ran a litle river of sweet and excellent good water: by which river we stayed certaine dayes to discover the things which were worthy to be seene, and traffiqued dayly with the Indians: which above all things besought us that none of our men should come neere their lodgings nor their gardens, otherwise that we should give them great cause of jelousie, and that in so doing, wee should not want of their fruite, which they call *Ananas*, whereof they offered us very liberally, receiving in recompence certaine things of small value. This notwithstanding, it happened on a day that certaine of our men desirous to see some new things in these strange countries, walked through the woods: and following still the litle rivers side, they spied two serpents of exceeding bignes, which went side by side overthwart the way. My souldiers went before

51

them thinking to let them from going into the woods: but the serpents nothing at all astonied at these gestures glanced into the bushes with fearful hyssings: yet for all that, my men drew their swords and killed them, and found them afterward 9 great foote long, and as big as a mans leg. During this combate, certaine others more undiscreete went and gathered their *Ananas* in the Indians gardens, trampling through them without any discretion: and not therewithall contented they went toward their dwellings; whereat the Indians were so much offended, that without regarding any thing they rushed upon them and discharged their shot, so that they hit one of my men named Martine Chaveau, which remained behind. We could not know whether hee were killed on the place, or whether he were taken prisoner: for those of his company had inough to doe to save themselves without thinking of their companion. Whereof Monsieur de Ottigni my Lieuetenant being advertised, sent unto to me to know whether I thought good that he should lay an ambush for the Indians which had taken or killed our man, or whether hee should go directly to their dwellings to know the trueth. I sent unto him after good deliberation hereupon, that he should not attempt any thing, and that for divers occasions: but contrariwise that he should embarke himself with al diligence, & consequently al they that were on land: which he did with speed. But as he sayled towards our ships he perceived along the shore a great number of Indians which began to charge them with their arrowes: hee for his part discharged store of shot against them, yet was not able to hurt them, or by any meanes to surprise them: for which cause he quite forsooke them, and came unto our ship. Where staying untill the next day morning we set sayle following our wonted course, and keeping the same, we discovered diverse Isles conquered by the Spaniards, as the Isles of S. Christopher, and of the Saintes, of Monserrate, and La Redonda: [. . .]

¶ [*After fifteen days' sailing they reached Florida, 'to witte, on Thurseday the 22 of June about 3 of the clock'.*

Although the islands, particularly Dominica, were undoubtedly visited again by this constant stream of shipping seeking fresh water and supplies after the Atlantic crossing, it is not until twenty years later that we have a further description of the Amerindians by English voyagers.

Francis Drake (1545?–1596) had been with Hawkins on his third voyage and accompanied him again during the 1595 expedition (see below). His fame had been established by the raid on the Darien peninsula in 1573, aided and abetted by both black runaway slaves ('maroons') and the local Amerindians. In the interim he had circumnavigated the world and risen to be one of the English Crown's most important naval advisers. For the expedition of 1585–6, from which the following accounts are taken, he intended to lead a fundamental assault on Spain's positions in the Indies. In the event he came away with less booty than on other occasions but having done serious damage to Spain's prestige in the Caribbean.

Two extracts relating to that voyage are reproduced here; the first from Hakluyt's

Principal Navigations *and the second from Keeler's (1981) transcription of the* Primrose Journal, *which was the record of the ship captained by Martin Frobisher, vice-admiral of the expedition. We join Drake as he leaves the Canaries.*]

[. . .] From hence putting off to the West Indies, wee were not many dayes at Sea, but there beganne among our people such mortalitie, as in fewe dayes there were dead above two or three hundred men. And until some seven or eight dayes after our comming from S. Iago, there had not died any one man of sicknesse in all the fleete: the sicknesse shewed not his infection wherewith so many were stroken, untill we were departed thence, and then seazed our people with extreme hot burning and continuall agues, whereof very fewe escaped with life, and yet those for the most part not without great alteration and decay of their wittes and strength for a long time after. In some that died were plainely shewed the small spots, which are often found upon those that be infected with the plague: wee were not above eighteene dayes in passage betweene the sight of Saint Iago aforesaid, and the Island of Dominica, being the first Island of the West Indies that we fell withall, the same being inhabited with savage people, which goe all naked, their skinne coloured with some painting of a reddish tawney, very personable and handsome strong men, who doe admit litle conversation with the Spanyards: for as some of our people might understand them, they had a Spaniard or twaine prisoners with them, neither doe I thinke that there is any safetie fro any of our nation, or any other to be within the limits of their commandement, albeit they used us very kindly for those few houres of time which wee spent with them, helping our folkes to fill and carry on their bare shoulders fresh water from the river to our ships boates, and fetching from their houses great store of Tabacco, as also a kind of bread which they fed on, called Cassavi, very white and savourie, made of the rootes of Cassavi. In recompence whereof, we bestowed liberall rewards of glasse, coloured beades, and other things, which we had found at Saint Iago, wherewith (as it seemed) they rested greatly satisfied, and shewed some sorowful countenance when they perceived that we would depart.

From hence wee went to another Island Westward of it, called Saint Christophers Island, wherein we spent some dayes of Christmas, to refresh our sicke people, and to cleanse and ayre our ships. In which Island were not any people at all that we could heare of. [. . .]

¶ [*The second extract relating to Drake's voyage, from the* Primrose Journal, *gives some further detail on the sailors' interactions with the Amerindians on Dominica.*]

[. . .] The 21 of December wee fell with an Iland called [Dominica]. the people ar all as redd as Scarlet, Wee ankered there to refresshe our men. wee fownde verie goodlie rivers there, & there wee tooke in water for our neede. wee woulde have tarried there longer for to have refresshed our men but wee coulde finde no convenient place to keepe them in from the people of the countrie, for they ar greate devowrers & eaters of men And the Ile is all woodes.

Wee withe our boate met with 8 of these men at sea who as soone as they espied us waved us unto them & put forthe a flagg of truce beinge a cake of Cassado bread, Wee borded them presentlie, there boate was a Cannow that is made like a hogges trowghe, all of on[e] tree. These people go naked withowte anie manner of clothe abowte them, There manner is when they kill anie of there enemies they knocke owte the teethe & were them abowte there neckes like a chaine & eate flesshe for meate.

When wee had borded them as before they gave us a kinde of Bottle full of water & Cassado bread that is made of a tree & wee gave them Bisket & a can of Beare, which they did presentlie bothe eate & drinke & then wee Departed from them & went rowinge close aborde the shore where the people of the countrie came runninge to the water side wounderinge greatlie at us. Then we came to a goodlie river of fresshe water & thither came 6 men of the countrie unto us & emongst them there was on[e] that commaunded the reste. On[e] broughte a cocke & a henne a nother browght Potatos, an other, Plantaine fruite. They did swime over the River to us & came to our boate & the Captaine cawsed a combe to bee geven them, which was Doonne & the cocke required for hit [it], but they woulde not, Then the Captaine gave a loking glasse to be geveen them, for which they gave ther cocke & the Captain Intised them to comme into the boate, which on[e] of them did & woulde have gonne with us but that his companions called him & would not suffer him, so he lepte into the sea with his bow & arrowes in On[e] hande & swame to shore with thother. Then we departed from them for that time.

The next Daie wee wente to serche further into the lande & the people ranne alonge the sea side before us. then the Captaine commanded a trumpet to be sownded which Doonne, the People hier [higher?] in the land gave a greate showte & kept a whistlinge & blew a thinge like a horne, then they came to the sea side & shott at us. Wee sowght for some good place but fownde none to serve our turne & so departed.

Thys Ile is full of woodes and busshes, Wee saw manie of there howses. We fownde snakes of great bigness with Newtes and other venomous worms. [. . .]

[*Drake's subsequent actions against the Spanish at Santo Domingo (again with the aid of local maroons), Río de la Hacha, and Cartagena were certainly successful, but by the 1590s there had been a change in the balance of forces as the Spanish improved their American fleet and the defences of their colonial settlements. Accordingly the subsequent voyages of John White, Amias Preston, and John Hawkins, to which the following extracts relate, have achieved less notoriety in the history of the region. None the less the prominence of Dominica as a base for re-supply remains undiminished.*

In the first extract we join John White en route *to the Virginia colony founded by Walter Ralegh. White had no plans to become embroiled with the Spanish in the Caribbean and, indeed, Hakluyt reproduces a letter from White to this effect, complaining that the supply of the Virginia colony was being jeopardized by these other 'adventures'. Leaving England on 20 March 1590 he followed the familiar route to the Canaries, leaving Gran Canaria on 9 April.]*

[...] The last of Aprill we saw Dominica, and the same night we came to an anker on the Southside thereof.

The first of May in the morning many of the Salvages came aboord our ships in their Canowes, and did traffique with us; we also the same day landed and entered their Towne from whence we returned the same day aboord without any resistance of the Salvages; or any offence done to them.

The 2 of May our Admirall and our Pinesse departed from Dominica leaving the John our Vice-admirall playing off and on about Dominica, hoping to take some Spaniard outwardes bound to the Indies; the same night we had sight of three smal Ilands called Los Santos, leaving Guadalupe and them on our starboord.

On Thursday being the 19 our Viceadmirall, from whom we departed at Dominica, came to us at Saona, with whom we left a Spanish Frigate, and appointed him to lie off and on other five daies betweene Saona [Española] and Mona [Puerto Rico] to the ende aforesaid; then we departed from them at Saona for Cape Tyburon. Here I was enformed that our men of the Viceadmirall, at their departure from Dominica brought away two young Salvages, which were the chiefe Casiques sonnes of that Countrey and part of Dominica, but they shortly after ran away from them at Santa Cruz Iland, where the Vice-admirall landed to take in ballast. [...]

¶ *[When they finally reached Virginia they found the settlement had been destroyed by the Amerindians and, though planning to winter in the Caribbean, they were driven off course by storms on the return south, eventually being forced to return directly to England.*

Our next extract is from Robert Davie's account of Amias Preston's and George Sommers's raid on the Spanish Caribbean, in the Hawkins/Drake tradition. Dominica was once again the preliminary resting place before they went on successfully to attack Coche, Coro, S. Iago, Cumaná, and Jamaica. We join the narrative as the expedition leaves the Canaries in 1595.]

[...] So we departed altogether with joy the 13 of April, & set our course for the West Indies. And the 8 of May next ensuing, we arrived at the yland of Dominica. In all which time nothing happened unto us saving this, that the 18 day of April at midnight, our admiral lost her long boat in towing. We staied at Dominica til the 14 of May, to refresh our sicke men. Here the Indians came unto us in canoas made of a whole tree, in some whereof were 3 men, in some 4 or 6, & in others 12 or 14, and brought in them plantans, pinos, and potatos, and trucked with us, for hatchets, knives, & small bead-stones.

Here in refreshing our men, we found an hot bath hard joyning to a cold river side: wherein our sick men bathed themselves, and were soone recovered of their sicknesses. This is a goodly yland, and something high land, but al overgrowen with woods. The 14 we departed from thence. [...]

¶ [*As the great age of the privateers draws to a close in the Caribbean, so the foremost practitioners of this art are themselves extinguished. The final voyage of Drake and Hawkins began on 28 August 1595; we join the expedition a month later, as they leave the Canaries.*]

[...] we came in the height of the Islands of Cape Verde, and then more Westerly for Martinino, one of the Islands of the West Indies, which we saw the 27 of October: but the night before we had a storme, in which sir Francis with foure or five other ships bearing on head of the fleete was separated. Then we stood for Dominica, an Island full of inhabitants of the race of the Canibals, not past ten leagues distant from Martinino. In it groweth great store of Tabacco: where most of our English and French men barter knives, hatchets, sawes, and such yron tooles in trucke of Tabacco.

Before we came to Dominica our Generall Sir Francis Drake altered his course, and went for Marigalante, which we had sight of the 28 day, and came to anker on the Northeast side a saker [cannon] shot off the shore in 13 fathomes water faire sholding. There the Generall went on shore in his barge, and by chance met a Canoa of Dominicans, to the people whereof he gave a yellow wastcoate of flanell and an hankerchiefe; and they gave him such fruits as they had, and the Dominicans rowed to Dominica againe. They came thither to fetch some fruits which they sowe and plant in divers places of that Island, which they keepe like gardens.

The next morning by breake of day we weyed and stoode betweene the Todos Santos, which are 4 or 5 little Islands betweene Guadalupe and Dominica. There is nothing upon these Islands but wood. We came to the Southeast side of Guadalupe and there ankered hard aboord the shore: the Southwest side of the Island is deepe water and good ankorage: where that day sir John Hawkins came to us againe standing up from the South side of Dominica. There we watered, washed our ships, set up our pinnesses, and refreshed our souldiers on shore. [...]

¶ [*From here they were pursued by Spanish frigates, some of the English being captured at sea. On 8 November they anchored off the Virgin Islands, where Hawkins fell sick. They departed southward on the 12th and Hawkins died four days later within sight of Puerto Rico. The expedition continued on into the new year but on 28 January 'at 4 of the clocke in the morning our Generall sir Francis Drake departed this life' just off Puerto Bello.*

The next account really lies outside the privateering tradition, having been written by Lawrence Keymis (d. 1618) as part of a wider description of his second voyage]

to Guiana in 1596 which was undertaken to consolidate the Amerindian alliances,
and further the discoveries, that had been made by Walter Ralegh in his first voyage
to the Orinoco in 1595. However, the role of the Caribbean islands as staging posts
in the Atlantic crossing, in both directions, is well illustrated here, as is the growing
consciousness of the need to treat the Amerindians well if colonial enterprises are to
succeed; prior experiences on Dominica being explicitly cited by Keymis as an
example of such lack of foresight. The following extract begins as Keymis turns
homeward from the Guiana coast.]

[. . .] Our English that to steale the first blessing of an untraded place, will
perhaps secretly hasten thither, may bee beholding to mee for this caveat, if
they take notice thereof. They may bee assured, that this people, as they no
way sought our harme, but used our men with all kindnesse: so are they
impatient of such a wrong, as to have any of their people perforce taken from
them, and will doubtlesse seeke revenge. The example of the like practise
upon the coast of Guinie, in the yeere 1566, and againe at Dominica, where
Alderman Wats his shippe hardly escaped being taken, may serve for our
warning in like case to looke for no good, before they be satisfied for this injury.

When wee had taken aboorde us such victuals as were in the Pinnesse: wee
set fire in her, (for her Rudder could serve her to no longer use) and stopping
the floodes, plyed to windwarde with the ebbe neere the shoare, untill wee
were sixteene leagues to the Eastwarde of the Rivers mouth, and then standing
off to Sea, wee fell in twentie foure hourse sayling with Punta de Galera the
Northeastermost part of Trinidad. But having Tabaco-island in sight, wee first
went thither. This Island is plentifull of all things, and a very good soyle. It is
not nowe inhabited, because the Charibes of Dominica are evill neighbours
unto it. They of Trinidad have a meaning and purpose to flie thither, when no
longer they can keepe Trinidad. Their only doubt is, that when they are seated
there, the Spaniard will seeke to possesse it also. The Governour of Margarita
went lately in a Pinnesse to viewe this Island. Gilbert my [Amerindian] Pilot
who sometime lived there, noteth it for the best and fruitfullest ground that
hee knoweth.

Thence wee returned to Punta de Galera and ancored in tenne fathome
under the North side of the Island some five or sixe miles from the sayde point.
The flood-tyde striketh alongst the coast to the Eastward very strongly. Wee
discharged a peece of ordinance, and afterwards went to shoore in our boat:
but no Indian came unto us. I would have sent John of Trinidad to procure
some of them to speake with us: but he was altogether unwilling, alleaging
that their dwellings were farre within the mountaines, and that hee knewe no
part of that side of the Island. From this place we set sayle for Santa Lucia, but
fell with Granata, which wee found not inhabited.

Saint Vincent we hardly recovered, by turning under the lee of the island.
The Tabaco of this place is good: but the Indians being Canibals, promising us
store, and delaying us from day to day, sought onely oportunitie to betray,

take, and eate us, as lately they had devoured the whole companie of a French shippe. This their treacherie being by one of their slaves revealed, from thenceforth they did all forbeare to come unto us. To sit downe on their lowe stooles, when they by offering such ease, will seem to shewe curtesie, abodeth death to strangers, that shall trust them. At Matalino or Martinino we found not any inhabitants. Lastly, wee came to Dominica, where we could get no good Tabaco. But having intelligence of a Spanish shippe, that was taking in of fresh water, at the Northwest side of the Island, wee wayed ancor to seeke him. Hee discrying us, stole away by night. The Indians of this place have determined to remoove, and joyne with them of Guanipa [river in east Venezuela], against the Spaniardes, who lately dispeopled one of their Islands, and at our being there one of the Canoas returned from Guanipa, and certified us, that the tenne Spanish shippes at Trinidad doe ride, some of them at Conquerabia, the rest at the small Ilands neere the disemboging place. Herehence we steered North and by East, taking the directest course to shorten our way homcwards.

Thus have I emptied your purse, spending my time and travell in following your lordships directions for the full discoverie of this coast and the rivers thereof. [...]

¶ [*The final extract relates to George Clifford, Earl of Cumberland (1558–1603), who was one of the most active English privateers, having organized twelve expeditions to the Caribbean between 1587 and 1598, and spending some £100,000 in the process. This expenditure was at last rewarded with the taking of Puerto Rico in 1598, which Drake had attempted but never achieved.*
The following account, written by Clifford's chaplain Dr Layfield (or 'Eglambie' according to Purchas's contents page), is taken from an extensive description of this last voyage, Clifford's flotilla having stopped at Dominica to refresh themselves prior to the assault on Puerto Rico. The extract includes a surprisingly detailed description of the native Dominicans at the end of the sixteenth century, and even includes the first recorded linguistic observation of them that is not simply lexical. As was noted in the Introduction, the phrase 'Wilde Majesty' occurs as a marginal note made by Samuel Purchas to this account.]

[...] By two in the afternoone wee were come so neere aboard the shoare, that wee were met with many Canoes, manned with men wholly naked, saving that they had chaines and bracelets and some bodkins in their eares, or some strap in their nostrils or lips; the cause of their comming was to exchange their Tabacco, Pinos, Plantins, Potatoes, and Pepper with any trifle if it were gawdie. They were at first suspicious that wee were Spaniards or Frenchmen, but being assured that wee were English they came willingly aboard. They are men of good proportion, strong, and straight limmed, but few of them tall, their wits able to direct them to things bodily profitable. Their Canoes are of one Tree commonly in breadth, but containing one man, yet in some are seene two yonkers sit shoulder to shoulder. They are of divers length: some for three or foure men that sit in reasonable distance, and in some of them eight or nine persons a rowe. Besides their Merchandise for exchange, every one hath commonly his Bowe and Arrowes; they speak some Spanish words: they have Wickers platted something like a broad shield to defend the raine, they that want these, use a very broad leafe to that purpose, they provide shelter against the raine because it washeth of their red painting, laid so on that if you touch it, you shall finde it on your fingers.

That night, having with much adoe found land, within a quarter of a mile of the shore, we ankored for that night onely, for though there were a good watering place, and a very sweete riveret fast by us, yet his Lordship ment to way ankor the next morning, and to beare in to another watering place, wherewithall we certainly looked for a hot Bathe. Their Oares wherewith they rowe are not laid in bankes as Ship-boates have, but are made like a long Battledoore, saving that their palmes are much longer then broade, growing into a sharpe point, with a rising in the middest of them a good way; very like they are to blades of bigge Westerne Daggers, that are now made with graving. The shankes of these Oares are of equal bignesse, and at the top crosset, like a lame mans crutch. These they use alwayes with both their hands, but indifferently as they finde cause to steere this way or that way. The next morning wee bore in to the North-west end of the Iland, where we found a goodly Bay able to receive a greater Navie then hath beene together in the memorie of this age. There his Lordship found the hote Bathe fast by the side of a very fine River, which within three or foure yards runneth into the River, which within a stones cast disburdeneth it selfe into the Sea. Here our sicke men specially found good refreshing. In this place his Lordship staid some six dayes in watering the whole Fleete, which in that time was all come saving the Frigat, one of the blacke Pinnaces, and one of the Flemmings (which we hoped to be before us, for they have directions.) It was held convenient here to take a Muster of our companies, and something better to acquaint every one with his owne colours; but the weather was so extreamely foule, that in three or foure dayes spent to this purpose, there could be nothing done. Upon Wednesday therefore, being the last of may, it was resolved to stay no longer there, but to come againe to ankor at the Virgines, and there bestow one day in training our men. For that was our way to Saint John de Puerto rico, whether his Lordship now declared it was his purpose to goe first of all. By this time (for his Lordship would not have anything done in that foule weather) the other blacke Pinnace was taken down for a long Boate to serve for the more convenient landing of our men.

That evening and the next morning all our men were brought aboord, and on thursday night our sailes were cut for the Virgines. To describe this Iland [Dominica], it lieth North-west and South-east, the soile is very fat, even in the most neglected places, matching the Garden-plats in England for a rich blacke molde: so Mountainous (certaine in the places where we came neere the Seacoasts) that the Vallies may be better called Pits then Plaines, and withall so unpassably wooddie, that it is marvailous how those naked soules can be able to pull themselves through them, without renting their naturall cloathes. Some speake of more easie passages in the Inland of the Iland, which make it probable that they leave those skirts and edges of their Countrie thus of purpose for a wall of defence. These Hils are apparelled with a very goodly greene of Trees, of many sorts. The tallnesse of these unrequested Trees make the hils seeme more hilly then of themselves happily they are: for they grow so like good children of some happy civill body, without envie or oppression, as that they looke like a proud meddow about Oxford, when after some irruption, Tems [Thames] is againe cooched low within his owne banks, leaving the earths Mantle more ruggie and flakie, then otherwise it would have bin; yea so much seeme these natural children delighted with equalitie and withall with multiplication, that having growne to a definite stature, without desire of overtopping others, they willingly let down their boughes, which being come to earth againe take roote, as it were to continue the succession of their decaying progenitors: and yet they doe continually maintaine themselves in a greene-good liking, through the libertie partly of the Sunnes neighbourhood, which provideth them in that neerenesse to the Sea, of exceeding showres; partly of many fine Rivers, which to requite the shadow and coolenesse they receive from the Trees, give them backe againe, a continuall refreshing of very sweete and tastie water. For the Inhabitants of this Countrie. A Captaine or two watering neere the place where his Lordship first anchored, found a leasure to rowe up a River with some guard of Pikes and Musketers, till they came to a Towne of these poore Salvages; and a poore Towne it was of some twenty cottages rather than Houses, and yet there was there a King, whom they found in a wide hanging garment of rich crimson Taffetie, a Spanish Rapier in his hand, and the modell of a Lyon in shining Brasse, hanging upon his breast. There they saw their women as naked as wee had seene their men, and alike attired even to the boring of their lippes and eares, yet in that nakednesse, they perceived some sparkes of modestie, not willingly comming in the sight of strange and apparelled men: and when they did come, busie to cover, what should have bin better covered. The Queene they saw not, nor any of the Noble wives, but of the vulgar many; and the Maidens it should seeme they would not have so squeamish, for the King commanded his Daughters presence, with whom our Gentlemen did dance after meate was taken away. This withdrawing of their wives seemeth to come of the common jelousie of these people; for (it is reported) that though they admit one man to have many wives, yet for any man to meddle with another mans wife, is punished with death, even among them. And no mervaile if the severitie of law be set instead of many other wanting hinderances. It seemeth that themselves are wearie of their naked-nesse, for besides the Kings apparrell, they are exceeding desirous to exchange any of their Commodities for an old Waste-coate, or but a Cap, yea or but a paire of Gloves.

It is pretie that they say is the difference twixt the habit of a Wife and a Maide. The Maide weareth no garter (and indeede she needeth none) but the Wife is the first night she is married (which is not done without asking at least the consent of her parents) so straightly gartered, that in time the flesh will hang over the list. The haire of men and women are of like length, and fashion. But of all other things it is most memorable, that whereas their Houses are private to all other uses, yet they have one common place, where all the men at least take their diet, nature teaching them that Law which in Licurgus his mouth was thought strange and perhaps needelesse. The King sitteth in the same great roome with the rest, but withdrawing himselfe into some more lovely part, accompanied onely with three or foure of the best esteeme; their meates are their fine fruites, yet have they Hennes and Pigges, but it should seeme rather for delight, then victuall: their drinke is commonly water, but they make drinke of their Cassain, better of their Pines (and it should seeme that might be made an excellent liquor,) but the best and reserved for the Kings cup onely of Potatoes: their Bread is Cassain. The last report of them shall bee what I have seene in experience, namely their great desire to understand the English tongue; for some of them will point to most parts of his body, and having told the name of it in the language of Dominica, he would not rest till he were told the name of it in English, which having once told he would repeate till he could either name it right, or at least till he thought it was right, and so commonly it should be, saving that to all words ending in a consonant they always set the second vowell, as for chinne, they say chin-ne, so making most of the monasillables, dissillables. But it is time to leave them who are already many leagues of. [...]

6. *The Voyage of the* Olive Branch *(1606–1607)*

¶ *The story of the Guiana adventurers who had such a long and torrid stay on St Lucia offers the most detailed and valuable account of Carib–European contact before the full-scale attempts at settlement on the islands of the Lesser Antilles in the 1620s. It also shows that divisions existed not only between different states but also between different classes and interest-groups, here categorized as 'land-men' and 'sea-men'.*

William Turner offers a semi-official report in which dissension is not denied but no mention made of the captain's seeming incompetence in failing to find Guiana. The brief and sympathetic account of native hospitality is very much in keeping with the earlier reports of trading and watering on these Carib islands.

Turner presumably did not expect to see the land-men again. Nicholl's pamphlet contradicts several of Turner's assertions, which must have passed for 'fact' before the return of Nicholl and his three companions. The length of Nicholl's absence, the trauma of his experiences, and his almost miraculous 'delivery' clearly made his story worth publishing. Especially interesting is the detailed account of Carib agriculture and smallholding, showing how successfully traditional crops had been combined with European introductions. Recent archaeological work has suggested that Nicholl's 'village' was near the present site of Vieux-Fort on the south coast of St Lucia (Bullen 1966).

Established themes make their appearance: one group perishes (presumably) in the search for gold; cannibalism is imputed to the Caribs despite lack of any evidence. Nicholl's prayer at the end of his extract that the Lord would guide them 'to some Christian Harbour' was answered. Unfortunately the Christian Spaniards in Venezuela gave them just as hard a time, if not harder, than the St Lucian Caribs.

Turner's report was collected in Samuel Purchas's 1625 anthology of travel-writing and is reproduced from the early twentieth-century reprint; Nicholl's pamphlet has been transcribed from the 1605 printed original with only minor changes: the old 's' has been modernized; 'j' and 'v' have been introduced; European names have been given consistent spellings. Its full title was An Houre Glasse of

Indian Newes, or A True and Tragicall Discourse, Shewing the most
Lamentable Miseries, and Distressed Calamities Indured by 67 Englishmen,
which were Sent for a Supply to the Planting in Guiana in the Yeare. 1605.
Who not Finding the Saide Place, were for Want of Victuall, Left Ashore in
Saint Lucia, an Island of Caniballs, or Men-Eaters in the West Indyes, under
the Conduct of Captain Sen-Johns, of all which Said Number, onely a 11. are
Supposed to be still Living, whereof 4. are lately Returnd into England. Written
by John Nicholl, one of the Aforesaid Company.

---

1. WILLIAM TURNER

The fourteenth of August, about two in the afternoone, we had sight of the
Barbados, which bore of us South South-west. The Land hath two points
bearing East and West one from another; and from the middle of it, it riseth like
Tenerife, and is tenne leagues broad, and is barbarous without any inhabitants,
having great store of Hogges, Piggeons, and Parrats. We bore for the West-
ermost part of this Iland, and so wee steered away West North-west, and North-
west and by West amongst for Saint Lucia.

The fifteenth day, being thursday, we had sight of Saint Lucia, bearing West
North-west of us. This Iland of Saint Lucia is a very fertile Ile, bearing many
sorts of fruites, as Plantons, Potatoes, Pinos, Guanos, Pompins, Cassado, and
many other fruites. It hath also great store of Cotten wooll, and Tobacco, but
their Tobacco is not very good. It hath also many wilde Beasts in it, as Tygars,
Guanes, Alagartos, and other Beasts, which time would not permit us to see.
It hath also great store of Pigeons, Parrats, Pellicans, Cats, and Dogges. The
people goe naked, having very long haire, and are very honest, kinde hearted
people. In this Iland wee set our passengers ashoare, and furnished them with
all things necessary that our distressed Shippe could afford them. But they like
treacherous idle disposed people, not regarding our kindenesse, nor pittying
our necessitie, betraied our Boate from us one morning as wee went ashoare,
my selfe and three or foure other Gentlemen being in her; and then they
detained three Saylers which were drawing in the Boate keeping them for their
owne use, and afterward sent us aboord in a Canoa, which we were faine to
buy of them for Knives. The Master and the Captaine seeing this their treacherous dealing, and being out of all hope to get their Boate againe, about
thursday in the evening, being the three and twentieth of August, gave them
a Peece of Ordnance with intent to beate downe their houses. We had no
sooner let flye at them, but presently they shot at us againe, the bullet whereof
came betweene our maine Mast and our Poope, but it hurt no body. So that
night we waied, and went to a Baye some two leagues to leeward of this roade
where we first ankored. In this Bay there are halfe a dosen of Indian houses
very pleasantly scituated upon the top of a hill, with a fresh water River at the
foote of the same hill; and in this Baye we had very good trafficke of linnen

cloath, and many pleasant fruites, for our Hatchets and Knives. After we had roade here some sixe houres, we might plainly discerne our Boate under saile, whereupon we presently fitted our small shot, hoping that their intent was to come aboord, and betray our Shippe, but they tacked in, and rowed alongst the shoare, till they came to the very Bay where we roade, and there they stopped, and we were in good hope to recover our Boate againe, but they tarried there trading for their commodities in the face of our Ordnance: whereupon we seeing their daring boldnesse to be so great that they presumed to trafficke in our owne Boate before our noses, and to goe about as it were to stop us from trafficke; we let flye at them sixe peeces of Ordnance, and a vallie of small shot; but what harme we did amongst them, we know not, for they rowed away, and got out of sight of us. We tearmed the Baye where we put these men a shoare Rogues Baye, & the Cape we called Cape Knave, and the River, River of Rascols.

This very same day being the foure and twentieth of August, we waied anchor, and steered away South South-east, and South-east and by South amongst for Saint Vincents. And upon Saturday, the five and twentieth day, in the afternoone we arrived at the Iland of Saint Vincents, where we came within a Ships length very nigh the shoare, which put us all in great feare, for if God had not sent us a gale from the shoare, we had runne a ground, and we had had all our throates cut by the Indians of that Iland. So that night we tried it off at Sea with our fore-top-saile, and fore-saile, intending next day, being Sunday, to stand it in againe for the shoare (because we had good hope of good trafficke there.) But the current had driven us so farre off at Sea by the next morning, and the winde blew so vehemently from the shoare, that we could by no means fetch the land; whereupon being foure leagues from the shoare of Saint Vincents, we steered away South South-west, and South-west and by South amongst for the Testigoes. And the next morning being monday, we had sight of the Granados, bearing of us South east, but we could not fetch the Testigos. The nine and twentieth being Wednesday morning, we had sight of five small Rocks, which bore of us West and by North some five leagues off: wee had also sight of the Iland of Blanco, whereby wee found that the Current had set us, and doth set to the North-east, and therefore your best course to goe from the Granados to the Testigos, is to steere away South-west.

2. JOHN NICHOLL

To make a long and tedious discourse of that which may be uttered in few words, experience teacheth, doth rather move a loathing in the Reader, then any way procure a liking either in reader or hearer: in which respect I have rather desired briefly to deliver a plaine truth, which of it selfe to the wise and discreete is ever most acceptable, then with filed phrases, or eloquent termes (which indeede in mee are wanting) to adde any thing more then is most true, neither to represent, or lay open to the view of the worlde, ought more then

AN
Houre Glasse of In-
dian Newes.
OR

A true and tragicall difcourfe, fhewing the
most lamentable miferies, and diftreffed Calamities *indured by* 67 *Englifhmen, which were fent*
for a fupply to the planting in Guiana in
the yeare. 1 6 0 5.

VVho not finding the faide place, were for want of vic-
tuall, left a fhore in Saint Lucia, an Ifland of Caniballs,
or Men-eaters in the Weft-Indyes, vnder the Conduct of Captain Sen-Iohns, of all which faid
number, onely a 1 1. are fuppofed to be
ftill liuing, whereof 4. are lately
returnd into Eng-
land.

Written by Iohn Nicholl, *one of the aforefaid*
Company.

Homo es? humani nil a te alienum puta.

LONDON
Printed for Nathaniell Butter, and are to bee
folde at his Shop neere Saint *Auftens* Gate.
1 6 0 7.

what my selfe, with my associates have had as wofull experience, as ever (in my judgement) had any creatures living under the Canopie of Heaven: only thus much I thinke it not impertinent to deliver, for the better explanation of that which followeth, I make no question, but that the greater sort of people, which either have travailed themselves, had conversation with travaylers, or imployed themselves to much reading, are not ignorant that in the maine of America, in that part thereof which is vulgarly called The west India, amongst many other large Teritories & Dominions, is the great and mightie Kingdome of Guiana, scituated neare about the middle of the saide continent, or somwhat more southerly, it being neare under the Equinoctial line, the Souther most part thereof, and extending it selfe to about some 5.036 degrees of North Latitude, being bordered on the South-west with Perue, on the South with Amazonis, on the North with Mexico, and on the East with the Ocean Sea.

The saide Countrey of Guiana was first discovered or made knowne to our English Nation, as farre as I can learne, about the yeare of our Lord 1594. at the charge and direction principally of Sir Walter Rawleigh: the same againe seconded by himselfe the yeare following: afterward againe by Captaine Keymish and others, at the charges of the said Sir Walter Rawleigh it being reputed to bee the chiefest place for golde Mines in all the West India: but the prosecution thereof being left off for a time, by what occasion I know not, it so happened that in the yeare of our Lord 1602, Captain Charles Leigh made a voyage thither, for the discoverie thereof, and finding a fit place for habitation, determined to procure the planting of a Colonie there in the River Wiapica, which said determination at his returne being put in practice, with the fur-therance and special charge of the worshipfull Knight Sir Olive Leigh, certaine men were sent thither, there to inhabite under the conduct of the aforesaid Captain Charles Leigh, who remayned there about a yeare and a halfe, where he with manie of his companie dyed. For a supplie unto which companie, was another companie sent, in the yeare 1605. at the chargee of the sayde Sir Olive Leigh, and certaine other adventurers, of which companie my selfe was one, all under the conduct and leading of Captaine Sen-Johns, who being embarked in the Olive Branch of Sir Olive Leigh, whereof was captaine and master under God, Captaine Catlin and Arthur Chambers.

Being thus readie, we set saile the twelfth of Aprill one thousand six hundred and five, nothing hapning worth note, till wee came as high as the North Cape, where an English Barke overtaking us, foure of our Gentlemen, by reason of their sicknesse, were desirous to returne home againe, so that getting their passage for Lisbone, they tooke their leave of us, whose names were, Maister Rogers, Maister Catlin, Maister Sanders, and another whose name I doe not now remember. So wee continued our course to the Canaries, and so to Cape Blancko in Barbarie, and from thence to the Ile of Mayo: in which time of our voyage it fell out as often it hapneth in such actions, that our companie being divided, (as being some sea-men, and the rest land-men, who are for the most part many times of contrarie natures) there was some heart-burning and malice one against another, which rested not onely in the common sort, but rather and most chiefly in our captaines, whose haughtie mindes not brooking contradiction on either side, had like to have growne to a daungerous discention, had it not beene appeased by the diligent perswasions of some other of the companie, whose plausible spirites were more addicted to unitie and peace, then any way liking of such daungerous and indirect courses, they well foreknowing that civill discorde have beene the overthrow of mightie kingdomes, and great common weales, and therefore well might have beene the biter subversion of our so weake & slenderly governed companie. But all parties being now (as it seemed) to the outward view quieted, we went a shore upon the said Ile of Mayo to take in fresh water and salt, where we found 5 Portugals, which had bin robbed by the French, and there set a shore, where having stayed five dayes hunting of Goats, and refreshing of our men, we departed to saint Iago, where we landed the five Portugals, in reward of which kindnesse of ours, the Inhabitants tooke three of our men, and kept them as prisoners while they sent seaven leagues into the Countrey to know the Governours pleasure, and at night sent them aboad againe, having taken certaine commodities from them, which they had to buy some of their fruits.

From thence (having weyed our Anchor) with a merry gale we sailed towardes our desired place to the countrey of Guiana: but missing our expectation, here began the first scene of our ensuing miseries: for whether it was our Masters want of knowledge that we fell not with the prefired place, or that the current which our master alledged to be the reason, that setting verie strongly to the North-wards, put us so farre short thereof, or whither (as of all others that is most certaine) it pleased God in that place at that time, and in such a manner, to let us feele some part of his heavie displeasure, conceyved against us for our times formerly misspent: so as I say the ending of our hopes was the beginning of our miseries: for plying to and againe, wandring as it were in a wildernesse of woe, betwixt hope and dispaire, the time passed away & with the time our victuals, the onely hope of our health exceedingly wasted: thereupon our allowance was greatly shortned, & with the same & other occurrences our mens minds very much distracted, which bred amongst us many fearfull & daungerous mutinities. And as one miserie commeth still in the necke of another, so fared it with us: for with our want of victuals, we being neare unto the Equinoctiall, and the Sun in that part of the Zodiacke which was neare unto the Zenith, it was so exceeding hot, that with the vehemencie thereof many of our men fell marvellous weake, and some of them died, namely our Carpenters mate John Browne, our Cooke, and Robert Paine, and many others were so weake, that they were not able to come above the hatches. This extremitie caused us (though against our stomachs) to entreate the master to bring us to the nearest shore he could. And so having beene seventeene weekes at sea, in stead of our hopefull expectations of attaining to a pleasant, rich and golden Countrey, and the comfortable companie of our friends and Countrey-men, there as we supposed them resident, we were

brought to an Iland in the West India somewhat distant from the maine, called
Santa Lucia, having about twelve degrees of North latitude, inhabited onely
with a companie of most cruell Caniballs, and man-eaters, where we had no
sooner landed anchored, but the Carebyes came in their Periagoes or Boats
aboard us with great store of Tobacco, Plantons, Potatoes, Pines, Sugar Canes,
and diverse other fruits, with Hens, Chickens, Turtles, & Guanas: for all which
we contented and pleased them well. These Carrebyes at their first comming
in our sight, did seeme most strange and ugly, by reason they are all naked,
with long blacke haire hanging downe their shoulders, their bodies all painted
with red, and from their eares to their eyes, they do make three strokes with
red, which makes them looke like divels or Anticke faces, wherein they take a
great pride.

The next morning we went a shore with all our weak men, where there was
five or seaven houses planted by a pleasant fresh water River, which Captain
Sen-Johns bought for a Hatchet of an Indian Captaine called Anthonie, who
could speake a little Spanish, and he told us he had beene a slave to the
Spaniard in the Ile of Margareta: so he and al his companie went to another
towne some three myles off.

Whilest our sicke men were a shore refreshing themselves, our Master would
have departed, and have left them to shift among the Carrebyes, but Captain
Sen-Johns, and the chiefe of our companie would not consent thereto. And
seeing it was in vaine all of us for to venter home in the Shippe with that small
allowance, wee were willing to come a shore, and there to live untill it should
please God to send some meanes to bring us a way: upon that condition they
should deliver unto us one great peece, and every man his Musket and weapons,
and halfe the munition in the ship, with all our Chests and commodities
whatsoever, which hee would not graunt, before we had subscribed to a
certaine Writing which he wrote to excuse himselfe at his returne into England:
so we receyved foure little Barrels of powder, and ten round Bullets for the
great Peece, which when wee brought a shore did much feare the Indians, for
they asked us if we brought it to kill them. But to please their humours, wee
told them it was to kill the Spaniards, and then they came and helped us a
shore with her, and with all our Chestes, of their owne accord.

Now after they had delivered all things a shore out of the Boat we thought
it good to stay her, and to keepe her for our owne use, for wee did not know
what neede we might have of such a commoditie afterwarde: so wee sent the
sailers aboord in an Indian boat, onely three would not goe, but would stay
with us: so we were in all left a shore threescore and seaven in the Isle of Saint
Lucca.

At night when we were all sitting togither at supper about a great fire, which
they could well perceve from the ship when it was darke: and as it should
seeme in revenge of their Boat, before they departed they purposed to let us
know they were not well pleased with the action, they shot a great peece at
us with a single Bullet, but as it pleased God it fell downe by the side of our

house, and missed us, which if it had come amongest us we sitting so thicke, it could not have chosen but have beene the death of many of us.

This made Captaine Sen-Johns discharge our peece at them, without intent to hurt them, but fairly overshot them: for he might have sunke them, and would if they had shot once more: then presently they weyed Anchor and departed.

The next morning Captain Sen-Johns went in the Boate, with fifteene more in his companie, to trade with Anthonio his father for Rone cloth, which he had saved at sea great store: but when we came there, contrarie to our expectation, we found our ship there trading with them, who had incensed the Indians sore agaynst us, telling them that we were bad people, and would take all they had from them, and would cut their throats.

And as we rowed alongst the shore, they discharged halfe a dozen peece of Ordenance, and a volly of small shot at us, but there great shot overshot us, and light upon the rockes, and scarred the Indians a shore mightily, and their small shotte light short without harming us. Their decermination was to drive us from our Boat, or else to have sunke her, for their great shot came so thicke that wee were forced to leape a shore into the Woods: then they manned their Periago, and came to take our Boat away, which wee perceyving entered her againe, and escaped all their malice: so wee returned home againe safe, and they departed towards Saint Vincent, the eighteenth or nineteenth of August, 1605.

After the departure of our ship we remained in peaceable manner amongst the Indians, dayly trading with them for all manner of victuall, as Plantons, Potatoes, Penas, Papaians, Pumpins, Callobashoes, Pappes, Mammies, Guiavas, with diverse other fruits, and Tobacco aboundance, all verie pleasant to eate. Also they brought Turtles, Guanas, Hens and Chickens, Woodcocks and Snipes, with some Pellicans.

As for the Turtles, we our selves did use every night by courses to send out sixe to catch them, which is easily done, by reason that every night they use to come a shore, and lay their egs in the sand, and by the heat of the Sun they are hatched. At their coming out of the water they do make as broad a tract as a Cart with their fins, by which meanes wee are ledde to the place where they doe sit, and so we turne them on their backes, which being done, they can doe nothing but so lie till they bee deade. The meate of them dooth eate like unto Veale, and I have seene taken out of one of them to the number of sixe or seaven hundred egges, which wee doe frie with the fat or oyle of the Turtle, and also with cassada wee did make exceeding good White-pots and Puddings, putting the Egges and Oyle into it. Also the Guana is proportioned like a Serpent, more then an ell long, with foure short feete. In eating it is like a Connie, and hath in his belly to the number of five and twentie or thirtie Egges.

This Cassada is a roote of a tree, whose juce is poyson: but being squeassed, the flower doth make an excellent kind of bread, and will keepe long.

The Indians did marvaile much at our manner of dressing our meate, and they would be familier, and would dine with us verie often, but by no meanes wee could not make them eate salt: for they use to eate all their meate seasoned with Ginnie Pepper: their women came verie seldome unto us, for they are verie jealous over them. Once or twice there came some women with them, unto whome wee gave shirts to cover their nakednesse, whereof they seemed proud: Their ancient women are verie ugly, by reason of their side breastes, which dooth lie like emptie bagges: but those which have not given sucke, are well proportioned and proper.

Also we had a Net, with the which wee would get at one draught as many fish of diverse sorts, as would serve all our companie a day.

A little before our arrivall, three Spanish ships were cast away, and much of the goodes these Indians had saved with their Boats, and hid it in the Woods, they had so much Roan cloath, that all their Periagoes had sayles thereof. They also had great store of stuffe, Sirge, and Spanish woollen cloath, cloakes and apparell: insomuch that if we had had a Barke of fortie tuns burthen, wee could have loaden her home with such commodities as would have made a saving voyage. All which we could have bought for hatchets, knives, beads, fish-hookes, and thimbles, with other trifles.

Thus for the space of five or six Weekes, wee went not much abroade, but cut downe the Woods about our houses everie day, and mounted our great Peece upon broade Tables, which wee our selves had sawne, least the Carrebyes should at any time assault us.

Soone after this, there came another Captaine from Saint Vincent, called Augraumart, which was brother to Anthonio, who was offended with him for selling the houses unto us: for the which cause Anthonio bid us kill him, and tolde us hee purposed to bring twelve Periagoes loaden with Carrebyes to kill us, but wee found this Augraumart verie kinde unto us, and was willing to doe, or tell us anything wee desired him, for he taught us to make a Grater, which he made of small sharpe flint stones beaten into a broade boord to grate our Cassada on, whereof we made our breade, and hee tolde us, that Anthonio would cut our throates, and therefore bid us kill him. This made us doubtfull which to trust to.

We had certain Articles drawne, which were to bee observed, wherein Captaine Nicholas Sen-Johns was Captaine. his brother Alexander Lieutenant, Miles Pet, and Philip Glascock were commaunders for the appoynting of our Watch: John Rogers was our interpreter for the Spanish tongue, and was to buy and bargaine with the Indians for all the companie, both for commodities and victuals, Maister Garret, Maister Tench, Francis Brace, and my selfe, were appointed to order the domesticall matters.

All the occasions that we made whereby the Carrebyes* should fall out with us, was that one of our companie did sell a sworde unto Captaine Anthonio, which was contrarie to the Articles we had set downe, for none was (upon

* Carebie signifies in their language, A valiant man.

paine of severe punishment) to sel either Sworde, Dagger or Hedge-bill: which when we knew, Alexander Sen-Johns with a dozen more went to his house, and found him in his bed, which they call an Hamaco, with a little fire under him because he was not well, and the Sword standing by him, which yong Sen-Johns tooke and brought forth to us. This drove him into a great rage against us, for never after that would he be familiar with us.

The Carrebyes did weare for an ornament upon the small of their naked armes a four-square plate, which maister Browne a Gold-finer told Captaine Sen-Johns had three partes of it Golde, who asked the Carrebyes where they got it: who presently pointed us to a great Mountaine on the North-west part of the Island whose toppe we might see from the place where wee dwelt: but Anthonio saide there was none. These contrarie tales made us suspect some villanie and that it was but a policie to drawe some of our companie thither, whereby they might the better deale with us: for at home they durst not attempt any thing against us, both for feare of our great Peece, and also wee would not suffer them to bring their bowes and arrowes within our Centinell. Yet our Captaine would not bee content till wee consented that hee should go to the Mountaine, and tooke with him all sortes of commodities to bargaine with the Indians for Cloath, and he tooke old Browne the Gold-finer, and his sonne George Browne, John Rogers, Maister Looking, the three sailers, whose names were, John Fleming, Thomas Butler, Owen a Welchman, James Garret, & one Joseph and Christopher, two Grocers, and one Maister Evans, with diverse more, to the number of sixteene.

And upon a Monday they all imbarked in the Boat taking eight dayes victuall with them, promising to return betwixt that and the next Monday, leaving his brother Miles Pet, Philip Glascock, M. Garret, M. Tench, and my selfe, to rule at home. Upon Tuesday & Wednesday the Indians did not come unto us with victuals as they had wont, which made us after suspect that they were at the slaughter of our men at the Mount: & upon Wednesday, my selfe with 3. more went to Anthonios house, where we found a great number of women, but not passing halfe a score men, making great preparation of victuals: some baking of Cassada, others roasting and boyling of great fishes and Turtles. I offred to buy some of them, but they refused and would not, neither would they looke of any commoditie we had, which made us much marvell: for before that time they never denied us: so we departed, & by the way we light of a narrow path wherein we travelled a little, and all along the way did grow aboundance of Guiava trees, whose fruit is as big as an Apple, and verie pleasant to eate: the greene ones are wholesome for the bloodie fluxe.

Wee had not travayled a Mile, but wee entered downe by a Thicket into a most pleasant Garden of Potatoes, which drove us into greate admiration to beholde the manner of it, for it was made round like a Bower, encompassed with a greene Banke, so equally, that made us thinke some Christians had made it for a strength to save them from the Indians: and uppon the toppe thereof did growe a companie of the moste tallest Trees that ever I behelde, which did naturally growe so neere one to another, and so thicke from the roote to the toppe, that wee could not perceyve the skie through them. But following the path, wee perceyved it to passe through a narrow cut in the banke, where wee traveyled two or three miles further, passing through many goodly Gardens, wherein was abbundance of Cassada, Potatoes, Tobacco, Cotton-wool-trees, and Guiava trees, in diverse places as wee travayled wee did marvaile to see the huge and great trees that were there: for most of them were five or sixe fathoms about, and fearing that wee shoulde bee benighted, wee returned the same way againe, with as much greene Tobacco, Potatoes, and Cassada, as wee could carrie, which did much content our men at home for the Indians had not brought any victuals in three dayes before.

At night sixe of our men went to seeke for Turtles, and founde two verie great ones, but could not bring them home. For when they had turned them on their backes, it beganne to raine, thunder, and lighten so extreamly, that they had much a doe to get home themselves, and so it continued all night, with the moste horriblest thunder-claps that ever I heard, with lightning and raine as light as day, which caused us to awake, and after prayers to sit all night by greate fiers, drinking of Tobacc, with extraordinarie mirth amongest our selves, little foreseeing the daunger that befell to us the next day.

Earely the next Morning, wee went to bring home our Turtles, and there wee founde a great number of Carrebyes on the shore, and three or foure Boates by them, roasting of lande Crabbes, for what purpose they were so gathered together wee knew not, but least we should suspect them of any bad intent towardes us, they willed us to eate with them, and brought home our Turtles to our houses.

All that fore-noone wee kept good watch, for there was verie many which came both by Sea and land and Augraumart and his father came with a great number of Indians, and brought in his hande a quarter of a Turtle, and a hundred Egges, and gave them to young Sen-Johns, and tolde him, that if hee would goe to his Brother Anthonius house, hee should have greate store of victualls, and that hee should see his wife, and the more to persuade us to goe, hee promised that we should have Hamacas for to sleepe in, which is the beds they use.

Their Women dooth make them of Cotten that growes naturallye on the Trees, wereof they have aboundance. Wee manye times made sute unto them for their Hamacas, because they would bee a meanes to save us from the Stings of a certaine Flye called a Musketo, the which would so torment us with their poysoned stings, and cause us to swell as though we had the Leprosie, for they would sting through three payre of Stockings, but they were not willing till now on the suddaine that wee should have any. And because they were so kinde to us, wee took them all into our houses, and were verie merrye and pleasant with them, and gave them Aqua vitae which they delighted much in.

But Maister Tench (who had wont to bee a curious corrector of us in our merriments) did show himselfe so extraordinarie pleasant, that hee fell a singing of Catches with the Carrebyes, and caused them to drinke carouses of Agua vitae and water.

If wee had beene determined to have kild them, wee might have done it at that time with small danger, wee had a hundreth and above of them within our houses without either bowe or Arrowes. And when some of our companie, made such a motion as to put them to the Sworde (for some of us was halfe and more jealous of them, that they had done some mischiefe to our captaine, by reason one of our companie did say, that hee heard an Indian say, that the Captaine of the English had his hande cutte off at the Mount) but this was not regarded, but was imputed that hee had misconstrued the Carrebyes language. Maister Tench was agaynst it, saying: God would not be pleased with such a bloudie Act, agaynst such harmlesse people, and therefore willed us not to doe it without they gave the first occasion, wherein hee wronged himselfe and us all, in seeking to save the lives of them, who within three houres after most cruellye murthered him.

Before Dinner they all departed, but Augraumart and his father, who dined with us. And presently after dinner, eighteene was chosen to goe to Anthonios house with Augraumart and his father, who had neither bowe nor arrow: onely his father had a Brasell sworde.

This they did least wee shoulde suspect their treacherie. But wee not fearing anie treason, because wee had beene often times well used there before, went on boldly.

And some of our companie thought that the verie sight of our Peeces was sufficient to terrifie them, for attempting any villany against us. And therfore did not regarde either to charge them, or to light our match.

In this carelesse and secure manner wee travayled through a little necke of land which runnes farre into the Sea, and then wee entered upon the sand, which was so extreame hote with the reflexion of the Sunne that wee were not able to travail apace, being loaden with our Peeces.

But Maister Alexander had put off his Doublet, and gave his Boy his Peece, & went jesting and playing arme in arme with the two Carrebyes a good space before us, until wee came to a point of Land a quarter of a mile from Anthonios house, and then hee called us to come forward, but hee beeing light and coole, did keepe a greate way before us still. And when hee least suspected daunger, Augraumart made as though hee would imbrace him, And suddenlye clasping helde with one hand on his Rapyer, and the other on his Dagger, and his Father with a great Brassell Sword strooke him downe before we could come at him, but he recovered againe.

Then came the Arrowes so thicke out of the wood, that we could not get our match in the Cocke for pulling the Arrowes out of our bodyes: so amongst us all was but five or six peeces discharged, which when the Indians saw give fire, they did fall flat on the ground, shouting and crying with a moste hellish noyse, naming us by our names when they hit us.

Then wee retyred backe to a poynt of land, thinking there to have fitted our

8. *Murder of the Crew of the* Olive Branch. From Theodor de Bry, *America* (Frankfurt-on-Main, 1634), xiii. 46. The Bodleian Library: Mason B.B. 62.

peeces, and to have given them a volley of shot, But there came another Ambush on our backes, and round about us, insomuch that wee were inforced to forsake our peeces, and betake us to our swords, which did much incourage them, for when they see wee could not hurt them with our peeces, they would come so neere us, as though they purposed to make choyce in what place to hit us, of some they shot in the faces, others through the Shoulders, and of others, they would naile their feete and the ground together.

Maister Budge and Robert Shaw ranne into the sea, and there were both drowned and kild with Arrowes, Maister Tench had a little Buckler, with the which hee did save himselfe a long time, but at the last an Arrowe passed through both his legges, that hee could not goe, and stooping to pull it out, they kild him, and if anye of us offered to runne at one or two of them, they would runne away, and of a suddaine twentie or thirtie would enclose us, and still shoote Arrowes in them til they were downe, and then they with a great Brassell sword beate them to death, and after would rifle them: Maister Kettleby did behave himselfe verie gallantlye, for hee did not respect what arrowes he received in his bodye, so hee could but reach one stroke at a Carrebye, but they were too nimble for us in regard they were naked.

Yet neverthelesse, wee runne through them all, thinking that if wee had escaped that ambush, there had been no more to trouble us, but as I was pulling Arrowes out of his bodye, to the number of twentie at the least, there came the third ambush out of the woodes from whence came an Arrowe and hit him in the Breast, which hee perceived would be his death, for hee could not stand but as I held him, but I was forced to let him goe, and shift to save my selfe.

Then I over tooke young Sen-Johns his bodye almost full of Arrowes, of which I pulled out a number, But what for the bloud that runne from him, and the extreame heate he was in by his running, hee was not able to overtake the rest of our companye that was before.

And still the Carrebyes did gather ground uppon us, and the Arrowes came thicke on everie side.

Then hee willed mee to intreat them stay, and when I had overtaken one, I caused him to stay, which he was unwilling to doe, for hee tolde mee his Sword would not come foorth of the Scabberd, so I tooke hold of the Hilts, and betwixt us both pulled it out, but before wee had made an ende, these cruell and bloodye Carrebyes had encompassed yong Sen-Johns yet (to my griefe) I did stand and beholde his ende, who before hee fell did make them run like so many Currs from a Lyon: for looke which way hee ran, they all fled before him: his body was so loaden with Arrowes, that he fell to the ground: and upon one hand and knees, hee did keepe them from him with his Swoord, so much hee scorned so basely to dye at their handes.

We two were then the onley markes they aymed at: for having rifled young Sen-Johns, they pursued us very hotly, which caused us make haste to foure of our fellowes, who were entred into a narrow path, which leadeth through the woods, from the sandes to the Houses where wee dwelt: but there was in the path an other Ambush, which drove them backe to the sandes againe: and when they saw us so hardly chased, they entred the path with us againe.

The one side of the path was a high Mountayne, the other went downe a low Valley. The first foure took up the Mountayne, by which meanes, they were a fayre marke for them to hitte, who dropped downe one after another.

All this time, neyther Harry which was M. Stokeleys man (a Marchant now in Bucklersbery) nor myselfe was shot: but as we thought desperatly to run through them in the narrowe path, there came an Arrowe and pearced quite through his head, of the which he fell suddenly, and I ran to lift him up, but he was dead without speaking one word to mee at all.

Then came there two Arrowes and hitte mee in the back, the one directly against my hart, the other through my shoulder blade: so (with my sword in my hande) I ran upon them desperatly, thinking (before I had died) to have ben the death of some of them. And in my running, I saw Captaine Anthony, with an Arrow in his Bow drawne against me, who stood untill I came very neere him (for he purposed to have sped mee with that shot) which when I see come, I thought to put it by with my sword, but it light on my hand, & passed therein the handle of my sword, and nayled both together: but I continued running at him still; and before he could nocke another, I made him, and all the rest turne their backs, and run into the sands againe: which oportunity when I espyed, I leapt into the wood, downe to the valley, where I found a great Lake: And hearing them, with great showts and cry, which they use in signe of triumph and victory, pursue mee still, I leapt into the Lake, with my sword nayled to my hand, and two arrowes in my backe, and by the helpe of God swamme over, but with much ado: for the further side was shallow water, but I waded in mud up to the waste, which had almost spent me.

Now when I was over, I convayd my selfe into the thickest parts of the wood, making all the haste I could, to give my fellowes, which were at home, warning, lest the Indians should set on them unawares: and in my going, I came into a path, and sought for a great tree, to see, if by the ayme of the Iland, I could perceyve which way our houses stood. Then suddenly I heard a great noyse, which made me stand behind a tree, and there I saw two or 3. C. Indians go by me, which I imagined were going to set on them at home: but it pleased God I got home, & gave warning before their coming: so Miles Pet charged our great Peece, and al our men were in redines for their coming. Then presently, they all came in sight upon the sands, whome we sent away (by shooting of our great Peece) & came no more in 3. daies: in which time, we fortified ourselves with our Chests: And upon Munday morning (before wee had made an end of praier) there came to the number of 13. or 14. C. Indians (both by sea and land,) & there beset us round, making a noyse with their Hornes, and made most horrible cryes, which they do use, the more to terryfie their enemies: and we did answere them agayne with the lyke cryes, devyding our selves into 4 parts, according as we had made our Forts of our Chests, placing five in every

Forte, and three to the great Peece, where Miles Pet, my selfe and another was. Then they shot their Arrowes among us as thicke as hayle, and lest they should follow in upon us and make use of those Arrowes agayne, we gathered them all together, & made great fires with them before their faces, and many times they purposed to rush in upon us by multitudes, & to have beaten us downe with their Brazell Swordes: But our great Peece was so mounted, that very readly we could turne it which way we pleased, and looke which way their greatest company went, we let her flye amongst them. So perceiving that they could not prevaile against us, they put Cotten wooll upon the end of their Arrowes, and put fire on them and shot at our Houses which were made on long Canes or Reedes, and suddenly tooke fire by reason of the heat of the day, & burned downe to the ground, fastning on our Chests which were our Forts, and burned all downe to the ground, the extreme heat of the flame did make our men forsake their Forts, and retyre behinde the great Peece, to the Sea-side, which incouraged the Carrabies mightily. M. William Kettleby lay close unseene of the Indians upon the sand, and with a long Peece hee would reach them 12. score paces, & galled them much: other wise, they would have come on the backes of us by Sea, but he shot their Boats thorow and scard them for entring that way. Now, when al our men were fled behind the great Peece, onely Philip Glascock & Richard Garrat stood behinde the smoke, and marked where they purposed to enter, & eche of them discharged halfe a score times at them: At last, Philip Glascock received an Arrowe in his head, and Richard Garrat one in his Brest, and two in his backe. And when the Indians saw that all were fled but them two, they purposed to enter through the smoake upon us: but in the entring, hee gave a warning to Miles Pet to turne the Peece against the smoake: which presently we did, and let fly amongst them and drove them all backe, with most lamentable shrikes and cryes: no doubt but that shot was the death of many of them: for she was charged with stones. Then they blew their great Hornes, and all retyred backe to their Boates, without shooting one Arrowe at us.

After that our house was burned and all our Chests, which before were our Fort, we fortified our selves with the remnants of the stakes, and thatch which we saved from burning, setting it in the ground slope wise, covering it with Sand & Earth, which saved us ever after from their Arrowes.

In all these extreme dangers and imminent Calamities which all this while we endured, let the Christian Reader judge in what a perplexed state we were plunged, seeing still one misery to follow another, and each misery farre exceeding the former: As first, our danger at Sea to be famished: then a comfortlesse remedy against Famishment, to be left in a farre remote and unknowne place, amongst a cruell, barbarous and inhumane people, without hope of ever having any meanes to recover the sight of our native and deare countrey and friends: Then the losse of our Captaine (and others) which before (in all extremity) was still some comfort unto us: And now (lastly) these lamentable stratagems of the massacre of our fellows and friends, therin seeing as in a Glasse, the utter ruine and Butcherly murtherings of our owne selves, being we made most assured accompt to drinke of the same Cuppe: But this was the least of our feares, and not the greatest of our miseries: For being now for a time rid of our bloudthirsty* enemies, our provision of victuals being al wasted, spent and spoyled, and having no meanes to get any more, it would have moved the heart of the cruellest Tirant in the world to compassion. But in the midst of all this unendurable misery, it pleased God (contrary to our expectation, in some sort) to relieve us even by our enemyes: For when all the rest were out of sight, one Periago returned very well provided of victual, and three or foure came on land, with as much as they were able to carry of Cassada, Potatos & Plantons, and cryed unto us to exchange with them, first holding up their Bowes, and after laying them on the ground againe in signe of peace: which we perceiving, sent out three likewise to bargain without weapons, carrying Knives, Beades and other trifles: Which being done, they departed, and we returned, giving prayse to God (thus miraculously) for to feede us, for wee had no meanes of our selves to get any.

Then, the Nette (with the which we had wont get as much fish of all sorts as would suffice us all for a day) the Indians tooke from us.

Thus for the space of 6. or 7. days, every day fighting for the space of three or foure houres, and then our victuall began to faile againe, which caused us to hold out a Flag of truce: which the Indians perceiving came in peacable maner unto us. Then one Francis Brace (by meanes of his French tongue) made them understand that our desire was to give them all that wee had, if they would let us have a Periago to carry us away, which one Captain Anthony willingly consented unto, and the next day after brought her, drawing her ashore within the compasse of our Fortes, we giving them, of Hatchets, Knives and Beads untyll they were contented: And to please them the more, we gave them every one a Shovell or a Spade, and so they departed.

And then wee went all to worke, some to make the Sayle, which wee made of very good Roane-cloath, and some to make the Mast: and every one did labour all that he could, to bee ready against night: for Anthonio told us, that his Brother Angrauemart would come the next day from S. Vincent with twelve Perriagos, all laden with men and Arrowes: whose words we always found true, for he could not dissemble.

And wee concluded, rather than wee would stay and dye so miserably at the Carrabies hands, who thirsted for nothing but to eate our flesh, and drinke our blood, as they had done with many other of our fellowes, wee promised unto the LORD (who had all this tyme fought for us,) to betake our selves unto his mercy, and doubted not but that hee would guide us safely to some Christian Harbour.

And upon the xxvi. of September. 1605. at one a clocke after midnight, we embarqued all xix. in that little Vessel or Boate which the Indians had made all of one tree, shee was not so broade as a Wherry, but it was almost as long

* Which departed in their Periagos.

agayne: Our Roapes for our Sayle were our Garters, and our Yard a Lance: Shee had a little Rother or Helme, but not one of company had skyll howe to use it, neyther had wee Compasse to direct us, but sayling by the Sunne in the day, and by the Starres in the night, keeping always betwixt South-west and West: For wee imagined, the maine Land of the West-Indies lay so.

PART II

At the beginning of the seventeenth century the Caribs still had exclusive occupation of their islands, but events over the course of the next hundred years resulted in the gradual and permanent usurpation of these territories by the European colonialists. At the forefront of the forces of this invasion were the missionaries, whose writings form the bulk of this section of the anthology. Thus, in contrast to the sporadic and limited contact experienced by the Caribs during earlier times, they now encountered not only increasing numbers of permanent settlers, but also sustained missionary interest in their lifestyle, language, and customs.

As a result of the latter kind of activity we may observe the advent of serious ethnographic endeavour and the emergence of the first rounded accounts of Carib society. Accordingly there is an abundance of material to choose from and the following extracts have been selected so as to try and cover all aspects of Carib society, while also giving greater prominence to some of the lesser-known or less-appreciated accounts. However, the very sophistication of these published ethnographic accounts can obscure, as much as illumine, the nature of Carib society at this time and therefore can be profitably read in the context of material from the archives of the French and English administration in the Caribbean (Nos. 8, 14).

A further contrast might be drawn between the missionary (Nos. 7, 9, 11, 13) and lay ethnographers and commentators (Nos. 8, 10, 12) on the Caribs, particularly as regards the manner of Carib religion, the origin and nature of their polity, and the vexed question of their linguistic repertoire. In general the missionaries tend to disparage native belief-systems and question their capacity for constructing an effective social order, while emphasizing the importance of linguistic description in the process of conversion. Lay commentators tend to present us with much more detail on their religious life (No. 12), to represent the political capacities of the Caribs pragmatically (No. 8), and to offer alternative perspectives on Carib origins and language (No. 10). It is thus one of the aims of this anthology to alert readers to the variability of the available data, rather than to offer authoritative judgement on its relative worth.

However accurate these various descriptions may have been, they only captured to an uncertain degree the nature of seventeenth-century Carib society, and, often avowedly, only as regards a 'traditional society' that was already disintegrating under the pressure of colonial occupation. By the end of the century Carib ethnicity was fracturing into a number of new identities that might be dubbed 'Black Carib' (No. 14), 'White Carib' (No. 8), and 'Red Carib'. It is therefore with a 'Golden Age' of Carib social and genetic 'purity' that Part II deals and in subsequent sections of the anthology it will become apparent how powerfully the images created at this time have endured in both European literature and Carib memory.

Further Reading

For the historical background to the period see Nellis Crouse's two books, 1940 and 1943, and Boromé 1967. On the missionary history, see Rennard 1929 and 1954. A good Spanish translation of the French missionary writings is Cárdenas Ruiz 1981. For comparative material on mainland Carib (Kariña) ethnicity, Whitehead 1988 and 1990a.

7. Thomas Gage
The Jesuit Massacre on Guadeloupe
(1648)

¶ *Thomas Gage (d. 1656) was sent by his father to study as a Jesuit in Spain in 1612. However, this experience only provoked a profound aversion to the Jesuit order and, against his father's wishes, he became a monk of the order of St Dominic, in Valladolid. In 1625 he was inspired to become a missionary to the Philippines by the head of the Dominican monastery in Jerez, Andalusia. However, the King of Spain had forbidden the passage of any Englishman to the Americas, so that it was necessary for him to be smuggled on board ship for Mexico in an empty biscuit barrel. He accordingly left Cadiz in July 1625, in the company of twenty-seven other Dominican missionaries and a number of Jesuits hoping to reach the Philippines via Mexico. He never did, but stayed in Mexico as a teacher in Chiapas and later as a parish priest in Amatitlan, where he learnt the native languages of Cachiquel and Poconchi.*

The following extract from the second edition (1655) of his New Survey of the West Indies, *the first being published in 1648, describes the events on Guadeloupe at the beginning of this journey; an interlude which probably did little to alter his early view of the Jesuits. The appearance of this second edition, which was promoted by Cromwell's Council of State, also suited the interests of the English government, since it displayed both the riches and the defencelessness of the Spanish colonies in America. Gage himself, having abandoned Catholicism and returned to England in 1637, actually became chaplain to the expedition of General Venables against Española in 1655. The assault on Española failed, but Jamaica was seized instead and it was here that Gage died the following year.*

Aside from the general interest his account of the massacre of Jesuits on Guadeloupe holds, it is notable for the description of the 'mulatto' Lewis, who is also referred to by Rochefort (No. 10) as an example of the 'inconstancy and lightness' of native conversion; a view strongly rejected by du Tertre (No. 11).

Of Our Discovery of Some Islands, and what Trouble Befell Us in One of Them

The Admirall of our fleet wondering much at our slow sailing, who from the second of July to the 19 of August had not seen nor discovered any land, save only the Islands of Canaria, the same day in the morning called to Councell all the Pilots of the ships, to know their opinions concerning our present being, and the neernesse of the land. The ships therefore drew near unto the Admirall one by one, that every Pilot might deliver his opinion. Here was cause of laughter enough, for the passengers to hear the wise Pilots skill; one saying, we were three hundred miles, another two hundred, another one hundred, another fifty, another more, another less, all erring much from the truth (as afterwards appeared) save only one old Pilot of the smallest vessell of all, who affirmed resolutely, that with that small gale wherewith we then failed, we should come to Guadalupe the next morning. All the rest laughed at him, but he might well have laughed at them, for the next morning by sun-rising we plainly discovercd an island called Desseada by the Spaniards, or the desired land, for that at the first discovery of the India's it was the first land the Spaniards found, being then as desirous to find some land after many dayes sailing as we were. After this island presently we discovered another called Marigalante, then another called Dominica, and lastly, another named Gua-dalupe, which was that we aimed at to refresh our selves in, to wash our foul clothes, and to take in fresh water, whereof we stood in great need. By two or three of the clock in the afternoon we came to a safe rode [anchorage] lying before the island, where we cast our anchors, no wayes fearful of the naked Barbarians of that and the other islands, who with great joy do yearly expect the Spanish fleets coming, and by the moones doe reckon the months, and thereby make their guesse at their coming, and prepare some their sugar canes, others the plantin, others the tortois, some one provision, some another to barter with the Spaniards for their small haberdash, or iron, knives, or such things which may help them in their wars, which commonly they make against some other islands. Before our anchors were cast, out came the Indians to meet us in their canoas, round like troughes, some whereof had been painted by our English, some by the Hollanders, some by the French, as might appear by their severall armes, it being common rode and harbour to all nations that sail to America.

Before we resolved to go to shore, we tasted of those Indian fruits, the plantin above all pleasing our taste and palate. We could not but much wonder at that sight never yet seen by us of people naked, with their hair hanging down to the middle of their backes, with their faces cut out in severall fashions, or flowers, with thin plates hanging at their noses, like hog-rings, and fauning upon us like children; some speaking in their unknowne tongue, others using signes for such things as we imagined they desired. Their signe for some of our Spanish wine was easily perceived, and their request most willingly granted to by our men, who with one reasonable cup of Spanish sacke presently tumbled up their heels, and left them like swine tumbling on the deck of our ship. After a while that our people had sported with these rude and savage Indians, our two cock-boates were ready to carry to shore such as either had clothes to wash, or a desire to bathe themselves in a river of fresh water which is within the island, or a minde to set their feet again upon unmoveable land, after so many dayes of uncertain footing in a floating and reeling ship. But that day being far spent, our Fryers resolved to stay in the ship, and the next whole day to visite the island; many of the mariners and passengers of all the ships went that evening to shore, some returning at night, and some without fear continuing with the Indians all night on shore. The next morning my self and most of our Fryers went and having hired some Spaniards to wash our clothes, we wandred sometimes all together, sometimes two and two, and sometimes one alone about the island, meeting with many Indians, who did us no hurt, but rather like children fauned upon us, offering us of their fruits, and begging of us whatsoever toies of pins, points or gloves they espied about us. We ventured to goe to some of their houses which stood by a pleasant river, and were by them kindly entertained, eating of their fish, and wild deers flesh. About noon we chanced to meet with some of the Jesuites of Santa Gertrudis ship in the midst of the mountain, who were very earnest in talke with a mulatto all naked like the rest of the Indians. This mulatto was a Christian, born in Sevill in Spain, and had been slave there formerly to a rich merchant, his name was Lewis, and spoke the Spanish language very perfectly. Some twelve years before, he had run away from his master by reason of hard and slavish usage, and having got to Cales [Cadiz], offering his service to a gentle-man then bound for America, the gentleman fearing not that his true master should ever have more notice of him from a new world, took him a ship board with him as his slave. The mulatto remembring the many stripes which he had suffered from his first cruell master, and fearing that from America he might by some intelligence or other be sent back again to Spain, and also jealous of his second master (whose blowes he had begun to suffer in the ship) that he would prove as cruell as his first; when the ships arrived at Guadalupe, resolved rather to die amongst the Indians (which he knew might be his hardest fortune) then evermore to live in slavery under Spaniards. So casting his life upon good or bad fortune, he hid himself among the trees in the mountain till the ships were departed, who after being found by the Indians, and giving them some toyes which he had got by stealth from his master, he was entertained by them, they liking him, and he them. Thus continued this poor Christian slave among those Barbarians from year to year; who had care to hide himself at the comming of the Spanish fleet yearly. In twelve years that he had thus continued amongst them, he had learned their language, was married to an Indian, by whom he had three children living. The Jesuites by chance having met with him, and perceiving more by the wooll upon his head, that he was a mulatto, then by his black and tauny skin (for those Indians paint themselves all over with a red colour) they presently imagined the truth that he could not

85

come thither but with some Spaniard: so entring into discourse with him, and finding him to speak Spanish, they got the whole truth of him. Then we joyning with the Jesuites, began to perswade the poor Christian to forsake that heathenish life, wherein his soul could never be saved, promising him if he would goe along with us, he should be free from slavery for ever. Poor soul, though he had lived twelve years without hearing a word of the true God, worshipping stockes and stones with the other heathens; yet when he heard again of Christ, of eternall damnation in hels torments, and of everlasting salvation in heavens joyes, he began to weep, assuring us that he would goe with us, were it not for his wife and children, whom he tenderly loved, and could not forsake them.

To this we replyed, that he might be a means of saving likewise their souls, if he would bring them with him; and further that we would assure him that care should be taken that neither he, his wife, nor children should ever want means competent for the maintenance of their lives. The mulatto hearkned well to all this, though a suddain fear surprized him, because certain Indians passed by, and noted his long conference with us. The poor and timorous mulatto then told us, that he was in danger, for having been known by us, and that he feared the Indians would kill him, and suspect that we should steal him away; which if they did, and it were noised about the island, we should soon see their love changed into cruell rage and mutiny. We perswaded him not to fear any thing they could do to us; who had souldiers, guns and ordinance to secure ours and his life also, wishing him to resolve to bring his wife and children but to the sea side, where our men were drying their clothes, and would defend him, and a boat should be ready to convey him with his wife and children a ship board. The mulatto promised to do as we had counselled him, and that he would entice his wife and children to the sea side to barter with us their wares for ours, desiring some of the Jesuites (whom he said he should know by their black coates) to be there ready for him with a cock-boat. Lewis departed, as to us he seemed, resolute in what he had agreed. Our joy likewise was great with the hope of bringing to the light of Christianity five souls out of the darknesse of heathenish idolatry. The Jesuites who had begun with this mulatto were desirous that the happy end and conclusion might be their glory. So taking their leaves of us, they hastened to the sea to informe the Admirall of what they had done, and to provide that the cock-boat of their ship might be in readinesse to receive Lewis, and his family. We likewise returned to the shore to see if our shirts and clothes were dry. Most of us (among whom my self was one) finding our linnen ready and our boat on shore went aboard to our ship, leaving two or three of our company with many of other ships on shore, especially the Jesuites waiting for their prey. When we came to our ship, most of the Fryers with what love they had found in the Barbarians, were inflamed with a new zeal of staying in that island, and converting those heathens to Christianity, apprehending it an easie businesse (they being a loving people) and no wayes dangerous to us, by reason of the fleet that passeth that way, and might enquire after our usage. But by some it was objected, that it was a rash and foolish zeal with great hazard of their lives, and many inconveniences were objected against so blind and simple an attempt. But those that were most zealous slighted all reasons, saying that the worst that could happen to them could be but to be butchered, sacrificed and eaten up; and that for such a purpose they had come out of Spain to be crowned with the crown of martyrdom for confessing and preaching Jesus Christ. While we were hot in this solemne consultation, behold an uproar on the shoar; our people running to and fro to save their lives, leaving their clothes, and hasting to the cock-boats, filling them so fast and so full, that some sunke with all the people in them. Above all, most pitifull and lamentable were the cryes of some of our women, many casting themselves into the sea choosing rather to venture to be taken up by some boat, or at worst to be drowned, then to be taken and to be cruelly butchered by the Indians. We wondering at this suddain alteration, not knowing the cause of it, at last perceived the arrowes to come out thick from the wood from behind the trees, and thereby guessed at the truth that the Barbarians were mutinied. The uproar lasted not half an hour, for presently our Admirall shot off two or three peeces of ordinance and sent a company of souldiers to shoar to guard it and our people with their muskets; which was well and suddainly performed, and all the Indians soon dispersed. Three of our Fryers who had remained on the land, our cock-boat brought them to us with more of our passengers, among whom one Fryer John De la Cueva, was dangerously shot and wound in one of his shoulders; this Fryer had been earnest with me to stay on shoar with him, which I refused, and so escaped that cruell and fiery onset of the Indians. Besides those that were drowned and taken up at shoar (which were fifteen persons) two Jesuites were found dead upon the sand, three more dangerously wounded, three passengers likewise slain, ten wounded, besides three more of the fleet which could never be found alive or dead, and were thought to have been found in the wood by the Indians, and to have been murthered by them. Our mulatto Lewis came not according to his word; but in his stead a suddain army of treacherous Indians, which gave us motive enough to think, that either Lewis himself had discovered the Jesuites plot to take him away with his wife and children; or that the Indians suspecting it by his talke with us had made him confesse it. And certainly this was the ground of their mutiny; for whereas Lewis before had said, that he would know the Jesuites by their black coats, it seems he had well described them above all the rest unto the Indians, for (as it was after well observed) most of their arrowes was directed to the black markes, and so five of them in a little above a quarter of an hour [were] slain and wounded. All that night our souldiers guarded the coast, often shooting off their muskets to affright the Indians, who appeared no more unto us. All that night we slept little, for we watched our ship; lest the Indians in their canoas should set upon us and take us asleep. Some lamented the dead and drowned, others pitied our wounded Fryer John De la Cueva, who all that night lay in great torment and misery, others laughed and jeared at those zealous Fryers, who would have stayed in that island to convert the Barbarians, saying they had their full desire of martyrdom. For had they been but that night with the Indians, doubtlesse they had been shread for their suppers. But now we perceived their zeal was coole, and they desired no more to stay with such a barbarous kind of people; but rather wished the Admirall would shoot off the warning peece for us all to take up our anchors, and to depart from so dangerous a place. In the morning all the ships made hast to take in such fresh water as was necessary for their voiage yet to America, a strong watch being kept along the coast, and a guard guarding our men to the river; and all the morning while this was doing not one Indian could be found or seen, nor our three men that were missing, appeared. Thus at noon with a pleasant and prosperous gale we hoisted up our sails, leaving the islands and harbour of Guadalupe.

8. *The Case of 'Indian' Warner (1657–1676)*

¶ *Almost all narratives of culture contact throw up a figure who inhabited that treacherous zone 'between' cultures which, at least in the early stages of colonial history, often meant moving uncertainly between two worlds, being seen at times on both sides as a valued intermediary, sometimes as a potential traitor. An early and paradigmatic example, who has always haunted the margins of Caribbean history, is Thomas 'Indian' Warner, supposed son of Sir Thomas Warner, Governor of St Kitts, and a Carib woman.*

Despite quite extensive documentation, little is known for certain about 'Indian' or 'Carib' Warner, although his very existence was a fertile source of ideological uncertainty for the English, as the drama of official attitudes to his case reveals. His parentage was disputed, his political loyalties questioned, his death the subject of a major scandal. The strong possibility that he was murdered by his white half-brother Philip Warner adds to the story's almost mythic status.

The complexities of Indian Warner's tale are perhaps best introduced by the earliest printed English account of this affair, which appeared in the second volume of Captain William Dampier's A New Voyage round the World *(1699–1709); although, contrary to the opinion of the family biographer Aucher Warner (1933), this is not actually the earliest printed account, being preceded by J. B. du Tertre's 1667 description of his early life and capture by the French (quoted below), as well as that of J. Clodoré (1671).*

We join Dampier in 1674 as he sails past the islands of St Vincent and St Lucia.

[...] We passed between them; and seeing a smoke on St Lucia, we sent our Boat ashore there. Our men found some of the Caribbe-Indians, and bought of them Plantains, Bonanoes, Pine-Apples, and Sugar-Canes; and returning aboard again, there came with them a Canoa with 3 or 4 of the Indians. These often repeated the Word Captain Warner, and seemed to be in some disquiet about him. We did not understand the meaning of it; but since I have been informed that this Captain Warner, whom they mentioned, was born at Antego, one of our English Islands, and the Son of Governour Warner, by an Indian Woman, and bred up by his Father after the English manner; he learned the Indian Language also of his Mother; but being grown up, and finding himself despised by his English Kindred, he forsook his Father's House, got away to St Lucia, and there lived among the Caribbe-Indians, his Relations by the Mother side. Where conforming himself to their Customs he became one of their Captains, and roved from one Island to another, as they did. About this Time the Caribbees had done some spoil on our English Plantations at Antego: and therefore Governour Warner's Son by his Wife took a Party of Men and went to suppress those Indians, and came to the Place where his Brother the Indian-Warner lived. Great seeming Joy there was at their Meeting; but how far it was real the Event shewed; for the English-Warner providing plenty of Liquor, and inviting his half-Brother to be merry with him, in the midst of his Entertainment ordered his Men upon a Signal given to murder him and all his Indians: which was accordingly performed. The Reason of this inhumane Action is diversely reported; some say that this Indian-Warner committed all the Spoil that was done to the English; and therefore for that Reason his Brother kill'd him and his Men. Others that he was a great Friend to the English, and would not suffer his Men to hurt them, but did all that lay in his power to draw them to an amicable Commerce; and that his Brother killed him, for that he was ashamed to be related to an Indian. But be it how it will, he was called in Question for the Murder, and forced to come Home to take his Tryal in England. Such perfidious Doings as these, besides the Baseness of them, are great hindrances of our gaining an Interest among the Indians. [...]

¶ [*As we shall see, the issue of Indian Warner's ambivalent attitude towards the English recurs throughout the contemporary descriptions of him, and particularly as regards his alleged involvement in the massacre of English settlers on Antigua; an ambivalence undoubtedly compounded by his position as a 'musteech' (i.e. person of mixed race) who was none the less commissioned by the Governor of the English West Indies, Lord William Willoughby, as Governor of Dominica. How this remarkable situation arose is made somewhat clearer by the early printed accounts of du Tertre and Clodoré referred to above. The content of these French accounts is virtually the same and it seems likely that Clodoré may have 'borrowed' from du Tertre's earlier work. Equally though, du Tertre had no personal knowledge of Indian Warner but relied on information given to him by a fellow missionary, Philippe de Beaumont, in whose account of the political history of Dominican 'Caraïbe' support for the French Warner is frequently mentioned but not personally described. Accordingly it is to du Tertre that we must turn for the biographical elements of Indian Warner's early life.*]

HISTORY OF A HALF-CASTE, NAMED WAERNARD, MADE GOVERNOR OF
THE ISLAND OF DOMINICA BY THE LORD WILLOUGHBY

General Warner [*Waernard*], contemporary of General de Poincy, had a son by
a female Indian slave from the island of Dominica: he recognized him as his
son, gave him his name, & raised him in his house with his other children.
Although this bastard was born of a female Savage & slave, there appeared in
him nothing of the Savage but the colour of his skin and hair, & although he
had very black hair, he combed and dressed it, contrary to the custom of the
other Savages: his build was medium, but it was perfectly proportioned in all
parts: he had a long face, a large forehead, & an aquiline nose, clear & wide
eyes; and one noted a certain gravity in his face that made known the grandeur
of his courage and his spirit. He lost his father in his adolescence, & Madame
Warner, who did not love him, & who had not disclosed this to his father,
began to persecute him & treat him with such inhumanity that she made him
work in the fields with the slaves of the household.

Warner, who with the good qualities of his spirit, & of his body, was a
trustworthy and enterprising man, bursting with vexation to see himself
reduced to such an unhappy & abject condition, took flight with other fugitive
slaves: but, after his recapture, Madame Warner put him in chains and fixed
a terrible pair of irons to his feet, & at the same time made him work in this
outfit. His captivity lasted until Monsieur Warner, the legitimate son of General
Warner, who governed in the island of Montserrat, came to St Christopher
where, having found him in this state, out of compassion he delivered him
from his chains & took him from Madame Warner, giving him some authority
over the other domestic servants.

This poor unfortunate, now freed, had hardly enjoyed the happiness of his
brother's presence, but once he had departed, the rage of the woman
redoubled, & she treated him with such cruelty that he was constrained to
follow the counsel with which his natural mother had inspired him, which
was to withdraw among the Savages of Dominica. He was well received there
thanks to his mother; & as he had the spirit, he quickly rose in the hearts of
the Savages in that part, which was on the leeward side of Dominica and,
along with others, was warring with the English, just as he arrived. This
Warner tried to reconcile them, & succeeded so well that he brought them all
together, & won the admiration of the Savages, over whom he held such
ascendancy that he engaged them with a marvellous facility to undertake the
most difficult tasks [...].

The Lord Willoughby, knowing what he was capable of, took him on a
voyage to England, making him appear at Court, where he comported himself
as a Christian with the English, & dressed as they did; but being returned he
rid himself of these clothes, & comported himself as an infidel with the
Savages, & went naked & covered with roucou as they do; but he never touched
a single woman.

The English, seeing the growth of their colonies, & moreoever their being restricted by the treaty made between ourselves & the Savages to expand into the islands possessed by the infidels, believed that Warner was a most appropriate individual to get round this treaty, & to take possession by these means of the island of Dominica: to that end they gave him a commission to subject these peoples to the King of England without settling here any natural Englishman. The Lord Willoughby cherished him, impressed him strongly, & obliged him to accept the commission as the Governor of the island of Dominica. [...]

¶ [*Du Tertre then concludes his account with a French translation of Indian Warner's commission from Lord Francis Willoughby dated 16 April 1664 and giving him 'full powers' to establish an English administration on Dominica. This was renewed, following Francis Willoughby's death at sea in 1666, by his son Lord William Willoughby. However, France and England were now at war in the Caribbean and Dominica became pivotal to that conflict. Accordingly, when the French appeared off Dominica in force in this same year, Indian Warner was captured and held by them for two years. It is probable that it was this event which stimulated the rumours among the English colonists that Indian Warner had already accepted a French commission, which circumstance, together with the evidence of his indifference to repeated Carib attacks on the English colony of Antigua throughout this period and his alleged revelation of a gold or silver mine on Dominica (CSP 1669–74: 496, Labat 1724: ii. 103), are highly significant factors in any understanding of his death in 1674. Although his loyalty to the English, which as we have seen may at best have been ambivalent, was complicated by his loyalty to the leeward Carib of Dominica, there is little reason to suppose that it also extended to the French and their 'Caraïbe' allies on the windward side of the island. This is made clear by the following extract from du Tertre's account of his capture, also briefly described by Philippe de Beaumont (1668: 235).*]

THE UNFORESEEN CAPTURE OF WAERNARD, GOVERNOR FOR THE ENGLISH, OVER THE SAVAGES OF DOMINICA

I have made mention in the first book which precedes this one of a *mestis* named Warner [*Waernard*], whom the Lord Willoughby had honoured with a commission as Governor of the island of Dominica for His Majesty of England with full powers to make obedient, as well as to chastise & punish with death the mutinous and seditious who oppose his authority. This Governor was established in the leeward of the island, & had adroitly managed a peace between the English and the greater part of the Savages of this area, & used all their industry, & employed all their forces, in order to oblige the other Savages (who mortally despised Warner & all the English) to follow his lead, until he committed several murders, & ate the flesh of other Savages who wished nothing to do with him.

This continued for some time, & the poor Savages who held to the French party were already coming to implore our assistance to deliver them from this cruelty, when nine pirogues full of Savages arrived on Guadeloupe, of whom four were going to Antigua, to make war in their fashion, & the other five retracing their route to surprise Warner, whom they had seen leaving to go to war, inattentive to the danger. These joined with other Savages their friends to attack Warner unawares, & they pressed him so vigorously that, without an English corsair who came late to his side, he would certainly have been roasted, grilled, & eaten in his turn by these barbarians.

The Governors of Martinique and Guadeloupe, as well as the Commissariat, who had received a hundred complaints about this rogue, strongly desired to go down and seize him; & there was an opportunity to effect this with the ship of Captain Bourdet, equipped for war & on which was Monsieur de Monville, lieutenant of the Auxiliary Company, with forty brave soldiers of that Company. He went to Martinique for orders from the Commissariat, & stayed some days in Guadeloupe in order to disembark some Irishmen.

I do not know exactly how they made their approach to trap him, but I do know that this Captain had ordered Monsieur de Chambre to make an attempt in passing &, in case this was fruitless, to advise Monsieur Clodoré on what means he ought to employ to arrest the cruelties of this barbarian; so that on 20 May or thereabouts, Captain Bourdet, being broadside to Dominica, saw an English ship of 100 or 120 tons ready for battle with nine pieces of ordnance, & upwards of seventy-five soldiers, to whom he quickly gave chase [...] and made all these people prisoners of war.

There was very little to pillage in this ship, as it was equipped for battle; all their booty was made up of some chests & packets belonging to the soldiers, some munitions, & a good number of firearms in decent condition; but the victory was notable, in that once the prisoners were secured, the Reverend Father Beaumont of our order saw a Savage among them; & having studied him a little, he recognized that it was the fellow that they sought, that is Warner, who being seen was laughed at by the other Savages, for having thought to save himself in this ship for fear of falling into their hands. He immediately warned Captain Bourdet, who was most happy with this prize, containing & guarding him most carefully, & returning forthwith to Guadeloupe to place the other prisoners as well into the hands of Monsieur de Lion, who on the spot hunted out the best pair of irons that they had in their prisons: & as bracelets gave him a strong pair of handcuffs, & put him in a dungeon, from where unless by a miracle, of which there are none for such people, it was impossible for him to escape. Also found in this capture was Monsieur Bary, physician for Guadeloupe, with five soldiers who were taken in a barque some days earlier.

A few days after the capture of Warner, the four pirogues of Savages that Monsieur du Lion had sent to Antigua returned to Guadeloupe with a considerable booty of negroes & weapons that they had taken from the English:

after surprising & storming the Guard Corps, they spiked the cannon, killed, roasted, and ate many English, of which they had kept two hands, roasted & dried like wood. They all claimed that they should have Warner & serve him in the same way: & it was with some diligence that they restrained themselves; one of them approaching him, gave him a blow with one of the cured hands of the English on the side of the head, from which a trickle of blood quickly sprang, & said to him, 'There, here is a blow from one of your friends.' Warner endured this blow with a gravity of stoical constancy: & without stirring said to him in his language, with a scornful look; 'You are a coward. If you have something to say to me, you ought to come and find me in my *carbet*, & not strike at me in the condition in which I am now.'

He then spoke to Monsieur de Malassis: 'These people are beasts, a rabble, & wretches unworthy of me; & I am not involved with them, other than to avoid the persecution of Mrs Warner. Furthermore I am Governor, I have a letter testifying to this commission; & Monsieur du Lion has the right to treat me as he wishes, since I am a prisoner of war'; & being asked if the heavy irons were not uncomfortable, he replied: 'I am accustomed to them, I have worn them twice for a long time in St Christopher's; but I will soon grow strong from here, & know well how to avenge myself.' Monsieur du Lion was advised to send him to France, & that he should spend his life in the galleys, that it was no more than he deserved. But Monsieur de la Barre arrived a little time after; he kept him until the end of the war, by which time he had repented and was returned to a condition where he lived as an Englishman, & not as a *Careybe*.

Monsieur du Lion bears witness to this much in a letter written to Monsieur de Cre, saying that he was growing very weary of guarding such a fellow: 'This rascal', he says, 'is the reason that I do not sleep well; since even though he is chained by the hands & feet, & in a dungeon under the eye of a sentinel: when I think that a *Careybe* has jumped fifty-two feet off a fort, & that he is still in good health: I believe that Warner would do as much if he were unchained.'

The affair of this skilful Savage jumper of which Monsieur du Lion speaks here happened at the beginning of September 1665, when a pirogue full of Savages came to Guadeloupe where, getting drunk on rum as they usually do, they met with a well-dressed Frenchwoman, whom they dragged aside, tore her clothes, & tried to violate; but she let out such loud cries that her husband & some Frenchmen came to her aid, swept up our savages like children from a good home, separated the one she complained about most, & took him to Monsieur du Lion, who had him shut away at the top of the fort with some guards; he waited until they were asleep & trusting in his *mabouya* [devil-spirit] leapt from a window fifty-two feet up; but his devil did not prevent a hole being made in his head; so that Warner, being a quite different man from this one, Monsieur du Lion had cause to be uneasy about him. [. . .]

¶ [*It is evident enough from du Tertre's account that there can have been little likelihood that Indian Warner was in fact in receipt of a French commission as the English colonists of Antigua accused him of claiming. However, it should be noted that it was on Antigua that Indian Warner was born and where he suffered at the hands of his stepmother, and also where the English had massacred the native population in their first occupation of the island, Indian Warner being brought up with the son of the slain Carib king of Antigua and St Christopher's; in this context a lingering antipathy towards the English on Antigua may well have been part of Indian Warner's personal outlook, reflected in his lack of intercession with other 'Caraïbe' groups on their behalf. Therefore, before turning to the accounts of Indian Warner's extraordinary death, we reproduce the 'Remonstrance' of the Antiguan colonists that was presented to the Court of Barbados in 1676. Although, ironically, it postdates the death of Indian Warner, it does make clear some of the complex background to this event, as well as the grounds for persistent English suspicion of their 'musteech' compatriot, and so too the origins of his ambivalence towards them.]*

It is to well knowne as well to the inhabitants of this island as to the other merchants and traders amongst us since its first being inhabited by Christians, or very near that time that the said Indians have not ceased by their continual incursions and very many horrid murders, ripping up women with child, burning of houses, and carrying away into miserable captivity, their children and others, almost to the utter ruine of this collony, whilst Indian Warner of late going under the name of Thomas Warner was a chief leader and actor amongst the said Indians untill the year of our Lord 1657 when some of the inhabitants of this Island with the assistance of Mountsarrat and others went against them although by their subtility it proved almost ineffectual, yett in the year 1660, the said Indian Warner with other Indians came to Coll. Christopher Reynall then governor of this Island, to make peace which was then agreed unto and wee had for some small tyme rest from their allmost continual Alaroms, but they soon fell to their accustomed cruelltys by robing, murdering and carreing away others of the inhabitants, so that we were again constrained to make war against them to our exceeding charge and the losse of crops at which tyme we requested Coll. Philip Warner to goe in pson against them in the hopes he might by faire means have brought the said Indian Warner to have been helpful to our party in finding out and persueing those othere breakers of the sd peace, but all our endeavours proved fruit-lesse and procured us nothing more but fair promises, but he would not go or appear against those that himselfe would say are our enemies, but on the contrary would give them notice of our arrival, although we spared not, at any tyme, to furnish him and those he called his friends with what necessaries they wanted.

Notwithstanding in the yeare 1666 they began again their old villainies and outragious practices, not regarding that peace, but rather looking on us as their tributaries, a barbarous conclusion drawn from our kindnesses, Indian Warner being all this while amongst them, and would never give us any notice of the designs against us, which drew us to conclude he was still against us, by consent, if not in pson, for those by him protected as his friends and nearest relations, were chief in comitting many outtrages murders, rapes and burneings, by which means we were wholly putt from labour, which if at any time we attempted to follow their poisoned arrows were soon in some of our sides, which spake nothing but death, soon after the said Indian Warner was carried prisoner by the French to St Christopher's being however his friends and nearest relations still persued their bloody practises against the poore Inhabitants of this Island for as often as the men engaged the French enemy, the said Indians were committing their murders, rapes and other villanys amongst the women and children, and when the Ffrench had subdued the Island and disarmed our inhabitants and carried away our negroes and what else they thought fitt, then did these Indians prosecute all villanies imaginable against our naked inhabitants haveing nothing but the mercy of God to protect ourselves from their cruelties, at which time, we having submitted to the Ffrench on their promise of safety from the barbarisme of the said Indians, the said Indians came to the house of Coll. Cardine late Govern'r. of this Island who cyvilly treated them, but at their departure desired him in friendship to walk with them to the sea-side, where they cruelly murdered him, and those that were with him, cutting off Coll. Cardine's head, broyled it and carried it to Dominica in triumph. But before their departure returned to Coll. Cardine's house, and carried away his wife children and others, with them into captivity, where some of them perished.

Neare to this same tyme they went to the house of Mr Thomas Taylor pretending friendshipp and by him they were kindly entertained, but before they departed they murdered the said Mr Taylor, Mr Thomas Beadle minister, Mr Robert Boyers, wounding others with poisoned arrows to death and carried away Mrs Taylor and children, Mrs Chrew and children, Mrs Lynt and children, with many too tedious to relate, and in these and the like bloody practises they continued untill a peace was proclaimed betwixt our more gracious king, the Ffrench, and Dutch. All of which bloody cruelties were acted and done by the Chiefs of Indian Warner's friends, without the least cause or provocation on our part.

And since the peace made with them by the Lord William Willoughby, although they have been kindly received and entertained by our inhabitants out of respect for the said peace, yett they soon begain their accustomed cruelties fore comeing to Parham Hill plantation in agreeable manner were civilly and librally entertained at their departure murdered several seamen that were taking tobacco, and planters that were carrying the same to the boats with out any manner of provocation.

Some of the said Indians being soone after apprehended at Mountserrat by our generall, who intended to have given them a due reward for the said murders, but such was our clemency towards them, that if by any means wee could have brought them to live peaceably by us, wee made our humble addresses unto our generall to lett them goe, which we hardly obtained from his Excellency, but no sooner were they loose but they committed roberies upon the said Island.

Such hath always been their requitalls of any kindnesses or civilities shewn them, and amongst these Indians were the friends and associates of the said Indian Warner and by him then interceeded for alledging they were not persons that had done the said murders, although afterwards appeared that these whom he a called his friends were the men that commited the said murder.

And to manifest the truth thereof, one of his nearest allies, in the yeare 1674 came with other Indians to the plantation of Coll. Philip Warner and killed severall Christians and carried away sixteen negroes, and one Christian child, whom they afterwards cruelly murdered, and at the return of the said Indians from this Island, Indian Warner mett them at Guardeloup and craved share of the booty they had brought from Antigua, and afterwards some of the goods [illegible] Coll. Warner's boyling house at their being last there comitting of murders aforesaid were found in the village belonging to Indian Warner in Dominica and were brought back by Coll. Warner's servants.

Thus hath the said Indian Warner often dealt treacherously, pretending friendshipp, but proving an absolute enemy, not only to this Island, but to our whole nation, for himself declared that he had a Ffrench commission, and said that he would rather serve the Spaniards than the English and finding ourselves to be neare our utter ruine by his fraud and treachery, we were constrained humbly to crave ayde of our captain generall to give us his commission to make war against the said Indians, without exception that we might labour by his just power to redeem ourselves from those cruel practices which wee had long laine under, which he was pleased to grant.

We then besought Coll. Philip Warner, our governor to goe in person against them, which at our earnest request he was pleased to undertake and with very great difficulty and hazard did doe such service upon them which hath procured our ease and rest in some measure to this tyme, although not without continuall watching and warding to our great charge and trouble, they still threatening a bloody revenge upon this place.

And it is evident, had not Coll. Warner's party beene quick in giving the first blow, upon those our bloody enemies, he and those with him had received the same measure from our pretended friends but utter enemies. Who had agreed with those hee called our enemies to destroy Coll. Warner and his party and to that end had them at rediness at hand, but God Almighty prevented them, not suffceringe him any longer to raigne in his barbarous practices of which this Island might give a large accompt for neare forty yeares past and whether the said Indian Warner with his associates received not a due recompense for their villanys and barbarous practices wee appeal to God and all the world.

[signed] Richard Boraston and 15 others. 1676.

¶ [*None the less, so important were the Caribs to the colonial prospects of both the English and French that Lord Willoughby saw the possibility that Indian Warner might win them to the English cause. Accordingly in the period from 1668, when he was formally commissioned by Willoughby as Governor of Dominica, until 1676 and the acquittal of his half-brother Philip on charges of his murder, the case of Indian Warner is prominent in English colonial records. The following extracts from the printed Calendar of State Papers (CSP) for this period are transcribed from the original manuscripts in the Public Record Office; these summary transcripts have been checked against the originals and could not be bettered by the editors. We have decided to let the material speak for itself since the realities of these events are probably now unknowable and there can be no attempt at historical authority.*

The first extract illustrates the place of Indian Warner in French–English rivalry and is taken from correspondence between the French General de la Barre and Lord William Willoughby in January 1668.]

M. De la Barre to Lord Willoughby.

Has received his letter, and congratulates him on his happy arrival at Nevis and good inclinations towards peace, to which he on his part will contribute all in his power. Wishes he could show his sense of the favour and courtesy shown to the Rev. Père Grillet. Captain Warner has never lived as a Christian but as a Caribbee, and De la Barre does not consider him included in the treaty of peace. Would send him at once, but is sure he would cause a broil with the natives, and returning to Dominica raise a party against the Caribbees, who the French must support, as they have ceded the island to them, and Englishmen must not inhabit, but if his Lordship will pass his word he shall not return thither. De la Barre will send him willingly, if not, believes he must be sent to his Majesty in England. Warner is now sent under parole of Mr Stapleton [Commander in Antigua] to send him back if he will not settle amongst the English, and no longer live as a savage.

Lord Willoughby to M. De la Barre.

Owns his civility in Capt. Thos. Warner's [i.e. Indian Warner] discharge, also his promise concerning the peace, which was this day solemnly proclaimed in Nevis. Cannot allow that any of his Majesty's subjects should have their habitations appointed by the French; so that since Dominica is within Lord Willoughby's Government, though not yet settled, knows no reason why the English should not settle there. Conceives it to be De la Barre's mistake that Warner is not included in the peace, for though it was his hard fate to meet with a step-mother that forced him to an ill course of life, that cannot deprive him of his birthright; being born in his Majesty's dominions, the 'deputed' son of Sir Thomas Warner and educated with him till 30 years of age, he took oath of allegiance to his Majesty, and received a commission from Lord Willoughby's predecessor to be Deputy Governor of Dominica. Could not have answered it if he had not insisted on his release, but will comply so far as to command Warner to use a Christian and a civil life, and show good behaviour towards the French. (CSP 1661–8: 535–6)

¶ [*However, it would appear that Indian Warner's position among the Caribs of Dominica was very uncertain after his period of captivity with the French. We learn the following from Willoughby's instructions for Major James Walker's expedition from Antigua to Dominica in February 1668.*]

To take Capt. Warner formerly of Dominica with him on board the Portsmouth frigate, and if he can beget a good understanding between Warner and his allies, leave him there with orders to bring the French party over to peace with our nation, and to procure a general release of the English captives. If unsafe after trial of the humours of the Indians to leave Warner, to bring him again to Barbadoes with such of the captives and Indians as he can, attacking and destroying the Indians and their towns. (CSP 1661–8: 546)

¶ [*In Willoughby's letter of 11 February 1668 to the Secretary of State, Lord Arlington, we learn more about the role of the French.*]

Antigua is of great consequence to his Majesty in these parts, and M. De la Barre has not forborne repenting ever parting with it. His care must now be to preserve it from the Indians, 'who are yet the French stalking horse', but the blow Sir John Harman gave the French at sea has staggered the Indians who are apt to side with the stronger. Has sent a small vessel to Dominica to demand the captives from Antigua, Montserrat, &c., and employed Capt. Warner, an Indian, but a loyal subject, whom the French, though their prisoner, could not corrupt or reduce in that affair; and will reduce Dominica if, by fair means, he cannot obtain the English captives, but that will take time, for they are pitiful enemies, and he expects to meet French conductors among them. (CSP 1661–8: 547)

¶ [*Some five years pass before Indian Warner is again referred to directly in government correspondence, when we learn that his commission is renewed following the death of Lord William Willoughby (CSP 1669–74: 487, 493–4) and that the President and Council of Barbados 'have only commissioned an Indian [. . .] to avoid giving distaste to the French', although their letter to Indian Warner states that 'they have thought good, in reward of past services, to continue his power'. This, and further correspondence between the President of the Council, Sir Peter Colleton, and the administration in England (CSP 1669–74: 495–6), suggests that Indian Warner had had some successes in his diplomatic mission among the Caribs, since there are references to 'Articles of Submission' to the English from the 'Indians of Dominique, [. . .] St Vincent and Sancta Lucia', possibly alluding in part to the 1668 treaty with the 'chief captains' of St Vincent (CSP 1661–8: 554).*]

However, at the end of 1674, there is an indication that storm clouds are already gathering around Indian Warner, as the following piece of intelligence emerges from an English source in Guadeloupe, suggesting that his 'Antiguan antipathy' may have come to dominate his motivations after the death of his supporter Lord Willoughby.]

M. Bovine of St Christopher's told [him] yesterday of a design the Indians have against Antigua 'this full of the moon'. They told him that what they did last at Antigua was only to make an inspection, and they were resolved to do more mischief there yet. Fourteen days since M. Bovine had occasion to hire a *periago* [pirogue] of Indians on Grandterre [Guadeloupe], but they said they could not stay because they must go with the rest of the *periagoes*, to the number of 20, to war against Antigua, and desired him to spare them some arms and ammunition, and what purchase they took he should share; which he denied them: he also not long since saw them at their houses at Grandterre making ready and poisoning arrows, and says they are Warner's Indians, [. . .]. The rogue that does all this has been a slave on Antigua, and will never give over till he has them in keeping that kept him. He speaks good English, and has at Dominica an English boy taken when they were last at Antigua, who might be had away if inquiry were made [. . .]. (CSP 1669–74: 624–5)

¶ *[In the light of this information the 'Remonstrance' of the Antiguan colonists (quoted above) seems altogether more justified in some of its accusations. At the very least it would seem that political and ethnic hostility to Indian Warner was beginning to outweigh his utility to the English administration in the West Indies; factors that had anyway only ever achieved a precarious balance. In fact the intelligence of an imminent attack on Antigua was absolutely accurate, though the degree of Indian Warner's personal involvement remains uncertain. Nevertheless the manner of his death in the ensuing revenge raid on the Caribs of Dominica ensured that the 'case' of Indian Warner was not yet closed. The first news of this event comes in the report of Sir William Stapleton, Governor of Antigua, to the Council of Plantations.]*

Need not recite the often repeated grievances of these Islands bleeding for redress, but beseeches them to consider them in this conjuncture of peace. The Indians of Dominica have again committed murders and rapines upon Antigua a little before Christmas last, whereupon we empowered the Deputy Governor, Col. Philip Warner, with 6 small companies of foot, to go to Dominica to be revenged on those heathens for their bloody and perfidious villainies, who killed 80, took some prisoners, destroyed their provisions, and carried away most of their periagoes and canoes, as their warlike vessels are called; his pretended brother, Indian Warner (reputed natural son to Sir Thomas), fell amongst his fellow heathens, who, though he had an English commission, was a great villain, and took a French commission, which makes him suspect that these Indians have been put on by those who made use of them in the late war [with France]. (CSP 1675–6: 171)

¶ [*However, a very different version of these events quickly emerges from the letter of the Governor of Barbados, Sir Jonathan Atkins, who writes that he:*]

Doubts they have for ever lost those people [Caribs of Dominica], whose friendship was so necessary in time of war, to the great damage of the French. But by the intemperate actings of one Warner [Philip], Lieutenant Governor of Antigua, by an action of the greatest inhumanity, who, from what provocation he cannot yet tell, transported 7 companies to Dominica, a dependent of this Government, without taking any notice of or complaint to Atkins, Warner's brother, whom he assassinated, having a commission from Barbadoes as Lieutenant-Governor for the King, and being the only person in these parts that asserted the English interest and suffered imprisonment and irons during the war for his service to the King, and coming ashore, his half-brother, for they had both one father, joined him with the Leeward Indians to take account of the Windward Indians for injuries done on Antigua; but after the action he invites him and his party to a treat, and having made them drunk with rum, caused them all to be massacred, not sparing his brother or little children. Encloses the examination of the master of the sloop, who was in the whole action, wherein he will find a very tragical but he fears very true story, the man being a serious and intelligent man of his quality. Had required a reason from his superior of the affront done to himself in his Government, but the King's honour and interest being so much concerned, thought it more fit to present the matter to his Majesty.

¶ [*Encloses the following:*]

Deposition of Wm. Hamlyn, commander of the sloop Betty, of Antigua, aged 23, before his Excellency and Council. In December last deponent was pressed by Col. Philip Warner, Deputy Governor of Antigua, to go with letters to Col. Stapleton at Nevis, and on his return was again pressed to carry 34 men in his sloop to Dominica, in company with two ships carrying in the whole 300 men, who arrived there on Xmas Day. Said vessels were met by Thomas Warner [Indian Warner], Deputy Governor for his Majesty, who understanding Col. Warner's design was the 300 men should fall upon the Windward Indians for some injuries supposed to be done by them to him on Antigua, agreed to assist him with 30 Indians, and ordered 30 more to attend them to carry orders. Four Windward Indians were slain, and believes 30 at least were killed, besides three that were drawn by a flag of truce to come on board and there killed. After the dispute was over, Col. Warner invited Thomas Warner and his Indians, to the number of 60 or 70 men, women and children, to an entertainment of thanks, and having made them very drunk with rum, gave a signal, and some of the English fell upon and destroyed them. Afterwards an Indian calling himself Thomas Warner's son came on board Col. Warner's ship, and told him he had killed his father and all his friends, and prayed him to cause him also to be killed, holding his head of one side to receive a blow, which by Col. Philip's order was given him, and he was thrown overboard. Deponent took an Indian boy in his arms to preserve him, but the child was wounded in his arms and afterwards killed; believes this slaughter was by the sole direction of Col. Warner, against the consent of his officers, several of whom he heard declare against it. In pursuit of the Windward Indians, two or three English were killed in fight. Said Thos. Warner being advertized that Col. Warner designed to kill him, replied he was better assured of his kindness and fidelity, being his half-brother. Deponent heard Col. Warner order Cornet Saml. Winthorpe to kill Thos. Warner, who refused to do so. Col. Warner and his men being in great distress for provisions, were provided by Thos. Warner and his Indians with what they could. (CSP 1675–6: 175–6)

¶ [*Such a divergence in testimony naturally required a special interest on the part of the metropolitan government and a 'Special Commission of Oyer and Terminer' was directed to the Attorney-General by the King, and a signed letter to Sir Jonathan Atkins 'to pass such sentence and judgement as shall be agreeable to law and justice' in the matter (CSP 1675–6: 228) was entered in the Plantation Book. Equally, the damage that had been done to Carib–English relationships on Dominica, whatever the truth of the killing of Indian Warner, prompted a remarkable response on the part of the English Crown, relayed in a letter from the Secretary of State, Lord Coventry.*]

[. . .] his Majesty is highly offended, and commands that a speedy and exemplary justice should be done upon the person guilty of this inhuman act, and his Majesty's pleasure is that the Governor effectually takes order that the offenders be proceeded against according to law and give such an account as his justice may appear to have been vindicated and the innocent blood that hath been so barbarously spilt be fully avenged. And since there is reason to believe that the Windward Indians may have been much alienated from the English by this action, his Majesty leaves it to the Governor to give that people some signal and public demonstration of his justice upon the authors by sending them some heads and by some other proper way which he shall think fit that they may be satisfied of the detestation his Majesty and the whole nation hath of this proceeding of Col. Warner's, and how ready his Majesty will be to punish severely any of his subjects that shall infringe the good understanding he desires to have preserved between them and his subjects. (CSP 1675–6: 248)

¶ [*Not surprisingly, when Philip Warner returned to England towards the end of June 1675, he was imprisoned in the Tower and 'charged with the murder of his brother*

Thomas Warner, an Indian, and the destruction of other Indians, His Majesty's friends' (CSP 1675: 293–4). In the event the trial was actually held in Barbados where Philip Warner was duly shipped (CSP 1675: 293–4). However, Governor Stapleton sent the following very strong letter on Philip Warner's behalf to the Council for Plantations in December 1675, followed by another in April 1676, enclosing further depositions to the same effect (CSP 1675–6: 382–5), that well expressed the attitudes to be found in the local Caribbean context, in which Warner was to be finally acquitted.]

Beseeches them to weigh in particular what he wrote of the Caribbee Indians, who have murdered on Antigua the King's subjects of both sexes, ravished women, carried away men, women and children, kept them slaves, burned houses, and committed other enormities; for which causes he sues for their grave advice to his Majesty for the release of Col. Philip Warner, whom he understands to be a close prisoner for taking some revenge on these treacherous and bloody malefactors, for that it is suggested that he has killed his brother, and that in cold blood. Both assertions are equally untrue, for the Indian Warner was not Sir Thomas's son but his slave, and the blood could not be cold, Col. Warner having twice fought the Indians out of pallisadoed trenches and pursued them to the leeward part of Dominica, where they found them harboured by this Indian Warner, who before had given notice to the Windward Indians of the design against them; he fell amongst them, and not by Col. Warner's hand nor aboard; the son pretended to be killed is at St Christopher's. A clause in Stapleton's Commission will justify his empowering Col. Warner; besides 3 several addresses made to him by the Deputy Governors, Councils, and Assemblies of the respective islands. But 8 days since the Marquis of Temericourt, Governor of Marigalante, delivered him 4 negroes carried away from Antigua by those heathens, having redeemed them for 4,000 lbs. of sugar. Hopes to give a fuller account of the matter of fact by the next opportunity, but in the interim desires their Lordships to peruse the annexed depositions concerning Indian Warner's fraternity with Col. Warner, who, had he destroyed all Caribbee Indians, had done the best piece of service for the settlement of these parts. The subject requires more time and more energetic lines than he is able to offer.

¶ *[Encloses the following:]*

Deposition of Walter Carwardine. Came over with Sir Thos. Warner to the Indies about 46 years since, and waited on him about 4 years, and Sir Thomas had in his family of Indian slaves a male child commonly called Warner, or Indian Warner, who, at their arrival at St Christopher's, was not above 6 months' old, and was never baptized or looked on as any other than a slave or negro's child, and was not reputed the child of Sir Thos. Warner. 1675, Dec. 18.
    Deposition of Lieut. Robert Choppin. To the same effect; and that shortly after

their arrival in St Christopher's Sir Thomas called all his Indian slaves before him, to the number of 24, and named a child (the first-born in his family of slaves) Warner; he was afterwards carried off by his mother and others who ran off, and some years after brought from Antigua by Capt. Fletcher, and lived as a slave, fishing and fowling with Sir Thos. Warner, after whose death he served his lady (now Lady March) and is reputed to be killed at Dominica. 1675, Dec. 18.

   Deposition of Sarah Choppin, wife of the above. Was servant to Sir Thos. Warner. Indian Warner always lodged in the Indian house, and never was reputed Sir Thomas's son, but remained a slave with him and Lady March till with 2 Indians more he ran away. 1675, Dec. 18.

   Deposition of Col. Randal Russell, Deputy Governor of Nevis. Arrived out of Europe in the yeare 1637, and lived in Sir Thos. Warner's employ for several years, and took account of his family, both of Indian slaves and others. Several ran away, one being the mother of Warner, so called because he was the first-born slave in the General's family in St Christopher's. To the same effect as the preceding depositions. 1675, Dec. 20. (CSP 1675: 319–20)

¶ [*The following petition to the king was also drawn up by Philip Warner at this time; it reveals further nuances in his defence.*]

He has been accused by the malice of a profligate seaman of crimes committed upon the Indians in Dominica, of which he is innocent, the witnesses at the last hearing having left out several circumstances, as also the distinction of time of 14 days between drinking with the Indians and killing them. Prays that his case may be re-heard, in order that he may prove his innocence. (CSP 1675: 321)

¶ [*So it was that Philip Warner's innocence was indeed proved, at least to the satisfaction of his fellow colonists in the Caribbean, for in a letter from Barbados dated 12 September 1676, written by Philip Warner himself, we learn something of the reasons for his acquittal.*]

His long silence has not been occasioned through want of respect, but his troubles, which have drowned his thoughts of all others things. This brings the good tidings of his deliverance after full twelve months' imprisonment in England, and on the 8th instant he was brought to public trial. His judges were 25 gentlemen from the Leewards and this place, the jury from this island only. Great search to find evidence against him, but none found but to his advantage. Proved Hamlin a perjured rogue, so the grand jury acquitted Warner, and he was discharged by proclamation. Is returning in a few days to Antigua, where he promises himself a great deal of future content in a private retired life. (CSP 1675–6: 447)

¶ [*And thus is the strange 'case' of Indian Warner concluded but far from explained.*

Such explanation is not the proper role of this anthology and must await further historical study, but we may end this presentation with one further extract, Jean Baptiste Labat's famous description of the mother of Indian Warner, whom he encountered in Dominica in 1700. Of the many ironies that have emerged in the 'case' of Indian Warner among the most poignant must be that the one person whose testimony would have been treated today as definitive in regard of Warner's paternity is also the very person whose opinion was never sought, and doubly so in that she outlived them all.]

We set sail again on the morning of the 9th [January 1700], & anchored at Dominica in front of the Carbet of Madame Ouvernard [Warner] the same day at two in the afternoon.

This female savage was, I believe, one of the oldest creatures in the world. It is said that she was very beautiful at one time, being now a little over 100 years & that she was the reason that an English Governor of St Christopher's was supported by them for such a long time, & because of that had a number of children, & among others a certain Ouvernard [Indian Warner] of which Father du Tertre speaks in his history. This half *Caraibe* was killed a long time before I arrived in the islands. They have always continued to call his mother Mrs Warner, since the English sent her back to Dominica after the death of the Governor who was supported by them. Her agedness, more than her position as mistress of an English Governor, has gained her a lot of credit among the *Caraibes*. She had a lot of children by this Warner, such that her Carbet, which is very large, was peopled with a marvellous number of sons, grandsons, and great-grandsons.

We hurried there as soon as our feet touched the shore. I made the greeting, & I believe it was well received, since it was accompanied by two bottles of rum, which is the most welcome gift for the Savages. She asked me when Father Raymond [Breton] was coming. He was one of our missionaries who had resided many years amongst them, working futilely for their conversion, but he has been dead some thirty years. I said that he would come soon. My reply gave pleasure to this good woman. Since to say that he was dead is something that neither she nor all the other *Caraibes* would be able to believe, because they hold that someone who they know is always alive, until they have seen them in their grave. It is like banging your head against a brick wall to make them believe otherwise.

This good woman was completely nude, & so naked that she had not two dozen hairs on her head; her skin was like a parchment, wrinkled & dried in the fire. She was so bent that I could not see her face except when she leant back to drink. However, she had plenty of teeth, & still lively eyes. She asked me if I wished to stay in her Carbet, & I responded that I would remain while our barque was at anchor; she had a hammock brought for me, I thanked her, but since I did not want to be covered in roucou like a *Caraibe*, I chose another part of her Carbet, where I could hang mine. Five or six other persons who were also going to Guadeloupe did the same; so we were all established at Madame Ouvernard's house, where we were at leisure to observe their customs, & to get to know them; thus we stayed here seventeen days.

9. *The First Missionary*
Raymond Breton (1647)

¶ *Raymond Guillaume Breton (1609–79) was ordained in 1631 and chosen for the new Guadeloupe mission in 1635, for which he embarked in May of that year. He returned to France nearly twenty years later, in 1654, following disputes over the role of the Dominican order with the Governor of Guadeloupe from 1643 to 1664, Charles Houël. In this time, Breton produced the key linguistic works on the 'Caraïbes', principally in the form of a two-part dictionary with extensive explanations of some of the basic cultural concepts of the 'Caraïbes' of Dominica, with whom he was the most familiar, as is made clear in the extract that follows.*

However, Breton's part in the authorship of this manuscript is far from clear, as Rennard (1929) discusses, for it represents something of a collective effort on the part of the French missionaries, being submitted as a report for the Superior of the order in 1647. Rennard suggests that this report was based on the experiences of Breton, among others, and that two later descriptions of the Guadeloupe missions, in Latin, were the individual effort of Breton, though showing clear identities with the earlier work. Accordingly only those sections of the 1647 work that also appear in the Latin relations are included here; being chapters 1, 2, 5, 6, and 12 of the twelve chapters of part II of this three-part work. It should also be noted that there are two versions of this latter work, one in the Bibliothèque Nationale, and one in the archives of Propaganda Fide in Rome (Rennard 1929); differences between these versions are indicated as appropriate, after Rennard, whose transcription has been utilized for this translation.

Clearly the most satisfactory procedure would have been to include only those items that might be unambiguously attributed to Breton, but a dictionary, grammar, and catechism do not make for agreeable reading, and in any case the focus here is the 'Caraïbes' and not the literary biographies of their observers. However, it should be emphasized that Breton appears to have had very strong views on the linguistic ethnography of the natives of Dominica, especially as regards the origin of the men's jargon and its relation to the natal language, undoubtedly stimulated by Rochefort's (No. 10) earlier account. It is therefore of some significance that the divergences in the manuscripts in Rome and Paris should centre precisely on these questions and that the modern scholarship of Douglas Taylor (1954) should indicate that, notwithstanding Breton's exemplary ethnographic credentials, he actually misunderstood the linguistic situation that he set out to describe.

Of the Origin, Mores, Religion, and Other Customs of the *Caraïbes* Commonly Called Savages, Ancient Inhabitants of Guadeloupe

Since our mission has been established principally for the instruction of the infidel savages, it is necessary to give some knowledge of their origin and customs, since a judgement may more easily be formed as to the success the mission will one day have through understanding the character of those with whom we are dealing. We say nothing that is not to be relied upon. The Revd Father Raymond Breton, monk of this mission, who has conversed with them almost two years and has advanced tolerably in their language during this time, has been able to learn about their customs and ceremonies, almost all of which he has seen or learned of from themselves, at least as regards those of Dominica, for in the other islands they have different reveries, as we know from the report of Reverend Father Meslan, a Jesuit who has been among the savages of Martinique.

Of the origin and disposition of the Savages

Nothing can be learned from collecting all their dreams and fables touching upon their origin except that they are descended from closely neighbouring peoples of the islands who come from the mainland. This much is completely certain. The friendship that they have with them and the trade of the one with the other are some indication as well as the uniformity of the name by which they both call themselves, namely *kallinago* following the language of men and *kalliponam* following the language of women; although, for some distinction among themselves and those of the mainland, they call the latter *Balouöouri*, from the word *Ballouö*, which means the mainland, as one would say a Parisian Frenchman, or of *Langrois*. Thus they say a *kallinago* of the mainland. We call those from the mainland who are friends of our savages *Gallybis* and our savages *Caraïbes*.

If you ask them how they derived from them and were carried over into the islands, they will not be able to give a reason for it. Duly, they all say that their first father *Kallinago*, having left the mainland accompanied by his family, set up home on Dominica. Here he had a long line of descendants and here lived the nephews of his nephews, who through an extreme cruelty killed him with poison. But he was changed into a fish of monstrous size that they call *Akaiouman* and he is still full of life in their river. This fable makes known at least that they are descended from peoples of the mainland.

It is the belief of many Frenchmen that there were other inhabitants in these islands before the *Caraïbes*, by whom they were driven out. And they base this on the fact that (and the same is certainly said by the savages) there are yet in some islands some of those people, who have retreated into the mountains, and who are white like the French and have long beards. Monsieur d'Esnambuc, Governor of St Christopher, assured Father Raymond that there were some on St Christopher. The *Caraïbes* vouchsafe that there are some on Guadeloupe and that they are above the great river at Goyave and at Grandeterre. And it is certain that there are some on Dominica since they often see them. When Father Raymond was on Dominica the first time in 1642 the savages surprised some of them—a man, a woman, and a girl. They killed and ate the man and made slaves of the woman and girl. And last year, the same day that he arrived here, these Mountain-men came down, burnt down a hut, and carried off some property.

Our *Caraïbes*, however, say through a well-established tradition amongst themselves that they have killed the *Allouagues* (first) inhabitants of the islands* and that these ones in the mountains are from their slaves who ran away into the mountains and there multiplied; which means that they now but rarely pardon the male slaves, but kill them and eat them. And if they are white it is perhaps because of the cold.

As regarding their persons, they are of good stature and well proportioned, strong, robust, ordinarily fleshy, and healthy. They have no other deformities, except that many of them are flat-nosed as a result of their mother's flattening the forehead and the nose at birth. Their natural colour is sallow, strongly tanned. They appear more red as a result of the roucou with which they redden themselves everyday. They have completely black hair and will not tolerate red or blond hairs. There are very few bald-headed people among them and they mock those who are. They are no more thieves than the French and as yet less so.

As for that which concerns their character, they are all melancholic, sad, sombre, and even their face shows it. They speak little if not spoken to. They are not overly stupid for savages. They are inquisitive and very capable in those things they apply themselves to, like making beds, baskets, fishing, hunting, shooting arrows. They are very sprightly and agile at climbing, jumping, and swimming, and without doubt are capable of greater things.

A young captive man among them related to them some of the story of the Holy Scripture; they questioned him thereupon and created in him some doubts which were not impertinences.

They are generous enough amongst themselves and give one to another from whatever they have: also they demand freely. They are not like that with us French, since they give us nothing and always require something and are not disheartened by refusal.

As to their nature, they are not cruel, unless it is against their enemies. They

---

* In the Roman version of the manuscript: 'Our *Caraïbes* ... say ... that they are the first inhabitants of the islands and that it is those ones who are in the mountains ... etc.'

are dangerous while they are in their cups and fight each other, but beyond that, it is easy to enjoy their company.

They are extremely idle and prefer to have the poorest fare and to work less. They scarcely think of the morrow and make no other provision than of manioc and sweet potatoes that they plant in season. Yet rather often they find themselves short. They do not care about either gold, or silver, or precious stones.

They have their work divided among the men and women: they make it a point of honour if one does not take them at their own estimation. The men never touch the everyday work of the women, believing that they would degenerate. Among all this, they live content and would certainly be happy, if the Christian religion had tempered a little their barbarity and coarseness.

One will ask perhaps how they are so few, given the multitude of their women. They reply to you that the Christians are the cause of it, since, as one of them was saying to Father Raymond, the Spanish have twice massacred all the savages on the island of St Christopher; once those on Guadeloupe, from which survived a woman and her children who took refuge in the mountains and here multiplied as they say. They tried to do as much on Dominica and there massacred well over half. Since, they have been burdened with smallpox, which they call *variola*, from which some have rotted and died, not knowing yet any remedy for this evil. Finally it is because everyone carries them off or kills them: the Flemish, the English, the Spaniards, and their *Allouagues* who are their enemies.

Of their language

The language of our *Caraïbes* is different from that of the *Gallibys* of the mainland. It is difficult to learn for many reasons. The first is that they couch none of it in writing nor with any other sign so that great patience is required in order to distinguish their utterances, which they hurl out loudly, and a capacious memory in order to retain that which one is able to gather. The second is that they have diverse sorts of languages. The men have their own and the women another, and yet another for orations and matters of consequence that the young people likewise do not understand well. The third is that they have no words to express the powers of the soul, such as the will, the understanding, nor that which concerns religion, [or] civility. They have no honorific terms like Our Lord. They express however some acts of the understanding and of the will, such as to remember, to wish. In other things, the language is copious and fine enough. They sometimes sing songs in a single pitch that is not agreeable and is simplistic. They sing whatever comes to mind without rhyme and very often without reason, especially against their enemies.

They name each other with terms that signify the degrees of consanguinity or affinity, like my father, my brother, my cousin; the others they call my compere.

They never call anyone by their name, particularly if he is related. If they are constrained to name him, they say no more than half the word. They often take the name of the person with whom they contract friendship or particular comradeship.

They have a jargon or specific language* through which they deal with us, which is Spanish, French, *Caraïbe* pell-mell at the same time.

Of the food on which they live

I do not think that there could be a nation in the rest of the world that would make more meagre fare than this one, although it has the means to maintain itself well; but what does it matter, since they are in good health, are fleshy and robust without these delicacies.

They do not rear cattle, nor sheep, nor goats, nor swine, and they never eat them among themselves, although they had a quantity of pigs on Dominica, no more than poultry, chicken eggs, butter, cheese, milk, oil, nor fat. They salt nothing among themselves; when they are present among us, they eat nearly everything, although those who have infants abstain, as we will relate in the following chapter. Among themselves, they eat turtle and white eggs from the turtle, but not the yellow, certain birds, crabs, *tourlourets*.[1] They never well cook what they eat, particularly the crabs. They cook the birds whole on two small prepared sticks, a little above the fire, after having singed the plumage. Once cooked, they wrap them with leaves and put them in the smoke; when they wish to eat they empty them out and boil them with their manioc and pepper juice, as they do with other things. They make a certain sauce which they consume with everything that they eat. They throw the bones of the fish that they have eaten in a pot with a handful of pepper, some manioc juice and some of the most refined flour, mixing everything together and soaking their bread and meat therein. They call this a *tomaly*. What is in earnest, is that there is always some hair of the old women and some roucou [in it], since they are extremely unclean. Their bread is just cassava fresh every day; their drink *ouicou* made with cassava and water. Sometimes they crush pineapples or sugar canes and drink the juice, likewise also water mixed with honey. While eating they do not reckon it at all impolite to belch.

They have only one regular meal a day, knowing it is the morning as soon as it is daylight. The rest of the day, they eat when they want and when they have the opportunity; they are always ready. The men eat apart in the great longhouse and the women in their little huts with their children.

They use but little *petun* [tobacco] in smoking, but they dry it in the fire, then make it into powder and mix a little with sea-water and put it between the lip and the gum, and the result is very strong.

---

* In the Roman version of the manuscript 'corrupt language'.

[1] Small red crabs, from the *Caraïbe* 'itorourou', giving also the French 'toulourou' = 'common soldier' or 'private', as in English 'soldier-crab' or 'hermit crab', due to its red markings.

Of their marriages and education of their children

As there is no polity or law among our savages, they also have no fixed rule for their marriages. There is no prohibited degree [of relatedness], or at least if they restrict themselves from some, such as between parents and their children and between brothers and sisters, it is rather by the powerful action of Nature that they are restrained than by reason of piety or continence. And there are some who notwithstanding the voice of Nature have joined themselves with their daughters and have by them children, and some mothers who have married their sons. But those persons are very rare ordinarily. Therefore none of the parents are now joined with their children nor brothers with their sisters. The first cousins once removed of sisters to them are wholly spoken for; those who are daughters of brothers are considered as sisters. Many marry the two sisters; a few the mother and daughter.

They have as many wives as they wish, and especially the chiefs and their children. And similarly they have them on different islands. They live in various little huts and sleep successively with their husbands, one one month, another the next. The one who sleeps with him serves him during this time and follows him all over, even to sea. If they surprise their wives in adultery or if they are pregnant by another man, they usually kill them, though sometimes they leave them one or two years without going to see them. The men are at liberty to leave their wives and they [the wives] are at liberty to remarry; but the women do not have any such prerogative. Although they have many wives, they [the wives] are seldom if ever jealous.

The husband never talks with the father, the mother, and the brothers of his wife unless they be either drunk or children. If they encounter them on the same path, they remove themselves and make a large circuit. If necessity obliges them to speak, as when they are at sea, they turn their face away and cut it short. They use no ceremony in marriage; if the girl is not absolutely promised to them as are the cousins of their sisters, they ask the father or the mother. They do not know what love is. They rarely marry without the consent of their father and mother. The men do not sleep at all with their wives, unless they are truly nubile and capable of having children. While the women are giving birth, the husbands withdraw from them, and they do not sleep together at all for five or six months from this point. And both undertake a fast, which is one of the most celebrated, especially when they have a boy for the first child. The man fasts more rigorously than the woman for fear that the infant should suffer by him. Father Raymond was at the house of Le Baron [*Caraïbe* chieftain] on Dominica, going to see one of these fasters, and as the Father was speaking to him of this fast, the savage told him that some abstained entirely from drinking and eating for the first five days after the confinement of their wives, and on the other days until the tenth, they take nothing but *ouicou*. After this they eat nothing but cassava and drink *ouicou* for the space of a month or two. And note that they only eat the heart of the cassava and hang up the rest with a cord for the festival. It is true that after they begin to eat, they eat and drink when they wish, but nothing except cassava and *ouicou*. When the day of the festival has arrived and their friends are assembled, all the skin of their bodies is cut with agouti teeth, as with a knife, until it bleeds; then they are rubbed all over with pepper-juice which causes them great pain, and they are sometimes so despondent with this fast and this blood-letting that it is necessary to lead them home by the hand, and, while the others get drunk at their expense, they continue to fast for some days yet. Once the fast is over, they still eat no fish or birds, as long as their infants are still feeble and weak, excepting crabs and also female chickens if they must.

The person fasting gave Father Raymond some very good reasons for it. It is, he said, because the children would have stomach illness or defective limbs like those of the animals that their fathers ate. For example, they would have a long and round snout if they were to eat eel, small and round eyes if parrots. (And for the same reason, they never eat sea-cow for fear that their children would have small, round eyes like this great fish.) They would have crooked feet if they were to eat pig and so on with other things.

We will also interpolate here this pleasing trait in passing. There is a species of caranx[2] which is a fine fish with the bones of the spine somewhat bent; when they eat this fish they take good care to dispose of its bones a long way off; they put them in the ground very gently for fear that they should become hump-backed and are astonished that the French mock them for this.

After the women have given birth, they press the forehead of their infants with their hand and thus make it match up with the crown of the head and force it to flatten. So it comes about that they have a large forehead. In order to keep them in this posture, they make them sleep by day on their knees, the head on one knee pressed by their hand, and their feet on the other knee. By night, they hold them to their side, from whence it comes that being accustomed to sleep so warmly, they will cry dreadfully when they [the mothers] go away even a little from their sides.

After two or three weeks they invite [someone] like a godfather or godmother who pierces the ears, the nose, and the underneath of the lip of these little infants and cuts their hair in front and gives them a name. They in exchange rub him with oil on the head and neck. The mothers never cover their infants when they go somewhere. They carry them under the arm with a little bed of cotton [hammock] that they pass over the shoulder in a sling.

When the children are one or two, the father holds a festival called *Elétoaz* at which their hair is cut entirely and their nose, ears, and under-lip are pierced if their weakness had hindered them being pierced when little.

The boys, when they are bigger, eat with their fathers and the girls with their mothers. They do not teach them any kind of manners nor do they say good day or good night nor thank you very much. They raise them with such

---

[2] Genus of *Scomberidae*, a family also uniquely distinguished by the *Caraïbes* with the term 'coulilaouarou'.

dissoluteness that they will only do as they please, and will obey their parents only at whim, and the parents do not chastise them at all. The mothers sometimes mistreat them, but this is only out of anger or spite, not by way of discipline.

When the girls begin to menstruate, they make them fast for a month or two, as they do the boys when they reach their adolescence, and they have them cut with agouti teeth, as we will relate when we speak of their drinking-parties.

When the father dies or leaves his wife, all the children stay with her; she takes charge of them and the husband no longer concerns himself with them.

There are amongst the savages women who prostitute themselves. There are no indecent expressions among them. They all, big and small, girls and boys, call things by their names without any shame.

Of their illnesses, death, mourning, burial, and reveries concerning the soul

Almost all of them are affected by that disease that one refers to as of Naples, or as others say, pians,[3] which is scarcely better, which is also common enough amongst the negroes. And some French people have also caught it from them. Yet this does not come, at any rate always, from Venus, seeing that they get it when they are still small. To cure themselves of it they do not sweat at all, but grate some *lambies* [sea-shells] that they gulp down with water. They rub themselves with genip, or with reed leaves burnt with the liana that they call *mouchao* or *miby*. They are not cured as quickly as those who are made to sweat.

One sees very few other illnesses amongst them, and it is a marvel that, leading so wretched a life, they are so healthy and well fed and live so long. For it is certain that they commonly live a very long time. It is only four or five months since Baron's father died and his wife, Baron's mother, is still alive. Le Baron, whose wife is still living, has a daughter; this girl has another and this other already has some children. So that the Baron is twice a grandfather and his mother three times a grandmother and the daughter of Baron who is a grandmother herself still has her grandmother alive. And this is not the only example that could be supplied. Their long life must be attributed to their lack of assiduousness.

They lay the blame for their illnesses on their *Rioche* [magic figurines] and, if the illness is long-lasting or serious, they call the *Boïyako* [priest-doctor] in order to consult him about it. They have a number of remedies for their sicknesses that the women apply to them, but they do not treat them any more gently than the healthy.

The kin never, or very rarely, visit their sick; and generally married people do not go there at all because, they say, there comes from their bodies a property that further afflicts the sick. This is why, when one of the sons of Baron was ill, neither his brothers, nor his sisters, nor his father would go to

[3] Also 'yaws' in English, possibly linked to the *Caraïbe* term 'yaya'.

see him; there was only his mother who treated him and who did not communicate at all with the father.

When some of their own die in battle, they do what they can to reclaim their bodies and bury them. But, here is what they do when they lay out their dead.

They make a round trench three feet deep, and inside a house so that he [the dead person] might be under cover. They wash the body, covering it with roucou all over, anoint the hair with oil, and fit him out as decently as at their great feasts. They wrap him in a brand new cotton bed and then put him in the grave in almost the same posture as the infant in the belly of its mother, not turned upside down, nor likewise with the face in the dirt, but upright, the feet below, the head above supported on the knees, and they cover the hole with a plank. This done the women sit all around, on their heels, and cry; their husbands embrace them with the left hand and pass the right hand under the arm as if to assuage their grief. And everyone intones a lugubrious chant mixed with sighs and shrieks. As they lament they [the women] throw earth with their hands into the grave and then make a fire on top. They burn his old clothes or they give them away. If he had slaves they [the men] kill them; but these usually take to their heels and they are not pursued.

The children of the deceased or his wife cut their hair as a sign of mourning. They also fast for one or two months. When Father Raymond asked them if their fast served some purpose for the deceased, they said no; but that those who did not fast would age more quickly or would not be steadfast, would not see the fish in the water, and their enemies would take them by surprise. And these reasons still seem pertinent to the old ones.

If one of the family is not able to attend the funeral, he comes to visit the tomb and there cries along with the family of the dead. When they think that the corpse has rotted, they gather again at the tomb and weep and trample on the grave. And this is their anniversary, at the end of which they wish to drown their sadness and the memory of the deceased in an abyss of *ouicou*.

Furthermore, concerning the soul after death they have this idle fancy: that each man has three souls. One in the head, that can be felt beating against the temples; another in the arm, which manifests itself in the pulse; and the other at the heart, which does enough to make one conscious of the movement.

The soul in the heart goes straight to the sky in order to be happy, although they are not able to say what this felicity consists of. The souls in the arm and the head become *mapoya*, that is to say evil spirits that torment them. They fear them greatly, since they attribute to them all their terrors that they have: such as happened to one who was lying on his left side and pressed on his spleen while asleep, which caused him to have bad dreams. Father Raymond observed this and woke him up and the savage was most grateful to him for having recalled him from the clutches of *Mapoya*, of whom he recites these wonders. However he was not able to believe that it was no more than a dream.

They believe that there are also other evil spirits at the edge of the sea who shipwreck them, that they call *Oumokou*. They also maintain [a belief in] some sort of torment in the bowels of the earth whence come the fiends that they call *Touvalik*.

We are informed of nothing further at present of the customs of our savages which merits being written down. It is true that we have set down a number of their stupidities which perhaps were not indispensable or even worthy of being written down. We appreciate it, [and] this is why we have omitted many others out of which a fair volume might be made. We have not however left everything out, whatever we might have wished, since otherwise you would not have been able to understand either their moods or their barbarism, if we had not represented somewhat clearly their customs, although brutal and truly savage.

10. *Relative Values*
Charles César de Rochefort (1658)

¶ *Charles de Rochefort's (d. 1690) Histoire naturelle et morale des Îles Antilles*
was first published in Rotterdam in 1658, although his name appears only on the
second edition of 1665. Much controversy surrounds the production of this work,
as well as the opinions and theories that it expounds. Certainly Rochefort's
Protestantism, if nothing else, sets him apart from the Catholic missionary
chroniclers who were his contemporaries. Moreover, his close identification with the
anti-clerical Governor General of the French Caribbean from 1638 to 1660, Philippe
de Poincy, to whom the first edition of his work is dedicated, adds an important
political dimension to the fierce criticisms that du Tertre (No. 11), in particular,
made of the work.

Subsequent commentators, no doubt because of the ethnographic authority that
du Tertre's own work appeared to have in virtue of his association with Raymond
Breton (No. 9), have largely accepted du Tertre's judgement as to the unreliability
and lack of originality in Rochefort's publication. However, we are now able to
appreciate that Breton and du Tertre also had a particular view of the Caribs which
they were keen to promote, especially as regards the issues of Carib origins, which
were supposedly reflected in the distinct modes of speech employed by men and by
women, and of their lack of capacity for socio-political organization (or 'polity').
Thus Rochefort explicitly contradicts du Tertre on this latter issue, as can be seen
from a comparison of the extracts reproduced in this anthology, and elsewhere
raises the possibility of northern, as well as southern, continental affiliations in the
origin of the seventeenth-century Caribs. This latter suggestion, while certainly
contradicting modern as well as earlier scholarship, in point of fact remains to be
properly researched and so must still be considered unresolved.

Notwithstanding these empirical controversies in the ethnology of Rochefort, his
theoretical orientation is notable for being comparative and not merely descriptive,
as with the missionary writers. In this sense he is a precursor of that better-known
comparative ethnologist Joseph Lafitau (1724), who also made extensive use of the
data on the Carib in his own examination of American ethnology (cf. Plate 12).

The following extracts were selected to illustrate some of these controversies, as well as to present some of the linguistic material whose interpretation is still at the heart of the many disagreements over the historical anthropology of the native Caribbean. The extracts are taken from John Davies's (1627?–1693) contemporary translation (1666) of Rochefort and have been checked for overall accuracy against the second edition (1665) of the original French text. Davies, described as 'a genial, harmless and quiet man', travelled in France between 1646 and 1652 and his knowledge of the French language appears to be commensurately competent. This translation has been used in the hope that his seventeenth-century English usage may perhaps occasionally bring us closer to those times than a modern translation ever could.

Certain remarks upon the Caribbian language

It is our intention at the end of this history, for the satisfaction of the more curious reader, to add a large vocabulary of the *Caribbian* language. And therefore, in this chapter, we shall make only some principal remarks upon it, such as may in some measure discover the grace, the smoothness, and the proprieties thereof.

1. The *Caribbians* have an ancient and natural language, such as is wholly peculiar to them, as every nation hath that which is proper to it.

2. But besides that ancient language, they have fram'd another bastard-speech, which is intermixt with several words taken out of forreign languages, by the commerce they have had with the Europeans. But above all they have borrowed many words of the Spaniards, for they were the first Christians that came among them.

3. Among themselves, they always make use of their ancient and natural language.

4. But when they have occasion to converse or negotiate with the Christians, they always make use of their corrupt language.

5. Besides that, they have also a very pleasant intermixture of words and expressions when they would undertake to speak in some forreign language. As, for example, when they use this expression to the French, saying, *Compere Governeur*, that is *Gossip Governour*, using the word *compere* generally towards all those who are friends or allies. In like manner they would say, without any more ceremony, *Compere Roy*, that is *Gossip, or Friend, King*, if there were any occasion to do it. It is also one of their ordinary complements to the French, when they say with smiling countenance, *Ah si toy bon pour Caraibe, moy bon pour France*, *If thou art good for the Caribbian, I am good for France*. And when they would commend, and express how much they are satisfy'd with those of the same nation, they say, *Mouche bon France pour Caraibe, France is very good for the Caribbian*. They say also, *Maboya mouche fache contre Caraibe, Maboya doth much against the Caribbian*, when it thunders, or in a hurricane. And, *Moy mouche lunes, I have lived many moons*, to signifie that they are very ancient.

They also have these words often in their mouths, when they find that the French would abuse their simplicity, *Compere, toy trompe Caraibe, Friend thou deceivest the Caribbian*. And they are often heard to say when they are in a good humour, *Moy bonne Caraibe, I am an honest Caribbian*.

6. Yet it is to be observ'd, that though the *Caribbians* of all the islands do generally understand one another, yet there is in several of them some dialect difference from that of the others.

7. There is no great use made of the letter *P.* in their language; but that only excepted, there is no want of letters, as there is in the language of Japan, Braseel and Canada, which want the letters *F. L. R.* Or in that of Peru, wherein *B. D. F. G. J.* consonant and *X.* are wanting, as historians affirm.

8. The language of the *Caribbians* is extreamly smooth, and for the most part pronouinced with the lips, some few words with the teeth, and in a manner nothing at all from the throat. For though the words we shall set down hereafter, seem to be rough, as they are written, yet when they pronounce them, they make elisions of certain letters, and give such an air thereto as renders their discourse very delightful to the ear. Whence it came, that Monsieur du Montel hath given this testimony of them: 'I took great pleasure', said he, 'in hearkning unto them when I was among them, and I could not sufficiently admire the grace, the fluency, and the sweetness of their pronunciation, which they commonly accompany with a little smiling, such as takes very much with those who converse with them.'

9. The *Caribbians* who are inhabitants of the islands have a sweeter pronunciation than those of the continent, but otherwise they differ only in dialect.

10. By the same word, according as it is diversly pronounced, they signifie several things. For example, the word *Anhan* signifies, 1. *Yes*, 2. *I know not*, 3. *Thine*, or *take it*, according to the pronunciation that is given it.

11. The Europeans cannot pronounce the *Caribbian* language with the grace and fluency natural thereto, unless they have learnt it very young.

12. They hear one another very patiently, and never interrupt one the other in their discourse. But they are wont to give a little hem at the end of every three or four periods, to express the satisfaction they have to hear what is spoken.

13. What advantage soever the Europeans may imagine they have over the *Caribbians*, either as to the natural faculties of the mind, or the easiness of pronunciation of their own language, in order to the more easie attainment of theirs, yet hath it been found by experience, that the *Caribbians* do sooner learn ours than we do theirs.

14. Some of the French have observ'd that the *Caribbians* have a kind of aversion for the English tongue, nay so far, that some affirm they cannot endure to hear it spoken where they are, because they look on them as their enemies. And whereas there are in their corrupt language many words taken out of Spanish, a people whom they also account their enemies, it proceeds hence that they learn'd them during the time they held a fair correspondence

with that nation, and before they began to treat them as they afterwards did.

15. They are very shie in communicating their language, out of a fear the secrets of their wars might be discovered; nay, those among them who have embrac'd the Christian religion, would not be perswaded to reveal the grounds of their language, out of a belief it might prejudice their nation.

16. We shall set down here some of the most particular properties of their language. In the first place, the men have many expressions proper only to themselves, which the women understand well enough, but never pronounce. And the women have also their words and phrases, which if the men should use they would be laugh'd at; whence it comes, that in this discourse one would think that the women spoke a language different from that of the men, as will be seen in our vocabulary, by the difference of the expressions which the men and women use of to signifie the same thing. The Savages of Dominico affirm that it proceeds hence, that when the *Caribbians* came to inhabit these islands, they were possess'd by a nation of the *Arouagues*, whom they absolutely destroy'd, save only the women, whom they married for the repeopling of the country; so that those women having retain'd their own language, taught it to their daughters, and brought them to speak as they did; which being practis'd to the present by the mothers to their daughters, their language came to be different from that of the men in many things. But the male children, though they understand the speech of their mothers and sisters, do nevertheless imitate their fathers and brethren, and accustom themselves to their language when they are five or six years old. To confirm what we have said concerning the cause of this difference of language, it is alledg'd that there is some conformity between the language of the *Arouagues* who live in the continent, and that of the *Caribbian* women. But it is to be observ'd, that the *Caribbians* of the continent, as well men as women, speak the same language, as having not corrupted it by inter-marriages with strange women.

17. The old men have also some forms particular to themselves, and certain affected expressions, not at all us'd by the younger sort of people.

18. The *Caribbians* have also a certain language which they make use of only among themselves, when they entertain any warlike resolutions. It is a very hard kind of fustian-language. The women and maids know nothing of that mysterious language, nor yet the young men, till they have given some assurances of their generosity, and the zeal they have for the common quarrel of their nation against their enemies. This is to prevent the discovery of their designs before the appointed time.

19. For the variation of their cases, persons, moods, and genders, they have no distinct particles as we have, but they lengthen their words by certain syllables or letters at the beginning or end of the word, and sometimes by the change of the letters. Thus they say in the imperative, *Bayoubaka, Go*; but in the indicative, *Nayoubakayem, I go*. In like manner, *Babinaka, dance*; *Nabinakayem, I dance*; much like the formation of Hebrew verbs.

20. Indefinite and absolute nouns are not much in use among them,

especially the names of the parts of the body; but they are always in a manner restrain'd to a first, second, or third person.

21. The first person is commonly expres'd by the letter N. at the beginning of a word, as *Nichic, my head*; the second by B., as *Bichic, thy head*; and the third by an L., as *Lichic, his head*.

22. The neuter and absolute gender is expres'd by a T., as *Tichic, the head*; but this is not much in use.

23. They have different names in speaking to persons when they are present, and others when they speak of them; thus they say *Baba*, Father, speaking to him, and *Youmaan*, speaking of him; *Bibi*, Mother, speaking to her, and *Ichanum*, speaking of her; which, with the difference there is between the language of the men and women, the young and the old, their ordinary discourse, and that us'd by them when they are engag'd in military deliberations, must needs cause a great multiplication of words in their language.

24. Their proper names are many times deriv'd from certain accidents, as we shall see more particularly in the chapter of the birth and education of their children.

25. They never name any one when the party is present; or at least, out of respect, they do but half name him.

26. They never pronounce the whole name of either man or woman; but they do those of the children; so that they will say, the father or mother of such a one; or else they say half the name; as for instance, *Mala*, instead of saying *Malakaali*, and *Hiba* for *Hibalomon*.

27. The uncles and aunts, as many as are of the collateral line, are called fathers and mothers by their nephews; so that the uncle is called *Baba*, that is to say, *Father*. But when they would expresly signifie the true and proper father, they many times add another word, saying, *Baba tinnaca*.

28. Consequently to the precedent appellation, all the he-cousins are also called brothers, and all the she-cousins, sisters.

29. But between he-cousin and she-cousin, the former calls the latter *Youe-illeri*, that is to say properly, *My Female*, or my betrothed, for naturally among them the she-cousins become wives to the he-cousins.

30. The months they call *Lunes*, that is *Moons*, and the years *Poussinieres*, that is the *Seven Stars*.

31. We shall now give a taste of the naturalness and elegance of their language, setting down the signification of their words, without expressing the words themselves, so to avoid the setting of them down twice, as reserving that for our vocabulary.

32. To signifie that a thing is lost or broken, they commonly say that it is *dead*.

33. They call a Capuchin Friar, Father *Aioupa*, and the word *Aioupa* signifies in their language a covering or a penthouse; as if they said, it is a man by whom one may be cover'd, by reason of his great *Capouche*. By the same name they also ironically call an ape or monkey, by reason of his long beard.

34. A Christian, *a man of the sea*, because the Christians came to them in ships.

35. A Lieutenant, *the track of a Captain*, or *that which appears after him*.

36. My son in law, *he who makes me little children*.

37. My younger brother, *my half*.

38. My wife, *my heart*.

39. A boy, *a little male*.

40. A girl, *a little female*.

41. The Spaniards and the English, *deformed enemies, Etoutou noubi*; because they are cloath'd, in opposition to their enemies who are naked, whom they simply call *Etotou*, that is to say, *enemies*.

42. A fool, *Him who sees nothing*, or *who hath no light*.

43. The eye-lid, *the covering of the eye*.

44. The eye-brows, *the hair of the eye*.

45. The ball of the eye, *the kernel of the eye*.

46. The lips, *the borders of the mouth*.

47. The chin, *the prop of the teeth*.

48. The neck, *the prop of the head*.

49. The arm and a wing are express'd by the same word.

50. The pulse, *the soul of the hand*. The Germans make such another composition, when they call the glove *the shooe of the hand*.

51. The fingers, *the little ones*, or *the children of the hand*.

52. The thumb, *the father of the fingers*, or *that which is opposite to them*. Of that kind is the ἀντίχειρ of the Greeks.

53. A joint, *a thing added*; they call also by that name a piece set on a garment.

54. The bladder, *the urine vessel*.

55. The ham, *that which draws the leg*.

56. The sole of the foot, *the inside of the foot*.

57. The toes, *the little ones*, or *children of the foot*.

58. The number ten, *all the fingers of both hands*.

59. Twenty, *the fingers of the hands, and toes of the feet*.

60. A pocket-pistol, *a little arquebusse*.

61. A candlestick, *that which holds somthing*.

62. Thorns, *the hair of the tree*, or *the eyes of the tree*.

63. The rainbow, *Gods plume of feathers*.

64. The noise of thunder, *Trerguetenni*.

65. This language hath also in its abundance and its naturalness some imperfections which are particular thereto; yet are they such as that some of them do not so much deserve blame as commendation.

66. The *Caribbians* in their natural language have very few words of injury or abuse, and what they say that is most offensive in their railleries is, *Thou art not good*, or *thou hast as much wit as a tortoise*.

67. They have not so much as the names of several vices; but the Christians have sufficiently supplied them therewith. Some have admir'd that in the

language of Canada there is no word answerable to *Sin*, but they might have observ'd withal, that there is not any whereby to express *Virtue*.

68. They have no words to express winter, ice, hail, snow, for they know not what they are.

69. They are not able to express what does not fall under the senses, save that they have certain names for some both good and evil spirits; but that excepted, they have no word to signifie spiritual things, as *understanding*, *memory*, *will*; as for the *soul*, they express it by the word *heart*.

70. Nor have they the names of Virtues, Sciences, Arts, Trades, nor those of most of our Arms and Tools, save only what they have learn'd since their commerce with the Christians.

71. They can name but four colours, whereto they make all the rest to relate; to wit, white, black, yellow, red.

72. They cannot express any number above twenty & their expression of that is pleasant, being oblig'd, as we said elswhere, to shew all the fingers of their hands, and toes of their feet.

73. When they would signifie a great number, which goes beyond their arithmetick, they have no other way than to shew the hair of their heads, or the sand of the sea, or they repeat several times the word *mouche*, which signifies *much*; as when they say in their gibberish, *Moy mouche mouche lunes*, to shew that they are very ancient.

74. In fine, they have neither comparatives nor superlatives; but for want thereof, when they would compare things together, and prefer one before all the rest, they express their sentiment by a demonstration which is natural and pleasant enough. Thus, when they would represent what they think of the European nations which they are acquainted withall, they say of the Spaniards and the English, that they are not good at all; of the Dutch, that they have as much goodness as a mans hand, or as far as the elbow; and of the French, that they are as both the arms, which they stretch out to shew the greatness thereof. This last nation they have a greater affection for than any other, especially those of it who have gone along with them to their wars; for they give those part of their booty. And as often as they return from their wars, though the French had not gone along with them, yet do they send them part of the spoil.

Of what may be accounted polity amongst the Caribbians

1. There are in every island of the *Caribbies*, inhabited by the *Caribbians*, several sorts of Captains: 1. The Captain of the *Carbet*, or of a village, whom they name *Tiouboutouli hauthe*. This is when a man hath a numerous family and retires with it at a certain distance from others, and builds houses or huts for to lodge it in, and a *Carbet*, where all of the family meet to be merry, or to treat of the affairs which concern it in common; thence it is that he is named a Captain of a family, or of houses.

2. A Captain of a *piraga*, that is, either he to whom the vessel belongs or he

who hath the command of it when they go to the wars; and these are named
Tiouboutouli Canaoa.

3. Amongst those who have every one the command of a vessel in particular,
they have also an admiral or general at sea, who commands the whole fleet:
him they call *Nhalene*. In fine they have the grand Captain, or Commander in
chief, whom they call *Ouboutou*, and in the plural number, *Ouboutounum*. This
is the same whom the Spaniards call *Cacique* (and we in this History call *Cacick*)
as some other Indians, and sometimes also our Savages do in imitation of them.
He is during his life, from his first election to that charge, the General of their
armies, and he is always highly respected among them. He appoints the
meetings of the *Carbet*, either for merry-making or deliberations in order to go
to a war. And he always goes abroad attended by all of his own house, and
some others who do him the honour to wait on him. Those who have the
greatest retinue are the most highly honoured. If any one gives him not the
respect due to him upon account of his charge, it is in his power to strike him.
Of these there are but two at most in an island, as at Dominico. They are also
commonly the Admirals when a fleet goes out. Or haply that charge is bestowed
on some young man, who is desirous to signalize himself upon that occasion.

This charge is obtain'd by election, and commonly he who is advanced
thereto must have killed divers of the *Arouagues*, or at least one of the most
considerable persons among them. The sons do not succeed their fathers in
that charge, if they be not worthy thereof. When the chief Captain speaks all
others are silent; and when he enters into the *Carbet*, every one makes [for]
him way. He hath also the first and best part of the entertainment. The
Lieutenant to this Captain is called in their language *Ouboutou maliarici*, that
is to say properly, the *track of the Captain*, or *that which appears after him*.

None of these Chiefs hath any command over the whole nation nor any
superiority over the other Captains. But when the *Caribbians* go to the wars,
among all the Captains they make choice of one to be General of the army,
who makes the first assault. And when the expedition is over, he hath no
authority but only in his own island. True it is, that if he hath behav'd himself
gallantly in his enterprises, he is ever after highly respected in all the islands.
But heretofore, before the commerce between the *Caribbians* and forreign
nations had alter'd the greatest part of their ancient politie, there were many
conditions requisite to obtain that degree of honour.

It was in the first place requisite that he whom they advanc'd to that dignity,
had been several times in the wars, and that to the knowledge of the whole
island whereof he was to be chosen Captain, he had behaved himself coura-
giously and gallantly. Next to this it was necessary, that he should be so active
and swift in running, as to surpass all competitors in that exercise. Thirdly, he
who stood for the Generalship of an island, should excell all others in swimming
and diving. A fourth condition was, that he should carry a burthen of such
weight as his fellow-pretenders should not be able to stand under. Lastly, he
was obliged to give great demonstrations of his constancy, for they cruelly cut

and mangled his shoulders and breasts with the tooth of an agouty, nay his best friends made deep incisions in divers parts of his body. And the wretched person who expected that charge was to endure all this, without betraying the least sign of resentment and pain, nay, on the contrary, it was requisite that he receiv'd all with a smiling countenance, as if he was the most satisfied man in the world. We shall not wonder so much that these Barbarians should endure such torments, in order to the acquisition of some dignity, when it shall be considered that the Turks do not shew themselves somtimes less cruel towards themselves, upon the account of pure gallantry, and as it were by way of divertisement; witness what is related by Busbequins in the fourth book of his *Embassies*, which were too tedious to set down in this place.

To return to the *Caribbians* of the islands. This ancient ceremony, which they observed in the election of their chief Governors, will no doubt be thought strange and savage, but there is something of the same kind observable in other nations. For in the kingdom of Chili they chuse for the sovereign Captain him who is able longest to bear a great tree upon his shoulders. In the country of Wiapoco [Oyapock], towards the great river of the Amazons, to be advanc'd to the dignity of Captain, he must endure, without the least stirring of the body, nine extraordinary strokes with a holly-wand from every Captain, and that three several times; but that is not all, he must also be put into a bed of cotton, over a fire of green leaves, the thick smoke whereof ascending upwards, must needs be very troublesome to the wretch who is so mad as to expose himself thereto. And he is obliged to continue there till he be in a manner half dead. This speaks a strange desire to be Captain. Nay, heretofore among the Persians, those who were desirous to be admitted to the Fraternity of the Sun, were requir'd to give proofs of their constancy in fourscore several sorts of torments. The Brasilians, without any other ceremony, make choice of him for their General who hath taken and kill'd most enemies. And now also in some of the *Caribbies* the *Caribbians* themselves laugh at their ancient ceremonies at the election of their Captain. For having observ'd that their neighbours think that kind of proceeding ridiculous, they now make choice of him for their Chief, who having behav'd himself valiantly in the wars against their enemies, hath acquired the reputation of a brave and gallant person.

As soon as the *Cacick* is receiv'd into his charge, he is highly respected by all, insomuch that no man speaks if he do not ask or command him to do it. And if any one cannot forbear speaking as he ought, all the rest immediately cry out *cala la bocca*, which they have learn'd from the Spaniard. But it suffices not to be silent in the presence of their Chief, but they are also very attentive to his discourse, look upon him when he speaks, and to shew that they approve of what he says, they are wont to smile, and that smile is accompanied by a certain *hun-hun*.

These expressions of respect are such as are not to be accounted savage, as being us'd generally all over the world. But the Maldiveses have a particular way of honouring a person. For as they think it a kind of disrespect to pass behind any one, so to express a great submission they take their passage just before him, and making low obeisance, say as they go by, *may it not displease you*. The Incas, a people of the kingdom of Peru, to express respect they bear their god, enter into his temple backwards, and go out of it after the same manner, quite contrary to what we do in our ordinary visits and civilities. The Turks account the left hand the more honourable among military persons. The inhabitants of Java think the covering of the head is the greatest act of submission. The Japonneses think it a great incivility to receive those who would honour them standing. They take off their shooes when they would express how much they honour any person. In the kingdom of Gago in Africk all the subjects speak to the king kneeling, having in their hands a vessel full of sand, which they cast on their heads. The Negroes of the country of Angola cover themselves with earth when they meet with their Prince, as it were to signifie, that in his presence they are but dust and ashes. The Maronites of Mount Libanus meeting their Patriarch, cast themselves at his feet and kiss them. But he immediately raising them up, presents them with his hand, which they taking in both theirs, and having kissed it, lay on their heads. But they who live about the streight of Sunda have a very strange custom, which is, that to honour their superiors they take them by the left foot, and gently rub the leg from the anckle-bone to the knee. And that done, they in like manner rub the face, and the fore-part of the head; an action which I doubt would be far from being thought respectful in these parts.

From what hath been said it may be deduc'd, that this worlds honour, whatever it may be, virtue excepted, conflicts only in opinion and custom, which differ, and somtimes clash, according to the diversity of mens humours.

But to return to the Captain of our *Caribbians*. It is his business to take the resolutions of war, to make all preparations in order thereto, and to go upon any expedition in the head of his forces. He also appoints the assemblies of his island, and takes care for the reparations of the *Carbet*, which is the house where all resolutions that concern the public are taken. In fine, he it is who in the name of the whole island, as occasion serves, gives answers, and appoints the days of divertisement, as we mentioned before.

The administration of justice among the *Caribbians* is not exercis'd by the Captain, nor by any magistrate, but, as it is among the *Tapinambous*, he who thinks himself injur'd gets such satisfaction of his adversary as he thinks fit, according as his passion dictates to him, or his strength permits him. The public does not concern itself at all in the punishment of criminals. And if any one among them suffers injury or affront, without endeavouring to revenge himself, he is slighted by all the rest, and accounted a coward, and a person of no esteem. But, as we said before, there happen few quarrels or fallings out among them.

A brother revenges his brother and sister, a husband his wife, a father his children, so that when any one is kill'd, they think it justly done, because it is done upon the account of revenge and retaliation. To prevent that, if a Savage of one island hath kill'd another Savage, out of a fear of being kill'd by way of revenge by the relations of the deceased, he gets into another island and setles himself there. Those whom they think sorcerers do not exercise that profession long among them, though for the most part they are rather imagin'd to be such, than that they are really so.

If the *Caribbians* suspect any one to have stolen somthing from them, they endeavour to lay hold on him, and to cut him over the shoulders with a knife or the tooth of an agouty, as a mark of his crime and their revenge. These agoutys' teeth among the *Caribbians* supply the want of our rasors, and indeed they are in a manner as sharp. Thus the ancient Peruvians and the Canarians, before they had use of our iron instruments, made use of a certain kind of flint instead of scissers, lancets and rasors.

The husband suffers not his wife to break her conjugal faith towards him without punishment, but he himself acts the part of both judge and executioner, as we shall declare more particularly in the chapter on their marriages. They know not what it is to punish publicly, or to observe any form in the execution of justice. Nay, they have no word in their language to signifie justice or judgment.

11. *Jean Baptiste du Tertre and the Noble Savages (1667)*

¶ *Jacques du Tertre (1610–87), son of a Calais doctor, fought as both sailor and soldier in the navy and army of the United Provinces, distinguishing himself at the siege of Maastricht, before entering the monastery of Faubourg Saint-Germain in 1635, where he took the name Jean Baptiste. He first went to Guadeloupe as a missionary in 1640, returning to Paris in 1642 to seek help for the mission. A second stay (1643–7) was marked by political difficulties, notably his antagonism to de Poincy. He made a last brief visit in 1656–7.*

Du Tertre first wrote a history of the French colonies in the West Indies in 1654. In 1667 this was considerably expanded as Histoire générale des Antilles habitées par les François, *the second volume of which deals with natural history, including the chapters on the native inhabitants, some of which are translated here. Volumes iii and iv were added in 1671, dealing with the political history of the islands.*

Like Bartolomé de las Casas before him, du Tertre is willing to see a natural goodness in the Caribs, which can be contrasted to the rapacious behaviour of supposed Christians, especially the Spanish and English, although his compatriots are not always excused. The Caribs' 'natural' qualities—underlain by that complex opening paragraph to chapter 1—are powerfully presented. Du Tertre's book was an important reference point for Jean-Jacques Rousseau in his depiction of 'natural man' in the Discourse on the Origins of Inequality, *written in 1754. There he refers to the Caribs, 'who have as yet least of all deviated from the state of nature' (1973: 71), and paraphrases du Tertre's account of the Caribs' insouciant habit of selling their hammocks in the morning and asking for them back at night (56).*

1. About the Savages in general

Just as in centuries past some people have believed that the atmosphere of the torrid zone was composed only, so to speak, of fire, flames, & heat; that the earth underneath was just an awful wilderness, so sterile & so burnt that it only served to bury those who wanted to live there, that all its waters were hot, stagnant, & poisoned: in a word, that it was more an abode of horror and torment than it was a place of pleasure and charm. So, at the very word Savage, most people imagine in their mind's eye the kind of men who are barbarous, cruel, inhuman, without reason, deformed, as big as giants, as hairy as bears: in a word, monsters rather than reasonable men; although in truth our Savages are Savages in name only, just like the plants and fruits which nature produces without cultivation in the forests and wildernesses, which, although we call them wild, still possess the true virtues in their properties of strength and complete vigour, which we so often corrupt by our artifice, & change so much when we plant in our gardens.

Now, just as I have shown that the atmosphere of the torrid zone is the purest, healthiest, & most temperate of all the atmospheres, & that the earth there is a little paradise, always verdant, and irrigated by the most beautiful waters in the world, it is appropriate to show in this treatise that the Savages of these islands are the most content, the happiest, the least depraved, the most sociable, the least deformed, and the least troubled by illness, of all the nations of the world. For they are just as nature brought them forth, that is to say, with great simplicity and natural naïvety: they are all equal, with almost no sign of superiority or servitude; & one can hardly recognize any kind of respect, even between relations, such as by son for father. No one is richer or poorer than his companion, & all unanimously limit their desires to what is useful for them, & indeed necessary, & scorn everything which is superfluous as not worthy to be owned.

Their only clothing is that with which nature has covered them. No polity is seen among them; they all live in freedom, drink and eat when they are hungry or thirsty, work and rest when they please; they have no worries, I do not say for the morrow, but from breakfast to dinner, only fishing or hunting exactly what is necessary for the present meal, without troubling themselves about the one after, preferring to get by with little than to buy the pleasure of a good meal with too much labour.

For the rest, they are neither hairy nor deformed: on the contrary they are of good stature and well-proportioned build, stout, powerful, strong, and robust, so fit and so healthy that old people of 100 or 120 are often seen among them, who do not know what it is to give in or bow their shoulders under the burden of old age, & who have very little white hair, & a forehead scarcely marked by a single wrinkle.

And if some have a flat forehead and snub nose, this is not due to a fault of nature but to the artifice of their mothers, who put their hands on the forehead of their children to flatten and lengthen them at the same time, believing that by that laying on of hands, these poor little things receive all the beauty for their faces; & because this first face, impressed immediately after the child's birth, will change with age, the mothers very often have their hands pressed on the forehead of their infants, for fear it will not change.

The rheumy-eyed, the bald, the lame, and hunch-backed are very rare among them. You meet a few with curly hair, but not one with fair or red, two kinds of hair they hate in the extreme. Only skin colour distinguishes them from us, for they have bronzed skin, the colour of olives, & even the white of their eyes has a little.

Some people have asserted that this colour is not natural to them, & that being born white like Europeans, they only become so bronzed through painting and rubbing themselves with roucou. But a clear proof of the falseness of this proposition is that we have a number of Savage children among us, on whom none of those colours has been applied, who nevertheless are no less bronzed than the others.

They have good reasoning, and a mind as subtle as could be found among people who have no smattering of letters at all, & who have never been refined and polished by the human sciences, which often, while refining our minds, fill them for us with malice; & I can say in all truth that if our Savages are more ignorant than us, so they are much less vicious, even indeed that almost all the malice they do know is taught them by us French.

They are great dreamers, & carry on their faces a sad and melancholy physiognomy. They spend entire half-days sitting on top of a rock, or on the riverbank, their eyes fixed on land or sea, without saying a single word. They do not know what it is to go for a walk, & laugh their heads off when they see us going several times from one place to another without making ground, which they judge as one of the deepest stupidities they have been able to observe among us.

They stand on their honour, but only through imitating us, & since they noticed that we have people among us to whom we show much respect, and defer to in all matters, they have been pleased to have such people as comperes, that is to say as friends, whose name they take at the same time, to make them more commendable, and they give theirs in exchange, & try for the same reason to imitate them in some way.

One day one of the oldest men on Dominica, called Amichon, having seen the Governor of Martinique with a big sailor's kerchief round his neck, which we generally call a cravat, thought he had at home the wherewithal to have himself well thought of by imitating his compere: this was the remnant of an old cloth made from the sail of a launch, which he wrapped round his neck two or three times, letting the rest hang in front of him. In this outfit he came to Guadeloupe, where he spread laughter among all those who saw him attired like that.

I enquired of him in all seriousness why he was got up in that manner, & he replied in a truly serious and sober tone that it was like his compere, du Parquet. But in truth, whatever great desires they have to be honoured, they have no point of honour which their interest in a small knife, a piece of crystal, a glass of wine, or 'stomach-burn' (which is what they call brandy), will not trample underfoot.

They are naturally kind, gentle, and affable, and often sympathize to the point of tears with the ills of the French, only showing cruelty to their sworn enemies. [...]

6. About Savage commerce

They have among them no kind of commerce, they sell or buy nothing, giving each other quite liberally all the things with which they can relieve their compatriots without inconveniencing themselves too much; but, there never having been a nation which was more in need of all the things that art has made common in all the nations of Europe, they have always greatly desired commerce with the French, & with other nations of Europe; because before communication, if they needed to cut down a tree to make a house, they had only had stone axes; if they wanted to go fishing, they only had turtle-shell hooks; if they planned to make a pirogue to go to war against their enemies, they took all the trouble imaginable to cut down a tree, to shape it, to hollow it & to give it the form of a pirogue: nevertheless they do not trade with the ships in safety, because some of them have been carried off, with loss of freedom and sometimes life. Those who do them most harm are the English, against whom they make war, because they [the English] have occupied some of their islands to which they [the 'Caraïbes'] want to return. They have had several fights with them, where the English have always been disadvantaged: in revenge for this bad treatment, the latter, when they sail past Dominica, change flag so as not to be recognized, & in order to trap these poor wretches in their ships by this stratagem, & sell them as the most expensive merchandise of their trade.

Our Savages would very much like us French to do with them what they do with their compatriots, that is to say, give liberally whatever is asked of them; but as they [the French] have a quantity of good merchandise, & are more attached to their interests than these Barbarians, they cannot relish that way of doing things; and I fear that with time we French will make them give up this praiseworthy custom in order to embrace trade. Which they have already made a good beginning at among us; for we no longer have anything from them if it is not through receiving with one hand and giving with the other. For the rest, they are such beggars and so poor, that most of them carry all their chattels with them.

When they come to visit us, it is because they have designs on our commodities, such as axes, billhooks, knives, needles, pins, hooks, cloth to make sails for their pirogues, crystal, small mirrors, glass beads, & other small trifles of low cost.

In exchange they bring us cotton beds, turtles, pigs, lizards, fish, hens, parrots, local fruits, bows, arrows, small baskets, & carets,[1] which is better

[1] Probably shells of the marine turtle *Caretta caretta*, distinct from the edible turtle *Chelonia midas*.

9. *Visite des Sauvages aux François*. From Jean Baptiste du Tertre, *Histoire générale des Antilles habitées par les François*, 4 vols. (Thomas Jolly: Paris, 1667–71), ii, opp. 395. The Bodleian Library: BB. Art. Subl. 122.

merchandise, & more expensive. They also bring us what they have collected from their enemies, everything which is not to their liking, & some green stones, & they also hold on to what they need; and if a knife is needed, when you present them with two axes or two billhooks, which are worth twenty times as much, for a turtle, they will not give it; and will take a knife, because that is what they need, and is the possession among all others which is most necessary to them, since they are constantly cutting and shaping.

They are cheap to trade with, & some of us French have earned much from them. A turtle as big as can be is only worth a billhook or an axe, a good fat pig is not worth more; but where there is most profit to be made is on the cotton beds and carets.

As we French are quicker and more adroit than they are, they are easily enough duped; they never sell a bed in the evening, because since these good people see the need they have for one at the present moment, they would not give their beds for anything at all; but in the morning they give them cheaply without thinking that once the evening comes they would be in the same position as the preceding evening; in addition, they do not fail to return at the end of the day & to bring back what has been given them in exchange, saying quite simply that they cannot sleep on the ground, & when they see that no return will be made, they almost cry with vexation. They are very likely to retract from all the deals they make; which is why it is necessary to hide and remove everything that has been bought from them. In a word, all their commerce and all their trade is just a child's game; and quite often when they come among us, they cost more to feed than the value of the gain made from the commodities bought from them. They are very importunate in asking for what pleases them: I do not know however if it is through pride or shame that they never ask for anything again once it has been refused them. [. . .]

13. About the obstacles encountered in converting the Savages

It is easy to conclude from what we have said about the manners and customs of these poor Barbarians, with what ease they would make their way to Heaven if they were illuminated by the light of the Faith; since, notwithstanding the thick gloom clouding their understanding, & the corrupt nature which serves them as guide in the conduct of their whole life, they undertake such frightful austerities, such painful fasts, such strange mortifications, such cruel blood-lettings, that many saints in possession of glory could not have undertaken so many in this life.

What if, instead of demons, they had Jesus Christ as master, & if, instead of the superstitious ceremonies in which the demons involve them, they had the holy maxims and innocent practices of the Gospels; what would they not do by means of this light, and what would they not undertake in view of the eternal rewards which it promises; since, without hope of a better life nor of any reward, they observe so precisely all the things prescribed for them by these spirits of delusion and deceit; & from what vices would they not disentangle

133

themselves through learning of the unending tortures of a wretched eternity, since although they recognize and confess every day to the cheating and impostures of the demons, & of their agents, none the less the fear of fleeting evils, with which they are threatened, makes them carry out with great punctiliousness what is required of them. Will they not raise themselves with good reason on judgement day against Christians, & particularly against those who converse and treat with them every day, & will they not condemn with justice their ambition, their greed, their lust, their dissoluteness, their treacheries, their envies, & a thousand other sins, which are not even known among them?

In a word, if what is found most difficult in the practice of virtue, & which presents most of an obstacle to our spiritual advancement, has no hold on their minds, what favourable surmise must we not draw to the advantage of these Barbarians, if in place of the countless reveries which completely encumber and confuse their minds, they had knowledge of the equally ineffable and adorable mysteries of our salvation; & if in place of the demons who tyrannize them, they had an incarnate God as model for their manners and all their actions?

These are the thoughts that hold the attention of so many of the monks, who regard themselves as happy in their labours, which cannot be imagined by those who do not witness them; & who consider their lives usefully employed, & their death glorious, providing they can contribute to the instruction and conversion of this barbarous people.

But if I am now asked how it comes about that after so many years Christianity sees little progress among the Savages, I reply that, even though it may not be visible and apparent, because of the obstacles that have been encountered, as much on their part as through various other happenings which I have related in this history, it is nevertheless much greater than we had expected; for, beyond the fact that the chiefs of these people, through political considerations, have often prevented or retarded the missionaries from preaching the gospel, it is certain that there are two main reasons on the part of the Savages themselves, not counting a thousand other little difficulties which the fire of love consumes, & not to mention those which Satan presents to us every day.

The first, & what is now almost the only [reason], is the poor impression the Savages have formed of the bad lives of the Christians; because they have seen men come to take possession of their lands, & those of their neighbours, with unheard of cruelty, who sought only gold, and whose way of life was somewhat more barbarous than their own: hence, even in our time, they felt such horror at the name Christian that the greatest insult they could pay to a man was to call him Christian; so that, however good the face they put on when they were asked if they wanted to be Christians, & replied yes, this was only, however, to be obliging, & to get from us what they had need of: because privately the very name Christian makes their heart pound and their teeth grind. From which it must be inferred that even though well over two-thirds of the Savages of Dominica are instructed to the point of responding that there is only one God in three Persons, that He made heaven and earth, that He punishes the wicked in hell with eternal torment, & that he rewards the good in paradise; though they know the commonest prayers, such as the Apostle's Creed, the Lord's Prayer, and the Hail Mary, & though they even make a holy sign of the cross; nevertheless, until they are more fully informed about the mystery of our redemption, and have removed from their hearts the hatred they bear to the holy name of Christian, it would be too risky to baptize them. This is why the monks are very careful not to hurry in a matter of such importance, besides knowing very well that most of the Savages would receive baptism in return for a small knife, or for some other trifle, & afterwards would mock the holy sacrament when the least thing was refused them.

This is what makes all the missionary monks bring all imaginable circumspection to bear, & makes them take on the part of the Savages all the care and precautions which they believe necessary, so as not to give them the holy sacrament in vain, nor to expose it to the blasphemy of these Barbarians.

Father Raymond affirms that in ten or twelve years he only baptized four of them, and that even these were all close to death. I know for sure that the Jesuit fathers who now exert themselves there proceed in this way more than the other missionaries; this is why there is good reason to be astonished at the boldness and temerity with which S. de Rochefort dares to tax the monks for causing the sacrament not to be held in the esteem due to it, through having baptized somewhat without proper consideration, & brings as proof for his proposition two notorious falsehoods, of which the first is that *Maraboüis, son of Baron, was baptized in Paris with great solemnity and in the sight of several gentlemen who honoured that event with their presence*; the second, that he was sent back to his country, laden with presents and fine clothes, but as little Christian as when he had left it, because he had not properly *understood the mystery of the Christian religion, and had no sooner set foot on land than he mocked all he had seen as a farce, saying that the Christians indulged themselves in stupidities, & then returned to the company of the other Savages, and had himself covered in roucou.*

This demonstrates great imprudence on the part of the monks, if what I put forward is true, but it equally demonstrates impudence and effrontery if it is nothing but falsehood: I would forgive S. de Rochefort, if he had only sold his book in Holland, or in distant countries, where his story could have passed for true, but to advance boldly before the eyes of all Paris that *Maraboüis, son of Baron, was baptized in Paris with great solemnity and in the sight of several gentlemen who honoured that event with their presence*: this is what cannot be tolerated.

So I would gladly ask him in what church he was baptized, who was the prelate who performed the ceremony, who gave him the name Louis, & who were *these gentlemen who honoured that event with their presence*: this is how one substantiates these kinds of claims, which cannot be concealed, having been made with ostentation; however, there is no one in Paris who has the slightest knowledge of this baptism of *Maraboüis*, whatever S. de Rochefort has said about it, having no doubt been misled on this particular, as well as on so many other points that he has given us in his book.

Because I do not want to believe that he has planned to give this fable of the baptism of *Maraboüis* in order to have the opportunity to declaim against the missionary monks concerning the administration of the sacrament of baptism; who, through what I am going to say about this very *Maraboüis*, make clear with what prudence and with what restraint they act in the dispensation of the sacraments.

So, this poor Savage having come to France, after having been saved from the wreck of the boat carrying Father Coliard, who was bringing the young man, he was taken to Paris and received into the monastery of the Dominican fathers in the new street of Saint-Honoré, where, for nearly ten months, they worked to instruct him in the mysteries of our holy religion; after which, having fallen ill, as he was abandoned by the doctors & on the point of death, it was thought that he should be given the holy sacrament of baptism: this is why he was asked whether he wanted to receive it & to die a Christian; having replied yes, as they began the task of baptizing him, he clearly showed that he was not so uninstructed as S. de Rochefort suggests, *& that he had well understood the mystery of the Christian religion*: for he gave to understand that he well knew that this sacrament was not repeated, saying that he thought that Father Coliard had baptized him during the shipwreck, & that he had thrown water over his head; but that it had been done so quickly that he did not remember it very clearly, but nevertheless that he wanted to die a Christian: which is what obliged the late R P Joseph Roussel, a monk of a probity and prudence renowned in Paris, to baptize him conditionally, so as not to do things unthinkingly. This is, quite simply, how things happened, in the presence of three or four monks, in one of the rooms of the monastery, where *Maraboüis* was ill, & to which is reduced the *great solemnity* spoken of by S. de Rochefort, who was no better informed about the return of this young man to the islands, since it is in no way true that he had no sooner set foot ashore than he mocked everything he had seen as a farce, saying that the Christians only indulged in stupidities: indeed, on the contrary I have learned from the monks who took him back to the islands that, having reached Martinique, they had often seen him sighing, crying, and deploring the blindness of the Savages, saying that they lived like beasts, & that he would often say during the crossing that a Savage who died among the Capuchins had died a good Christian, & that he had really wanted to die the same way.

It is none the less true that having reached Guadeloupe, his mother did so much that she lured him to go to see his relatives, & to take a cotton bed which she had made for him, & that shortly after he had arrived, his mother and all the other Savages gained such power over him, that they made him marry, as if by force, one of his first cousins, who belonged to him according to the custom of the country; but, some time later recognizing his mistake, scorning that woman, & doing all he could to get himself back among the Christians, his own relatives poisoned him. R P Raymond confirms this in his Dictionary, saying that it is wrong to accuse him of dying apostate; so that S. de Rochefort has been as ill informed about the baptism and return of Maraboüis as about the fine clothes and presents he brought back from France, seeing as the whole lot was not worth 100 francs.

In the first edition of my book I had put down as a second obstacle the difficulty of learning the language of the Savages, which was not the lesser in those times: because of the few monks we had, hardly sufficient for the Christians in the colony, it was almost impossible for us to send any among the Savages to learn their language, all the more difficult as it is for being impoverished and imperfect; but Father Raymond has remedied this so successfully through his care and indefatigable labours, in the extensive Dictionary and the excellent Catechism which he has given us in it [the language], that the missionaries can make themselves very competent in instructing them, without neglecting the duties that they are obliged to perform for the Christians in the islands where they reside. Besides the number of monks of various orders being much greater than it has been so far, there is room for hope that God will bless the work of our missionaries and that it will soon be seen that most of the poor Savages embrace the Christian religion, & that, with us, they will perform acts of immortal grace to Him who by His infinite goodness will have delivered them from blindness, & from the jaws of hell.

12. *An Account from the Jesuit Missions*
Sieur de la Borde (1674)

¶ *Sieur ('Mr') de la Borde is a shadowy figure known to the editors only from his description of the 'Caraïbes' which first appears as part of a collection,* Receuil des voyages en Afrique et l'Amérique, *made by Louis Billaine and published in Paris in 1674. Another version was issued by Adrian Broakman in Amsterdam in 1704, and edited by F. Louis Hennepin, 'Missionaire recollect & notaire apostolique', with the endorsement of Richard Ligon, historian of Barbados. The title-page to these printed works reads:* Narrative of the Origin, Mores, Customs, Religion, Wars and Voyages of the Caraibes, Savages of the Antilles Islands of America. Made by the Said DE LA BORDE, Employed in the Conversion of the Caraibes, being with the R.P. Simon Jesuit; and Taken from the Library of Mister Blondel. *The original manuscript apparently derives from the collection of François Blondel (1618–86), a naval engineer in the King's service who was sent, among other places, to the Caribbean in 1666 to make maps of the islands and assess the need for fortifications. It was presumably at this time that he encountered de la Borde.*

The Jesuit priest Simon, also referred to on the title-page, certainly appears in the French colonial correspondence of the period as being involved in the conversion of the 'Caraïbes' of Dominica and St Vincent (ANP Colonies F3–44, fo. 462, 1665), though no reference to the nature of de la Borde's employment in this mission has been found. One may conjecture that, as laity 'employed' in the conversion of the 'Caraïbes', he was either part of the French military and naval presence or a functionary of the local administration.

Whatever the case his account is notable for being one of the few extensive non-missionary descriptions, along with that of Rochefort (No. 10), to have survived from this period. As with Rochefort and du Tertre, and all the more acutely given the lack of provenance for this account, the issue of originality inevitably arises, as de la Borde appears to acknowledge in his opening sentences. However, while there are obvious parallels with earlier accounts, there are also many original pieces of information, not least in the detailed section on religion and 'diabolical superstition', which greatly amplifies the limited descriptions of the missionary-ethnographers, who might well be expected to have had the greater difficulty in dwelling extensively on heathen religious conceptions. None the less his debt to the Jesuit Father Simon is fully acknowledged in the final section, where he also tantalizingly alludes to the existence of the latter's lost linguistic works on the 'Caraibes'.

All but three sections from de la Borde's narrative have been translated here, representing over two-thirds of the entire work. The illustrations that accompany the text were commissioned by Billaine from an anonymous illustrator 'who has taken care to reside a long time amongst them, & understands their language extremely well'.

There are so many descriptions of the islands that it is quite pointless to repeat what has so often been said about them. If, none the less, it seems that I do so on certain occasions, it is that things are represented as other than they are, for want of having seen them, or for other reasons & considerations they are misrepresented to us, & tell things more or less as they are not. I do not intend to speak here of the air, the climate, and the nature of the country; others have spoken enough, I shall only make some remarks in order to satisfy those who wish it, about the customs & superstitions of the Savages, & what I speak about, I am able to assure its truth by reason of the great familiarity I have with them & by reason of having been sufficiently curious to pay attention to them & to inform myself about them. This curiosity is not reprehensible as long as one may draw some profit from it; because when I consider that the *Caraibes* are hospitable, without ambition, very simple, without avarice, very sincere, without thievery, without deceit, without blasphemy, without lies, I cannot but admire them, & imitate them in their morality detailed in the points above; but if they have their perfections, they also have their vices, of which we will speak in the following discourse. When I consider their self-delusion, & that they have neither faith, nor law, nor King, I feel obliged to give thanks to my Creator for having given me knowledge of a God & for causing me to be born into the true religion & a subject of the greatest King in the world.

Of the origin of the Caraibes

I will not try to uncover the origin and descent of the *Caraibes*, island savages of America; besides, they themselves know nothing of it. They have as little curiosity about the past as about the future, & authors speak so diversely that I see nothing but obscurity & little certainty. Some have even imagined that they are descended from the Jews; because in practice their female relations are naturally intended as their wives, & because they eat no pork.

Old Savages have told me that they derive from *Galibis* from the mainland, neighbours of their enemies the *Alouagues*; because the language, the customs, & the religion have a lot of conformity with their own, & because they have entirely destroyed a nation of these isles, except for the women whom they took for themselves, & this is the reason that the language of the men does not resemble that of the women, in several particulars. I also believe that what has made such narratives so diverse has resulted because, since the *Caraïbes* consorted with strangers, they have changed their habits and manner of behaving, & renounced what used to be most esteemed amongst them. Yet there are those who do not change at all, & these tell the others that the cause of all their sorrows, of their illnesses, & the war that the Christians make against them, comes from no longer living as *Caraïbes*.

Of their religion, & the conception they have of the creation of the world, & the stars

Although they have an extremely changeable spirit, very trifling, & inconstant in all their enterprises, nevertheless they have the character of heretics in the matter of religion; because they are so obstinate and attached to their *Chemeen*, & to all their other superstitions, that all that one can say to show them that it is the Devil who deceives them under this name, is not adequate to make them give it up. They are not unlike the Calvinists, with neither priest, nor altar, nor sacrifice; I believe that this is never seen amongst all the other pagans. Through their brutal passions, their barbarous habits, & their bestial lives, they have stifled all knowledge, & the light of the divinity that nature gives, which is astonishing, & which I would not believe, if I had not seen it every day, & although they have been preached to for twenty years, they do not wish to believe, nor recognize their Creator, & source of all good. They fear the evil one who is the Devil, which they name *Maboia*, but they render him no worship.

Judging from many of their fables, there is reason to believe that they were formerly guided by the light of the Gospel; aside from the fact that what they relate of *Louquo*, whom they reckon to have been the first man & *Caraïbe*, was tiresome and was also against decorum, & could shock the ears of the chaste: I will only report some things about him.

Louquo was the first man & *Caraïbe*; he was not made from anybody, he descended from the sky to here below where he lived a long time. He had a large nostril from which came forth the first men, in the same way as [they did] by [his] making an incision in his thigh. Many events happened in his life which were shameful, & infamous to recite. He made fishes from scrapings & little morsels of manioc, which he threw in the sea, & big ones from large pieces: he resuscitated three days after his death, & returned to the sky: the terrestrial animals came forth afterwards, but they do not know from where.

The *Caraïbes* were formerly long-lived, & if they did not become aged, they died without being ill; also they ate nothing but fish, which is always young, & never ages.

Afterwards they found a little garden of manioc that *Louquo* had left behind; as they recognized nothing of this plant an ancient appeared to them and taught them its usage, & told them that by breaking the wood into little pieces, &

planting them in the earth, other roots would come back. They say that in the beginning this manioc took no more than three months to mature, that later it did so in six, & finally nine, as it does at present, before it was good for making bread or cassava, that they call *Aleba*, & the women *Marou*.

They believe that the sky has existed for all time, but not the earth, & the sea, nor either one in the noble form they have at present. Their moving force & principal intermediary *Louquo* had firstly made the earth soft, smooth, without mountain; they are not able to say from where he got the material. The moon followed forthwith and esteemed itself very beautiful, but after it had seen the sun, it concealed itself from shame, & ever since only shows itself at night.

All the stars are *Caraibes*: they make the moon masculine, & name it *Nónun*, & the sun *Huóiou*: they [the *Caraibes*] attribute eclipses to *Mapoia*, to the Devil who tries to make them die, & they say that this wicked seducer cuts their hair by surprise, & makes them drink the blood of a little child, & that it is when they are entirely eclipsed that they have many maladies, & that they also become sick when not warmed by the sun's rays & its light.

They prize the moon more than the sun, & at all the new moons the moment that it begins to appear they all come out of their houses in order to see it, & exclaim: 'Behold the moon.' They take certain tree leaves which they fold like a little funnel, & trickle a drop of water down into their eyes, while looking at it; this is very good for the sight. They regulate their days by the moon like the Turks, & not by the sun; in place of saying a month, they say a moon: they never say, 'how many days to make your journey?' but, 'how many nights will you sleep?'

Their counters are their fingers: in order to express twelve they show their hands and two toes: if the number exceeds the feet and hands they are much hindered, they say *Tamieati*, a lot, & if there is a great quantity they show their hair, or a handful of sand. When they prepare to go to war, & to be at the rendezvous on the appointed day, each one takes a number of pebbles according to their decision, puts them in a calabash, & on each morning removes one, & eventually there are no more, that is to say that the time fixed until departure has expired, & he must take the field. Sometimes they make marks on a piece of wood, or else each one ties knots in a small cord, & they undo one of them each day.

Thus, in the beginning the earth was soft, the sun has made it hard, just as it has with the sky; for there are on high more beautiful gardens than here, grand savannas, fair rivers: there *Oüicou* flows without ceasing (a beverage like beer), water is never drunk, the huts & houses are better made there, where their *Zemeens* dwell, & as they themselves do after death: they have more women than here, & a great number of children. No work is done, everything grows here without sowing, one does nothing but sing & dance, & one is never ill.

What they say about the origin of the sea, & about the creation, & generally about all the waters, relates in some manner to the Flood. The great Master of

Chemeens, who are their good spirits, angered & in a rage that the *Caraïbes* at this time were very wicked, & no longer offered him cassava, nor *Oüicou*, made it rain many days such a great quantity of water that they were nearly all drowned, with the exception of a few who saved themselves in small boats and pirogues on a mountain which was the only one left. It is the deluge of the hurricane which made the *mornes*, the *pitons*, & the cliffs which we see. *Mornes* are hills, *pitons* are the high pointed rocks or high mountains in the form of a sugar-loaf. It is he who separated the islands from the mainland. If you ask where these waters came from, they will reply to you that there are rivers on high, & that the first waters came from the urine and the sweat of the *Zemeens*, & it is this which is the cause of the saltiness of the sea, & what makes the water sweet is that the sea escapes underneath the earth, & here purifies itself.

Racumon was one of the first *Caraïbes* made by *Louquo*. He was changed into a large serpent, & had the head of a man: he was always on a *Cabatas*, which is a massive tree, very hard, high, and upright; he lived from its fruit, which is a large plum or small apple, & which he gave to passers-by: now he is changed into a star.

Savacou was also a *Caraïbe*, he was changed into an *Erabier*, which is a large bird, it is the captain of hurricanes & of thunder; it is he who makes the great rains; he is also a star.

Achinaon Caraïbe, at present a star, makes light rain and great winds.

Couroumon Caraïbe, also a star, makes the great 'lames' and overturns canoes. 'Lames' at sea are the long waves which are not at all cut across, & formed in such a way that one sees them strike land all of a piece from one end of the beach to the other: so that however little strength the wind has, a shallop or a canoe is almost unable to come ashore without overturning, or being filled with water. It is he also, by means of his wind, who makes the ebb and flow of the sea.

Chirities, the Pleiades, they reckon by, & observe the years by this constellation; nevertheless they are not able to say how long it is since the first of their nation came from the continent to inhabit the islands: moreover they are not able to say how old they are, they record nothing of all this, & see no point in all these notions. They are not much concerned as to where we come from, they call us *Balanaelé*; that is to say men from the sea, & believe in effect that we were born from the sea, & that we have no other dwellings than those of ships. They believe at this time that we come from another world, & that our God who made the sky & earth is not theirs, nor made their country.

As they have never believed that there were countries other than their own, the first time that they saw ships, & heard cannon, they believed that it was demons, & that the vessels, & the men who dressed and behaved differently from them, had emerged from the depths of the sea & had come to carry them off, & take their land; they took refuge in the woods. They have since recognized that they deluded themselves on one point, & that the other is genuine: they wish that we had never set foot in their land, & whatever they may pretend, they hold us in great aversion, but they are no longer to be feared: for many have been destroyed. I think there are still a good 4,000: of the twenty or thirty islands that they possessed, they now only occupy two or three. The French, the Spanish, the English, & the Flemish currently have them all. The first time that they saw a man on horseback, they believed that the rider & the horse were all one, & that the man was part of the beast; they only saw this contrivance walking from a long way off, & still at present there are those that do not dare to approach one; similarly there are those on St Vincent who have not yet seen Christians. It is very difficult in these sorts of narratives not to make some digression; let us return to our stars.

They call the sun ruler of the stars, & say that it is he who through his great light prevents them appearing by day. Nevertheless they believe that they withdraw & descend by night: lightning bolts are made by *Savacou* when he breathes out fire in a huge cannonade: thunder is made when the master or captain of the *Zemeens* chases other smaller *Zemeens* which are not *Manigat* [astute] & it is while they are being chased, & falling to the ground, out of fear that one hears this great noise: they [the smaller *Zemeens*] also shake the ground, & they are changed into beasts; they are strangely afraid and hide themselves when it thunders.

Coüalina is captain of *Chemeens*: *Limacani*, a comet sent by the captain of *Chemeens* to make mischief when he is annoyed.

Joulouca, [the] rainbow *Chemeen*, who thrives on fish, lizards, pigeons, humming-birds, is completely covered with beautiful feathers of all colours, particularly his head; it is this half-circle & rim which appear, the clouds prevent the rest of his body being seen. He makes the *Caraïbes* ill when he finds nothing to eat on high; if this fine Iris[1] appears when they are at sea, they take it as a good omen & say that she has come in order to accompany them, & to give them a good voyage, & when she appears on land, they hide themselves in their huts, & think that it is a strange *Chemeen*, who has no master; that is to say a *piaye*, as I shall explain afterwards; & thus he can do nothing but mischief through his evil influences, & is looking for someone to kill.

Of Chemeen & of Mapoia, who are their good and evil spirits, & of some of their diabolical superstitions

In order to demonstrate that the *Caraïbes* are bestial men, or rather beasts that have the form of men, it may be said that they never want to go to enjoy the delights which they say are on high, because they would have to die, & as they have no other desires than those of the present life, it is also for the same reason that they get annoyed when one speaks to them about going to paradise: they do not wish at all to leave the good things of the present for the benefits to come, to leave what they possess for what is unknown; to leave the pleasures which they feel every day for the eternal delights which they cannot see, & which do not titillate their senses.

[1] Rainbow goddess and messenger of the ancient Greeks.

They are very careful of their health, & are so apprehensive about death that they will not allow anyone to speak of it, for fear that it would arrive sooner: they would give themselves up to the Devil in order to live a long time; they never pronounce the names of the dead from a fear of being obliged to think of death, which would make them ill straight away; but they say the husband of so-and-so, or the wife of so-and-so is dead.

There is a certain wood the pith of which they would not dare to rub on the body or chin; that thing, they say, would make their beard grow, & age them before their time.

They are never ill without believing themselves bewitched, & merely for a headache, or stomach upset, if they are able to seize the woman whom they suspect, they kill her or have her killed; it is usually a woman, because they dare not attack a man so freely. But before having her killed they practise strange cruelties on this poor wretch: their kin & friends go to take her, they make her rummage in the ground in many places, maltreat her until she has found what they believe her to have concealed, & often, in order to deliver herself from these executioners, this woman confesses what is not true, picking up several pieces of shell, 'Burgaus', 'Lembies', 'Erabes',[2] or other fish bones. 'Butgos' is a species of shell very common in the Antilles, & on the mainland, & is found on the sea shore. 'Lembies' are the large shells that one sees in Paris on show in several Apothecaries' shops. They use these 'Lembies' in two ways; as trumpets by means of which one often hears them from over a league away, & even further. They have different tones by which they make known their needs, the success of their enterprises, whether in war or hunting or fishing; &, following which, their women prepare for them, often an hour or two before they arrive, either the cooking-pot, or the buccan, or whatever is needed if they are wounded; & in order to conclude the remarks on the usage of 'Lambies', a rather long digression must entangle us: you will not be displeased to hear that the fabled patience of Griselda does not approach theirs in the making of certain necklaces with which they adorn themselves during their feasts & ceremonial days. They call them *Clibat*, & the savages of Canada *Pourcelaine*. They are made of small pieces of these 'Lembies' that they wear down on some rocks until they have become round, and about two 'lignes'[3] in diameter, & half a 'ligne' thick, in a necklace of a reasonable size; because they have many rows across, there are between 3,000 and 4,000 of these pieces in each necklace, & they could not make one properly, & pierce it with the tools that they use, in less than three days: it is notable that amongst the whole lot, one does not find an inequality of thickness of a single hair [. . .] [see Plate 10].

They also make these kinds of necklaces from the seeds of black palms, which glisten like jet when they are polished: these pieces are a little bit longer, & less in diameter, & notched on the extremities [. . .].

---

[2] Possibly refers to the lamellibranch molluscs.
[3] The twelfth part of an inch.

When the women taken as sorcerers pick up the fragments of 'Burgaus', & of 'Lambies' or of 'Erabés', they say that it is the remains of what they have eaten, that the supposed sorceress had put it in the ground. After they have made incisions on her body, the agouti teeth covering her in blood, they hang her by the feet and cover her with *Piman*, a natural species of very strong pepper, which they rub in her eyes, & leave her for several days without food; finally one of these executioners comes half-drunk and smashes her head with a *bouton*, or club, & they throw her in the sea. I know this from having saved two from their hands.

As has been said, they have the *Chemeen* that they esteem as their good spirit; that is to say they consult the Devil by the intercession of their magicians or *Piaye* doctors or *Boyé* who abuse them under these names, & they carry out these damnable ceremonies on many occasions. Firstly on the issue of their maladies in order to keep healthy, in order to know where they are while lost at sea due to bad weather, on the issue and outcome of their wars, & in order to learn the name of the man or woman who has bewitched them, whom they kill as I have just said; it is often a pretext to undo their enemies. Each *Piaye* or *Boyé* has his particular *Chemeen* or rather a demon familiar, & they are governed by the baneful advice of these detestable oracles; they also give them the name of *Eocheiri*.

Therefore in order to know about the outcome of their maladies they have a *Piaye* come to them at night, who first extinguishes all the fire in the house, & makes the suspected persons leave: he retires into a corner, where he makes the sick person come, & after he has smoked a bit of *petun* [tobacco] he crushes it in his hands & blows it into the air, shaking and making his fingers click. They say that the *Chemeen* never misses coming to the odour of this incense & perfume through the medium of this *Boyé*, who without doubt makes a pact with the Devil; & being interrogated, he responds in a clear voice, as if it comes from a long way off, to all that is asked. Afterwards he approaches the sick person, feels, presses, & manipulates the afflicted part several times, always blowing on it, & extracts something, or makes a feint of taking some thorns, or little pieces of manioc, of wood, some bones or fish-bones that this Devil put in his hand, persuading the sick person that this is what caused the pain. Often he sucks this painful part, & goes out of the house hurriedly in order to vomit what he calls the venom; thus the poor invalid awaits curing more through imagination than in reality. It is notable that he does not cure fevers, nor wounds caused by arrows & *boutou*, and by knife; not a word must be said in these diabolical assemblies: not a noise must be made, not even by those at the back, otherwise the *Zemeen* would flee. I had surmised, after once surprising them, that the *Piaye* himself was counterfeiting the voice, & that often he was only stamping his feet on the ground in order to create the belief in the others that he was travelling to on high to fetch the *Zemeen*. One of these *Boyés* later confessed to me that truly he never budged out of the house, but that it was the Devil who responded. I am astonished nevertheless how the *Caraïbes* think

10. *Upper left (from top)*, lambi shell (*clibat*), bow and arrow, black palm seed necklace, fish arrow, paddle; *upper right (from top)*, *coüy*, plate; *lower left*, large *canary*; *lower right*, two small *canary*. From Sieur de la Borde, *Relation des Caraïbes sauvages des Isles Antilles de l'Amérique* (Louis Billaine: Paris, 1674), following 20. The Bodleian Library: AA. 41. Art.

11. *Upper left*, *hibichet* (flour carrier); *upper right*, baskets; *lower left*, *boutou* (club); *lower right*, *matoutou* (low table). From Sieur de la Borde, *Relation des Caraïbes sauvages des Isles Antilles de l'Amérique* (Louis Billaine: Paris, 1674), following 20. The Bodleian Library: AA. 41. Art. The first three items later appear in Labat.

that the *Piaye* goes on high, & that he only comes back after this *Zemeen* has returned; it must surely be that the Devil deludes both the invalid & the curer.

To the *Zemeen*, & to the *Piaye* for the trouble of having called him forth, they offer *Oüicou* and cassava on a *matoutou* in their houses, without any ceremony [...] [see Plate 11]. The *matoutou* is a small table of aromatic wood or reeds one or two feet square & half a foot high; they leave it all night, & even though they find it the next day just as they had left it, they persuade themselves that the *Zemeen* has taken his fill from it, but that he has eaten and drunk only in spirit: at the same time if they offer him a knife or axe, the *Piaye* takes it for himself & makes them believe that the *Zemeen* has taken it for his spirit & heart. They so revere these profane offerings, which they call *Alakri*, that it is only the old ones & the most considerable among them who dare to taste them. They have sometimes asked me to drink it; I have done so in order to disabuse them of the silly superstitions of this sacrifice, of which one is to drink of this *Oüicou* on an empty stomach, otherwise one would burst; & expressly I ate before drinking it; the other is, to take care to hold the cup, or *Coüy*, upright, & not pour it, or the neck would become crooked, & the eyes would shed tears without ceasing: I expressly let it overflow, & held the *Coüy* crookedly.

If the sick person is cured, & returns to health, they make a feast for the *Mapoia*, at which the *Piaye* lacks nothing. At the end of the banquet they blacken the convalescent with genip apples, & he is made as fine as the Devil.

They also offer to the *Zemeens* the first fruits of their gardens, & that without ceremony or saying a single word. When they have a great drinking-party, which is their debauchery, they always put to one side a *Canary*, earthenware, or some calabashes for the *Zemeen* [...] [see Plate 10].

They take trifling things as spirits; they believe that the bats that they call *Boulliri*, which flutter round their houses by night, are the *Zemeens* which guard them, & that those who kill them will become ill. They have so many sorts of *Boule-Bonum*, that could be said to be bad omens, that I cannot decide to report here all their reveries & nonsense.

In order to create a *Piaye* or *Boyé* the ancient *Boyez* educate the apprentice from his youth to this detestable ministry, making him fast five months on bread & water in a little hut, where he sees no one, his skin scratched with agouti teeth. On several occasions they make him swallow tobacco juice, which makes him vomit up his insides & roll around until he faints, when they say that his spirit goes on high to talk to the *Zemeen*; they rub his body with gum, & cover him with feathers in order to render him adroit at flying, & to go to the house of the *Zemeen*; if some matter arises, that is to say some illness, they show him how the operation is carried out, how to feel, to suck, & to blow the patient, & the manner of summoning and speaking to the *Zemeen*.

In the end, what is worthy of compassion [is] to see the profound delusion in which these wretched people are enveloped; they are not [a people] of great consequence, & they do not fear the *Zemeen*, because he is good, & and does them no wrong; but they are curiously apprehensive of the *Mapoia* who does

12. First initiation of a 'Caraïbe' divine. From Father Joseph François Lafitau, *De Zeden du Wilden van Amerika* (trans. from *Mœurs des sauvages amériquains, comparées aux mœurs des premiers temps* (1724), 2 vols. (G. van der Poel: The Hague, 1731), 169, pl. 15. The Bodleian Library: 4 Delta 223, 2 vols., i. 344.

Lafitau accompanies this illustration with an account of the initiation drawn from a report written by Father le Breton, a Jesuit missionary who spent many years on St Vincent. According to Lafitau, the Carib women hang three hammocks in a clean hut, one for the *piayé* or shaman, one for the proselyte, and the third for the *maboya*, or spirit. The *maboya* enters the hut in the middle of the night with the noise of a thunderbolt. All three have a long conversation in which the spirit talks in an artificial voice, like a puppet-master. The *maboya* then takes possession of his hammock, shaking the whole hut as he does so, and eats the food that is offered him with a great gnashing of jaws and teeth, though the food remains intact. The shaman requests that the *maboya* make another spirit descend so that the young proselyte may serve him, and a second *maboya* appears, promising to protect the young man, but also to be his enemy if he is not served faithfully. The spirits vanish in another violent thunder clap. All the villagers then crowd into the room to revive the trembling pair, warming them with fire and giving them food and drink.

them harm, & I believe that it is in order to appease him that some wear his hideous & horrible image round their neck, & paint him or carve him in relief on the front of their pirogues. They told me that it was to create fear in the *Alloüagues*, their enemies, when they went to war, that seeing this ugly grimace, the jaws gaping, they would be frightened of being devoured by him, & they would all remain so terrified that they would not be able to paddle any more, & that thus they would easily capture them. *Alloüagues* is the name of a nation situated towards the banks of the river Orinoco, perpetual enemies of the *Caraïbes* & *Galibys*.

They often have frightful & terrible dreams, where they seem to see the Devil. I have heard them sometimes at night, two at the same time, moan, cry out, & wake with a start, & tell me that the Devil had wanted to beat them. They carried on screaming when they were wide awake & made enough noise to chase him away: their melancholic humour contributes strongly to all these visions.

Sometimes they put in a calabash the hair or some bones of their deceased kin which they keep in their Carbet, which they use for sorcery, & they say that the spirit of the dead speaks from within there, & warns them of their enemies' plans.

They believe that they have several souls: the first in the heart, which they call *Youanni* or *Lanichi*; the second in the head; & the others at all the joints in the body, & where there is pulsation of the arteries: that it is only the first that goes on high after death, & takes a beautiful young body all new, that the rest remain on earth changed into beasts or into *Mapoia*, & that all these sorts of spirits are of different sex, & multiply [...]

Of their wars, voyages, & adornments

They never go to war without first having held a great drinking-party, & it is there that they hold counsel, that they resolve & conclude all the affairs of state. All their wars consist of rapid attacks on the enemy: they never make them in the open; but fox-like, hiding themselves in the woods & trying to surprise. As soon as they have killed someone or burnt a house, they withdraw promptly: if they are discovered, or if they just hear a dog bark, they take care not to press their point, & retreat without doing anything; they carry away their dead, & it is at this time that they lose most of their people. (To hold a Carbet, have a drinking-party, & hold counsel are in their view equivalent synonyms, the one never being done without the other.)

If they themselves serve as tombs for their enemies, it is rather through rage than through any relish that they find the most valiant of them, cure them over a fire, break them open, & eat them; usually they keep some in their baskets, a foot or a hand well dried and smoked. A savage from St Vincent showed me the foot of an *Alouague* which he had in his basket: they eat only *Alouagues*, also savages from the mainland towards the river of Orinoco. They say that the Christians give them stomach ache; nevertheless they ate the heart of some Englishman less than a year ago. There are some of this nation among them whom they carried off very young, & they have learnt their way of life so well that they do not wish to return at present.

There are a great number of negroes who live with them, particularly on St Vincent where their stronghold is. They have so multiplied that at present they are as powerful as them [the *Caraïbes*]. Some of them are fugitive maroons who were taken in war; these are slaves of the *Caraïbes*, whom they call *Tamons*; but the greater part came from some Flemish or Spanish ship which was wrecked close to their islands.

They have as weapons the bow & arrows, the *Boutou*, & at present the knife. The *Boutou* is a sort of club of greenwood, or hard Brazil-wood, massive, heavy, two or three feet long, three fingers wide, & towards the end flat like the hand, an inch thick, & carved according to their custom. [. . .] [See Plate 11].

They fill in this carving with a white paint, & with a single blow they kill a man. They make a great store of arrows, which they prepare long beforehand: they consist of a tube which grows at the top of certain reeds as thick as the little finger, four or five feet long, polished & without any knot, yellow & light as a feather. In the fat end of this tube they fit in place of iron a piece of greenwood half a foot long, & on it make with a knife a number of little darts or harpoons, so that they cannot be pulled out. They poison the end of these arrows with the liquid of a tree called 'Manceniller', & the fruit 'Mançanille', the name which the Spaniards have given to it because this fruit resembles apples. So that at the beginning of the discovery of the Indies a lot of Europeans poisoned themselves through having eaten indiscreetly. They make an incision in the rind [and] the juice which comes out as white as milk is a poison more dangerous than that of serpents. They also put in some of their arrows certain fish-bones as long as a finger, that they find in the tail of a sort of ray which is quite common here. This fish-bone carries its own venom, & is as dangerous as the others. Their bows are also of Brazil, & of palm. They do not undertake any voyage without being adorned in their best *Caconnes* [beads, etc.], they paint themselves, deck themselves out, rub themselves with roucou. As soon as they arrive at some Carbet, the master promptly hangs some hammocks for the chiefs, the women bring something to drink, & to eat; & as soon as it has been presented to their men, & been placed in front of the captain of the pirogue, the crew, without waiting any longer to be told to take it, carry off everything, so swiftly that if the host has no more to offer to them, & if pressed by hunger, he is constrained to put aside his dignity & to come to eat with the others. Afterwards he goes back to his position, & the crew bring back the *Coüis* to him, & [place] the *Matoutou* in front of him. He lets it be known that he is full, & calls those who were presented to him to gather everything up & take it all away. Their hosts never eat anything with them during this ceremony, still less their women; but afterwards they eat pell-mell: when they are full they say the *Maboüy*, that is to say, give their regards, paying a *Huichan* likewise, one after the other, which means adieu. While they are at sea, they blow a large shell, which is named *Dambis*, in order to inform their neighbours that they are friends, & are voyaging; & they carry their beds everywhere.

If a lone *Caraïbe* arrives in a Carbet, he will be received in the same way, & if the cassava which is presented to him on the *Matoutou* is folded it is a sign that he ought to leave the rest; if it is spread out, he may carry it away; but before leaving, a woman will come to cover him with roucou, to comb his hair, & to dress him.

When they are at sea, & making some crossing to go to another island, such as St Lucia, St Vincent, or the mainland, they eat neither crabs, nor lizards; because these are animals who always lurk in their lairs & in crevices; thus these would prevent them, they say, from reaching another land. They drink no pure water, & take great care not to spill any in the canoe or in the sea: this would cause it to swell, & would bring rain & bad weather. They drink a 'patrouillis'[4] & some *Maby* that they boil, & liquefy with the hand rotating like a pestle. After they have pressed it they place what remains in a *Coüy* and eat it separately, as a delicacy. When they approach land, they must not name it or point to it, except through a pouting mouth; & saying, *Lyca*, it is there: for otherwise they might not be able to land there. There are certain spots at sea where, as they pass by, they never fail to throw something overboard to eat. It is, so they say, for *Caraïbes* who perished there in former times, & who have their huts at the bottom of the sea; otherwise they would not be able to go any further, or the canoe would overturn. When they see some cloud about to burst, they all blow in the air, & drive it away with their hand in order to divert the rain to another direction; in order to calm the sea, & appease a tempest, they chew some cassava & spit it into the sky & sea in order to appease the *Zemeen*, who is annoyed, perhaps, because he is hungry. If they do not have a good wind an elder of the group takes an arrow & hits the stern of the pirogue, after which it goes like a bolt from a crossbow; if some gust of wind makes them lose land, & some tempest takes them by surprise, they bring forth the *Zemeen*, that is to say they consult the Devil; when they lack fire, they make it with two small pieces of dry wood, resting the end of one on the other, & turning it quickly between their hands.

In truth the *Caraïbes* have quite well-made & proportioned bodies, of middling height, broad of shoulders & hips, nearly all in good condition, & robust. One encounters among them very few disabilities & deformities: most people [have] round & full faces, quite generous mouths, the teeth perfectly white and compact, the complexion naturally tanned or olive. This colouring even extends to the eyes, which are black, small, & lively; but they have the nose & forehead flattened artificially, for their mother squeezes them at their birth, & continually during all the time that she suckles them, imagining that there is in this something of beauty. They have large and spaced out feet, very tough, because they walk barefoot; the hair extremely black & long, which they often comb &

---

[4] Some muddy water, i.e. a drink taken while patrolling (with thanks to Mrs Elfrida Dubois for this identification).

oil; they cut it across the front in the form of a rope end, leaving two small pieces on each side of the temple; all the rest is pulled back behind & very nicely dressed with long lanyards of cotton, at the end of which are small bunches of glass thimbles or other trinkets. They wrap this bundle of hair with well-finished cotton, & fix parrot feathers in it, & on top a large red one from the tail of a duck. They do not have a beard, they pull it out bristle by bristle, as I have said, with the point of a knife, & before they had our razors to use they would employ a keen-edged & sharp-cutting grass.

They change their natural colouring with a red hue soaked in oil that they apply to their bodies, & they call this to 'roucou' oneself; the old ones just apply it with the four fingers & the thumb, from the head to the feet; the young ones seek a little more workmanship, they daub their faces & give themselves moustaches in the Spanish style, put some slashes & some motley on the cheeks, & from forehead to ears; they also rub themselves with roucou around the mouth & the end of the nose; you would say that this looks like a hog's flayed snout. They darken one eye with black & the other with red, & with this they esteem themselves more handsome & valiant; in place of roucou, others blacken themselves all over with genip, in such a way that they look like Devils.

They all have the ears & the bit between the nostrils pierced, as well as that part on the underside of the lip below to the right where, on other occasions, a small tuft of beard is left; this is done when they are still at the breast: fifteen days after her confinement the mother invites a skilled woman to perform this ceremony for her infant. As soon as she has pierced it with a palm thorn, she passes through a small thread of cotton; if it is a girl she names her; if it is a boy, it is a man who gives him the name of a tree or of an island, or of a fish, or of a bird, or of some occasion: I have seen one named an étui, because he was so small when he came into the world. They never take their father's name; each one has his own particular name.

They hang small *caracolis* from their ears, & a long filament of cotton from their lip down to their waist; they pass through the bit between the nostrils a small finger-ring of silver or of pewter, they wear *caracolis* as big as a hand on their neck, set in wood, & a large bundle of 'rassade', which are little beads of glass, black, white, of all colours. These *caracolis* are little pieces of metal in the form of a crescent, thin as paper, shining like well-polished brass, or rather like gold, which never rusts nor fades. They get them from the Spaniards, & sometimes give a negro in order to have one; they value them more than any of their ornaments. They wear in the form of baldric a great set of teeth of all sorts of animals, & of tiger claws. They put their bracelets above the elbow, & the garters at the ankle. They also wear behind the back the complete wings of a bird dried & cured, or even a dozen of their feet, put close together & attached by a small piece of tiger skin. There are some old ones who have round their neck some small bones of *Allouagues*, their enemies whom they eat, from which they make fifes. The first time that I saw some *Caraibes* loaded with all this baggage, I thought of our performing mules in a pageant.

The hair-style of the women is similar to that of the men: when they do not put feathers in it, they do rub their hair with oil, & also fasten a bundle of cotton to it, at the end of which they put several shells, & a quantity of thimbles, in the same way that at their waists they fashion some 'rassade', or hang about fifty hawk-bells which make a great noise while they are walking and dancing; they also wear necklaces, but of large beads of crystal & green stones which come from the mainland, towards the river of Amazons, & which have the virtue of curing epilepsy: it is their most precious jewel, & they only put it on at festival gatherings & on visits. They have a certain half-hose or webbed boot of cotton thread, that they redden, which runs from the ankle to the calf, & another four fingers wide between the calf and the knee: this thing presses on them with such force that it will not expand, & it renders the calf plump & round like a ball at the end of this footwear, on which the leg sits beautifully shaped, & which they never remove; & a kind of stiffened band of the same fabric, large as a saddle-seat, which makes them splay the legs a little while walking; this workmanship is woven on the leg itself & without very exact needlework.

They also 'roucou' and blacken the body, & make above their forehead a manner of head-band which comes to a point on the nose; in such a way that it seems that they have crapes like widows, & around the eyes some small black lines which set off & enhance their brightness, & make them appear much more sparkling. I am reminded of those ladies in France with beauty-spots: they also pay great attention to the making of their eyebrows. They also take pleasure in adorning their children with this colour, making a thousand small, very slender figures on their bodies, with little paint-brushes made of their hair, which are rather crude. They devote a whole day to making this garb which only lasts nine days. [. . .]

Remarks on their languages

Although there is some difference between the language of the men & that of the women, as I have said in the chapter on their origin, nevertheless they understand one another. The old men have a jargon when they are dealing with some plan of war, which the young do not understand at all. Their language is very destitute: they can only express what is obvious. They are so materialist that they do not have a term to designate the workings of the spirit, & if the beasts were able to speak I would want to give them no other language than that of the *Caraïbes*. They have not one word to explain matters of religion, of justice, & of what pertains to the virtues, the sciences, & a great number of other things about which they have no notion. They are not able to converse, as I have said elsewhere: they name only three or four colours. By means of these few remarks made on their languages, one may judge what they are.

The Reverend Father Simon of the Company of JESUS, who has laboured much, & who yet labours every day with great zeal & fatigue for their conversion, has made in it [their language] an entire dictionary of precepts in the form of a grammar, a very full catechism, & many simple discourses on the divine mysteries of our faith; this work will be useful to those who might plan to acquire some awards in the conversion of these infidel peoples, as I have said formerly.

I could make this narration still longer: but these are, it seems to me, the most necessary remarks to make known the *Caraïbes*: there is no more than a small remnant of this nation, & apart from the fact that they are destroying themselves every day, the English labour to exterminate them utterly. I believe that God allows this, without fathoming his judgements, & that the whole of Europe should invade their lands; because they are too great an insult to the Creator through their bestial way of life, & because they have no wish to recognize Him at all. Although it has been possible to speak to them for the last twenty years, they ridicule Him; & if there were reason to hope that they could be made Christians, it would first be necessary to civilize them & make them into men. Divine Providence will provide for this when it pleases: it has His purposes in all things.

13. *Jean Baptiste Labat*
A Sojourn on Dominica (1722)

¶ *Jean Baptiste Labat (1663–1738) arrived in the French Antilles in 1694 and returned to France in 1705. In the intervening years he carried out various duties as a Jesuit priest in both Guadeloupe and Martinique, becoming Superior of the Guadeloupe mission in 1702, and Procurator of Martinique, for the second time, in 1703. In 1704 he was made Superior of the Martinique mission, as well as Chief Administrator.*

The first, six-volume, edition of Labat's Nouveau Voyage aux isles de l'Amérique *was published in Paris in 1722 and was quickly followed by a two-volume edition in 1724 published at The Hague, a further eight-volume edition being issued in Paris in 1742. Its lively tone and vivid descriptions have ensured that a number of abridgements and translations have already appeared, earning Labat such nicknames as 'The Smiling Monk' or 'The Pirate's Priest' (Labat 1931, Young and Helweg-Larsen 1965). In similar vein the accessibility of Labat has meant that many of his accounts of incidents with the natives of Dominica have been recycled frequently in the ethnographic literature, acquiring thereby the patina of authority that his brief soujourn there, of seventeen days, hardly justifies.*

Nevertheless, he is admirably forthright in acknowledging his lack of first-hand experience of Dominica as compared to his forerunners, such as Breton, and anyway made constructive use of local and native informants; a key technique for modern ethnographers as well. His personal encounter with the mother of 'Indian' Warner, although included not here but in the section on Warner himself (No. 8), also adds force to this consideration, as well as neatly illustrating the intimacy and intricacy of relationships across what can appear to be a fragmented region.

The Author goes to cul-de-sac François. Description of the Carbet of the Caraïbes

I left Macouba on 12 December [1694] after I had said mass. I charged my neighbour Father Breton with the care of my parish, I dined in passing at La Grand Ance, & I arrived in good time in the town of La Trinité at the house of

Monsieur de Mareuil, in order to go with him to sleep at the house of Monsieur Joyeux at the river Gallions.

We left there the following morning. As Monsieur Joyeux did not reside in the area we were going to, & as he had only an overseer and some negroes at his house, which we would not have accommodated from our usual provisions, he had been careful to put some stop-gap provisions, of which we might have need, in his canoe, so as not to be obliged to go to the house of any of his neighbours before the business was finished. A wise precaution, of which we saw the utility when we were three-quarters of the way to cul-de-sac Robert, since we were surprised by such a violent gust of wind from the west that if we had not reached the point at La Rose in order to get under cover, I do not know what would have become of our canoe & those who were in it.

This point at La Rose is a headland which forms the eastern coast of cul-de-sac Robert. A *Caraïbe* who lives there has taken the name, or he has given his to it; I am not sure which of the two. But what I know very well is that this point was a great help to us; here we beached our canoe, & while the negroes unloaded it in order to drag it higher up, we went into the Carbet of Monsieur La Rose. After the recent fright, I was not too vexed by this adventure, which gave me the means of seeing the *Caraïbes* in their houses; after having seen them in their pirogues.

The *Caraïbe* La Rose is Christian, as is his wife, & ten or twelve children that he has had by her, & some others which he had before being baptized. They received us very civilly: he was wearing cloth pants over a brand new covering of scarlet from head to toe, that is to say that he had just been rubbed with roucou, it being scarcely after nine o'clock when we entered his house. His wife was wearing a lap around her loins which reached half-way down the legs. We saw two of his daughters, 15 or 16 years old, who wore nothing other than the ancient costume of the nation when we appeared, that is to say, the loin cloth, leggings, & bracelets; but a moment later, they showed themselves with laps. The lap is a piece of cloth with which the women wrap the body below the armpits, ordinarily twice round, & whereof the ends that cross each other are coiled inside in order to hold it firm, & which extends normally to the middle of the legs. There are some shorter laps, but rarely longer ones. This type of dress is most commodious, being put on and taken off easily; the men and the women use it in the same way along the whole coast of Guinea. La Rose had four big boys well covered in roucou, with the strip of cloth in a small cord. The rest of the children were small, & dressed as they had come into the world, with the exception of their belt of glass beads. We found a large company in this Carbet; there were nearly thirty *Caraïbes* who had returned there, for the occasion about which I will speak presently.

The houses of the *Caraïbes* are called Carbets; I know nothing of the etymology of this name,[1] I have never heard it said that there was any other in

---

[1] 'Tinobone' and 'raboui' were the terms respectively used by male and female *Caraïbes*; the French derivation is probably from nautical usage since 'carbet' is a ship's large cabin.

Caraïbe
ou Sauvage des Antisles de l'Amérique.

Fleche

Arc

Caracoli

Femme Caraïbe des Antisles de l'Amerique.
A *Bracelets*. B *Colier de Rasade* C *Camisa*
D. *Espece de Brodequins*.

A

B

C

D

13. *Caraïbe* and *Femme caraïbe*. From Jean Baptiste Labat, *Nouveau Voyage aux isles de l'Amérique*, 6 vols. (P. Husson *et al.*: The Hague, 1722), i, following 3. The Bodleian Library: Meerm. 447.

the whole of Martinique than that of La Rose. This Carbet was around sixty feet long, by twenty-four to twenty-five feet wide; it was made a little bit like a market-hall. The small posts rose nine feet off the ground, & the large ones in proportion. The rafters touched the ground on both sides, the lathes were of reeds, and the roofing, which was of palm leaves, also came down below the rafters. One of the ends of the Carbet was completely closed off with reeds, & covered with palm leaves, reserving one opening for going into the kitchen. The other end was almost all open. At ten paces from this building there was another of about half the size of the first, which was partitioned in two by a palisade of reeds. We entered here, the first room serving as a kitchen; seven or eight women or girls were busy making cassava. The second room apparently housed all those ladies with infants who were not yet admitted to the great Carbet; there was no furniture other than baskets and hammocks just as in the great Carbet. La Rose had close by a coffer, a musket, a pistol, a sword, & a cartridge belt. His four large boys were also armed, & had done their duty perfectly well when the English had attacked the island. A number of *Caraïbes* were working on some baskets: it is there that I observed for the first time the manner of making them. I also saw two women who were making a hammock on a frame, as I have described [elsewhere]. The bows, the arrows, & the clubs were in great profusion, neatly attached to the rafters. The floor was beaten earth, very clean & very even, except under the wall-plate where there was a small declivity. There was a rather good fire a third of the way down the Carbet, around which eight or nine *Caraïbes* squatted like when one does the necessary; they were smoking while waiting for some fish which is called 'coffre' [coffer-fish][2] to be cooked. These gentlemen made their customary civilities to us without changing posture, saying to us: 'Good day comrade, want some grog.' They knew Monsieur Joyeux, & liked him, because when they went to his sugar-mill he gave them some syrup to make their *ouycou*, & never missed giving them something to drink, which is an infallible means for gaining their friendship.

The fish of which I have just spoken were set across the fire between the wood and the embers in higgledy-piggledy fashion. I took them at first for some bits of log, not being able to persuade myself that one would cook in so strange a fashion. I said this to the comrade of La Rose, who answered that it was their practice; & that when I had tasted these fish, he was sure that I would find them good, & that I would admit that the *Caraïbes* were not such bad cooks as I supposed. Permit me here not to repeat precisely his words; I believe that the sense suffices, & is just as I have said.

Meanwhile the dinner hour approached, & the sea air had given us an appetite. So I told Monsieur Joyeux's negroes to bring over a table-cloth, & seeing a nice mat laid out in a corner of the Carbet I thought that it was the spot where these gentlemen were coming to take their meal, & that in the meantime until they had need of it, we would be able to make good use of it. I

[2] 'Toucoucouyou' being the *Caraïbe* term, family *Ostraciontidae*.

threw down the table-cloth with some serviettes; bread, salt, and a plate of cold meat were brought. Monsieur de Mareuil & Monsieur Joyeux pressed me to take my place, that is to say to sit down on the mat. After the usual niceties I sat down, these gentlemen doing likewise; & we had already started to eat when we noticed that these *Caraïbes* were looking across at us, & were speaking to La Rose with some degree of discomposure. We asked him the reason, & he told us that there was a dead *Caraïbe* under the mat where we were sitting, & that this had very much angered his relations. We got up at once, & took away all our things. The fellow La Rose had another mat brought which was spread in another place, we sat down here, & continued our meal at our ease, giving drink to Monsieur La Rose & the whole company, so as to make amends for the offence we had given them in sitting on their dead. In this manner we became friends again just as before.

In the conversation we had with La Rose while we were eating, we learnt that all these *Caraïbes* were assembled at his house to hold the funeral of a *Caraïbe* who was under the mat where we had sat down earlier, & that they were only waiting for some of his relatives from the island of St Vincent finally to inter him. Because it is necessary that all his relations see that he is dead from natural causes in order to believe it; so that if a single one is found who has not seen him, all the others together would not be sufficient to persuade this one; on the contrary he would believe that they had all contributed to his death, & he would believe himself obliged by honour to kill someone to avenge the death. This custom & this point of honour appeared to us most tiresome & very arrogant. I believe that our host would have sincerely wished that this *Caraïbe* had not done him the honour of choosing his Carbet to die in, because this large company diminished his manioc greatly, of which he had perhaps no more than just enough for his family.

After we had dined, I asked whether like a friend of the deceased we would not be able to see him. La Rose told me yes, & that it would be a pleasure for the whole company, especially if we drank & made toasts to his health; forthwith he lifted the mat & the planks which covered the grave. It was fashioned like a well, about four feet in diameter, & six to seven feet deep. The corpse was here nearly in the same posture that I have described for those who were around the fire. His elbows rested on his knees, & the palms of his hands supported his cheeks; he was appropriately painted with roucou with moustaches and black streaks, in a different dye from the ordinary one, which is only genip. His hair was tied behind his head; his bow, his arrows, his club, & his knife were beside him. He had sand only up to his knees, in so far as was apparent, which was necessary to sustain him in that posture, since he did not touch the edges of the grave at all. I asked if it was possible to touch him, & was allowed such liberty in full. I touched him on the hands, the face, & the back, all of which were very dry, & gave off no bad smell, although they assured me that they had taken no other precaution than that of covering him with roucou the moment that he expired, after which he had been put in the grave as we saw him. The first of his relations who had come had removed the sand in order to inspect the corpse; & as he gave off no bad smell, they had put none of it back again so as not to have the trouble of taking it away for each new relation who arrived. We were told that when everyone had seen him, the grave would be filled completely & permanently. We did not fail to drink to & to make the company drink to the health of the deceased, after which they replaced the planks which closed the grave, & the mat above. It was close to five months since he had died. I wished very much that some relation had arrived while we were there, so that we might have witnessed their ceremonies, but none of them came.

Meanwhile the fishes which were on the fire being cooked, & these gentlemen being hungry, the women brought two or three *matatous* full of fresh & still hot cassava, with two large *coüis*, of which one was full of *taumali* [stew] of crabs, & the other of pepper sauce. This was accompanied by a large basket of boiled crabs, some coffer-fish which were on the fire, & some large scaled fish cooked in the same fashion.

Although I had dined well enough, I did not forbear to approach the *matatou* so as to taste their fish & their sauce. What is accommodating about these people is that their table is open to all: one has no need of being invited nor of being known in order to sit down; they never invite anyone, but also they do not prevent anyone from eating with them. Monsieur de la Rose & his four boys made the sign of the cross & said the Benediction, the others dispensed with it because they were not Christians, although they may have already been baptized, & moreover would be ready to be so as many times as they were given a glass of brandy.

I will explain what the *taumali* is when I talk about crabs. As for their pepper sauce, it is gravy of boiled manioc with lemon juice, in which they crush such a great quantity of pepper, that it is impossible for anyone other than themselves to make use of it. I have said before that this was their favourite & universal sauce. It is necessary to make a further remark, which is that they never use salt; this is not because they lack it; there are some natural salt-pans in all the islands where they would be able to supply themselves, but it is not to their taste, any more than boiled meat or fish. I have been informed by them that, apart from the crabs which form the better part of their diet, they eat nothing that is cooked in water: everything is roasted or smoked. Their manner of roasting is to pierce through morsels of the meat, or whole birds when they are small, with a skewer of wood, & to plant it in the ground in front of the fire, & when they judge the meat cooked on one side, they make a half turn so that the other side cooks; but when it is a slightly large bird like a parrot, a wood-pigeon or a chicken, they do not take the trouble to pluck them nor to gut them. They throw them into the fire fully clothed and shod, & when the plumage is roasted, they toss them on top of the cinders & embers & they leave them in that state the time that they judge necessary for their cooking, after which they take them off; they easily lift the crust that the feathers & the skin have made on the flesh, they remove the gut & the crop, & in this way eat the bird. I have eaten them several times in this manner; I have prepared them myself as I am about to tell, & I have always found that the flesh completely crammed with its juice was of an admirable tenderness & delicacy. Those who do not believe me are easily capable of making the experiment, & convincing themselves of the truth or falsity of what I report.

I tasted some fish with large scales, which strip off as if taking them from a sheath. The flesh was very good, well cooked & so juicy that you would say that it had been filled with butter. It is true that this fish is ordinarily oily enough; but it must be acknowledged that when it is cooked, without water, the butter or oil changing the excellence of its juice, by mixing itself in, it can only be described as much better.

The coffer is a fish so called because it is covered with a fairly thin, dry & very tough scale. From the tail as far as the head, which is joined to the body without any obvious division, it is triangular, & its head has the same shape. When one of those which had been served on the *matatou* was opened by a corner, you would have said that it was a hot pasty that had just been opened; the smell was good, the flesh white & well cooked, & although this fish does not pass for one of the better ones, perhaps because there is more scale than flesh, I found it very good & very succulent.

It was a real pleasure to see this large band of *Caraïbes* squatting on their backsides like monkeys, eating with the appetite of invalids, without saying a single word, & peeling the smallest crabs' claws with admirable skill & speed. They got up with as little ceremony as they had used in sitting down; those who were thirsty went to drink some water, some admired themselves while smoking, a portion went to bed, & the rest began a conversation in which I understood nothing, because it was in the *Caraïbe* language.

The women came to take away the *matatous* and the *coüis*, the girls cleaned the place where we had eaten, & together with the little children withdrew to the kitchen where we went to see them eating in the same posture & with as good an appetite as the men had just shown. I was a bit surprised that the women would not eat with their husbands, or, if it is a rule among the nation, why Madame La Rose as a Christian & mistress of the house had not been excepted from it. I told my thoughts about it to her husband, who replied to me that custom did not allow it; that the women must never eat with their husbands; & that even if he had been alone, he would have eaten just with his grown-up boys, & that his wife, his daughters, & the rest of his children would have eaten in the kitchen. This custom, which appears utterly extraordinary at first sight, is not overly savage; after some reflexion it appeared to me full of good sense, & most proper in order to contain this proud sex within the bounds of duty & respect that is owed to men. The *Caraïbes* are not the only ones who use them in this way; I will report in another place some examples where the Europeans must make adjustments in order to keep well clear of vexations.

We stayed at the La Rose Carbet until almost three in the afternoon. The wind completely calmed down, it was only the sea that stayed very swollen; but the eldest son of La Rose offered to come with us, & three other *Caraïbes*, attracted by the hope of some brandy, made the same approach to us, & we took them at their word. Although we already had seven negroes in the canoe, we judged that this help would not be without utility; that the young La Rose would pilot better than Monsieur Joyeux's negro, & that the number of our paddlers being increased by four would make us go more quickly & more safely.

Diverse customs of the Savages

The time that I spent in the Carbet of Madame Ouvernard [Warner] & of several other *Caraïbes* has given me the opportunity to see close up & to examine at leisure their mores & their ways of behaving. I am going to inform those who will read these memoirs about them, without imposing order, but just as I find them written down in my journal.

They all get up very early in the morning, that is to say, a little before sunrise, & leave the Carbet forthwith for their necessities: they never do it near their houses, but in some place a little way away, where they make a hole that they cover over afterwards with earth. They go immediately to bathe in the sea, when there is no river for their convenience, since when they find one, they do not go at all to the sea. When they return, they sit down in the middle of the Carbet on a small stool made of a single piece of wood, fashioned a little like a chocolate bicorn hat. They wait there until the air & the wind dry them; after which one of their wives, or someone else, comes with a small pot full of roucou diluted in carap oil or *Palma Christi* [copaiba], so as to cover them in roucou. She begins by combing, or at least by disentangling their hair, & after it has been rubbed a little with carap oil, she ties it with a cotton cord, & makes it into a bunch above the head; then, taking the pot with the paint in the left hand, & a paint-brush, like a small bale of feathers, in the right, she daubs him all over his body beginning with his face. When all the upper part of his body is painted, the *Caraïbe* gets up so that his thighs & shanks can be painted; & when that is done, he sits down again on his stool, & himself daubs the parts which modesty has not permitted his wife to touch.

According to his fancy he fastens his hair behind his head, or leaves it to hang, & according to the weather & the occasion, he will make himself some moustaches or other black marks on the face & on the body, with genip juice.

When they find lice while painting or rubbing themselves, they crack them between their teeth to give them tit for tat, & to avenge themselves for their bites. It is not only the *Caraïbes* & negroes who have a claim to lice in these islands: these animals live on everyone else, as soon as the tropic has been passed. I have often heard that point argued against; but since I have heard nothing that has satisfied me, I will not report it.

Whilst one party of women is occupied in covering the men with roucou, the other lot make cassava for the meal, since they eat it hot. If they have been fishing during the night, or catching crabs, or there is something from the previous day, they hurry to cook whatever there is, & bring it as soon as the master of the Carbet orders. They all eat as soon as they are 'roucoued', without saying anything to one another, without making any gesture of civility or religion: neither the young boys nor the very old are set apart. After they have eaten, the women bring something to drink; & then some get back into their hammocks, others place themselves around the fire squatting on their heels, like monkeys, their cheeks resting on the palms of their hands, & stay for hours at a time in that position & in silence, as if they were in a profound meditation; or instead they whistle with their mouths, or with a kind of flute or reed-pipe, & always in the same pitch: nothing in my opinion is more disagreeable & more boring than this music. Others are found who put themselves to work on some baskets, or making arrows, & bows, clubs, or something else of that kind, each one according to his particular bent, & with no one taking the liberty of ordering anyone else to do anything. It is in this way that they work, always for present needs, always in a negligent & indifferent manner, without attaching themselves in the least to what they are doing, & giving it up directly they begin to become tired of it.

Their conversation, when they have it, is extremely modest and most calm: there is but one who speaks: all the others listen to him with great attention, at any rate in appearance, without interrupting him or contradicting him, responding to him only through a sort of humming that is made without opening the mouth, which is the mark of approbation that they give to the speech being made to them. When that person has concluded, if anyone else takes over, whether he speaks in conformity with what the first one has said, or whether he says just the opposite, he is assured of being greeted with the same hum of approbation. I fully believe that they only behave like this in unimportant matters, & that they act differently when it concerns them more closely, for they understand their interests perfectly well, & gain their ends by ways that are not at all savage. I have never seen them argue, nor quarrel amongst themselves: I admired this reserve. But what is really remarkable is that without speech & without rows they very often kill & massacre each other. It is principally in the assemblies that they call Vins[3] that this happens.

These assemblies have no set time for being held: this depends on the caprice of the man who wants to bear the expense. No one is obliged to attend, even if invited, except those who have the inclination to drink & to get drunk, or to behave badly. They are sometimes held to resolve on a distant voyage, that is to say, for trade, or for visiting, or for war. The organizer takes care some days earlier to inform all his neighbours, sometimes the whole nation, to turn up. Whoever wants to, comes: everyone is welcome there, & leaves when he pleased. Nevertheless, the host provides a quantity of *oüicou*, sweet potatoes, yams, bananas, figs, & cassava. He & the people of his Carbet, & even his neighbours, if they judge it opportune, go fishing & hunting, & smoke every-

---

[3] In fact obviously a French word, that replaced the *Caraïbe* equivalent 'ouycou'; specific festivals would have different names, though 'coulouca' is perhaps the most general term.

thing they catch. It is rare for them to eat anything that is boiled, except crabs. They eat little meat, although they can eat as much as they want, since they raise enough poultry & pigs: nor do they lack wild pigs, or agoutis, & other animals, & they have an abundance of wood-pigeons, parrots, thrushes, & other birds that they kill with their arrows as skilfully as we do with our muskets, & without so much noise. But they keep their poultry, their pigs, & their other animals, that they catch during the hunt, in order to take them to the French Islands, & barter them for things they need; so that one can say that crabs & fish are their most usual sustenance, except at the time of their festivals, when they spare nothing to entertain those they have invited.

As I was not present at any of these sort of assemblies, I can only speak of them on the report of others. Those from whom I have learnt more about the circumstances are firstly a *Caraïbe* who had retreated to Martinique, after having killed someone on Dominica; & this Frenchman who had fled to Dominica for a similar reason, who served me as an interpreter all the time I stayed in Dominica.

After all the company is assembled, & has eaten well & drunk *oüicou* to excess, & tafia, when they are able to have it, the master of the Carbet makes the proposal for which he has invited them. Whatever it may be, it never fails to be well received & approved in the usual manner. If it is a war-party that is proposed, some old woman never fails to exhibit herself & to harangue the guests in order to excite them to vengeance. She gives them a long detailed account of wrongs and injuries that they have received from their enemies, she joins to this the enumeration of their relations & friends who have been killed; & when she sees that all the company, already extremely overheated by the drink, is beginning to give signs of fury, & that they live only for the blood & death of their enemies, she throws into the middle of the assembly some cured limbs of those whom they have killed in war, on which they swoop immediately like furies, scratching them, cutting them in pieces, biting them & munching them with all the rage of which cowardly, vindictive & drunken people are capable. They approve the project with great shrieks, & all promise to return on the appointed day, in order to leave together, & to go to exterminate all their enemies.

The other projects are resolved in a more tranquil manner; but when it comes to their execution, this depends absolutely on caprice, or on the mood they happen to be in when the moment comes to put the matter in hand; for they are entirely free & independent, & no one has the right to command the others: their fastidiousness on this point is inconceivable.

It is an error to believe that the Savages of our islands are anthropophagi, & that they go to war expressly to make prisoners in order to gorge themselves with them, or that having taken them, without this intention, they make use of the opportunity when they have got them in their hands for devouring them. I have proof to the contrary more clear than daylight.

It is true that I have heard it said by several of our freebooters that towards the Isthmus of Darien, Bocca del Toro, the Isle d'or, & some other places on the coast, there are wandering nations that the Spanish call 'wild Indians', who have never wanted to have dealings with anyone, [and] who eat without mercy all those who fall into their hands. This [is] perhaps true & perhaps also false; for if they have no dealings at all with anyone, how is it possible to know? And even though this may be true, what would it prove in relation to our *Caraïbes* of the islands, so far removed from these people, both through the distance between their dwelling places, & through their manner of life. Why should they be alike on this point rather than on the others?

I know that the Marquis de Maintenon d'Angennes, who commanded the King's frigate *The Sorcerer* in 16.., lost his shallop with eighteen or twenty men who were in it, who were carried off by these Indians when they tried to take some water from a river; one may conjecture that in carrying them off as they did, the dead men & the living, it was in order to be satiated with their flesh, like certain negroes of the African coast who there keep open butchery at least according to what some historians say.

I also know, & it is very true, that when the French & English were starting to establish themselves in the islands there were many people of both nations who were killed, cured, & eaten by the *Caraïbes*; but it was a completely extraordinary action amongst these peoples: it was rage that made them commit this excess, because they were only able to avenge themselves fully of the injustice that the Europeans had done them in chasing them from their lands, by putting them to death, when they seized them, with cruelties which were not ordinary or natural to them; for if that existed in those times, it would also be done today; & yet they are not seen practising it, neither on the English with whom they are nearly always at war, nor even with their greatest enemies the *Allöuagues*, who are Indians from the mainland beside the Orinoco river, with whom they are continually at war.

It is true that when they kill someone, they cure his limbs, & fill up calabashes with his fat, which they carry away to their homes; but this is as a trophy & a mark of their victory & of their valour, a little like the savages of Canada carrying off the scalps of their enemies when they have killed them, & of their prisoners, after they have killed them with extraordinary cruelty. Our savages are more humane: when they take women, of whatever colour or nation they may be, very far from doing them wrong, it is certain that they treat them with gentleness, & that if they [the women] wish, they marry them & regard them as if they were of their nation. When these [prisoners] are children, they bring them up amongst themselves without dreaming of killing them, & the worst that may happen to them is to be sold to the Europeans. As regards the grown men who are found & taken carrying weapons, it is certain that they kill them in the heat of combat, without hampering themselves by making them prisoners, as do the Iroquois, in order afterwards, at leisure, to sacrifice them to their rage & to their cruelty. I repeat it therefore one more time: if they cure some limbs of those whom they have killed, it is only in order to conserve for a longer time the memory of their combats & of their victories, & to stimulate themselves to vengeance, & to the destruction of their enemies, & never to gorge themselves with them.

It is rare that any of these festivals go by without some murder being committed: this is done without a lot of ceremony. It suffices that one of the guests, overheated by the drink, recollects that one of the bystanders has killed one of his relations, or that he has given some cause for vexation, in order to induce him to vengeance; no more is necessary. He gets up without ceremony, he approaches his enemy from behind, splits his head with a blow from a club, or stabs him with a knife, without any one of those present endeavouring to prevent him, or to detain him after he has struck the blow.

If by chance the one who has just been assassinated has children, brothers, or nephews in the assembly, they sometimes throw themselves on the assassin, & kill him; but it is rare that this happens, since the one who makes a sudden attack in this manner carefully observes that there is no one in a position to give tit for tat. He waits until they are drunk, asleep, or absent. If those who have an interest in the deceased are present, & they fear that the assassin may have support, & that there may be too great a risk for them to take vengeance in the open, they hide their resentment, & put off to another occasion giving the murderer the same treatment, unless he changes country. It is fortunate, though, if he gets out of it like that, since neither forgiveness, nor compromise, is known among them; & often when they are unable to avenge themselves on the individual, they do it on someone who belongs to him. That is what makes their quarrels & their divisions everlasting, & means that their country is not populated the tenth part of what it ought to be, seeing the quantity of women that they have, & the particular characteristic they have of multiplying themselves a great deal.

Such is the usual end of their assemblies or feasts, from which they retire only when there is nothing more to eat or drink at the house of the person who has invited them. After this each returns home. When the feast is made for a voyage of war, those who have agreed to it, & who have appeared the most ardent for the enterprise, do not remember it any more, & do not think at all to present themselves on the day chosen for setting out, unless the whim of the moment may make them; for they may do it, or they may not do it, there is no one who would be able to find fault. They are all equal; & although someone is captain, that person is not more respected, nor better obeyed.

There are none but the women who are bound to obedience, & of whom the men are the absolute masters. They take this superiority to excess, & kill them for very trifling matters. A suspicion of infidelity, well or badly founded, suffices with no other formality for them to have the right to crack their heads. This is a little savage in truth; but it is a most proper restraint for holding the women to their duty. It is usually the old women who are the cause of all the disorders that happen in the households: however small a grievance they have against a young woman, they quickly find the means to disparage her in the mind of her husband, & give birth to an infinity of suspicions in him; & when they have nothing more positive to say against the young ones, they accuse them of being sorceresses, & of having killed someone: no more is necessary, all other scrutiny is superfluous, the accused is deemed convicted, her head is split, & no more is said about it.

The old women are called *Bibi*, that is to say, grandmother, or pre-eminent mother of all: in the same way the old men are called *Baba*, that is to say, pre-eminent father. Old age is the only quality that allows them, or which gives them, a little importance.

When they begin to feel the onset of hunger, some go hunting, & others fishing, each one following his bent. It is almost unheard of for a father to tell his son, as soon as he is 16 to 18 years old, to go hunting or fishing, or for the master of a Carbet to presume to tell those who reside with him, to go here, or accompany him there: he could expect a most curt refusal. If he wants to go fishing or hunting, or necessity constrains him to do so, he simply says, like St Peter: 'I am going fishing'; & those who have the inclination to go, reply to him as laconically as the Apostles: 'we are going with you'; & follow him.

There is no other people in the world more jealous of their liberty, & who resent more actively & more impatiently the least affront that might be given them. Likewise they mock us, when they see that we respect & obey our superiors. They say that we must be the slaves of those whom we obey, since they give themselves the liberty to command us, & we are cowardly enough to execute their orders.

It is only the women who are commanded in this country; & although this is done in a gentle & seemly manner, & they are accustomed to obey from their tenderest youth, it must still be remarked that they feel all the weight of this yoke. Yet they obey without answer, or rather they know so well their duty, & carry it out with such exactitude, silence, meekness, & respect, that it is rare that their husbands are obliged to remind them of it. A great example for Christian women, who are preached to uselessly since the death of Sara, wife of Abraham, & who will be preached to, judging by appearances, until the end of the world as fruitlessly as one preaches the Gospel to the *Caraïbes*.

I must render this justice to these poor women Savages, that during all the time that I have been in Dominica in different Carbets, I have never seen them idle for a single moment. They work ceaselessly, & do it with such calm & meekness that, although they are no more mute than the other creatures of their species that one sees in other parts of the world, not a word of anger is heard between them, though very often they have irritating mishaps, & harsh & difficult jobs to put up with: for it must be taken into account that it is they who do everything that there is to do inside & outside the Carbet. The men only fell the trees, when there is a clearing to make, which happens rarely. They occupy themselves further with hunting & fishing, & with other small jobs of which I have spoken above, & that is all. If they are returning from a hunt, they throw down what they have caught at the entrance to the Carbet

167

without troubling themselves further with it; it is for the women to pick it up, & to prepare it. If they have been fishing, they leave the fish in the canoe, & go to lie down without saying a word. The women must run to the canoe, bring the fish, & cook it: for they must assume that the fisherman is hungry. One can say, in a word, that they are truly servants who have remained in the condition for which they have been created, without deviating from it up to the present day thanks to the superiority their husbands have always maintained over them.

PART III

Anglo-French rivalry continued almost without pause throughout the eighteenth century. England brought the Seven Years War to an end in 1763 by capturing the valuable French sugar islands of Martinique and Guadeloupe which, under the terms of the Treaty of Paris, were returned to France in exchange for recognition of British possession of the previously 'neutral' or unclaimed islands of Dominica, Tobago, Grenada, and St Vincent.

During the eighteenth century there are reports of Caribs on some of the smaller islands such as Marie Galante and Tobago, and on the mainland of South America, all probably refugees from war and natural disaster. However, by mid-century the Caribs were, in effect, a major presence only on Dominica and St Vincent. Before 1763 European settlement on these two islands—mainly French—had been small scale and piecemeal. English intentions were more grandiose, though difficult to put into practice. From the survey of Dominica drawn in 1763 by John Byres, it seems that the Leeward Carib—where 'Indian' Warner had his base (at what is now known as Massacre)—had removed themselves, or been removed: the two principal European settlements, Portsmouth—with its fine natural harbour—and Roseau—which the English tried to rename Charlotte Town—were both on this coast. Byres's survey optimistically divided Dominica into lots, for purchase in London by auction (a division that mostly ignored the inconvenient fact that much of the island is too mountainous and densely forested for plantations of any kind). One small lot, on the north-east coast, was designated as Carib land, presumably an indication that this was the site of the main settlement, although there were obviously other Carib groups elsewhere on the south windward. Like most Caribbean islands during this period Dominica was the site of Anglo-French warfare, slave-risings, and problems with maroons. The Caribs seem to have been peripheral to all this activity, though contact with the numerous maroon groups would not necessarily register in the colonial archives. Joseph Senhouse's diary (No. 15) therefore offers an especially valuable glimpse of the Dominican Caribs, one of the very few that punctuate the 150–year gap between Labat (No. 13) and Ober (No. 21).

The picture on St Vincent was very different. For one thing the terrain there is less severe, and new sugar plantations were in theory possible on a large scale. However, the major complicating factor was the presence of a powerful group of so-called Black Caribs, the product of interbreeding between the native Caribs and escaped or shipwrecked black Africans, a grouping that probably had its origins in the early sixteenth century, but which began to flourish at the start of the eighteenth, as our first chapter here shows (No. 14). By 1763 these Vincentian Black Caribs were in firm occupation of precisely the land on the windward coast deemed most suitable for the development of new plantations. The story of British conflict with and eventual removal of the Black Caribs from the islands is told in the remaining chapters in this section. Conflict was slight and intermittent for several decades, and close intercourse between Caribs and planters was clearly possible. In 1773 the boundaries of Carib territory were redrawn (see Plate 14). The successful slave rebellion in Sainte-Domingue upped the stakes during the last decade of the eighteenth century, and, as a consequence, the planters were determined to remove the Black Caribs from the island altogether, as is apparent from the end of William Young's 1795 *Account* (No. 17). In 1796 over 4,000 Black (and some so-called 'Yellow') Caribs were removed to the small island of Balliceaux, and in the following year the survivors were deported to Central America.

Further Reading

William Young's *Account* was the standard work on the Black Caribs for many years. Recently alternative accounts have emerged, generally more sceptical of the planters' views and more sympathetic to the various indigenous groups: see Kirby and Martin 1986, Craton 1982 and 1986, Marshall 1973, Gullick 1976, 1978a, and 1978b, and Gonzalez 1988.

14. *First Reconnaissances of the Black Caribs (1700–1723)*

¶ *Although the presence and social integration of black runaway slaves within the Amerindian societies of the Caribbean certainly had begun as early as the mid-sixteenth century (No. 4), it was not until the eighteenth century that they became a distinct social element with separate, and at times conflicting, interests from the native population. Most of all on St Vincent, possibly due to the demographic consequences of the chance wrecking of a slave ship in the vicinity, the 'Nègres Caraïbes', or Black Caribs, came to form a powerful and enduring society whose story is reflected in subsequent sections of this anthology.*

The purpose of the following extracts is to illustrate the growing awareness on the part of the Europeans as to these developments and their attempts to exploit nascent divisions between these Black Caribs and the original native population. At the same time these documents suggest that such activities by the Europeans were themselves an important element in the formation of Black Carib identity; for, in the context of French and English rivalry over the settlement of Dominica, St Vincent, and Grenada, they represented a potent and novel element in colonial political calculations.

The first extract is taken from a report made in 1700 by Commissariat Officer Robert and the Governor General of the French Antilles, the Comte d'Amblimont, which alludes to the shipwreck off St Vincent as a possible origin for the considerable number of 'negroes' reported here. The first mention of this event was in a deposition of Major John Scott, who dates it as 1635 (C S P 1661–8: 534), with subsequent references in the publications relating to Sieur de la Borde (1674) and William Young (1795). However, Robert further suggests that the favourable currents from Barbados to St Vincent were an important factor in augmenting the black population here. This geographical circumstance helps explain the deep antipathy of the black Vincentians for the English that finally came to a head in the 'Carib Wars' of the 1760s–1790s (Nos. 17, 19).

The second extract is taken from the official correspondence of the French authorities on Grenada and introduces the affair of Caraïbe Olivier. *This incident clearly highlights the day-to-day tensions that existed between the French colonists and the native population, but does so in a way which also demonstrates the divergent interests of and the tensions between the Amerindian population and the black escapees from slavery. Equally, French circumspection in their dealings with both these groups underlines their importance to successful colonization of the area, while mention of the Galibi and Paria Amerindians reminds us of the wider, regional relationships still practised within the native polity, and not yet interdicted by the colonial frontier.*

The final extract is taken from A Relation of the Intended Settlement of the Islands of St Lucia and St Vincent in America; In Right of the Duke of Montagu and under His Grace's Direction and Orders in the Year 1722, *published by Nathaniel Uring in 1726. It comprises the report of John Braithwaite, which itself appears in a number of other sources, most notably being transcribed and translated by the French colonial authorities (ANP Colonies C10d–2, No. 2) within a few years of its original publication by Uring, as well as being reproduced by Southey (1827).*

As this persistent interest shows, there are a number of fascinating features to this account, particularly the light it throws on the changing nature of Amerindian allegiance to the colonial powers as well as the emerging ethnic contrasts between the 'Black' and 'Indian' inhabitants of the island.

Moreover, it is apparent that there was a sophisticated appreciation, on the part of both the 'Indian General' and the 'Negroe Chief' that Braithwaite encountered, as to the 'specious pretences' of European colonial expeditions, reflected anecdotally in their insistence that they drink wine not rum. Equally, that Braithwaite was at first led to entertain for several days a 'chief' of no consequence suggests that naïve diplomatic overtures were often and easily recognized as such by the native population.

REPORT OF INTENDANT ROBERT, 1700

There are a considerable number of negroes in St Vincent who established themselves here a long time ago, having their families and their *Carbets* in parts where they are separated from the *Caraïbes*; I will examine with the Marquis d'Amblimont [i.e. the Comte] the plan to carry off these negroes to sell them in the French colonies or to send them to be sold by the Spanish. Meanwhile I will give you, Monseigneur, some knowledge of the establishment of these negroes of St Vincent, in particular that which it appears to me you would most want. This island of St Vincent is the one where the *Caraïbes* maintain themselves in the greatest number since the establishment of the Europeans in the Caribbean, and similarly through the trade between the French, English, and *Caraïbes* it has been convenient that they have been left with their property, as also on Dominica, without anyone being allowed to trouble them there. It happened that there was a long time before this a ship full of negroes wrecked and lost on the windward of St Vincent, many of the negroes and negresses from the said ship escaped on shore and were received kindly by the *Caraïbes*; it is this event that began settlement of these negroes on St Vincent, where they live. There were negroes and negresses, they had children, and some of these negroes married *Caraïbe* girls, on account of which they have grown in number; it is true that many negroes who have deserted from the islands possessed by the Europeans have put themselves among those on St Vincent, but few have deserted the French islands and particularly not this one [Martinique]; St Vincent is to the south of Martinique and the winds and currents carry to the west, in such a way that the negroes who flee from here would not be able, save for a miracle, to reach St Vincent; of all the islands the one from which it is the most easy to reach St Vincent is Barbados, it is not necessary to do anything other than drift on the currents and by steering a canoe ever so little it is therefore possible to come very easily from Barbados; that is why among the negroes of St Vincent there are few who come from the French islands.

As far as removing all these negroes from St Vincent is concerned, the people, Monseigneur, who have written to you should have made known to you at the same time that it is not an easy enterprise, and the more one examines the means of trying it the more one finds difficulties with them. These negroes are settled on the windward of St Vincent and all this windward coast is full of dangers and obstacles; there is no place to anchor for the little barques, and one needs to have all the skill of these negroes in order to land here with their pirogues; so that one must not count on being able to make a landing anywhere on this windward coast, nor on attacking them by this route. It would be more practicable to disembark on the leeward side in the area occupied by the *Caraïbes* and then to make one's way inland; to cross the island to the windward part where the negroes are. This would also be very difficult, unless the *Caraïbes* here will allow it and will lend a hand, because there are in this island extraordinary peaks and cliffs, which form astonishing precipices; it is also completely covered in woods from top to bottom except for the clearings of the *Caraïbes* which are very few in number, and one can easily judge that on an island like this it is difficult to forge paths to cross it; that would need time, a lot of people and supplies, and above all persons able to stand up to this labour in a land of remote forest and consequently unwholesome climate. However, I believe it will be necessary to take that route if one wishes to make war on these negroes of St Vincent; but before attempting this journey it is necessary to be assured of the attitude of the *Caraïbes* of St Vincent, so as to not to have any commitment to an enterprise that brings war with them upon us. This would be a very great disturbance for all the French colonies, as one can judge by the injury that the English colonies suffer being at war with them, the

English likewise having done everything humanly possible in order to have peace with those of St Vincent. The most common opinion is that the *Caraïbes* of the said island wish that the negroes that are settled here would flee elsewhere; some of these *Caraïbes* who come here testify the same; it seems also that this would be in their interest, because they are subject to the fear that these negroes, who are multiplying and growing in number, will become stronger and more powerful than them and afterwards maltreat them. On the other hand it is not possible to be at all assured that this will occur because there are a great many of these negroes allied with some of the *Caraïbes* and who live together on good terms, and one ought not at all absolutely to rely on the specific words of these *Caraïbes*, who speak little, who take a long time to explain themselves, and who judge most cleverly what one desires them to say: they often say out of kindness what they believe you wish them to say. What is certain, and what makes me believe that these *Caraïbes* will never consent to allow the French to land on their part of the leeward coast and to give them passage to penetrate to the windward side, is that all their greatest consideration is given to not letting anyone set foot on their island, neither the French nor any other kind of person; it is a very steadfast sentiment that they prefer to see 2,000 negroes settled in their island than to see disembarking here only fifty armed Frenchmen. This is why one can certainly plan on having no agreement from these *Caraïbes* for this enterprise, and that in order to try it is necessary to risk war with them, as well as with the negroes of the said island of St Vincent. If one became master of these negroes it would be necessary to sell them to the Spanish; one would not be able to do anything else and they would want none of them in the French islands, besides it would be necessary to plan on a considerable expenditure for this enterprise, on a number of good men, on barques and pirogues supported by two or three warships. I have the honour to inform you, Monseigneur, it will be solely up to you to give me, as much in advance as possible, a plan for this most just project. I do not know if M. D'Amblimont will see here more advantages than appear to me; I wish to assure you that I was not exaggerating the difficulties at all; my intention is not at all to increase them but to take notice of all things on the footing that they are, in order that those measures and precautions are taken in the enterprise that are necessary for it to succeed. [...]

LETTER OF M. DE BEAUMONT ON THE *CARAÏBES* AND FATHER LE BRETON'S MEDIATION IN GRENADA, 3 SEPTEMBER 1705

I am now back from the islands of Grenada and St Vincent with a detachment which M. de Machault sent to me in a boat with Father Le Breton, a Jesuit, to inform us in Grenada about what caused the *Caraïbes* of that island to massacre some of the inhabitants and what has been done since.

We learned that one night the man named Olivier, a *caraibe*, returning to his area on the windward side with three others, met a local named Catinat, who was making his rounds, his musket on his shoulder. After they had all said good evening to each other this *Caraibe* came up behind Catinat, seized his gun, threw him to the ground and bayonetted him several times from which he thought him dead, carrying him away from the path; nevertheless he did not die of his wounds until a week later. After this attack this same *Caraibe* next met a sailor to whom he wanted to do the same, but being more robust he escaped from him and only had his hands cut a little by the bayonet. At once he informed M. de Bouloc, who having already learned what had happened from the local man [Catinat], dispatched a militia officer and some locals to arrest this murderer. This detachment, arriving in the district of the *Caraibes*, found that there were about eighty of them embarking; and as they had no orders to fire they went on to burn the Carbets. The order not to fire was very prudent, as we later learned; it is certain that the *Caraibes* who were escaping had no part whatsoever in this butchery, not wanting to let the murderer or even those who were with him embark with them. In order that he should be punished M. de Bouloc, who thought at that time that he had embarked, wrote about it to the governor of Spanish Trinidad. I do not doubt, My Lord, that he will report to you about it and about the answer he received in greater detail, as well as the fact that this murderer again fled on the eve of our arrival, which was the 25th of last month. He shot arrows at a resident's negro, who died of his wounds two days later, and also shot arrows at two of the residents' children, who fortunately were not wounded. This repetition of the offence therefore showed that this *caraibe* Olivier had remained in the island, which alarmed the neighbours and above all the women, it being forbidden to them to shoot unless in self-defence. Wanting to treat this nation with caution and to understand the matter in advance, it was agreed among us that Father Breton would go to the district of the *Caraibes* and take with him a savage from St Vincent whom I had on board as a passenger [and] to whom, he having been seen by the *Caraibes* remaining on the island as well as by the said Olivier, they would come [and] he would take them to Father Breton, well known among them [and] from whom, he having had a mission on St Vincent for almost three years, they would conceal nothing. As they did not appear at all during the two days that this monk was there he could not learn anything for certain. We were told only that it was believed the fellow [Olivier] was coming. Whereupon this murderer was put in prison, having been accused by a resident of killing one of his pigs, he having always claimed the pig that he had killed was stray.

There are others who told us that it [happened] because he had thought that a resident had carried off an Indian woman, a relative of his, about which he had complained to M. de Bouloc a few days before this first murder. That may well be; however, M. de Bouloc promised he would make an investigation of it and he has learned since that it was a savage who took her away. He has also written to the governor of Trinidad about it. That, Monseigneur, was all we were told about this matter.

On the 30th following we raised anchor for St Vincent and put off there eight savages, three men, three women, and two children, whom I had aboard; not including the savage passenger [from St Vincent], whom Colonel Jansson, commanding at Nevis, had sent to M. de Machault with the information that the savages of St Vincent had come to warn him that if he did not return them [the eight savages] they would kill three Englishmen, one a merchant captain, whom they were holding. These [eight] savages were taken by an English barque which had entered one of their bays under the French flag, and trusting this they went on board, and then were taken to Nevis. Our arrival at St Vincent gave that nation great joy. I returned the savages after having been given the remaining Englishman of the three. A few days before they had taken the captain to the general, and the other Englishman had died of an illness, according to what they [the savages] as well as the Englishman assured me. I do not doubt, Monseigneur, that the general has informed you of this.

I take the liberty also, Monseigneur, of informing you that the day I anchored at St Vincent, which was the 3rd of this month, forty to fifty armed savages came alongside in their pirogues. I received them and gave them suitable presents. They told us that they were going to the windward side, the district of the negro *caraibes*, to butcher the one who, two days previously, had murdered a savage. Father Breton, who was there the next day to get the Englishmen, learned that there had been a considerable massacre on both sides and that there was real war between them and the negroes. And during the two days that the Father [Breton] stayed during his trip I always had a considerable number of savages on board to cement friendship with them, which is what they wanted, to make them drunk, and to give them some presents; without making them aware of any mistrust I was, however, on my guard. I described to them the obligations that they ought to have to France, for having rescued their relatives and peoples from the hands of the English their enemies. They showed real joy and this nation will remember it forever. They had learnt of the action of the *caraibe* Ollivier. They thoroughly assured me that if they found him they would kill him. The *Paria* and the *Galibis*, who are at Trinidad, will do the same. These St Vincent savages seem to me to have a lot of confidence in us; they even indicated that if they were given help against the negroes they would accept it. That would be a good catch. It is claimed that there are about 3,000 negroes, all strong, fit to send to the Spanish mines. There is a war between them which can only be ended by a specific campaign, since it is based on the fact that these negroes kidnap the women of the savages, who are very jealous and never forgive. For this [enterprise] it will be necessary to have the forces to oppose any assistance that the English may give the negroes. In truth the communications between the two districts appear a little difficult for a surprise attack; but the savages being there and ruining the negroes' provisions and seizing their canoes and pirogues, they would not hold out long. Monseigneur, excuse me from telling you the measures

I would propose in such a case, not having the honour to be qualified to take such a liberty and being persuaded that whoever is put in charge will give you very good plans. I will always make it my glory and honour to carry out as zealously as possible the orders I am given, being utterly devoted to the service of the King and in order to merit, Monseigneur, the honour of your protection that I very humbly beg you to grant me, as well as my promotion.

Monseigneur,

Permit me to add to this copy that since my first [letter] M. de Bouloc has informed the general that the *Caraibes* of Grenada have again, in the last few days in the windward district, massacred a sergeant and a soldier of the garrison, along with a negro, who were on some land that I had recently given to M. de Jardin, a lieutenant, who happily for him was not found there, otherwise he might have suffered the same misfortune.

This same massacre is causing the inhabitants who are in the area to abandon their work and premises and, if order is not promptly restored, I predict that it will be hard in the future to increase the colony's settlement. I have just seen a few letters from the inhabitants who want to leave.

On this, I took the liberty of asking the general to be so good as to send a detachment to set up a strong guard in the windward district so as to contain these savages and draw them out in order to be able to keep the inhabitants in their homes and continuing their work. I would have applied myself with all possible zealousness to the execution of his orders but he did not agree [to this plan]. As I am not allowed to know his reasons, it would be well if it pleases you, Monseigneur, to give me the honour of telling you that if the leaders were properly united everything would combine for the good of the administration and the colonies.

I am, with a very profound respect and all the submissiveness that I owe you, Monseigneur, your very humble and very obedient,

M. de Beaumont

REPORT ON THE PROCEEDINGS AT ST VINCENT BY CPT. BRAITHWAITE

In pursuance of a Resolution in Council and your order for so doing, the day you sailed with his Grace's colony for Antego, I sailed with the Griffin sloop, in company with his Majesty's ship the Winchelsea, to St Vincent. We made the island that night, and the next morning ran along shore, and saw several Indian huts, but as yet no Indians came off to us, nor could we get ashore to them, by reason there was no ground to anchor in. Towards the evening two Indians came on board, and told us that we might anchor in a bay to leeward, and when we were at anchor they would bring their General on board; here we came to anchor in deep water, and very dangerous for the sloop. One whom they call General came on board, with several others, to the number of twenty-two. I entertained them very handsomely, and made the chief some trifling presents, but found he was a person of no consequence, and that they called him chief to get some presents from me. Here two of the Indians were so drunk they would not go ashore but stay'd on board some days, and were well entertained. After this, little winds and great currents drove us off several days, but at last we came to an anchor in a spacious bay to leeward of the island; the draught of which I ordered to be taken by our surveyor for your better understanding, the place being the only one where a settlement could be made. The ship and sloop were scarce come to anchor, before the strand of the shore was covered with Indians and amongst them we could discover a white, who proved to be a Frenchman. I took Capt. Watson in the boat with me, with a Frenchman and immediately went ashore. As soon as I came among them, I asked, why they appeared all armed? for every man had cutlashes, some had musquets, pistols, bows and arrows, etc. They with very little ceremony, inclosed me, and carried me up the country about a mile, over a little rivulet, where I was told I was to see their General. I found him sitting amidst a guard of about a hundred Indians; those nearest his person had all musquets, the rest bows and arrows and great silence. He ordered me a seat, and a Frenchman stood at his right hand for an interpreter. He demanded of me, what brought me into his country, and of what nation? I told him, English, and I was put in to wood and water, as not caring to say anything else before the Frenchman, but told him, if he would be pleased to come on board our ships, I would leave Englishmen in hostage for him, and those he should be pleased to bring with him; but I could not prevail with him, either to come on board or suffer me to have wood or water. He said he was informed we were come to force a settlement, and we had no other way to remove that jealousy, but to get under sail. As soon as I found what influence the Frenchman's Company had upon them, I took my leave, after making such replies as I thought proper, and returned to my boat under a guard. When I came to the shore, I found the guard there was increased by a number of Negroes, all armed with fusees. I got in my boat without any injury and went on board to Capt. Orme, and told him my ill success.

Immediately after I sent on shore the sloop's boat, with a mate, with rum, beef and bread, etc. with some cutlashes, and ordered a Frenchman to conduct them to their General, and to tell him, that tho' he deny'd me the common good of water and a little useless wood, nevertheless I had sent him such refreshments as our ships afforded. Our people found the Frenchman gone, and that then the Indian General seemed pleased, and received what was sent him, and in return sent me bows and arrows.

Our people had not been long returned, but their General sent a canoa, with two Chief Indians, who spoke very good French, to thank me for my presents, and to ask pardon for his refusing me wood and water and assured me, I might have what I pleased; and they had orders to tell me, if I pleased to go a-shore again, they were to remain hostages for my civil treatment. I sent them on board the man-of-war, and with Capt. Watson went on shore. I was well received, and conducted as before, but now I found the brother of the chief of the Negroes was arrived with five hundred Negroes, most armed with fuzees; they told to my interpreter, they were assured we were come to force a settlement, or else they would not have deny'd me what they never before deny'd any English, viz. wood and water; but if I pleased, I might take in what I wanted under a guard. Finding them in so good a humour, I once more introduced the desire I had to entertain them on board our ships, and with some difficulty prevailed with 'em, by leaving Capt. Watson on shore, under their guard, as a hostage. I carried them on board the King's ship, where they were well entertained by Capt. Orme, who gave the Indian General a fine fuzee of his own, and to the chief of the Negroes something that pleased him. Capt. Orme assured him of the friendship of the King of England, etc. The Negroe Chief spoke excellent French, and gave answers with the French complements. Afterwards I carried 'em on board the Duke's sloop; and after opening their hearts with wine, for they scorned to drink rum, I thought it a good time to tell 'em my commission, and what brought me upon their coast. They told me, it was well I had not mentioned it a-shore, for their power could not have protected me; that it was impossible; the Dutch had before attempted it, but were glad to retire. They likewise told me, two French sloops had, the day before we came, been amongst 'em, gave 'em arms and ammunition, and assured them of the whole force of Martinico for their protection aginst us; they told 'em also that they had drove us from St Lucia, and that now we were come to endeavour to force a settlement there; and notwithstanding all our specious pretences, when we had power, we should inslave 'em; but declared they would trust no Europeans; that they owned themselves under the protection of the French, but would as soon oppose to their settling amongst 'em or any act of force from 'em, as us; as they had lately given an example, by killing several: and they further told me, it was by very large presents the French ever got in their favour again; but they resolved never to put in their power, or any European, to hurt 'em. They advised me to think what they said was an act of friendship. This being all I could get from them, I dismissed 'em with such presents as his Grace ordered for that service, with a discharge of cannon, and received, in return, as regular vollies of small shot as I ever heard. In the night the Winchelsea drove from her anchors; which, as soon as I perceived, and had received Capt. Watson from the shore, I got under sail, and stood to the man-of-war. This is a faithful report of all I can recollect.

John Braithwaite.

15. *The Diary of Joseph Senhouse (1776)*

¶ *Joseph Senhouse (1743–1829) was the fifth son of a Cumberland family. He went to sea at 16, and then followed his elder brother to Barbados. Sir James Lowther was the family patron and, through his good offices, Senhouse was appointed in 1771 to the lucrative position of Collector of Roseau, in Dominica; in 1773 he became Comptroller of Customs. He left Dominica that same year and, apart from a brief trip in 1776—which provided the diary that follows—never returned, although he kept the Dominican job until 1786. During the 1780s he became manager of the Lowther family interests in Carlisle, was rewarded with a knighthood in 1783, and married into a wealthy Northamptonshire family in 1787.*

His graphic account of crossing Dominica from Roseau to Rosalie is followed by one of the few English accounts of the Caribs of Dominica to survive from this period. Senhouse goes out of his way to distance himself from the reports of Labat and du Tertre, and therefore to normalize the Caribs as harmless and inoffensive. Like many other European writers over the last 500 years he is deeply impressed by Carib basketry.

The diary now forms part of the Joseph Senhouse papers in the Cumbria Record Office, and is reproduced in the transcription made by James C. Brandow.

At the Bay near Bridge Town, Barbados
Sunday, June 2d, 1776. Pleasant, fair Weather.

Having previously engaged with Capt. Lock for his Sloop, the *Favourite*, to go down to Dominica for five Joes (or £12.10 Currency of Barbados), in the Afternoon of this day repaired on board the above vessel, Francis Craig, Master, & immediately got under Sail, passing under the Lee of this beautiful Island.

At Sea; in sight of Martinica, P.M.

About 10 A.M., saw the high Land of Dominica bearing N.W. The Master of the Sloop being unacquainted with this Coast, I undertook to stand Pilot and about 5 in the Afternoon, conducted the *Favourite* safely to an Anchor in Couanary or St David's Bay. The best Anchoring place in this Bay, wh. is situated on the most windward part of Dominica, is when the Middle of Russel or the Southernmost Island bears South & the Centre of North Island is situated East, in 8 or 9 Fathoms, Sand, and Clay. A current generally sets out of this Bay from the Rivers that empty themselves into it. Immediately upon Landing, walked to Castle Bruce, the Plantation of Col. James Bruce of ye 70th Regiment. Continued here inspecting into the state of Lowther hall until—

June 10, 1776.

Embarked this afternoon on bod. the aforemention'd Sloop at 11 A.M. & stood along Shore, towards the So.ern extremity of the Island called Cachacrou, which we reached before Sunset and arrived at Roseau about 7 P.M. Supped and remain'd with Mr Sam. Duer, Collector, about ten days and during that period dined with Gov. Will. Stuart, Judge Wilson, Mr Winston, Solicitor Genl., etc., etc.

Thursday, June 20, 1776.

This Morning abo. $\frac{1}{2}$past 7 o'clock, set forwards for Couanary on Horseback in Company with Liet. Gov. Stuart, Lieut Col. James Bruce of the 70th Regiment, and Mr James Laing. Crossed the Roseau or Queen's River at the Estate of Monsr. Lacoudry & rode up the Valley for nearly 2 Miles, passing by several deep wallsided, murky Vallies or rather dark, horrible Gullies, whose bottom can never enjoy the cheering Rays of the Sun in any other position than that immediately vertical. These have each a little Stream or run of Water, & their sides, notwithstanding the rugged steepness of them, are almost everywhere covered with Trees & Shrubs that wear a perpetual verdure and present many prospects strikingly Romantic. We now begun to ascend the Mountains and leaving the River on our right hand, continued advancing for full three Hours, when we reached the Grand Etang. The Road we had passed over in our way up is extremely croked & narrow, being for the most part made on the sides of very steep Hills & from necessity it runs in all directions. Notwithstanding which, it leads as directly to the Lake as the situation of the Mountains and the nature of the Ground will possibly admit of. In many places the Soil being of Clayey quality, We found it exceedingly Slippery from some Rain that fell last Night, and to render our Journey the more terrifying, several parts of this slippery Road led upon the brink of such steep precipices that with the least false step, the Horse and Rider must have been tumbled headlong down for many hundred feet below. At one of the most frightful of these perpendiculars, a Gentleman not long ago perceiving his Horse beginning to falter, very fortunately threw himself upon the Road but his Beast fell so far beneath as fractured every bone in his Body. We were besides so unlucky as to find upon some of those precipices, several huge Trees which having lost part of their foundation when this Road was cut, were fallen across it & rendered it necessary for us to dismount & crawl over or creep under in the best manner we could; but our Horses, that on such occasions were led, most wonderfully escaped from destruction. It was very observable in proportion as we rose up the Mountains, that the Trees constantly and uniformly diminished in height & thickness, and about a Mile from the Grand Etang, they begun to be covered as in Northern Climates with a species of grey Moss. In the Neighbourhood of the Lake, the Trees were dwindled almost into Shrubs, generally not more than 12 or 13 feet high & surrounded with a thick Coat of Moss. An abundance of Fern Trees flourish'd hereabouts. Towards the summit, the Road grew more level & Stoney, with only a very thin Stratum of vegetable Mould.

Having arrived at the most elevated part of the Road where we found the remains of a Hut, we dismounted to refresh ourselves & Horses near a Well cut out of a Rock in the shape of a Bason filled with most excellent cold and transparent Water. From hence we had the best view of the celebrated Lake, laying about 200 yards below, which I apprehend cannot be more than half-a-Mile long & not more than a quarter in breadth, but as it is so surrounded with Trees that grow everywhere close to the Water's edge, the view is very much obstructed upon that account. My Judgment of its size is therefore merely conjecture. About one Mile distant and not much above our level, we had a full prospect of Morn Vert. A great quantity of Fish, it is said, this Lake (which is very deep) contains and they are asserted to be of various kinds. Near its Southern extremity, the River Roseau takes its rise in consequence of a Cascade that falls out of this piece of Water. The air of this lofty part of Dominica we found extreamly cool and refreshing tho' the Sun was unclouded & nearly vertical, yet at Roseau and at several other places below, it was Raining from Clouds pendent in the lower regions of the Atmosphere. One of our Party having said he would bring a Thermometer to determine the degree of heat upon this Spot, it was therefore a very great mortification to us all to understood it was forgot. In this cool, solitary place we rested upwards of an hour, sharing the provisions we brought for Dinner with the Servants that attend'd & converted the Fountain into Grog for their benefit. We then mounted our Horses to descend the Eastern side of the Mountain and about 200 yards from the Well, had a view of the Sea and the Country on the windward side of the Island for a prodigious distance, Richmond Estate bounding the prospect to the No.ward. We had not advanced a Mile when the Road proved so exceeding bad that the Col. & Myself thinking it more prudent to trust to such Supporters as we had long been accustomed too & could confide in, than to depend upon the unsure footing of our Horses that we were but little acquainted with, and mine in particular having the character of a stumbler, we therefore alighted and walked a great part of the way down until we came to a considerable trace of level Land where we mounted again and continued our Journey to Rosalie, reaching that Estate about three o'clock in the afternoon.

The principal things that engaged my attention on this Plantation (the property of Col. O'Hara, Gov. Stuart, etc.) was the large, limpid River of Rosalie, having a handsome Bridge thrown over it, & the Hospital which seems a much better and more Roomy building than the dwelling House. Tho' this Estate has buried an extraordinary number of Negroes since the first settlement of it, the Surgeon, a very polite Prussian, informed me that it was then but thinly inhabited.

Col. Bruce's Pettiaugre waiting for us at the Waterside, he & myself took leave of the Governour and descended with some difficulty as well as danger on board of her from a Crane & rowed to the Northward. Proceeding along shore, we saw considerable Flocks of different species of Birds, such as Boobies, Noddies, Coblers, & Tropick Birds, flying out of holes or Nests in rugged perpendicular Cliffs that are elevated over the Mouth of St David's River & proceeded to Castle Bruce.

This Plantation, one of the best in Dominica, was settled by the present hospitable proprietor, Col. James Bruce, & is equal in its annual produce to 200 Hogshd. of Sugar. The Works are spacious & substantial, Where may be seen a very simple & ingenious contrivance upon the principles of the Persian Wheel, made use of in order to raise a Stream of Water of a sufficient height to run into the Worm Tubs. The River already mentioned affording a plentiful supply of Water, the Mill is set in motion by what is term'd an undershot Wheel of about 38 feet in Diameter, to the top of which, by the means of Boxes fixt on the back part of every other Waterboard, that element is raised where from the circular progression of the Water Wheel, they are alternately emptied into a Trough & from thence by a Spout, it is convey'd into the abovementioned Tubs. The Great Wheel is often employed only for this purpose while the Mill continues at rest.

One of the chief beauties this Estate can boast of is the large River of St David's which is filled with a pure, wholesome Water & well stored with excellent Mullets & other sorts of Fish; also an abundance of River Lobsters or Crayfish. However, to balance in some measure the many & great advantages that arise from possessing so fine a Stream, after a great fall of Rain in ye Mountains, this River will sometimes, on a sudden, rush down with such extraordinary impetuosity as nothing can possibly resist or stand before it, which was particularly the case in 1774 when a large part of the most valuable Cane Land was entirely destroy'd & swept into the Sea. However, such precautions or embankments have since been made as it is hoped the like devastation will not happen any more. To bathe in a Tropickal Climate in so fine a Stream as this, an exercise I have frequently indulged myself in, is a luxury not to be described and to be fully known must be Felt.

It is here and upon some other parts of the windward Coast of the Island that the few Caribbs of Dominica are settled, who probably in all do not amount to more than 10 or a dozen Families, one of which by permission cultivate a piece of Ground for their own benefit upon Lowther hall. These people have not any mixture of the Negroe as we find to be the case in St Vincent's and are descended unadulterated from the Aborigines or first Inhabitants of these Islands that they have given name too. They have a clear, olive Complection, little black piercing Eyes, with flat Foreheads & Noses, resembling very much the Malays or people of Sumatra & Java. They are of a strong, well-proportioned make, seldom exceeding the middle size. Their hair is perfectly black and coarse which they frequently wear long, hanging down to their Waist, taking much pains in Combing & keeping it clear but suffer none to grow upon their Faces or Chins. Their Dress is either a Shirt & pair of Trowsers or otherwise they appear almost stark naked.

The mode of Life pursued amongst these People is extreamly simple and artless, being content with very small, mean Cabbins or Huts, resembling the letter 'A' or the Roof of a House set upon the Ground, covered with the Branches of the Cocoanut Palm etc., which generally are open at one end and sometimes at both. Under this covering they swing in Hammocks of their own manufacture which are constructed tolerably neat but their greatest art is shewn in making a sort of Baskets or Paniers of different sizes with the bark of a kind of Willow that is stained of various colours and are at the same time useful & handsome.

The Settlements of these Indians are always near some River or Stream of fresh Water wherein they enjoy the delightful & wholesome exercise of washing themselves every Morning before Sunrise and near the Sea. The Water seeming to be as much their element as the Land, for when one of their Canoes is overset as is sometimes the case in Fishing or travelling from place to place by Sea, all the Men, Women & Children swim about it, the Women sometimes supporting one or more Infants, till it is put to rights & such is their dexterity that it very rarely happens that they lose the smallest parcel of their Lading. Their Weapons formerly were only Bows & Arrows, in the use of which they are still surprisingly alert and dexterous; with these they will shoot Parrots, Ramiers & even River Fish, with amazing success & the keeness of Sportsmen. Hunting is likewise one of their favourite diversions; their Game: wild Hogs, Indian Coneys, etc. Nor should we forget their eagerness in searching for Crapauds, a species of Frog held by them as well as the French Inhabitants of this Country, in high estimation.

When the Husband or Master of a Caribb Family returns home with any Venison or Fish, the Wife brings it from the Boat, dresses it & performs the most servile duties without murmuring. Every Husband having so unlimited a power over his Wife that he can even put her to death on the slightest offence and it is to be feared this horrid brutality too often happens amongst this barbarous people, especially when they are intoxicated with Spirituous Liquors which they are extravagantly fond of, because their number from long experience is evidently upon the decline. They seem, otherwise, to be a shy, reserved set of People, fond of their own customs and of enjoying a peacefull retirement, being unwilling to mix with any other Nation. In this respect they are by no means singular, for I apprehend Mankind in any state approaching that of

the English and them, are the worst and the most tremendous I ever rode. Sometime since, Mr *Baxter* had near lost his life in crossing them. His horse fell down a precipice of thirty feet perpendicular, and the hind legs of the horse were over the precipice before he was alarmed, when he immediately threw himself off. In one place we could not even lead our horses, till a company of Caribbs who were passing by, lent us their cutlasses, with which we at last cut open a way. When we had descended the great mountain, we came into one of the most beautiful plains I ever saw in my life. It is but seven miles long, and three broad, but I think it is as beautiful as uncultivated Nature can make it. It forms a bow, the string of which is washed by the Atlantic ocean, and the bow itself surrounded by lofty mountains. Here the Caribbs chiefly dwell. As we passed by their villages, they stood at their doors in ranks, crying out, '*Bou jou, bou jou:*' (a corruption of *Bon Jour*, a good day;) others cried out, '*How dee, How dee:*' and on many of them being asked, they delivered their cutlasses into our hands, which is the highest proof of confidence they can give. We had with us at this time one of the sons of the grand chief of the Caribbs (*Chateaway*). He has been under the tuition of Mr and Mrs Baxter for some time, and speaks a good deal of English. His name is *John Dimmey*, a fine young man, and of a princely carriage. His father the grand Chief was gone from home; if I could have seen the father I believe I should have obtained his consent to take his son with me to England. His sentiments are highly refined for a savage. 'Teach me your language, *Dimmey*,' said Mr *Baxter* to him one day 'and I will give you my watch.' 'I will teach you my language,' replied the young Chief, 'but I will not have your watch.'

When we entered into the house of one of the Chiefs whose name is *De Valley*, Mr *Dimmey* whispered to Mr *Baxter* that the family would not be satisfied if we did not take home refreshment, to which we consented: and they soon brought a large dishful of eggs, and a bowl of punch. Mr *Dimmey* alone could be with difficulty persuaded to sit down with us at table, the rest would serve. A little sone of the Chief also, (a very beautiful boy for his colour, who had been under the instruction of Mr *Baxter*, and had been already taught to spell) gave us high entertainment by the convincing proof he gave us of an infant genius.

But in the midst of all this kindness there was some degree of jealousy: for I perceived that Mr *Baxter* several times informed them that I received no pay from the King. Mr *Baxter* seemed to live in their affections; and as he has already made a considerable progress in their language, I could not help intreating him to spend two years among them, and give them a full trial. Great as the cross was to that good man who expected to return to his beloved Antigua, he immediately consented. On our return from the Caribb country, I visited our new School-House, and found it much larger than I expected, and far too large for one family. I therefore ordered the workmen to divide it: one half of which I appropriated to the use of Mr and Mrs *Baxter*, and the other half to that of Mr and Mrs *Joyce*. As Mrs *Baxter* intends to educate some of the

Caribb girls, we shall now have three teachers among them. The conduct of Mrs *Baxter* in this instance is not to be overlooked. Though born of a considerable family in Antigua, and brought up in all the softness and luxury of the country, she readily consented some years ago, that her husband should sacrifice a place of four hundred a year currency which he held under Government, that he might devote his whole time and strength to the work of God: and now was perfectly willing to go with her husband among savages, and spend her time in forming their totally uncultivated minds.

I was very uneasy when I found that little had yet been done by Mr *Joyce* in the education of the *Children*: but when all the difficulties were laid open, in the proper settlement of the land on which the house was built, in bringing the materials for building to the proper spot, the ilness of Mrs *Joyce*, and some other particulars, my mind was appeased, and I trust every thing will soon have the most favourable appearance through the blessing of God.

I feel myself much attached to these poor savages. The sweet simplicity and cheerfulness they manifested on every side, soon wore off every unfavourable impression my mind had imbibed from the accounts I had received of their cruelties. Cruelties originating probably with ourselves rather than with them. They are a handsomer people than the Negroes, but have undoubtedly a warlike appearance, as their women frequently carry cutlasses in their hands, and always knives by their naked sides.

We now returned to Kingston, preaching by the way, and being received by the planters with every mark of kindness and respect. Indeed the whole body of the people seems to wish us success. Many were the proofs of affection shown us at our departure, especially by one whose delicacy will not admit of my mentioning his name.

Having appointed Messrs. *Gamble* and *Clark* to labour in the English division of the Island (Mr *Baxter* now and then making a visit) I hired a vessel for Dominica; and with Mr and Mrs *Baxter* (who were desirous of making one visit to their old friends in Antigua before they settled among the Caribbs) and Mr *Lumb*, set sail on Tuesday the 16th for Dominica.

I am, dear Sir,

Your most dutiful,

Most affectionate, and

Most obliged Son,

THOMAS COKE

17. *William Young and the Black Charaibs (1772/1795)*

¶ *Sir William Young (1749–1815) was born into a family with West Indian connections. His father, also Sir William Young (1725–88), Governor of Dominica and one of the biggest landowners in St Vincent, had played some considerable part in Anglo-Carib relationships during the 1760s and 1770s. The second baronet was a Member of Parliament, author of several books, and, for many years, spokesman in England for the West Indian planters. In 1795—with interest in England newly aroused by the second Carib War—he edited his father's valuable papers on the Caribs, which appeared as* An Account of the Black Charaibs in the Island of St Vincent, *and from which these extracts are taken. For the most part we have summarized the narrative given by William Young (as we will call the son), and quoted extensively the documents he quotes from the 1760s and 1770s, during which decades his father, Sir William Young, was a prominent planter and colonial official.*

William Young writes with confidence and authority, but his accounts are clearly produced to serve the interests of the West Indian planters, who, by 1795, were firmly committed to removing the Caribs altogether from the island of St Vincent, a goal they were soon to achieve. The concerns of 1795 are apparent in the last section, where Young speaks in his own voice of the recent outbreak of hostilities on the island—which had already led to the complete destruction of one of his estates. Sir William Young's original papers, dating from the earlier period, demonstrate a much more nuanced attitude towards the Caribs in their response to changing political circumstances.

William Young begins his account by giving a brief history of English claims to St Vincent, and of the relationship between what he calls the 'Red Charaibs', who had ousted the native 'Galibeis' from the island, and the Negroes or 'Black Charaibs', descended from the cargo of a wrecked African slave ship. According to Young's clearly partial account, the Blacks were taken by the Caribs as slaves, but revolted, killed many of their masters, and escaped with Carib women to establish themselves

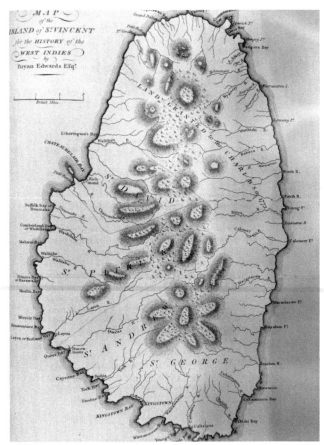

14. Map of the island of St Vincent. From Bryan Edwards, *The History, Civil and Commercial, of the British Colonies in the West Indies* (John Stockdale: London, 1794), i, opp. 392.

*in the mountain fastnesses from which they attacked the Red Caribs, eventually
succeeding in establishing themselves on the eastern half of the island. The French,
predictably enough, are seen as fomenting the differences between the two groups in
order to gain several footholds on the island. In 1763 St Vincent became British
under the terms of the Treaty of Paris, and Sir William Young was appointed to
head the commission that would carry the settlement into effect. The Caribs were
unimpressed by British claims: 'they yet obstinately persevered in declaring against
all interference within the country they called their own.' The commissioners
realized that patience would get them nowhere and that the sovereignty of the island
was in question.*

It was under these impressions, and urged by a strong sense of duty, the
commissioners addressed the Lords Commissioners of the Treasury, by letter,
dated August 10th, 1765, representing;

'That the Charaibs are altogether uncivilized, and the *Blacks* particularly of an
idle untractable disposition. They live in huts scattered in an unregular manner,
at a great distance from each other, without any established subordination,
claiming large tracts of woodland intervening, of which they make no use; and
are besides possessed of other lands in the cleared parts of the country, which
interfere much with the laying out plantations for sale. They had hitherto
occasioned no disturbance, but still we are in doubt if they ever can be made
useful; or whether in many instances they may not prove dangerous. The
measure that appears to us, from these considerations, to be the safest and
most for advantage of the colony, would be as soon as possible to remove as
many of them *as can be prevailed upon* to quit, on terms consistent with the
humanity and honour of his Majesty's government: and what seems the most
probable for accomplishing that end, would be to buy the cleared land, and
cottages, of those *who are disposed to sell*, satisfying them with money, or
whatever else may be acceptable, and offering at the same time other lands in
Bequia, where they cannot be hurtful, in lieu of those they quit; but not
permitting them to take up any land again in any other part of St Vincent's,
except in such places, and on such terms, as may confine them to proper
boundaries, and subject them to some regulations.

(S.S.) T. GREGG
Secty.
(S.S.) WM. YOUNG
ROBT. STUART,
ROBT. WYNNE.'

¶ [*Bequia was soon rejected: It had no rivers and therefore no water. The situation
remained unclear. Sir William Young went back to England for consultations, and
was required by Parliament to make an official report, containing a specific plan
with detailed arrangements of future procedure respecting the Caribs.*]

The commissioner accordingly drew up sundry propositions, which were *fully* approved of, and made the basis of the following instructions, dated February 2, 1768, and immediately transmitted to the commissioners in St Vincent's.

      I. That the commissioners shall survey and dispose of all the cultivated lands from Ribichi to Grand Sable, and round to Chatteau-bellair (the Charaib country.)

     II. That no step shall be taken towards the removal of any Charaib, till the whole arrangement and design shall have been notified and explained to the satisfaction of their chiefs; and they be made to comprehend the conditions on which the settlement was proposed, and that the plan be carried into effect with the gentlest hand, and in the mildest manner.

    III. That in fixing the quarter of the island, destined for the new settlement, every proper indulgence be shown them, and that the lands allotted for them in exchange, be convenient for their habitation, sufficient for their support, and, in point of situation, adapted to their manner of living.

    IV. Certificates shall be given to their principal persons of the situation and quantity of land allotted to them.

     V. The absolute property of the lands so allotted, shall be assured to them and their children, and in such manner as shall be found most to their satisfaction, and agreeable to their customs.

    VI. Until they shall have gathered in their provisions from their former lands, and built houses on their lands newly allotted, they shall be permitted to remain in their former situation, and five years shall be allowed them for these purposes.

    VII. Under these terms, the spots of cleared land they now occupy shall be sold, and make part of plantation allotments, with the woodlands which surround them; and on the final removal of the Charaibs shall make part of such property.

   VIII. Such spots of cleared land shall be sold at not less than £10. the acre; to be paid in two payments, one half down, the other at the expiration of five years.

   IX.X. Of the purchase money for such cleared land, 4 joannes, or £8 sterling per acre, shall be paid to the Charaibs who claim the lands, and be paid to the Charaib in two equal payments, one half at time of sale, and the other moiety in five years; or sooner, on certificate of his removal to the lands allotted him in exchange.

    XI. If at the end of five years, the Charaib shall not have prepared for removal, or built him a hut on the new lands allotted him, the governor, &c. may and shall direct the planter succeeding to the land, to build a hut for the said Charaib, accounting for the residue of the purchase money due to him.

    XII. No quit-rent shall be reserved for lands allotted to the Charaibs, but they shall be the absolute property of them and their descendants, or assigns, provided always that they may not alienate to any white person.

XIII. If in course of the arrangement the remains of the native, or Red Charaibs, desire for their security to be separated and settled apart from the free Negroes, it shall be done.

XIV. Returns to be made of the Charaibs, who receive allotments and take the oath of fidelity to the King.

XV. No fee whatever to be taken for Charaib allotments.

(S.S.) GRAFTON,

PRIS. CAMPBELL,

C. JENKINSON.

May 25th, 1768.

These instructions were proclaimed and published in English and French, throughout the island of St Vincent's. It is to be observed, that from long intercourse with the French all chiefs of the Charaibs speak that language.

¶ [*The Caribs discussed these proposals amongst themselves, and listened to the advice of the Frenchman, the Abbé Valladares, whom Young sees as having had some influence over their actions. Chatoyér is mentioned as the Carib chief, Jean Baptiste as his 'prime minister'. The Caribs were divided amongst themselves, although Young, with hindsight, is of the opinion that such divisions were part of an artful strategy to fool the English. If so, it worked. The English began to build roads into territory the Caribs regarded as theirs: the surveyors and their military escort were taken hostage and freed only when promises were made that the surveys would not continue.*]

July 17, 1769, the commissioners addressed a letter to the Lords of trade and plantations, giving a detailed account of the passed transactions, and the critical situation of the colony in St Vincent's. They write that 'The instructions we now have from your Lordships are, in our humble opinion, as proper as any that could have been devised for the purpose of settling the windward part of the country; but experience now shows us that it will be impossible, without imminent danger to the colony, to complete any settlement or arrangement with the Charaibs, let the terms proposed be ever so tender or advantageous, without a force sufficient to restrain and awe them into disobedience; for which purpose it will be highly necessary to have a considerable military force on the island, before we again attempt to carry our instructions into execution, as we find their numbers greatly exceed what we formerly apprehended.

We have the greatest reason to think that suffering the Charaibs to remain in their present state, will be very dangerous, and may at some period prove fatal to the inhabitants of the country, as their situation, surrounded with wood, makes any access to them, for the purpose of executing justice, impracticable; and they will from thence be capable of committing all outrages unpunished; of harbouring the slaves of the inhabitants of this island, as well as of all the neighbouring islands; of sheltering amongst those, vagabonds and deserters from the French, and in case of a rupture with France, it is probable they will join in distressing the inhabitants, and in an attempt to conquer the country.

(S.S.) WM. YOUNG,

JOHN HUNT,

ROB. STEWART,

ROB. WYNNE,

WM. HEWITT.'

¶ [*Shortly afterwards the Vincentian planters themselves sent a petition to the Secretary of State for the Colonies:*]

'To the Right Hon. the Earl of Hillsborough one of his Majesty's principal Secretaries of State, &c. &c. &c.

The Memorial of sundry proprietors of land in St Vincent's, on behalf of themselves and the planters of that island,

Humbly Sheweth,

That near two-thirds of the cultivable lands of St Vincent's remain in the possession of the Black Charaibs, but a very small proportion of which has yet been cleared of wood.

That by the culture of such lands, *as are at present and must for ever be unnecessary to that people*, his Majesty's revenue will be greatly increased, and from the accession of inhabitants, the island may be rendered in some degree defensible.

That in obedience to his Majesty's instructions to his commissioners, to sell such lands as should remain unoccupied, after allotting to the Charaibs very sufficient quantities for their support and happiness, every measure had been pursued by the commissioners, that could tend to conciliate their affections, and make them sensible of his Majesty's gracious intentions respecting them.

That they nevertheless, from groundless fears and jealousies assembled in arms, very much to the terror of the inhabitants; that they denied the sovereignty of the King, and obliged the surveyors to retire with precipitation from that part of the country.

That they live without order or any laws for their good government; that the barbarities exercised by them on the native Indians, who first afforded them protection, have been such that the few who are left alive have been compelled to seek an asylum amongst his Majesty's subjects.

That they applied to Count d'Ennery, the governor of Martinique, for assistance of men and arms to drive the English from the island, and proposed to him, on their parts, to set fire to their settlements.

That they seized and sold in the neighbouring French islands several Negro slaves belonging to the planters of St Vincent's, some of whom were very lately restored to their owners by order of the French governor.

That it is not the wish of your memorialists from what hath been said, that the Charaibs should be otherwise dealt with, than in a manner entirely becoming humanity. They pray only that his Majesty will be graciously pleased to extend his protection to themselves; that as they desire not the destruction of others, they may be secured in their own lives and properties, which they humbly conceive can never be effected whilst the Charaibs are permitted to remain in their present lawless state, and possessors of so considerable a share of the island, through which, in future war, his Majesty's subjects will at all times be exposed to the sudden incursions of an enemy.

That your memorialists believe, from their knowledge of the nature and dispositions of the Charaibs, that if a force sufficient to reduce them, was speedily to be sent to the island, they would acknowledge the sovereignty and domain of his Majesty, and that every necessary arrangement might be made with facility, and perhaps without the loss of one life, &c. &c.

Jan. 22, 1770.'

¶ [*At this stage certain private individuals seem to have tried to bypass the official commissioners and deal directly with the Caribs. Young's account is somewhat evasive about these events; eventually the Government, averse to coming to any decision, turned the matter over to Sir William Young for investigation and report.*]

From this report, dated Dec. 15, 1770, and which is of very considerable length, I shall transcribe a few extracts, sufficient to afford a just notion of the case, and of the argument on which Government annulled those purchases, which they were so powerfully and shamefully solicited to legalize and support.

The question is treated under the three heads of pretension to royal favour, of claim of right in the applicants, and of the policy of concession by Government.

On the first of these pleas the benevolent and able author of this report says,—'much attention and compassion is, in my humble opinion, due to the Charaibs of St Vincent's: for although many of them proved refractory, and without just or sufficient cause have opposed the execution of the King's orders, so replete with tenderness for them, and with paternal care for their proper settlement, maintenance, and comfort; yet when we reflect on the nature of their case, and the peculiarity of their manners, how important the whole transaction must have appeared in their eyes, and how many doubts must have arisen in their minds, filled with jealousy and dread, lest their repose should be disturbed by the intrusion of strangers, and themselves extirpated in the end, or reduced to slavery; I say, when all these matters are duly considered, much is to be forgotten, much forgiven them.

But upon what principles any degree of favour from the King can be expected by subjects, who appear, in the very case where favour is solicited, to have, as far as in them lay, *weakened* the King's pretensions of *right and sovereignty* to the island; who have acted in direct opposition to his known orders, and who have thus insulted his government, I am totally at a loss to discover. They pray that his Majesty may be made to confirm these purchases, made without his permission, and contrary to his pleasure, from the Charaibs: that is not a prayer of duty and respect; they are apprehensive their titles cannot be deemed valid without it, and therefore they solicit; they offend in the first instance,—they do not ask forgiveness;—they expect a reward from the crown in return for their disobedience to it.

From the jealousy and opposition of the Charaibs, and the danger the colony was thereby exposed to, his Majesty's commissioners have found it necessary to desist from the execution of his instructions, to report home a state of the case, and to await respectfully the King's further orders.

These memorialists have involved a delicate subject, already teeming with difficulties, with still further ones; and perhaps derive some expectation of success, even from the very difficulties they have helped to create.

If from the observations I have made, the memorialists have no reason to expect the King's confirmation of their purchase as a matter of *favour*, it remains only to be considered, whether they ought to obtain it as a matter of *right*, or from principles of *good policy*.

And first, as to the matter of right:—In the King's instructions to his commissioners, the island (St Vincent's) is said to have been settled contrary to the faith of treaties, and they are forbid to acknowledge any right in virtue of possession by the inhabitants.

In further instructions, since given to the commissioners, they are directed to allot good and sufficient lands to the Charaibs, for their support, maintenance, and comfort, which they are to hold by virtue of certificates under the crown, and with a restriction incapacitating them from selling or alienating the lands so allotted to any white person whatsoever.

The opposition of the Charaibs to the execution of these orders, and the transactions which have occurred in consequence, need not at present be repeated. But as the King's pretensions to the island, and his instructions, as I have stated them, were perfectly known, and publicly proclaimed in St Vincent's the *memorialists* cannot, I presume, enjoy the King's confirmation of their purchases as a matter of *right*.

It only remains to examine, whether they should enjoy it on principles of *good policy*.

It may be easy to determine who are best entitled to the possession of cleared and cultivated lands, since it is equitable, that those who have toiled should reap the fruits of their labour; yet it will be difficult to prove *any natural right or title to the large tracts of woodlands* in St Vincent's, which certain Charaibs may presume to claim: there is apprehension of endangering the peace of the island, from the disputes and contests among the Charaibs themselves.

The sellers of these lands, as set forth in the memorial, are only three

Charaibs: now it can no way be demonstrated, that others of them do not conceive they have an equal claim to the enjoyment of woods, perhaps esteemed amongst them a common right of nature; if so, it is probable that those who have received no share of the advantage arising from the sale, may be dissatisfied with their comrades, and oppose a precedent, which may gradually endanger their other possessions, by admitting strangers into their neighbourhood without the general consent of the whole.

As to the argument made use of in the memorial, that by the King's confirmation of these bargains, others may follow, and thus the *Charaibs* be *removed*. Let me be *their* advocate:—Will it be consistent with the dignity of the crown of Great Britain to encourage artful and designing men to delude the Charaibs out of their possessions, and that too under the mask of friendship?—With humble submission to your Lordships, I will be bold to assert that this plan can never be effected, without practices that disgrace humanity: how many collusive bargains, quarrels, and massacres, must come to pass before a whole race of men are deluded out of their possessions, and have no longer power to justify themselves? the thought engenders a train of monstrous consequences, as full of danger as of iniquity.'

Having gone through the subject more especially submitted for his opinion, the Commissioner closes his report, with a new proposition respecting the Charaibs, and which I shall more particularly refer to when stating the terms which closed the Charaib war, as it is in proof that the grants in that treaty did not arise from present weakness or fears, but out of original sentiments of clemency and bounty.

'For quieting if possible the fears and jealousies of the Charaibs, and restoring confidence and security to the colony, (and considering) the improbability of acquiring the friendship of the Charaibs by any other means than those of favour, and the danger the colony must be exposed to, unless their friendship is secured, or unless they are absolutely reduced by force of arms. The *proposition* is, that a royal proclamation be issued, declaring that the King has taken compassion on their ignorance, distrusts, and jealousies, and rather than be the author of their destruction, is graciously pleased, that they shall *continue to hold the lands they now possess* under his royal favour, on condition *only*, that they become his good and faithful subjects; and never sell, or alienate these lands but to himself, or to those he shall think fit to depute by his authority.'

¶ [*Land speculation still flourished to such an extent that the area of the whole island was purchased three times over. The Caribs were presumably puzzled by these examples of civilized behaviour. At a conference with the commissioners they resolutely opposed any European settlement on the island.*]

July 1771, the commissioners made an official and definitive report on these subjects, in which they say,

'We are of opinion, that the positive refusal of the Charaibs to agree to the terms offered by us, on behalf of the crown, or take the oaths of allegiance, added to their avowed attachment to the French, makes it absolutely necessary for the security of the lives and property of the inhabitants, that some steps should be immediately taken to prevent their committing outrages unpunished.

We think that the sale of lands is no longer the most important object, but that the honour of the crown now becomes concerned for the protection of its subjects, against a race of lawless people, who when prompted by liquor or ill designing persons, may commit any violence without being subject to control.

In our opinion, the most effectual means of reducing them to obedience, will be *to carry a road through their country*, under protection of a sufficient military force, and after allotting them lands for their ample subsistence, to sell the remainder, which will very fully repay any expenses incurred by the arrangement, and contribute to keep them in order, by mixing white inhabitants amongst them.

(S.S.) WM. YOUNG,
JOHN HUNT,
ROB. WYNNE.'

¶ [*Sir William Young, now governor of Dominica, was made President of the Council with a remit to carry out the road-building scheme, in effect a declaration of war on the Caribs. The resulting hostilities lasted five months, from September 1772 to February 1773, and seem to have ended in stalemate.*]

'*St Vincent's Gazette, February 27, 1773.*

On Wednesday the 17th inst. a number of Charaibs came into the grand camp at Macaricau, and a treaty of peace and friendship was then concluded by his Excellency General Dalrymple, on the part of his Britannic Majesty, and by the chiefs of Grand Sable, Massiraca, Rabacca, Macaricau, Byera, Coubamarou, Jambou, Colonrie, Camacarabou, Ouarawarou, and Point Espagniol, for themselves, and the rest of their people.—The Articles of which treaty are as follow:

    I. All hostile proceedings to cease; a firm and lasting peace and friendship to succeed.

    II. The Charaibs shall acknowledge his Majesty to be the rightful sovereign of the island and domain of St Vincent's; take an oath of fidelity to him as their King; promise absolute submission to his will, and lay down their arms.

    III. They shall submit themselves to the laws and obedience of his Majesty's government, with power to the Governor to enact further regulations for the public advantage as shall be convenient. (This article only respects their transactions with his Majesty's subjects, not being Indians, their intercourse and customs with each other, in the quarters allotted to them not being affected by it.) And all new regulations to receive his Majesty's Governor's approbation before carried into execution.

IV. A portion of lands, hereafter mentioned, to be allotted for the residence of the Charaibs, viz. from the river Byera to Point Espagniol on the one side, and from the river Analibou to Point Espagniol on the other side, according to lines to be drawn by his Majesty's surveyors, from the sources of the rivers to the tops of the mountains; the rest of the lands, formerly inhabited by Charaibs, for the future to belong entirely to his Majesty.

V. Those lands not to be alienated, either by sale, lease or otherwise, but to persons properly authorized by his Majesty to receive them.

VI. Roads, ports, batteries, and communications to be made as his Majesty pleases.

VII. No undue intercourse with the French islands to be allowed.

VIII. Runaway slaves in the possession of the Charaibs are to be delivered up, and endeavours used to discover and apprehend the others; and an engagement, in future, not to encourage, receive, or harbour any slave whatever: forfeiture of lands for harbouring; and carrying off the island a capital crime.

IX. Persons guilty of capital crimes against the English are to be delivered up.

X. In time of danger to be aiding and assisting to his Majesty's subjects against their enemies.

XI. The three chains to remain to his Majesty.

XII. All conspiracies and plots against his Majesty, or his government, to be made known to his Governor, or other civil magistrates.

XIII. Leave (if required) to be given to the Charaibs to depart this island, with their families and properties, and assistance in their transportation.

XIV. Free access to the quarters allowed to the Charaibs, to be given to persons properly empowered in pursuit of runaway slaves, and safe conduct afforded them.

XV. Deserters from his Majesty's service (if any), and runaway slaves from the French, to be delivered up, in order that they may be returned to their masters.

XVI. The chiefs of the different quarters are to render an account of the names and number of the inhabitants of their respective districts.

XVII. The chiefs, and other Charaibs, inhabitants, to attend the Governor when required for his Majesty's service.

XVIII. All possible facility, consistent with the laws of Great Britain, to be afforded to the Charaibs in the sale of their produce, and in their trade to the different British islands.

XIX. Entire liberty of fishing, as well on the coast of St Vincent's, as at the neighbouring keys, to be allowed them.

XX. In all cases, when the Charaibs conceive themselves injured by his Majesty's other subjects, or other persons, and are desirous of having reference to the laws, or to the civil magistrates, an agent, being one of his Majesty's natural born subjects, may be employed by themselves, or if more agreeable at his Majesty's cost.

XXI. No strangers, or white persons, to be permitted to settle among the Charaibs, without permission obtained in writing from the Governor.

XXII. These articles subscribed to and observed, the Charaibs are to be pardoned, secured, and fixed in their property, according to his Majesty's directions given, and all past offences forgot.

XXIII. After the signing of this treaty, should any of the Charaibs refuse to observe the conditions of it, they are to be considered and treated as enemies by both parties, and the most effectual means used to reduce them.

XXIV. The Charaibs shall take the following oath, viz.

We A.B. do swear, in the name of the immortal God, and Christ Jesus, that we will bear true allegiance to his Majesty George the Third, of Great Britain, France, and Ireland, King, defender of the faith; and that we will pay due obedience to the laws of Great Britain, and the Island of St Vincent's; and will well and truly observe every article of the treaty concluded between his said Majesty and the Charaibs; and we do acknowledge, that his said Majesty is rightful Lord and Sovereign of all the Island of St Vincent's, and that the lands held by us the Charaibs, are granted through his Majesty's clemency.

On the part of his Majesty,

W. DALRYMPLE

On the part of the Charaibs.

Jean Baptiste.	Simon.
Dufont Begot.	Lalime, Senior.
Boyordell.	Baüamont.
Dirang.	Justin Baüamont.
Chatoyér.	Matthieu.
Doucre Baramont.	Jean Louis Pacquin.
Lalime, Junior.	Gadel Goibau.
Broca.	John Baptiste.
Saioe.	Lonen.
François Laron.	Boyüdon.
Saint Laron.	Du Vallet.
Anisette.	Boucharie.
Clement.	Deruba Babilliard.
Bigott.	Canaia.'

15. *Chatoyer the Chief of the Black Charaibes in St. Vincent with His Five Wives*. Engraved from a painting by Agostino Brunias (*c*.1770). In Bryan Edwards, *The History, Civil and Commercial, of the British Colonies in the West Indies* (John Stockdale: London, 1801), iii, opp. 179. The paintings and engravings of Agostino Brunias provide the most important visual documentation of European travellers' perceptions of Carib life on Dominica and St Vincent during the second half of the eighteenth century. Comparatively little is known about Brunias's years in the West Indies. He worked for Robert Adam in Rome in 1756–8 and was brought by Adam to England, where he lived for several years before making his way to Dominica in the early 1770s. He was clearly connected to Sir William Young (see No. 17), who owned many of Brunias's paintings, and in all probability travelled with Young to his Vincentian estates. Brunias returned to England in the mid-1770s and exhibited at the Royal Academy. He continued active until around 1810 (see Huth 1962). He made engravings from many of his paintings, and Bryan Edwards used four of these in his history of the British colonies in the West Indies. Plate 15 shows Chatoyer, most famous of the Black Carib chiefs, with five wives and attendants. Chatoyer's evident skills as warrior and diplomatist by turns fascinated and terrified the English settlers. His death, supposedly in a duel with an English militia colonel (see Plate 16), was a major blow to the Black Caribs during the hostilities of 1795. Plate 17 shows a scene of Black Carib family life, with valuable details of dress and accoutrement.

¶ [*Young proceeds to an account of the period of French occupation, begun in 1778 with the connivance of the Caribs, still sympathetic to their old friends. He now moves from quoting from his father's papers to speaking from his personal experience. The Carib chief Chatoyer moves centre-stage, finally dying in the battle that marked the beginning of the second Carib War, only a few months before Young made his compilation. The* Account *builds to its dramatic conclusion, to which Young's narrative has irrevocably been leading.*]

In the year 1780, a most dreadful hurricane laid waste the whole island of St Vincent's: every cane was torn up from the ground—every building was laid low—every property was destroyed. The British planters labouring for the sustenance of themselves and Negroes, and for restoration of their estates from the effects of this dreadful calamity, had in their season of poverty and depression some respite from rapacity, and a more than ordinary plea to protection from a benevolent conqueror; and that protection, to those engrossed by the ruin of their fortunes, and of but ordinary sagacity and foresight, covered the evil spirit and malignity of *those* whom it checked, and controlled from overt acts of violence. It remained for time to develope general character, from partial and successive instances. It was not easy to persuade an honest Englishman that an entire nation could be perfidious and cruel. He could admit no such opinion from mere circumstances; he was doomed to adopt it from fatal experience. Myself with others have been deceived.

In 1783, by treaty of peace with France, the island of St Vincent's was restored to the crown of Great Britain, and therewith the Charaibs returned to its dominion, without any specification of conditions, on which they were so returned.

Let the conduct of the British Government be reviewed on this occasion. Did it raise the sword of justice? or did it even implead its laws of forfeiture? did it enforce one penalty on the treasons of the Charaibs? No!—it did not: it treated them as an ignorant and deluded people, whose conduct needed compassion rather than pardon; and who were to be acquitted (as by a jury on insanity) in humane consideration of weakness and of folly. A veil was thrown over the whole scene of perfidy; and the offended spirit of Government professed in its lenity to forget, what in its constitutional justice it might not dare to forgive.

Let the conduct of the British planters in St Vincent's be revised too on this occasion—Did they act with a vindictive spirit of retaliation? did they show a temper of resentment? did they show even an indifference of regard? No!—they returned good for evil, and treated the Charaibs with a benevolent attention, and with bounties; by which even their best services in the late war would have been amply repaid.

I pass by instances of courtesy and private hospitality; but some of a more general tendency should be noticed.

Hereditary feuds and animosities existed amongst many of the Charaib families, which, though ever laid aside in times of general war, and against a common enemy, were as constantly resumed in times of peace;—*pristina mala postquàm foris deerant, domi quærere*, belongs to this people, in common with others, and with the greater nation described by Livy.

Whilst the French possessed the island of St Vincent's, many of the weaker parties had fled the Charaib boundary, and settled on English estates in the neighbourhood. The English, when again in power, not only on application permitted them to remain on their lands, rent-free, and without conditional service, but gave them every assistance; and their canoes being of use in shipping articles of the estates, they engaged them on the most liberal terms, and which allowed to each Charaib a Spanish dollar for the day.

In the town of Kingston a marked attention was shewn to the Charaibs who brought articles for sale; I should say rather Charaib women, who, laden like beasts of burden, were driven with the flat of the broad sword from the Charaib boundary, fifteen miles, to the English market. No slavery is equally wretched with that of the Charaib women; but no better proof can be stated of the satisfaction given in this respect, than the increased numbers of these women, and their lordly drivers, resorting progressively to the English market.

The chief Chatoyér, with his brother Du Vallée, were assisted by loans or sureties of English gentlemen, enabling them to clear and cultivate a larger portion of lands; and each of them by these means had purchased slaves, and was comparatively rich.

The beautiful garden island near Calliaqua, called Young Island, with a convenient villa built on it, was by the proprietor allowed for the Charaibs to refresh, or sleep upon, going to, or returning from Kingston; and occasionally as a station for their fisheries.

The chief Chatoyér and his family, or tribe, in particular, received the most flattering attentions and hospitality from that gentleman and his family: himself and people had ever accommodation at the house, and on the estate of Calliaqua; and when Chatoyér fell, in March 1795, fighting against the English on Dorsetshire Hill, his hand grasped a silver-mounted broad sword, engraved with the arms of that family, and valued as a memorial of the gallant Lieutenant Henry Young, of the 62d regiment, who fell with it in his hand at Saratoga, and which would never have been given by his brother to Chatoyér, but on the faith of his employing it in loyal service to the King, and (as he promised) in particular defence of the family and its interests.

To enumerate further acts of conciliation, and of bounty towards the Charaibs, would extend this Essay beyond its original design. How far they were vain and nugatory, will appear from an anecdote too remarkable, and too strongly noting a rooted and envenomed antipathy to the English, to be here omitted.

Soon after the treaty in 1773, Captain Gordon, with consent of the family, which was of considerable influence and note, took a Charaib boy, of the name of Peter, into his house, and with intent to educate him, and engage him in his service. Peter Gordon (for so the boy was thenceforward named) accompanied his patron and kind master to England, and afterwards, on that officer being called to Gibraltar, served with him during the whole of the memorable siege of that fortress.

From what accident, or from what motives I am not informed, but in the beginning of the year 1788 Peter Gordon returned to St Vincent's, and immediately joined his family in the Charaib district.

Peter had left St Vincent's too young to have imbibed his country's prejudices, and having been treated with the greatest kindness by his late master, and having been a social favourite with the brave soldiery at Gibraltar, he truly loved the English; and he would with earnest gratitude talk to his countrymen of their good faith and kindness, and of their power and wealth in London, and of their valour at Gibraltar. A character of disciplined bravery, a mind enlightened by European intercourse and travel, and a natural eloquence, gave him an ascendancy with his tribe; and become the British advocate with his countrymen, he had shewn an influence, occasionally, conducive to the peace of the colony, and to the interests of Government. The legislature of St Vincent's in honourable retribution, voted a reward to the Charaib, Peter Gordon—that vote was the warrant of Peter's death! Soon after going on the sea with a numerous party of Charaibs, they reported, on their return, that Peter Gordon's canoe was sunk, and himself drowned. Of a large fleet of canoes, none other but that of Peter Gordon's was sunk:—*and why was not Peter Gordon saved?* It is not easy to suppose that a Charaib, who swims readily as he walks, should be drowned with any one canoe in sight!

A retrospect to this and to many past circumstances, might well render the inhabitants of St Vincent's not wholly unprepared for the consequences of another war with France.

As soon as intelligence arrived in March 1793, of the French declaration of hostilities, the governor of St Vincent's called together his council, and took every precaution to prevent communications with Martinique, and to secure the fidelity of the Charaibs. The chiefs were invited to meet the governor and council at Kingston, and a feast was on the occasion given them at the public expense. Their treaty of 1773 was then article by article recapitulated to them; compensation offered them for any tobacco or other articles they proposed selling at Martinique; and their grievances inquired into, which reduced to a single instance of trespass in the cutting some wood on the lands of Chatoyér, the attorney-general, Mr Keane was ordered to prosecute, and Chatoyér received forty pounds damages.

There were more than one of these feasts and conferences, and the Charaibs returned home from each with every assurance of peaceable conduct, and of fidelity to their engagements.

The expeditions from Great Britain in 1793, and the very superior force by sea and land throughout the West Indies the following year, for a time kept all quiet in St Vincent's.

The Charaibs, awed and depressed by the view of the British force, assumed a mien and language well suited to lull the caution of the wisest, who were not acquainted with the perfidy of their character; and even those who knew them best, were so inclined to hope for their reformation, that prudence nearly gave way; and but for the alarm-bell which sounded from Grenada on the 5th of March, 1795, it is probable St Vincent's might have been taken by surprise, and in the result (now authenticated) every English subject, even to the child at the breast, was to have been murdered, and our nation been extirpated from the island.

On the 5th of March the intelligence from Grenada induced the Governor of St Vincent's to call out the militia, and to declare martial law.

Different persons were sent round to address the Charaibs, and sound their intentions on subject of the alarm. The answer given by the Charaibs at Massaricau is remarkable, its accuracy cannot be doubted, being taken from the narrative published in St Vincent's under the respectable authority of D. Ottley, and H. Sharpe, Esquires.

The spokesmen of the Charaibs—'expressed their astonishment at the suspicions entertained against them: they had been already once deceived by the French, and pardoned by us for their misconduct during the last war: since the peace they had been treated with the utmost kindness and humanity. They in particular residing within the boundary, had been protected against their enemies in the Charaib country! had been allowed to live on the lands of the English, and to occupy as much as was necessary for their support, without paying rent, or receiving molestation: no possible advantage could be derived by their making war against us, and no pardon expected if they should attempt it: they could not answer for the conduct of the Grand Sable Charaibs, but they had received no intimation from them of an intention to disturb the peace of the colony.'

The reader who has attended to the very peculiar system of Charaib perfidy, noted in former pages of this Essay, will not be surprised to find, in continuance of this quotation, that three days after,—'These very men *were the foremost* in the attack upon the inhabitants of the plantation where the conversation had passed, and where they had lived, and had been encouraged and supported for ten years past.'

It is further remarkable, that on Sunday, March 8th (only two days before the general attack), a more than ordinary number of Charaibs crowded to Kingston market with different articles for sale, and assumed a more than common air of social ease and festivity.

Unhappily this conduct, and these circumstances, produced a confidence fatal to many; yet let not indolence or presumption be too hastily imputed to the unhappy victims; the attack was so unprovoked, the ravage so unprofitable, the barbarity so excessive, that to entertain a previous suspicion of it, in its full extent, was not within the computation of every good mind; and some might think to avert the ruin of their fortunes by remaining on their estates; and pleading to those whom they had benefited, to incur at least no personal hazard.

On the 10th of March, 1795, and following days, the Charaibs from different quarters made incursions like a torrent of fire into the settlements of the English; the canes, ripe throughout the land, nourished the conflagration, the Negroes fled their huts, moaning for their murdered fellows, and the route of the savage hord was literally marked out by a line of flame and massacre.

I will not expatiate on instances of cruelty in this dreadful career from the Charaib boundary to Dorsetshire Hill, where it received its check from British valour: the following proclamation found in the pocket of the chief Chatoyér, who there, on the 14th of March, fell by the bayonet of the brave Major Leith of the St Vincent's militia, will fully declare the purpose of this attack; and that purpose was but too faithfully executed in rapine and in murder, as far as occasion offered.

'Copy of the declaration of Joseph Chatoyér, chief of the Charaibs

Chateau-bellair, the 12th day of March,
and the 1st year of our Liberty.

Where is the Frenchman who will not join his brothers, at a moment when the voice of liberty is heard by them? Let us then unite, citizens and brothers, round the colours flying in this island; and let us hasten to co-operate to that great piece of work which has been already commenced so gloriously. But should any timorous men still exist, should any Frenchman be held back through fear, we do hereby declare to them, in the name of the law, that those who will not be assembled with us in the course of the day, shall be deemed traitors to the country, and treated as enemies. We do swear that both fire and sword shall be employed against them, that we are going to burn their estates, and that we will murder their wives and children, in order to annihilate their race.'

The dreadful and atrocious purpose of general massacre declared in this proclamation, and 'that those French who resist the invitation shall be treated *as enemies* (that is *as English*), their estates burnt, and themselves, wives, and children, murdered', cannot but, as it excites horror, arrest the chief attention— But let me call that attention to another point of view; to the language of a Charaib chief, under French nomination and authority, commanding an united army of French and Charaibs, and in direct terms calling on those French, *as brothers and as countrymen*, who themselves, or their fathers, in 1765, received their estates, and the liberties and rights of Englishmen, from the bounty of the King of Great Britain.

I have avoided in disgust, all details of massacre; they would fill a long and melancholy page; and the list of unfeeling and unprovoked slaughters might be closed with the last act of the savage life of Chatoyér; who, on his arrival at Dorsetshire Hill, had three prisoners brought forth (a blacksmith and two other English, whom he had taken unarmed some days before at Chatteaubellair), and himself hewed them to pieces, in wanton trial of the British sword which

16. The tombstone of Alexander Leith, Anglican Cathedral, Kingstown, St Vincent. Photograph by Peter Hulme. Col. Alexander Leith was credited with the death of the formidable Black Carib chief Chatoyer (Chattawae), and his own death, soon afterwards, was marked by this tombstone in the cathedral. Chatoyer had to wait rather longer for a memorial, a plain stele which was erected in 1985 on Dorsetshire Hill, near where he died. Chatoyer is now one of St Vincent's national heroes.

17. *A Family of Charaibes Drawn from the Life in the Island of St Vincent.* Engraved from a painting by Agostino Brunias (*c.*1770; see Plate 15). In Bryan Edwards, *The History, Civil and Commercial, of the British Colonies in the West Indies* (John Stockdale: London, 1794), i, opp. 391.

had been given him, and with a cruel art (as represented by a Negroe present), which protracted the agonies of death to half an hour.*

One further circumstance it is necessary to mention, and place in its true light: when it is told, that on the irruption into the plantations, Mr Forbes was murdered, and his wife spared, and afterwards returned in exchange for a Charaib prisoner, it is to be remembered, that Mrs Forbes was a catholic, was educated at Martinique, and speaking French as a French woman, was probably supposed to be one, and may have owed her life to that circumstance.

A detail of military operations enters not into the design of this Essay.

Thanks to Almighty God!—we have *now* intelligence, that by the bravery of his Majesty's troops, aided by the loyal and gallant militia of St Vincent's, and by their faithful Negroes in arms, after four months severe conflict, the French force had been subdued and wholly destroyed; and the Charaibs driven back to their woods.

In open war, and prepared with arms in their hands, I doubt not the loyal and brave planters, with proper military aid, continuing to retain, for their King and country, the sovereignty of St Vincent's.

But they cannot in peace set down to restore their ravaged estates;—their resources are gone,—their credit with British merchants is lost, whilst the Charaibs remain in the island, at pleasure to destroy,—and *whose forebearance can never more be trusted.*

And now, to sum up the inference of this short but eventful history of thirty years!

Sad and fatal experience has shewn that the combination of barbarous and of national enmity is not to be broken, and that the Charaib will ever be French.

Were peace with France to be proclaimed at this very hour, yet a foresight of destruction to every property on so ordinary a contingency as another war, must sicken all industry, and preclude all loans and commercial credit.

But even the interval, ere hostilities may again commence, is a season of danger to the British planter.

In the very sense of his past outrages, the Charaib will embitter his mind with stronger animosities, and satiate his antipathy with secret mischiefs.

The perpetrator of unprovoked wrongs forgives not the sufferer; him whom he hath wantonly attacked, he will maliciously persecute: the planter has to fear that his canes will be burnt in the night, and himself or his child shot from behind the bush.

It is the protection of laws which, in securing property, gives life to industry;

---

* Chatoyér reviled these unhappy victims, and the English nation, at each blow of the sabre, in exactly the same manner the Saracen Argante used the sword given by a Christian chief, as described by Tasso. When attacking the Christians, Argante exclaimed:—'Questa sanguigna spada è quella stessa | Ch'il signor vostro mi donò pur ieri; | Ditegli come in uso oggi l'ho messa, | Ch'udirà la novella ei volontieri, | E caro esser gli dee, che'l suo bel dono | S' è conosciuto al paragon sì buono; | Ditegli che vederne omai s'aspetti | Nelle viscere sue più certa prova; | E quando d'assalirne ei non s'affretti, | Verrò non aspettato ov'ei si trova.' Thanks to Major Leith, the donor of the British sword has no more to apprehend from the Charaib Argante.

no one will labour the field, if all may take the crop, or (what is the same), if any may *destroy it.*

Other considerations must operate yet more forcibly than those of property.

A national antipathy, aggravated by savage manners and disposition, is too terrible in neighbourhood to the father of an English family.

The participation of a small district hemmed in by the seas, with a people whom law can never reach, and of savage manners, must be ever dangerous; and if they have antipathies to us, founded in attachments to our enemy, *must in the end be fatal.*

What bold adventurer will *now* plant a cane?—or who will *now* hazard his wife or child, where the cruel and perfidious Charaib may prowl at pleasure?

These truths are so powerfully urged by late events, that without inter-position of the strong hand of Government, it is to be feared that the most healthy, rich, and beautiful islands of St Vincent's may, to all intents of national advantage, be lost to the crown of Great Britain

Mere regulations respecting the Charaib can no longer be deemed effectual.

Laws cannot reach them in their woods.

The British planters can no more trust to professions.

The nation can have no further confidence in treaty.

Under all these circumstances and considerations, the Council and Assembly of St Vincent's, in the instructions to their agent in London, declare the sole alternative to be,—

'That the British planters, or the Black Charaibs, must be removed from off the island of St Vincent's.'

18. *William Young's Tour of the Islands (1791)*

¶ *In 1791, before the beginning of the second Carib War, William Young visited the estates he had inherited in the West Indies and wrote an account of his travels,* A Tour through the Several Islands of Barbadoes, St Vincent, Antigua, Tobago, and Grenada, in the Years 1791, and 1792, *which remained unpublished for ten years. After a decade of constant ferment in the Caribbean, a new edition appeared of Bryan Edwards's* An Historical Survey of the Island of Saint Domingo (*which had been originally published in 1797*), *to which had been added as an appendix Young's* Tour through the Windward Islands. *A prefatory note by Bryan Edwards explains that these extracts are 'by favour of Sir William Young, transcribed literally from a rough journal, in which he entered such observations as occurred to him from the impressions of the moment. They may be considered therefore as a picture drawn from the life; and the reader must be a bad judge of human nature, and have a very indifferent taste, who does not perceive that it is faithfully drawn, and by the hand of a master.' This book also appeared as a new third volume of a new edition in 1801 of Edwards's* History of the British Colonies in the West Indies (*first published in two volumes in 1793*). *This third volume is the source of the extracts which follow. In 1807 Young was appointed governor of Tobago, a post he held at his death, on that island, in 1815.*

By 1795, when he compiled his father's papers (No. 17), the situation on St Vincent was reaching the climax that Alexander Anderson will describe in the next extract (No. 19). In 1791, when William Young undertook this tour, an uneasy peace still held. Four years of French occupation had ended in 1784, and the English planters were busy expanding their sugar works at the expense of both Carib and French smallholders. But it was not until 1793, when war broke out between Britain and France, that a further uprising became almost inevitable. Consequently, the tone here is domestic, almost pastoral, untinged by the retrospective hatred for the Caribs which taints many settler accounts of this period of Caribbean history.

[St Vincent] Friday 23 [December 1791].

This morning I passed an hour or more, observing the process of sugar making in the boiling house. Of the best cane juice, a gallon of liquor gives one lb. of sugar; of the middling-rich, 20 gallons give 16 lbs.; of the watery canes, 24 gallons give 16 lbs.

This afternoon ANSELM, chief of the Charaibes in the quarter of Morne-Young, and BRUNAU, chief of Grand Sable, at the head of about twenty, came into the parlour after dinner, and laid a *don d'amitié* at my feet of Charaibe baskets, and of fowls and pine apples. We treated them with *wine*, and afterwards about a dozen of their ladies were introduced, who preferred *rum*. I had much courteous conversation with Anselm, accepted a basket, and a couple of pines, and bought some baskets of the other Charaibes. They were all invited to sleep on the estate, and a keg of rum was ordered in return for Anselm's present, and for Brunau's, &c.

LA LIME, one of the chiefs who had signed the treaty in 1773, and a dozen others, had before visited me at different times, but this was a formal address of ceremony, and all in their best attire, that is, the men, and perhaps the women too, for though they had no cloaths, saving a petticoat resembling two children's pocket handkerchiefs sewed at the corners, and hanging one before and one behind, yet they had their faces painted red, pins through their under lips, and bracelets; and about their ancles strings of leather and beads.

December 25 [...]

This day, and almost every day, I had many Charaibe visitors tendering presents. I laid down a rule to receive no presents but from the chiefs, for the person presenting expects double the value in return, and the Charaibes are too numerous for a general dealing on such terms either with views to privacy or economy. I should not omit that yesterday morning the chiefs, Anselm and Brunau, who had visited me the evening before, came to see me, and politely having observed that they would not intermingle, in their first visit of congratulation, on my coming to St Vincent's, any matter of another nature, proceeded to demand *quelles nouvelles de la France*, and then *quelles nouvelles de l'Angleterre*; and thus proceeded gradually to open the tendency of the question, as relating to the designs of government touching themselves. It seems that for some persons of this colony, travelling into their country, and looking over the delightful plains of Grand Sable from Morne Young, had exclaimed, '*what a pity this country yet belongs to the savage Charaibes!*' and this kind of language repeated among them, had awakened jealousies and apprehensions, and some French discontented fugitives from Martinico and elsewhere had (as had been heard from the Charaibes at Kingston) given a rumour that I was come out with some project for dispossessing them by the English government. To remove these jealousies, I told them, 'That private a man as I was, and come merely to look at my estate, and settle my private affairs, I would venture, on personal knowledge of the minister, and character of our common king, and unalterable

211

principles of our government, to assure them, that whilst they continued their allegiance, and adhered to the terms of the treaty of 1773, no one dare touch their lands, and that Grand Sable was as safe to them as was Calliaqua to me: it was treason to suppose that the king would not keep his word, according to the conditions of that treaty; and if any subjects ventured to trespass on them, they would, on proper representations, be punished. For myself, I assumed a mien of anger, that they should forget their national principle in exception of me. If friendships and enmities descended from father to son, they must know me for their steadiest friend, and incapable of any injustice towards them.' They seemed very much pleased with this sort of language, and assured me of their strongest regard and confidence, and would hear no more lies or tales to the prejudice of myself, or of the designs of government. They invited me to come and taste their hospitality, and I promised to do so, and we parted as I could with—the best friends in the world. [. . .]

Friday, January 13, 1792.

The Charaibe chief of all, *Chatoyer*, with his brother *du Vallee*, and six of their sons, came to pay me a visit, and brought their presents; a stool of Charaibe workmanship, and a very large cock turkey of the wild breed, which with a hen I mean for England. Chatoyer and du Vallee were well dressed; as a mark of respect, they came without arms. We had much conversation with them, and I gave in return a silver mounted hanger to Chatoyer, and a powder horn to du Vallee. The latter is possessed of nine negro slaves, and has a cotton plantation. He is the most enlightened of the Charaibes, and may be termed the founder of civilization among them. Chatoyer and his sons dined at the villa, and drank each a bottle of claret. In the evening they departed in high glee, with many expressions of friendship. [. . .]

[Tobago] Sunday, March 15.

Early in the morning set out, and in the afternoon reached the *Louis d'or* estate. Twenty-two miles from Port Louis, from the very point of the Town of Port Louis, the country becomes hilly; and as you further advance, the hills rise into mountains not broken and rugged, as the convulsed country of St Vincent's, but regular though steep, and on a large scale of regular ascent and descent. The scene of nature is on an extensive scale, and gives the idea of a continent rather than an island. It is not alone its vicinity to the Spanish main that suggests this idea. The appearance of the island fully warrants the assumption, and the contiguity of South America, only more fully marks its being torn therefrom, and of its being, in old times, the southern point or bold promontory of the vast bay of Mexico.

Friday, March 16.

This day I rode over my estate; but previous to any remarks thereon, I must notice the radical words and languages of the Indian red Charaibe (Louis). There are three families of red Charaibes, settled in a corner of my Louis d'or estate, and their history is briefly this.—Louis was five years old when his father and family fled (about fifty years past) from the persecutions of the Africans or black Charaibes of St Vincent's. The family has since divided into three distinct ones, by increase of numbers. Louis the chief, is a very sensible man, and in his traffick for fish and other articles, has obtained some knowledge of the French language.

The following words I took from sound, and with accuracy; for on reading over the Charaibe words to Louis, he repeated them back in French to me.

God—naketi i.e. *Grandmere*	Wind—cazabal	Father—baba
The Sun—vèhu	Rain—conob	Mother—behee
Moon—mòné	Thunder—warawi arow	Son—wica
Earth—hoang	Mountain—wieb	Daughter—hania
Sea—balané	Tree—wewee	Life—nee
Fire—wat-ho'	Bird—fuss	Death—hela 'hal
Water—tona	Fish—oto'	Devil—qualeva

I interrogated Louis as to religion: he is now a catholic, but says the Charaibe belief was always in a future state.—Formerly, they used to bury the defunct *sitting*, with his bow, arrows, &c. 'But now', says Louis, 'we bury *au long et "droit"*, which is better; for when sitting, the body got *re treci* (this was his expression) and could not easily start up and fly to heaven, but being buried *long and strait*, it can fly up directly when called.' This argument was possibly suggested by the catholic missionaries, to make the poor Charaibes leave the old practice. Louis's belief in a future state is however ascertained. [...]

[Grenada] Tuesday, March 27.

Louis la Granade, chief of the Gens decouleur, and captain of a militia company, came to the government house. He seems a fine spirited, athletic fellow, and wears a large gold medal about his neck, being a gift from the colony, in reward for his various services and experienced fidelity on all occasions. The mulattoes have presented a most loyal address to the governor, stating their strong attachment to the King and the British constitution, and their abhorrence of all innovation.

Friday, 29.

At ten in the morning we sailed from Grenada in the Fanfan schooner, coasted the leeward side of the island from south to north; it seems well peopled, and in general it appears to be a rich sugar country; with less variety of ground indeed than St Vincent's and less verdure. Its mountains are but hills in comparison with those of St Vincent. A waving surface, hills gently rising and falling, characterize Grenada. Deep vallies shaded with abrupt precipices characterize St Vincent's.

[St Vincent] Saturday, March 30.

At three in the morning anchored in Kingston-bay, St Vincent's, and thence rode to the villa. From Grenada to St Vincent's, our schooner hugg'd the land of the Grenadines under their leeward side, with very small intervals of channel. The Grenadine isles and detached rocks, are supposed to be about 120 in number. Twelve of these little isles are said to produce cotton.

April 19.

Had much conversation this day about the Charaibes.

The windward estates, quite to the Charaibe boundary of Bayaraw, are of the richest land in the island, but the surf on the shore is at all times so heavy, that no European vessel can continue on any part twenty-four hours with safety, and no European boat can come on shore without the danger of being swamped. Hence, until lately, the supposed impracticability of landing stores and taking off sugars, prevented the cultivation of the lands; but since the Charaibes in their canoes, have been found to accomplish what Europeans cannot effect with their boats, these lands have risen to £60 sterling an acre, and every settler is growing rich. A sloop lays off and on as near as she may to the shore, and in one morning, from day-break to noon, a canoe manned by ten Charaibes, will make forty trips to the sloop, carrying each time a hogshead of sugar, &c. &c. and the expence for the morning amounts to ten dollars, being a dollar for each Charaibe.—The Charaibes thus begin to taste of money, and are already become very industrious at this work. Moreover, they plant tobacco, and want nothing but a market to encourage them to plant more. Chatoyer's brother (Du Vallee) has nine negroes, and plants cotton. Money civilizes in the first instance, as it corrupts in the last; the savage labouring for himself, soon ceases to be a savage; the slave to money becomes a subject to government, and he becomes a useful subject.*

Mr B. acting collector of the customs, informed me, that the value of British manufacturers exported from St Vincent to the Spanish and French settlements, was upwards of £200,000 annually. From the superior advantages of Grenada, with respect to situation, &c. the export trade of that island to the Spanish main, must be much more considerable. That of Jamaica out of comparison

* This must be admitted with some limitation. Before a negro places such a value on money as is here supposed, he must have acquired many of the refinements and artificial necessities of civilized life. He must have found uses for money, which, in his savage state, he had no conception of. It is not therefore the possession of money alone; it is the new desires springing up in his mind, from the prospects and examples before him, that have awakened his powers, and called the energies of his mind into action. I have thought it necessary to observe thus much, because the doctrine of my amiable friend, without some qualification, seems to sanctify an assertion which has been maintained by speculative writers, with some plausibility; namely, 'that if the negro slaves were allowed wages for their labour, coercion would become unnecessary'. What effect a system of gradual encouragement, by means of wages, operating slowly and progressively, might produce in a long course of time, I will not presume to say; but I am persuaded that an attempt to introduce such a system among the labouring negroes in general, without great caution and due preparation, would be productive of the greatest of evils.

greater. These circumstances are to be taken into general account, of the importance of the West India Islands to Great Britain.

April 24.

Went on board a Guinea ship, the Active, from Sierra Leone. On board this ship is a black boy, called Bunc, about ten years old, the son of an African chief; he is going to England for his education, and has two slaves sent with him by his father, to pay his passage by their sale. Captain Williams has another boy on board, who was sent to England two years ago for the same purpose. This voyage he was to take him back to Annamaboe; but the boy absolutely refused landing again in Africa, and he waits on Captain Williams as a free servant, and is going back to England with him. The slaves were in high health; Captain Williams is a superior man in this trade; as a fundamental trait of his character, I notice, that last year (1791) on receiving the parliamentary bounty for the good condition in which his people arrived, he gave out of his own pocket £50 as a gratuity to the surgeon of his ship.

Monday, April 30.

This day Dufond, Chatoyer's brother, and next to him in authority, particularly on the Grand Sable side of the country, made me a visit: he had been twice before when I was absent in other islands, and on his first visit had left his own bow and arrows for me. I gave him in return a pair of handsome brass barrelled pistols. He seems a very polite and sensible man, and speaks good French.

May 8.

Embarked on board the Delaford, and at 5 P.M. sailed for England.

19. *Alexander Anderson and the Carib War in St Vincent (c.1798)*

¶ *Many accounts of European contacts with the Caribs during the latter part of the eighteenth century are written from the inevitably very partial perspectives of either the planters—who wanted Carib land—or the colonial officials—for whom the Caribs were a 'problem'.* Alexander Anderson's Geography and History of the Island of St Vincent, *written in the late 1790s but only published for the first time in 1983, is for this and other reasons an especially valuable record of a time of turmoil in the Caribbean.*

Anderson (1748–1811) was by training a botanist. Educated at Edinburgh University, he worked at the Apothecaries' Garden in Chelsea before sailing to New York in 1774 to stay with his brother. He fled from the colonial revolution to Surinam, but was taken prisoner off Martinique by a privateer. Freed to St Lucia he found what he thought was the West Indian version of Peruvian bark, a source of quinine. This brought him to the attention of Sir Joseph Banks, and when St Vincent was freed from French occupation in 1784, Anderson was chosen to take over the management of the botanic garden.

The extract that follows is in three parts. The first deals with the Carib–French relationships, at this time closer and warmer than those between the Caribs and the English: Anderson is critical of the English planters' blinkered attitude to the islands' native inhabitants and to the powerful Black Carib group that had established itself on the windward coast. This improvidence is seen as a cause of the war that followed. The second extract details the influx of French Revolutionary ideas into the Caribbean, especially through the person of Victor Hugues. The abolition of slavery on the French islands was obviously seen as a dangerous precedent by the British, though again Anderson has critical words about English 'inattention and self-security'. The last extract details some of the events of the war that broke out in March 1795, and ends with a defence of British treatment of the deported Caribs, though Anderson admits that nearly half of the 5,200 removed to the island of Balliceaux died before the final deportation to Central America.

Anderson's manuscript is in the possession of the Linnean Society, London. It was transcribed by Richard A. and Elizabeth S. Howard, who modernized capitalization and punctuation, and published in 1983. We print that transcription with minor alterations made after consulting the manuscript.

During six years the French were masters of the island, the Carribs had constructed a number of large canoes, many of them capable of carrying from 30 to 40 men. With these they had constant and regular traffic with the French islands, and even as far as Trinidad, bartering their commercial articles for arms, ammunition and trifling bagatelles of dress. This trade it undoubtedly was wise policy in the French to encourage as much as possible. It attached these savages more closely to their interest and increased their hatred to the English. But no attempt was made ever to intercept or stop this connection. At that time they cultivated a considerable quantity of tobacco, which was more esteemed than that of any other country, the greater part of which was carried to Martinico and manufactured into the well-known Macuba snuff. These traffic and connections with the English inhabitants were trifling in respect to what they had with the French islands, which daily increased. Seldom any of their chiefs or principal men came to Kingstown, to such a height had their aversion to the English become. Although they knew the language so as to speak it equally well as the French, they would use only the last to the English. So little acquainted were the inhabitants with strength or transactions of this people within their territory that few Englishmen in the island know the surface of the earth within their bounds farther than Mt. Young, a few only out of curiosity ever attempted to go as far as it, or the farthest, Grand Sable. They made presents of rum or something else as a present for that permission. These [and] many other impolitic steps naturally led these savages to conceive that the English were afraid of them, consequently made them more bold and insolent, and so far had these ideas operated that an Englishman could not set his foot beyond the boundary without permission of the nearest chief, and then surrounded by an armed party, that at last none except some who lived near the boundary and were acquainted [with] their chiefs, making frequent presents of sugar and rum, would venture among them.

Notwithstanding this situation of affairs on the windward side of the island, the planters set themselves down in self-security, clearing, planting and building on to the very boundary, John Bull-like, thinking of no interruption to the calm until the storm bursts upon him, the too general prevailing idea with West Indians interest for the present moment only, without any regard for the future. Possessing a fertile soil which amply repaid their labour and expense, they dreamed of no accident or danger, the only object who should have the

217

most land in canes and send the greatest number of hogsheads of sugar to market, forgetting they were surrounded with mortal enemies who viewed their prosperity with chagrin and jealousy, from their long possession, regarding every foot of land the planter cleared as intrusion on their property, only waiting and anxiously wishing the favorable moment to be ended by their allies for extermination of the English name. Their hopes were founded on their own observation and knowledge of the English that in the hour of prosperity they make no provision for the moment of danger, as great part of the island (windward side) was in long possession of the Carribs when the planters began to cultivate it, they abandoning it with great reluctance, from attachment to the part they had long resided in [and were] born upon. Numbers of them never went beyond Byera but moved back into the woods behind the English and formed new settlements. Several families were drove off by force from spots the planter wanted for his works or cane land. This was sometimes done imprudently by burning their houses.

Instead of these harsh measures, it is more than probable that trifling presents and fair words would have accomplished the ends, or had they been left a short time until they had got their crops of ground provisions off, there is little doubt but they would have moved off of themselves and with their brethren formed new abodes in the woods. It may be a query if allowing these families who wished to remain among the English a small spot of ground as their own property, if it would not have been politic and wise, as many tribes of them might and probably [would] have detached themselves from their brethren and united themselves to the English interest. Such procedures might have averted the awful consequences that happened. Altho' they could claim no title or right to the lands, yet with the savage as well as with the civilized, long possession gives the idea of a claim—at any rate, hard measures should not have been used. For whatever a savage conceives as an injury or insult to him is never forgot; revenge is nursed in his breast until he has the opportunity of taking it. Had the treaty of peace been enforced as it ought to have been, and proper subordination over all their countrymen, such procedure would have been proper, as it would have shown them they were subjects to the British government, under which every man was to have his own, but no intrusion on another's property. The scheme I have mentioned would have little curtailed the cultivable land of the planters. One of the greatest errors in planters' life is planting more canes than they have negroes and mules to manufacture them. Besides, domesticated Carribs would have been useful, as those who remained among them proved to be to the planters in shipping their sugars on that boisterous, rocky coast, nor at first could it have [been] accomplished without them. Until taught by them, the negroes had not the hardness nor address to perform it. Instances may be produced against the policy, I maintain, in several families of Carribs who remained among the English inhabitants without molestation and yet were ring leaders in the rebellion. It is true and I will grant it, particularly among Mariqua, but these families were never put on the footing

I mention, but driven from spot to spot as the land became useful to the planter. They had no settled residence nor depend on one for a month.

The second remote cause that operated for the destruction of the colony was the criminal neglect in not attempting to civilize and instruct them in the principles of the Christian religion. It is certainly a reflection on those whose duty it was not to have used the means of instructing them and conveying to them some moral and religious information. Letting them remain in the state of ignorance and barbarism was reserving them as a lasting scourge to the island. Had they been sensible of the moral and religious ties which bind civilized nations, St Vincent would not have presented the melancholy spectacle it did in 1795 and '96. That their children are susceptible of education and improvement, as those of other people, cannot admit of a doubt. We well know that all the difference between civilization and barbarism is from education and example entirely. To maintain that some tribes of men are fitted by nature for the improvement of their mental faculties, and others not, is as repugnant to the omnipotent Creator as it is to common sense and experiment. We know the most enlightened nations of Europe at this day were some hundred years ago in a state of the grossest barbarism, and other nations, from science spread through the earth at present in intellectual knowledge, but little removed from the savage. But let us for a moment lay aside the idea of religion and our duty to communicate either it or any moral instruction to our fellow creatures and for argument's sake suppose ourselves infidels. Would not policy point it out to us as rational not to divest our independents of it? or in other words, to have them savages. If not, where is the coercion to them from murdering us or setting our houses on fire, if they can? if by that means they can acquire full liberty to their natural propensities. The savage knows the laws of nature for his own interest and preservation and those under which his tribe avenges from tradition and the protection of his wife and children. What can he know more? He can commit no crime if he complies with these, or can he with justice be punished for transgressing the civil laws of his neighbour when he knows not what civilization is nor sensible of a crime by the transgression? And whatever bounds may be set him, he can conceive himself under no laws or obligations to them but those handed down by his ancestors and of simple nature. [. . .]

To what I have said of St Vincent it may seem necessary to give a cursory sketch of the immediate causes which produced the horrid devastations and massacres which commenced on the tenth of March, 1795. The remote causes have been already mentioned—at that period a new combination of events matured the infernal story, formed plans for the destruction of the English inhabitants. That the situation of the island was singular pointed out the easy accomplishment of their schemes. The number of English inhabitants capable of bearing arms were scarcely 300 of all descriptions. There were at least as many French white men, exclusive of mulattoes and freed negroes associated with them. (For six months previous a number of French from the French islands had clandestinely come to the island, secreted themselves with the Carribs and their countrymen, and many settled themselves in the woods behind the English. Altho' many of this description were observed by many of the inhabitants and made reports of them, but no attention was paid to the reporters, but rather treated with contempt.) At this time, from some dispute or misunderstanding among the members of the colonial assembly, it misfortunately was dissolved, nor was there time to call a new assembly together, and appeared that an untoward fatality attended the unhappy island. The militia law had just expired. Therefore, the militia could not be called out, according to law nor martial law enforced. The military strength in the garrison, and in fact in the whole island, was about thirty invalids of the two flank companies of a batallion of the 60th Regiment, which were left from those that went to the misfortunate attack on Gaudeloupe, and about ten artillery men. There appeared a self security and relaxation for common safety less to guard against invasion or introduction of French principles of liberty and equality, which Victor Hugues was disseminating far and wide, and had given a conspicuous example as to slavery in one of the largest and most valuable colonies to the windward of Porto Rico. It was evident to every Englishman that every Frenchman in the island was a democrat. This they avowed openly and had frequent meetings or clubs in and about Kingstown. From the leveling principles which at this time Frenchmen of all descriptions inimical to monarchial government had imbibed, it might have been easily foreseen that they were as busy in forming plans for the destruction of the British government in these islands as their brethren were in Europe for the overthrow of the king and British constitution as well as all monarchial governments. If we take a dispassionate view of the relative situation of the English and French inhabitants in St Vincent and Grenada, the caring and desperate part the latter took for the annihilation of the former will not appear so strange as it otherwise would. As we must regard human nature much the same in all nations and tribes of men, when in similar situations similar impressions on the mind naturally will be produced. Can an Englishman say he would not have acted the same part under a similar government? There has always been and probably ever will be a natural antipathy and mutual jealousy between English and French men, and perhaps proper and necessary that national prejudices and dislikes should in some degree prevail. They certainly will never be equally attached to the same mode of government. However, it might have been supposed that the French inhabitants in these two islands, being natives under the British government and associates with Englishmen, had enjoyed many advantages they never could have had under the French government, and from nothing many of them had realized considerable fortunes. They would at least have remained neutral in case of an invasion nor could have been supposed abettors or instruments of instigating savages and slaves to murder their masters and destroy their property.

There were probably defects in the colonial laws which prevented the cementing the English and French inhabitants as they ought to have been under the same constitution. However that was the case or not, I cannot say, but it certainly is a solecism in politics to denominate the whole community subjects to the same power, yet many of the common immunities to [a] part, certainly arbitrary to govern the whole by laws the making of which a part has no voice in forming. Let it be granted that the French inhabitants of St Vincent and Grenada were as happy and probably happier than the English inhabitants in equivalent circumstances. But yet we will grant [that] a certain degree of subordination from local laws restraining from the common immunities of the society is more disadvantageous in idea than in reality. Yet if we view the manner in a moral or philosophic light, we must allow for the human propensity in a state of civilization. All partial restraints will be regarded unjust, altho' trifling. But no plea or excuse can be presumed in justifications of the horrid plans of devastation and scenes of massacre the French inhabitants of the two islands abetted and were accessory in. If a French army of regular troops had landed with design of a fair conquest, then joining or aiding would undoubtedly have been high treason, as they had long been British subjects and often voluntarily taken the oath of allegiance to the king of Great Britain. How then can they be vindicated, as attempts were made from secret plans among themselves and private correspondence with the French commanders in Guadeloupe, not only to reduce the islands under the French government but render them masses of ruins and in cool blood murder all the English inhabitants? Although every circumstance in Grenada and St Vincent conspired at the period to the accomplishment of their diabolical scheme, yet the interposition of the almighty and overriding Providence counteracted its general tendency.

To account for such a degree of human depravity, we must recur to the atheistical and leveling principles which were disseminated throughout the French government and pervaded her colonies as well as the mother country. During the reign of that diabolical tyrant, Robespierre, atheism was solemnly proclaimed and the Christian religion abjured. It was then their ideas of universal conquest and the overthrow of all the established governments of the world were formed, [and] assassination of all superior orders of men, both in a civil and religious capacity, was encouraged. The British nation was the only barrier to the accomplishment of their plans. In revenge, every means both private and open their powers possessed were used for the destruction of the British nation, and nothing could tend more to that than the destruction of her colonies. By that they destroyed her commerce. The words equality and property they conceived would be as fascinating to the English slaves in the West Indies as they had been to the unhappy peasantry of France and other unfortunate nations in Europe. For their designs in this quarter the favourable opportunity was offered by the very singular and astonishing event of Victor Hugues' arrival with 1800 men from France in two or three frigates, making himself master of Guadeloupe almost as soon as he landed in it. Than this commander, Robespierre could not have pitched on a fitter for his intentions.

The boldness of his designs and the rapid performance of his plans astonished everyone. To strong natural abilities were joined a quick penetration and thorough acquaintance [with] the dispositions and natural bents of the minds of the lower classes of mankind; nor was he less conversant with the abilities and plans of all our commanders in the West Indies. He was a man of undaunted courage, with great conduct and presence of mind, determined and steady in all his resolutions. He was more obeyed from fear than from love. All these were requisites and highly commendable for a commander possessing his orders, had they not been prostituted and tarnished in the perpetration of the most horrid crimes, massacres, and the cutting the bands of civilized society asunder. As to the murder of the many unhappy victims of loyalists that had joined the English army and fell into his power, perhaps it was their own fault. We have nothing to say. The order of his rulers necessitated him perhaps to perform the sanguinary deed. To the then existing government of France they were certainly rebels. Whether they had the means or aid of escaping or chose to join the republicans is not well known. But the premeditated murders and devastations he planned and encouraged in the English islands will brand his name with infamy to the latest posterity. As a prelude to his future operations on his landing in Guadeloupe, he proclaimed all the slaves free men, mustered and armed all those that suited his intentions, appointing officers of their own custom. On this certainly depended his maintaining himself in his conquest and the havoc he made on the English islands. However, his chief end was baffled in the hopes that it would be the means of producing a general revolt among the English slaves, altho' by his emissaries he soon learned all the French inhabitants with their negroes and coloured men of that description in St Vincent and Grenada were ready to cooperate with him. It will appear astonishing that their plans were formed and fit for execution, with quantities of arms, ammunition and men to discipline the mulattoes and blacks in both islands without the English knowing of it. In Grenada they had gone so far as to have a regular fortification mounted with cannon.

From the whole tenor of Victor Hugues' conduct after his arrival in Guadeloupe and his inflammatory proclamations, it might have been easily foreseen a storm was gathering to burst on the English lands. Yet the English in both St Vincent and Grenada were lulled into an unprecedented degree of inattention and self security. They dreamed of nothing but increasing their estates and calculating the growing revenue. All this was well known in Guadeloupe. For about six months previous to the insurrection, the English in St Vincent, particularly in and about Kingstown, had given themselves up to an unexampled degree of thoughtlessness and sociability, hardly any thing but general entertainments, and once or twice in the week maroon dinners, as they are called in this part of the world, everyone carrying a proportion to eat and drink to a riverside, under shady trees, assembled on the grass without ceremony, no table or furniture of any kind except plates, knives and forks. It was very observable at this time in St Vincent there was more social and less of party spirit than was before or has been since. It seems as [if] Providence had intended this general sociability for unanimous exertions and fortitude that soon was to be called for the general preservation. Had they not been united, such a handful of men never could have withstood the hordes of desperadoes and savages that poured on them from all quarters like a torrent. [...]

On the morning of the tenth of March a party of volunteers of between thirty and forty rode off from Kingstown toward the Carrib country to reconnoiter the maneuvers of the Carribs. They carried muskets and some ammunition, yet they had no idea they would have occasion for them. They went more like a party of pleasure to the Carrib country to observe their motions and if [there were] any war-like appearances among them. Nothing remarkable appeared until within two or three miles of their boundary, when they observed the buildings on the estate next to them in flames, a too clear indication of what was going on. They immediately halted, being joined by the white men from the neighbouring estates. They took possession of an eminence in the road, but they had only been there a few minutes consulting on the measures they should pursue when they were fired upon by large bodies of Carribs on the heights above them and from the bushes and canes. Being surrounded on all sides, greater part of them fell wounded or were taken and shockingly mangled in pieces with cutlasses. The few who made their escape by the swiftness of their horses gave the alarm as they went on. All fled that property [who] could with what was on their backs, not having time to take the more valuable articles or even the little cash they had. So rapid was the progress of the savage hordes that the few white men on that side of the island had not time to collect or take any station that could stop or retard their progress until assistance could be sent from Kingstown. Several unhappy managers and overseers fell into their hands who were immediately butchered and cut in pieces. The fate of a man with one arm was uncommonly affecting. He was advised to fly for his life. He answered no, he would remain with his property. As he was maimed and had no offence weapons, he was sure they would not hurt him; however, he soon experienced the fate of the others. The cruelty they committed is too shocking for narration, nor would they be credible if not too well authenticated. To show these savages in their true light, I will only mention one instance, how much soever it may affect the feelings of humanity. A misfortunate family fell into their power consisting of husband, wife and sucking child. After cutting the husband in pieces before his wife, they snatched the infant from the mother's breast and dashed out its brains on a stone at her feet. Her I believe they saved, by entreaty of some Carribs who knew her and to whom she had frequently given rum.

It was very remarkable that the day before these events, viz., ninth of March, several gentlemen had gone within the Carrib boundary and dined with one of the chiefs, to whom the Carribs were uncommonly civil and attentive, but they were observed to be collecting and in consultation in larger bodies than usual. From this it was evident that they were not quite prepared for their

223

operations. The affair at Mariqua plainly convinced them that their schemes were discovered, which no doubt forced them to commence sooner than they intended. The day these gentlemen were with them they had probably not had information from Mariqua, and happy for them it was not the case. From the suddenness of their attack next morning, they must have heard of the circumstance the very evening they left them. The Grand Sable, Rabacca and Mount Young Carribs with those behind the English settlements commenced the depredations to windward. The same day those of Owia and to leeward of it made their eruption on that side of the island under the command of Chateoy, commander in chief of the whole on the leeward side of the island. They were joined by all the French to the leeward of Kingstown at Chateaubelair, as those to windward by the French adjacent to Kingstown. The preservation of the English families to leeward was owing to a Frenchman having a commission from Victor Hugues, who in that instance showed humanity, altho' [he] was afterwards one of their chief officers during the war. A gentleman residing at Chateaubelair who had been in frequent social meetings with this Frenchman informed of his danger and [advised to] fly for his life instantly the Carribs in their canoes coming round a headland were in sight, from which intimation the English had no time to escape. Three obstinate and unthinking men, two mechanics, the other an overseer on an estate, not being armed, they trusted to the clemency of the banditti and conceived they might remain and carry on their occupation. These misfortunate men were brought alive to Dorchester hill, the rendezvous of the two parties, and there butchered.

It was fortunate for the colony that the leeward party did not burn or destroy in their progress, as those from windward did. This, no doubt, was owing to the sagacity of their chief and the policy of the French leaders with him. They only plundered the works for sugar and rum but burnt none of the buildings, but on two estates. But on the doors of all the buildings was written the name of the new proprietor. Chateoy, as commander, naturally had the largest claim, consequently several were designated for him. This principle of presuming property no doubt was owing to the French, as they naturally supposed they would be ultimately masters. They knew it was their interest to preserve and not destroy property. From this was owing the preservation of most of the buildings in Kingstown Valley. In course of a few days after the general insurrection, both hands met on Dorsetshire hill, threatening the total exter- mination of the English from St Vincent. Forever dark and gloomy was the prospect, but with the danger did the united energy of the few inhabitants increase, braved every danger, and dispensed this legion of marauders and murderers from that very spot on which all their future hopes of destruction and conquest rested. During the dreadful contest for about two years several contingent events providentially happened for the preservation of the colony at the most alarming and eventual periods. One of the most fortunate, at the time of the formidable junction of the barbarous armies on Dorsetshire hill, was the arrival of the Zebra sloop of war in Kingstown Bay. Her commander and crew contributed not a little in dispossessing them of this stronghold, on which depended the preservation of the island.

As it is not my intention and foreign to my design (of the present publication) to give regular detail of this savage warfare to its conclusion. I have merely brought circumstances so far as to give some idea [of] the remote and immediate causes of it and an account, as far as can be ascertained, of nature and disposition and principals [of] this adventurous tribe of blacks and by which they actuated from their first arrival in St Vincent until transported to the island Rattan. Sir Ralph Abercromby conquered their party and the most formidable body of the enemy on the Vigie in June, 1796, which led to the surrender of all the posts the French possessed in the island and ultimately to the surrender of them. Previous to that happy period, many were the dreadful reverses of fortune the island experienced, and numerous bloody conflicts in different parts of it. After his arrival there was not a moment lost for reducing the Vigie, the chief post the enemy then possessed. The situation is strong by nature, being several eminences commanded by higher ground, and every art had been used in forming breastworks with numerous ditches to render it as inaccessible and strong as possible. However, it was so situated as to be surrounded by a besieging army admitting no retreat for European troops, which was different with forces he had to [deal] with. It was surrounded by the British army. All their outposts attacked at daylight in the morning. About 2 p.m. three strong redoubts were taken, their strongest hold only remaining, from which they had no chance of escape. They sent out a flag of truce next morning; terms of capitulation were agreed upon. This garrison formed the principal body of the enemy. In it were most of the French white officers and the commander in chief, a black man, a native of St Lucia, [who] had been invested with the chief command by Victor Hugues on the death of the Carrib Chateoy. He was a brave and daring man of great military parts, with which was joined a quick penetration. Of his abilities as a general, there were too many convincing proofs to the British troops. As true bravery and humanity are always united, so were they in this black man. The English prisoners he treated with as much humanity and attention as his situation could admit and saved many of them from the barbarous ferocity of the Carribs, and that mercy which he showed to them he fully experienced when fortune put him in the situation he had them. During the engagement and in cover of the night a large body of the most desperate of the enemy made their escape through the trees and bushes, unperceived, and many had actually crept in the night time through the ranks without a possibility of seeing them. The Carribs, as usual, made their escape at the beginning of the action, and not an individual of them was found in the Vigie. This motley garrison, to the number of 500 when they marched out to ground their arms, had all the honours of war paid to them usual on such occasions to European troops. Perhaps the ceremony was no doubt disgusting to some of the British army and was censured by several. It was disgusting to a British soldier to go through the maneuvers to such a mixed gang which merited no better appellation than a banditti. However, the measure was wise and politic and had a happy effect. It was well known that the most daring and desperate part of them exclusive of the Carribs was still in the interior woods and on the most inaccessible parts of the island, from which no force could dislodge them but by hemming them in, depriving them of provisions and access to the sea. They would have been driven to desperation by harsh treatment or ill usage of those in our power, from which they would have had no idea of mercy to themselves. From the open candour and punctuality of the commander in chief in forming the articles of capitulation and in the performance of them, Marinier capitulated for all the other posts in the island under the command of French officers, which in consequence delivered them up according to the agreement, but as may be naturally supposed, none of the Carribs, island negroes and French mulattoes who were not in these posts considered themselves in this treaty. All the Carribs and desperadoes in the woods and a few from the French islands of a daring disposition joined them under the command of a black man, Maunpedos, native of St Lucia and brother-in-law to Marinier. He was a brave, fiery and daring fellow endowed with not a little of military skill and conduct. But the strength of the enemy was now broken, the remains of them not so formidable as to endanger the safety of the island. General Abercromby departed for the conquest of Grenada, leaving General Hunter with the command of the troops left in St Vincent, judged sufficient for the reduction of the remainder of the enemy, for which he was well fitted by his military abilities as well as by his vigilance, activity and humanity.

However, the reduction of them was far more difficult than at first appeared, as well from their numbers as obstinacy. In fact, the greater of them were desperadoes who from their savage conduct had no right to expect mercy, and long before they could be convinced, it would be bestowed upon them. Although many of them were killed and taken prisoners, it was found impossible to pursue them to their strongholds in the mountains or reduce them by force. Nor in such a warfare had European troops an equal chance with them, had their constitutions been adequate. Altho' several of the prisoners were sent to them at different times to assure them their lives would be saved and protected, yet they continued obstinate until a more efficacious mode was adopted, by daily sending out strong parties to destroy their settlements and ground provisions, but these parties were terribly harassed from behind trees and bushes. Of consequence many were killed in the contests. The rangers or black corps were chiefly employed. It was a service too severe for regular troops. Being thus deprived of the means of existence and constantly harassed by parties sent out in all directions, at length Marinpeder, their black commander, gave himself up with the greater part of his gang, but a number of the island negroes with some white men still remained with the Carribs. But [at] last, finding those who had given themselves up were treated with humanity after proclamations and offers of pardon, the greater part surrendered, but none of the Carribs as yet had shown any disposition to come in. Conscious of their horrid enmities, they could not be made to believe they would be forgiven. It is what savages have no idea of, as retaliation only actuates them. Being constantly hunted through the woods by the rangers and driven from their strongholds in the mountains, their provisions and huts constantly destroyed, many of them were killed, as the negroes on these occasions gave them no quarter. They were entirely cut off from the sea, as sea water was the succedance for salt with the Carribs yellow as well as black, without it they cannot exist. At last some of their chiefs ventured to come to the outposts, under the pretense to bargain for their tribes, but this was merely a pretext of these artful people, as their intentions were only to gain intelligence and to find out what reception they would have. They were treated with every possible attention and went back with the pretense to bring in the rest, but they returned no more. But being continually harassed and finding no mercy in the woods, at last one chief and his tribe surrendered and were gradually followed by most of the others.

Many of them were a dreadful spectacle of distress and misery. A number of them when they first came in were so weak as not to be able to crawl, but from the abundance of nourishment they were supplied with, they were in two weeks' time able to march to Caligua, from which they were sent to Balliceaux, a small island to the windward of Bequia which had been previously rented for them. Buildings and every possible accommodation were provided for them, canoes and fishing tackle for those that chose to catch fish for their families, of which there is the greatest abundance of the best kinds around the island. The maintaining them there was great expense to the island of St Vincent exclusive of the King's provisions. Vessels were in constant employ by the island in carrying them provisions and water. A surgeon from the garrison was sent to take care of their sick, and a committee of the council and assembly went over once in the week to see they had every necessary.

I mention these circumstances with the view of doing away any imputation of cruelty or inhuman treatment that may be alleged against the colony or military to this unhappy but barbarous race. It is more than probable they will not escape the pen of the historian. Many historians as well as philosophers, from bad information and conjectural ideas, are too apt to attach inhumanity where it should not rest. Tyranny, cruelty and inhumanity are favorite themes in the present day, and we are too apt to view our fellow creatures through the darkest medium as to their good qualities and to set off them bad in the clearest light. If these people were injured, it was by too much indulgence while they were captives, as they had no determinate quantity of victuals or rations, but as much as they could destroy. It is therefore a query if this was not the means of destroying many of them. If we regard their miserable situation for such a length of time in the woods, where the greater part of their food was leaves of trees and roots of all kinds that were in the least digestible, from this mode of existence to the abundance of animal food we must conceive injurious to them, for one extreme is as bad as another. Nor [can] there be any hesitation in ascribing the death of so many of them to the overabundance of food during their stay on Balliceaux. However, it was owing to the humanity of General Hunter, and I remember when the observation was mentioned to him. He said he [would] rather they should die by too much food than by too little and that there should be no imputation as to their want of the necessaries of life. A stranger, to have seen the care and attention to them in this local situation, he would have little conceived they had been the principal agents in the devastations and murders in St Vincent.

When they were all collected in Balliceaux, their number was 5200, near one half of which died during their abode in it. 2700 were embarked for Rattan. Every circumstance considered, this large decrease will not appear surprising. Besides too much food, we must conceive the origin of many diseases all during their miserable situation in the woods without shelter, their want of food, constantly harassed and pursued from one place to another. That those diseases did not show themselves at first is nothing strange, for we find many more of any army die after the campaign when enjoying ease and plenty of necessarys in quarters than during their hardships in the field. We have another powerful cause of the death of so many of them, and that was the agonizing reflection that they were to be forever transported from their native country to another they never saw, as these were the terms they surrendered on, nor is there any doubt but that the thoughts of their folly and bad conduct in bringing them to that situation operated strongly on their minds. Notwithstanding the dreadful life they had in the woods, yet the whole of them surrendered not 'til about two years ago. These small remains consist of two or three families only and have a small tract of land given them for their habitations and provisions. Until their reduction it was not conjectured they were so numerous as they proved to be. About 6,000 surrendered, and we may readily allow one third of them to have been killed and perished in the woods by wounds, hunger and fatigue. The shocking state a number of them were found in [in] the woods was awful, some expiring half putrid, many dead in their hammocks, some partly eaten by rats and their own dogs. Like all savages, they paid no attention to their sick and infirm on their march from the windward of the island. They would give no assistance to the sick who could not walk, and the soldiers supported and carried several on their backs.

The island of Rattan was determined upon for the future residence of them. From every account it is particularly well calculated by nature for them, having every advantage they could wish, being well supplied with game and fish, the soil fertile. If the Spaniards permit them to remain in quiet, in time they may be a much happier people than if they had remained in St Vincent. A sufficient number of ships for the transportation of them were prepared under the protection of a ship of war. Every article for convenience as well as use was put on board for them: seeds and roots of all the esculent plants they were accustomed to to supply their new colony and twelve months' provisions for their existence until they could reap the produce of them, with all the necessary implements for agriculture; arms, ammunition for their defence, as well as to supply them with game; also fishing tackle and every other thing that was supposed necessary or useful for them, and left in full possession of their new colony.

The fifth of April [1797] they sailed for their destination in the island Rattan, leaving their native woods and mountains never to see [them] again, and every moment disappearing more and more to their longing eyes. On that occasion could the human mind not divested of all sensibility but feel for their fate and forget their many crimes and errors that brought them to it and bewail the vicissitudes that nations as well as individuals are fated to? Altho' factions and rebellions may be the cause of extirpating a people from a government under which they might have ever remained free and happy, yet who can avoid melancholy sensations on a whole race of mankind transported forever from their native land inhabited by them for many generations and not conceive there has been something radically wrong in the principles of that government necessitated to that act?

The St Vincent Carribs were a peculiar race and from accidental causes different from all other tribes of men. Altho' originally Africans, from the mixture and connection with the American indians they were what we may call a hybrid race from the two. They adopted many of the habits of the aborigines, particularly in dress and mode of living. Their language differed from their native tongue and also from the indian. The forehead of their children they flattened after the indian manner, but this was more as a mark to distinguish them from the slaves than the principle of imitating the indians. Hence the negroes called them flat heads. From them alone no danger could have been dreaded to the colony. Altho' they were a cunning race, yet they were a cowardly. The negroes of the colony were an overmatch for them at any time [and], had they had permission, would have soon destroyed them. The negroes bore them a great antipathy. This no doubt originated from jealousy. The poor slaves, knowing them to be of the same extraction with themselves, yet being free and enjoying more liberty than the lower class of white men, going as gentlemen while they were laboring hard with sweat of their bodies. There was something natural to this dislike and was human nature only.

It was their connection with the French that rendered the black Carribs a dangerous people. In their hands they were instruments of revenge for the English whenever they had occasion for them. Had that connection been timely cut off, they might have been rendered useful to the colony and a singular tribe of mankind preserved that are now nearly extinct and will soon be forgot that such a race ever existed.

PART IV

The chapters in Part III mainly concerned the wars on St Vincent that resulted in the expulsion of large numbers of Caribs from the island in the last years of the eighteenth century. Those wars had taken place because the Caribs occupied land that the British wanted for growing sugar. On Dominica, a different topography led to a different situation. The Caribs did withdraw from certain parts of the island under European pressure but, despite the extensive sale of lands after the Treaty of Paris in 1763, large-scale agriculture was possible in very few places, and the Caribs were not harried into expulsion.

Thomas Atwood, writing in 1791, suggests that there are no more than twenty or thirty families of Caribs ('properly called "Caribbes"'). After a brief description he concludes:

> It is much to be regretted, that since this island has been in the possession of the English, so little pains have been taken to cultivate an union with these people, as they might be capable of essential service to its internal security, especially against the accumulation of runaway negroes in the time of peace; and in war they might be induced to join in its defence, should it be invaded. Yet they are permitted to roam wherever their fancies lead them, as much unnoticed as if no such people were in existence. They are men as well as we, are born with the same degree of sensibility; and by proper encouragement, might be of material benefit to a country which was originally their own. (1791: 223)

So little notice was taken of Atwood's advice that practically no written evidence remains of Carib life during the first three-quarters of the nineteenth century. Evangelical travellers were plentiful in the West Indies, especially in the period leading up to the abolition of slavery in 1834, but none took an interest in the Caribs. The sparse evidence that remains for the early and mid-century is included in the words of two Catholic priests writing in the 1850s and 1860s (No. 20(1) and (2)). Another priest who left brief but interesting evidence is Father Suaudeau (No. 20(4)), who seems to have encouraged some of the earliest photographs of the Caribs, taken by the first group of tourists to 'visit the Caribs'. Also from this period dates the only modern study of the Carib language 'as now spoken' in Dominica (Rat 1897).

Around the turn of the century the West Indies became tourist islands, at least for the rich, with the establishment of regular steamer services from England and the USA, and with the first series of modern travel- and guide-books published. North American interest in the area grew enormously in the years after the annexation of Cuba and Puerto Rico in 1898. A typical guide-book of the time was Frederick Ober's *Our West Indian Neighbours. The Islands of the Caribbean Sea, 'America's Mediterranean': Their Picturesque Features, Fascinating History, and Attractions for the Traveler, Nature-Lover, Settler and Pleasure-Seeker* (1904); but Ober was originally a naturalist, and it was he who had 'rediscovered' the Caribs during an ornithological field-trip in 1877, described in his earlier book *Camps in the Caribbees* (No. 21). After the Spanish–American war there were rumours that England and the USA were going to swap the Philippines and the British West Indies. Ober was a strong proponent of US annexation of the West Indies as a whole, a move that was backed by the *New York Herald*.

Meanwhile, after several decades of more or less complete neglect, Britain also began to look with fresh eyes at its West Indian possessions. Writers like Trollope (1860) and Froude (1887) had painted a tawdry picture of the West Indian colonies; Dominica, in particular, had gained a reputation for internal strife, enhanced by the property-tax riots in La Plaine in 1893 in which troops from HMS *Mohawk* shot into a crowd of protesters, killing four. A Royal Commission was set up under Sir Robert Hamilton, which produced a searching report. Joseph Chamberlain adopted Dominica as a test-case for his deter-mination to modernize the colonies, pushed a financial settlement through Parliament, and appointed a thrusting young Administrator, Hesketh Bell, as his instrument. Bell did much to promote Dominica: a new generation of settlers arrived, as did a new wave of British travel-writers such as Sir Frederick Treves (No. 23) and Symington Grieve (Plate 27).

Hamilton's report contains an intriguing glimpse of dissent within the Carib community, two letters forwarded to the commission by rival chiefs (No. 20(3)), a division which surfaces again in Hesketh Bell's own writings (No. 22). Bell took a life-long interest in the Caribs, and his establishment of the Carib Reserve is a clear landmark in modern Carib history.

Further Reading

There is little secondary material on this period, though Lennox Honychurch's *The Dominica Story* (1984) is a reliable guide to developments on the island, including those that affected the Caribs.

20. *Priests and Chiefs on Dominica (1856–1905)*

¶ *After Thomas Atwood's brief words about the Caribs of Dominica, written in 1791, little is heard about them for nearly a century: in 1880 Frederick Ober can present himself as their rediscoverer (No. 21). Almost the only accounts of these years that have survived are written by the Catholic missionaries who continued their efforts at conversion, more successful in the nineteenth century than they had been in the seventeenth. Father du Lettré's work in the 1850s seems to have been decisive in this respect. In the following decade Bishop Poirier managed to persuade Queen Victoria to grant a number of acres at Salybia to build the Catholic church of Sainte-Marie, near the site of a new Catholic church built in 1991. In 1865 Caribs roofed the Catholic cathedral in Roseau.*

The first of the four extracts in this chapter is taken from a report addressed by du Lettré to the Bishop of Roseau on the state of religion in the parish of St Andrew. The report begins with an account of du Lettré's lack of success amongst the Methodist communities established around Wesley and La Soie, on the east coast of Dominica, and to the north of the Carib communities, before speaking of the writer's difficulties in contacting the Caribs themselves. Du Lettré (1807–73) was a secular priest, born in France, who spent twenty-one years in Dominica. His letter was probably written within a few years of his arrival on the island in 1852, perhaps in 1856.

Once firm contact had been established with the Caribs, the Catholic priests seemed to go out of their way to re-establish the defunct office of Carib chief or king. The second document is a letter written in 1864 by Father Clément-Désiré Ardois (d. 1875), like du Lettré a companion of the Eudist Bishop Poirier, one of the most influential churchmen in the West Indies during the nineteenth century. Ardois recounts, at the end of a letter to his religious superior, news of the election of a new Carib chief who took the name of Canute. One of Poirier's own letters says that the new chief was a direct descendant of the previous 'king', who died fifteen years earlier. He was called Étienne, and chose the name Canute because the date of his election, 19 January, was the feast of St Canute, King of Denmark.

By the beginning of the twentieth century there were enough parish priests on the island to ensure fairly regular visits, and most of the Caribs were, at least nominally, Catholics. Father René Suaudeau came out from France as a young priest in the early years of the new century. He was parish priest at Wesley and made regular visits to the Carib villages to his south, especially to the church that had been established at Sainte-Marie (Salybia). He wrote regularly to his parents in France and, after his early death in 1908, they asked his religious order to publish the letters in his memory.

It was Suaudeau who arranged for the photograph of Auguste and his wife to be taken (Plate 19). In a letter of 15 March 1906 he wrote to his parents: 'You will soon receive a photograph of the king and queen of the Caribs. Several days ago I was in Sainte-Marie and an Englishman and his son belonging to a great and noble family came to see me. They had a photographic machine with them. I asked them to photograph the king and queen, which they were delighted to do.' This letter casts interesting light on the position of Carib chief at the time of Hesketh Bell's formalization of the Reserve.

The Carib 'king', Auguste François, often referred to as Ogiste, seems to have been a figure of considerable power in the later years of the nineteenth century. Although old, he made a strong impact on both Father Suaudeau and Hesketh Bell (No. 22(2)). An earlier glimpse is provided by the letter addressed to Sir Robert Hamilton during the course of his royal commission to Dominica in 1893, along with the one surviving indication of a rival chief, Bruni Michelle, who clearly had to do without the assistance of the official interpreter (3). Sir Robert G. C. Hamilton (1836–95) was a long-serving civil servant who had just retired as governor of Tasmania when he was appointed to head this commission.

---

1. The Report of Father du Lettré (1856)

[...] From this day onwards the Catholic religion, with no refuge in La Soie, found itself thereby emancipated. Not going any longer to Corel, I set off further afield to look for refuge amongst the *Caraïbes*. These are the remnants of the ancient inhabitants of Dominica before the discovery of the New World: in my parish they form three small groups of about forty people each at Nattien, Bataca, and Rivière-Gaulette. In general they are smallish in stature, with a slightly swarthy complexion, straight black hair, a broad face, and stocky body. They have almost forgotten their ancient language, which they only use amongst themselves and to keep secrets from others. It is spoken from the throat, and is very impoverished: it has no terms to express spiritual matters. For the rest they speak creole like the other inhabitants of the country. They used to be all, or almost all, Catholics; from time immemorial they carried their children everywhere, even to the neighbouring islands, to have them baptized. They cross the sea in a canoe which is not planked; when the canoe overturns they turn it back up; and it has become proverbial that a *Caraïbe* never drowns.

They have no resemblance to Europeans and even less to African peoples: it seems most probable that they are descended from the peoples of Asia. The first and even the second time that I turned up amongst them, especially at Bataca, they were so frightened that they ran away and hid deep in the woods, along the dreadful cliffs that overlook the sea. Fortunately I had a guide with me; he was a *Caraïbe* called Jean, more sociable than the others, who led me to their retreat by the edge of the sea. It was there that I found Walacre, a nestful of men, women, and children, who had taken refuge higgledy-piggledy under the shelter of the foliage: little by little they recovered from their fright, and agreed to come back to the houses they had abandoned when I had arrived.

The first time I visited them in Rivière-Gaulette, I stayed with them for several days: one of them called Augustin generously gave us a new house, reasonably clean, which we used as a chapel; and it is there, every Sunday since then, that they gather to say their prayers. I promised to come back again to have them make their first communion; and on 16 June 1853, after a retreat of twelve days, I gave fifteen of them their first communion; and on 25 March 1855, on Passion Sunday, I gave first communion to sixteen more *Caraïbes*. We no longer need to look for them in the woods; they come to us joyfully because they have found happiness in religion.

From the time when I stopped saying mass in Corel in 1853 we have been obliged to move around from one place to another: to Nattien where the *Caraïbes* have built a little chapel, to Melville-Hall to the house of a Catholic, to Marigot in a house which is part Catholic and part Protestant, to Morne-Sylvie in the middle of a wild forest where I have said mass for four years on some government lands at the house of Mr Smith, where a Catholic called André had offered me refuge to lead a retreat during the week after Low Sunday in 1854, but where the owner of the house, a Protestant, had quite honestly required me to leave. The agoutis have their lairs in the forests and the grisgris make their nests in the trees; but the Son of Man has no place in La Soie to have a mass said to Him and to rest in the sacrament of His love. In the month of November 1855, a Catholic from Morne-Sylvie called Benjamin Augustin had offered to sell me a clearing where a chapel could be built; his wife, a Protestant, refused to sign the deed of sale. All these misfortunes and set-backs in all parts of La Soie, far from damaging true religion, have been the means whereby Providence makes itself known in a heretical country, where no one had seen a Catholic priest.

2. LETTER FROM FATHER CLÉMENT-DÉSIRÉ ARDOIS (1864)

Roseau, 23 March 1864

Venerable Father Superior.

Almighty God has looked kindly upon us, and after sailing for eighteen days we have reached Fort-de-France without incident. The sky and the sea, the wind, the rain, the calm, good progress, little headway: these were our variants.

We were six priests on board and for half of the crossing we had the consolation of saying mass every day. A mass is important on a ship! All those who attend are touched and welcomed. Our attendance was made up in large part of soldiers on their way to Mexico, for the most part religious and refined officers.

Monseigneur had come to perform an ordination in Martinique, where we were forced to wait eight days for passage on the steamer that would carry us back to our poor but beloved mission. It was on Passion Sunday that we landed on Dominican soil, and I arrived back in time to celebrate the main mass in my much-loved parish. It was a wildly happy occasion; all the roads were covered with flowers and greenery, all the houses decked with flags, not to mention our guns, which had been firing ever since morning. I went into my house through seventeen triumphal arches. The church and the presbytery were covered with garlands and festoons with colours and devices. It's imposs-ible to convey the joy and delight of these good people. In Europe you just don't have any idea of these things. Almighty God will compensate the people here for the sacrifices they make in leaving their relatives and friends behind. I'd like to dwell on the subject, but we are right in the middle of Holy Week, and we will succumb under the burden. It's only hope that keeps us going; but if we don't get help we will succumb. This is just what M. Lehaire was saying to me again the other day. 'I can't take any more', he said to me, 'with these two parishes, in a few months' time I will either be dead or I'll have to abandon everything.' M. Guiller, who is coming to France, will give you an idea of the extent of these two parishes. Believe the expert. At the end of the day, dear brother, you are our hope! If you only knew what ravages the devil makes here in a parish which is without a priest for just a few months, and on the other hand, how much good a priest can do amongst our poor people when he can stay with them continuously! You people in France, you should consider how lucky you are! You will send people out to us as soon as possible, won't you? The government has put six passages at Monseigneur's disposal. For the love of God and for the health of these souls, come to our assistance, help us! Morbihau has been served for ages by the Holy Bishop. We really like our priests at Morbihau, now we have two who help us a lot. Before long we will probably send to you a young boy of about 9 who belongs to an honest but poor family here. He is wanted by an aunt who lives in Scotland, but she is a Protestant and will spoil the child. If there is a ship for France loading at Martinique we will put the little chap aboard, and send you notice by our next courier. We think about the same thing for some others, but we will try sending them to the little school in Nachecoul, where they can only do the first lessons, but where their board is free. Monseigneur takes on the impossible and anxiety consumes him; a good letter from you, dear Father, would give him some rest and sleep. Father Lehère is well, as is Father Marie. Father Prosper is as round as a ball, but better than that he has become a man of great importance. Listen to this. While I was away he went on an expedition to visit our savages, the *Caraïbes*, with a priest whom the bishop of Guadeloupe had given to help the

English government. They gathered all the Indians together in a field, and made them elect a king, which they named Canute I. Father Prosper has become his plenipotentiary in Roseau, and handles *Caraïbe* affairs with the government and the administration, and he is eloquent about his little Tabo II. He has a real swagger when he accompanies his copper-skinned majesty through the streets of his capital. I must end, there is much work to be done; after Easter we will have more time. Affectionate greetings to all our brothers.

I assure you of my most respectful sentiments.

P. Ardois

8th–9th m.a.

3. Letters Addressed to the Hamilton Commission (1894)

(*a*) *Letter from Carib chief*

Dominica, Dec 7 1893

SIR,

I, as CHIEF of the Caribs residing in the district of St Marie, in this island, have been asked to lay a few facts before your Excellency as a cause of discontent.

1. We require a school in the quarter, and as there is none, the children are brought up in ignorance.

2. A hospital is also much needed, and our sick are taken to town with great difficulty. The distance to town is considerable, and the roads are in very bad condition.

3. I conduct the affairs of the settlement, and receive no remuneration from the Government.

4. I very respectfully ask to be heard in person.

I am, &c.

(Signed) AUGUSTUS FRANCIS

His Excellency Sir Robt. G. C. Hamilton, K.C.B.

Her Majesty's Special Commissioner to enquire into Dominica Affairs

Read over to the above Augustus Francis by the Interpreter, and sworn by him to truly represent the wants of the Caribs.

(*b*) *Petition from Bruni Michelle, rival chief of the Caribs*

To HER MAJESTY.

In the name of God.

MY LORD,

We humble beg of your kindness to accept our petition of your poor people, Indians or Caraibe, of Salibia, to unbrace the favarable opportunity to address-ing to you to emplore the marcy of our Beloved Mother and Queen Victoria, for her poor and unfortunate childrens. We dont have nothings to supported us, no church, no school, no shope, no store. We are very far in the forest; no money, no dress, etc., etc. They call us wild savages. No my beloved Queen, it is not savages, but poverty. We humble kneel down in your feet to beg of your assistance. Accept from your humble childrens of Salibia, in the care of

MR. BRUNI MICHELLE

11 December 1893
Make at Salibia.

4. FATHER SUAUDEAU IN THE COUNTRY OF THE CARAÏBES (1905)

In my last letter, I described to you all the characteristics of my parishioners, particularly the *Caraïbes*: afterwards I rather regretted having described them so negatively. But having now seen the *Caraïbes* again, I have to say that as far as they, at least, were concerned there was no exaggeration. Thieves, yes, they certainly are, starting from the king. When I speak of the king of the *Caraïbes*, you must not imagine a king sitting on a throne with a crown on his head and a sceptre in his hand.

He is an old *Caraïbe*, blind for the last year, to whom, four or five years ago, the leadership of the *Caraïbes* was entrusted. He received his command from the Queen of England and collects 200 francs a year; but in reality he commands nothing. His wife is blind too. The first time I went to their house it was to take Almighty God to his wife and to confess the old king, who is called Auguste; but without knowing that they were king and queen of the *Caraïbes*. When I found out later, I was really surprised by their sickly appearance. At the same time I found out from the people of Sainte-Marie, and from Father Bellaudeau himself, that the king had been a thief all his life and that his son now stole for him.

About a month ago he killed a magnificent sheep just ready to lamb, and ate it in the company of several other *Caraïbe* families. This sheep belonged to the old woman who cooks for me when I go down there. At the same time there were other *Caraïbes* as well as her who came to complain that they had been robbed of a goat or some vegetables or some money. They knew the thieves, but none of the other *Caraïbes* would act as a witness. Even if they are not thieves themselves, they are frightened of the old king who, it seems, is also a sorcerer. What is certain is that people come to consult him from Martinique and from other islands.

Last week I had gone down there to say mass on Passion Sunday and to have them take the Easter sacraments. Only forty-eight *Caraïbes* had come out of 300 or 400. I visited the sick and, since I was passing Auguste's house, I stopped to ask how he and his elderly wife were getting on. He wanted me to come in. I said, 'No, I will stay on my horse, I do not wish to enter the house of thieves, that I wanted to have you take your Easter sacraments, but see myself prevented from taking Almighty God into your house.'

He told me that he had never stolen, and he took Almighty God as witness of what he was saying.

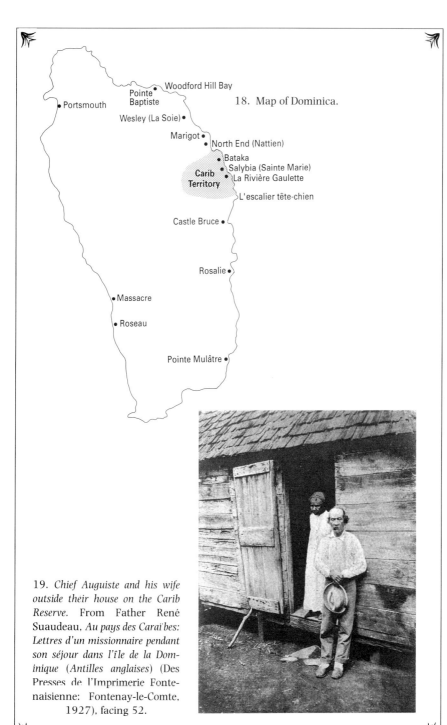

18. Map of Dominica.

Woodford Hill Bay
Pointe Baptiste
• Portsmouth
Wesley (La Soie) •
Marigot •
North End (Nattien)
Bataka
Carib Territory
Salybia (Sainte Marie)
La Rivière Gaulette
L'escalier tête-chien
Castle Bruce •
Rosalie •
• Massacre
• Roseau
Pointe Mulâtre •

19. *Chief Auguiste and his wife outside their house on the Carib Reserve.* From Father René Suaudeau, *Au pays des Caraïbes: Lettres d'un missionnaire pendant son séjour dans l'île de la Dominique (Antilles anglaises)* (Des Presses de l'Imprimerie Fontenaisienne: Fontenay-le-Comte, 1927), facing 52.

'Be quiet, old man,' I said to him, 'Almighty God knows well enough that you have always been a thief.

'Isn't it true that you said one day to Father Bellaudeau, on this very spot, that you had the right to take from other people's houses whatever you liked, because you were king of the *Caraïbes?*'

'That's right, Father, I am in command here.'

'After all, you are no more king than the king of England, and you've no more spirit than he has. In fact he doesn't steal like that, he is honest, and you, you are not. You know well enough that Father Bellaudeau said to you one day: I have more respect for the tail of my horse than I have for you. If you had been honest he wouldn't have said that.'

At this point he started to get angry and his wife came to the rescue. They told me that the *Caraïbes* hated them and that they are the ones who made them blind through poison.—'No, you haven't been poisoned, you haven't been bewitched, it is Almighty God who has cursed you; Almighty God hates thieves.'

'But after all, Father, I don't actually steal.'—'No, because you're blind, but you make your children steal. Everybody knows about it here, but they are frightened of you. I am not frightened of you and I tell you that if I was master you would all go to prison.' And with these words I left. So I'm no longer the friend of the *Caraïbe* king; but down there I have much more authority than he does. What I tell you about here is a summary of the conversation that I had with him.

On Friday afternoon, the governor of Dominica, to whom I had lent the presbytery at Sainte-Marie for two days, came here to thank me, and we chatted about all this.

He said to me: 'Father, it was I myself, two years ago, who got a pension of 200 francs for that old sorcerer direct from the king of England. And I'm really sorry I did so.'

21. *The Ornithological Eye*
Frederick Ober (1880)

¶ *The modern period of writing about the Caribs begins with the rather unlikely figure of Frederick Albion Ober (1849–1913), who almost literally stumbled upon the Caribs during an ornithological field-trip to Dominica. Ober had an early interest in natural history: a boyhood collection of stuffed and mounted birds from his local area in Massachusetts impressed Alexander Agassiz of the museum at Harvard University. From the early 1870s Ober worked for the Smithsonian Institute and wrote extensively for the journal* Forest and Stream. *He spent two years (1876–8) in the Lesser Antilles, discovering twenty-two species of birds new to science. His ornithological findings were printed in the annual report of the Smithsonian Institute, but he also produced a travel-book for the general reader,* Camps in the Caribbees: The Adventures of a Naturalist in the Lesser Antilles (1880), *from which the following extracts are taken. Ober later undertook the first extensive tour of the West Indian islands in search of ethnographic and archaeological material for the 1893 Columbian Exposition in Chicago (1893), published a popular* Guide to the West Indies (1908), *and had a successful career in real estate in Hackensack, New Jersey.*

In the preface to Camps in the Caribbees *Ober writes of 'leaving the beaten path of travel' in order to 'penetrate beyond the line of civilization'. He offers his readers the Caribbean forest, 'where everything reposes in nearly the same primitive simplicity and freshness as when discovered by Columbus, nearly four centuries ago'. 'My only claim is, that these sketches are original, and fresh from new fields— new, yet old in American history,—and that they are accurate, so far as my power of description extends. They have not, like the engravings, had the benefit of touches from more skilfull hands, and they may be crude and unfinished, and lack the delicate shadings and half-tones a more cunning artist could have given them; but they are, at least, true to nature' (pp. v–vii).*

Ober's account of life among the Dominican Caribs is full and sympathetic, though his scientific attitude is nicely caught by the way in which his lamentation over the death of the community's oldest inhabitant, from whom he had wanted to collect a

241

Carib vocabulary, is alleviated by the idea of exhuming her skeleton and taking it back for the Smithsonian Museum's collection. The second part of the extract sees Ober visiting St Vincent and undertaking some amateur archaeology on the small island of Battowia.

I had been a month in the interior of Dominica, living in the woods, hunting new birds, and enjoying the novel experiences of camp life in tropical mountains. From time to time came reports from the Carib country, that only strengthened the determination I had formed of penetrating to their stronghold. That they lived secluded from the world, held no intercourse with other people; naked they wandered at will in the forest; without houses, they slept on the ground on beds of leaves. Sending my collections of birds to the coast and ordering thence a fresh supply of provisions and ammunition, I left the Caribbean side of the island and marched over the mountains toward the Atlantic, with three stout girls and a man laden with my effects. The journey was to occupy two days, as the rivers were swollen. They had 'come down', in the language of the country; but when a river is 'down' in the West Indies it is *up*—having rushed down from the mountains, swollen up by some heavy rain, and flooded the lowlands.

The Carib reservation in Dominica extends from Mahoe River to Crayfish River, a distance of about three miles along the Atlantic coast, and away back into the mountains as far as they please to cultivate. Though each family has a little garden adjacent to the dwelling, any individual can select an unoccupied piece of ground on the neighboring hills, or mountain sides, for cultivation. All their provision grounds (as are called the mountain gardens where the staple fruits and vegetables are grown) are at a distance from the house, some even two miles away, solitary openings made in the depths of the high woods. As the soil in general is very thin, and does not support a crop for many successive years, these gardens are being constantly made afresh.

As I rode along, every house seemed deserted; no face appeared and I met no one save the ancient king, old George, who was named for King George the Third, tottering toward the plantations, to spend for rum some money he had earned. There were two sovereigns, in fact, for the Carib chief held in his hand a golden one, of English coinage. The houses are low and thatched deeply with calumet grass tied in bundles and lashed tightly upon frame-works of poles. Some of them were open at the sides, though a few were built up at the sides and ends, with wooden doors and shutters. Near each hut is the cook-house, a roof of thatch supported upon four poles; or again, merely a 'lean-to', the roof slanting up from the ground with just room enough for the cook to squat under while attending the fire.

Beneath this roof, on a few stones which support the cooking-utensils, is usually an old iron pot, which serves a variety of uses. Twice a day it is brought into requisition for the household; at other times it is open to the inspection of hogs and strangers. The rudest cabins, but at the same time the most pic-turesque, were those composed wholly of grass and reeds with wattled sides, looking like the huge stacks of grass one sees on marshes and meadows in America. Even the doors of these huts were made of canes and flags, wattled together with reeds, while the windows were merely loop-holes. The roads, though narrow bridle-paths, are good, as the Caribs seem to take a pride in keeping them in order. Either through fear or pride they obey all the laws imposed upon them by the crown and colony, and always perform their quota of road labor without a murmur.

The path turned suddenly, and at the base of the hill we came abruptly upon the Rivière Saint Marie, where, sporting in the water, were several naked children, and a girl and woman washing clothes. Of course, there was a general stampede as I crossed the river; and one could not have told, five minutes later, but for the garments drying on the rocks, that there had been a Carib near. I rode up a gentle eminence, and was introduced to the house in which I was to reside for a short time. But one family lived near, an old Carib woman with five children.

The first object conveying a hint of the proximity of Salibia, the Carib village, is a cross—indicating the religion of the people and the site of a cemetery. It stands up lone and majestic, a background of hills giving it prominence, its arms stretched out gaunt and bare, to which the continual trade-winds have given a color, gray and weather-beaten. Palm and plantain crop out on the hillsides beyond, and the former thrusts its head up from the river ravines below. Behind it, hid by the swell of the knoll, are the graves—not many, yet not few, for so small a settlement—simply raised hillocks of earth; and some have upon them a few flowers, which seem to be occasionally renewed. Upon the graves, all the trees have fallen prostrate, or have been felled, to cover them; with limbs stretched at the foot of the cross. I have never been in a cemetery that so appealed to my feelings as this. All is still, and solitude reigns.

From the slight depression of the surface here, nothing is seen evincing human occupancy of the valley, until the foot of the cross is reached. Many an evening, during my six weeks' stay in that lonely valley, have I climbed to the base of the cross and sat there enjoying the silence and solitude. From that point one overlooks the lower half of the valley, which is shut in on three sides by high hills covered with forest, abandoned fields, and provision grounds, alternating. Beneath, the most prominent object is a rude chapel, a loosely-built structure, to which comes monthly a lusty priest, to care for the souls and the silver of the people. Lower still, are the four or five thatched huts comprising the village of Salibia; but one of these is occupied, and the cocoa palms rustle their leaves in a desolate place; and their rustling, with the eternal roar of the ocean, is the only sound heard from morning to night.

There are sea-grapes there in perfumed bloom, among the satin leaves of which dart humming-birds, sugar-birds, and drowsy bees. This is the valley in which I became acquainted with the 'Cannibal Caribs' of Columbus, this secluded spot on the Atlantic coast of Dominica, in the month of April, 1877. [...]

None of the old writers mention the hospitality of the Carib, which at the present day is a virtue he possesses in perfection. I recall one of the many excursions made through the environs of the hamlet into the forest in my search for birds. The day was hot, but a cool breeze from the ocean, which always blows from ten in the morning till six in the evening, tempered the heat. Bordering the forest was a little open space, in the center of which, on a spur of the hills overlooking the sea, was a small thatched hut, inhabited by one of the few families of Caribs who have remained uncontaminated by negro blood. As I emerged from the forest I was met by a robust damsel with laughing eyes, who brought for me a wooden bench and placed it beneath the grateful shade of a mango. Then appeared her father, who welcomed me to his habitation, and then disappeared. A little later, when he re-appeared, he was driving before him a flock of fowls, and singling out the largest and plumpest, he requested me to shoot it. Thinking I had not understood him, I hesitated, but, at a repetition of the request, fired and tumbled the fowl in the dust. There was an instant scattering of the others, but the old man picked up the slain one and marched off with it to his wife. Then he knocked down a few cocoa-nuts, and, clipping off the end of one, brought it to me, with its ivory chamber full of cool and refreshing water, apologizing that he could offer me no rum or gin, which it is customary to mix with it.

In an hour or so I was invited to the hut, where, on a clean table, was spread a substantial meal of bread-fruit and yam, with the chicken I had so recently shot. This last was a luxury the Indian seldom treated himself to; and when I reflected to what extent my host had deprived himself, and upon the recent, the very recent, demise of the chicken, I could scarcely eat. My friends refused to sit at table with me, but attended upon my wants, bringing me fresh cocoanut-water, and mangos and guavas for dessert. To be sure, there was neither fork nor table-knife; but one living in the woods is never without his pocket-knife, and a fork can be quickly whittled from a palm-rib. After the repast I retired to the shade of the mango; the father gathered about him his materials for making baskets, and the daughter wove for me a curious cone of basket-work, used by the children in their games, which, being slipped over the finger, cannot be removed so long as it is tightly drawn.

The sun at noon is very powerful in that climate, and one quickly feels its somnolent influences. The people are up early, and work a little in the morning, but in the heat of the day little is done. No traveler passes, unless some one on a long journey; and no one works except the basket-maker, who can do so under the broad-spreading shade of a mango or tamarind. Even he, as noon draws nigh and breakfast is disposed of, stretches himself upon a board and dozes for an hour or two. Everything is hushed in universal calm, and even the insects and birds feel the influence of the solar rays and are silent, drowsy, and indulging in mid-day siestas. *Dolce far niente* is the life these people lead; the sweet-do-nothing more than is absolutely necessary.

Hospitality such as I have mentioned is not exceptional. If an Indian takes a liking to you, hence-forward you are his *compère*; all he has is yours—and what you possess, also, is reckoned as his, if he want it. When he offers to you his house and all in it, it is no idle custom without meaning, for even his household furniture, if there be any, is at your disposal.

The ancient Caribs, if we may credit the statements of early writers, believed in some sort of future state, and also that their departed friends were secret witnesses of their conduct. 'The brave had the enjoyment of supreme felicity with their wives and captives; the cowardly were doomed to everlasting banishment beyond the mountains. This was their next world. They dimly recognised a Divinity, a great creator of all things, and vaguely offered their homage and sacrifice.'

It is supposed that each person had his tutelar deity; it may have been a tree or a rock. The northern tribes, the Arowaks, had their *zemes*, or household gods, when discovered by the Spaniards. 'The Caribs erected a rustic altar of banana leaves and rushes, whereupon they placed the earliest of their fruits and choicest of their viands, as peace-offerings to incensed omnipotence. They could not be insensible to the existence of a great ruler, when the convulsions of nature were so great as they witnessed in the earthquake and hurricane.'

In religion, at the present time, the Caribs of Dominica are Roman Catholic, and are very observant of the rites of the church. Upon the occasion of the priest's monthly visit, nearly all flock to hear him, even if they do not obey his injunctions; and the sick are brought, and the dying, to obtain the sacrament. At the close of service, one Sabbath, word was brought the priest that Madame Jim, a middle-aged woman, was dying, with a request that he would hasten to administer the last rites of the church. But the priest was anxious to be away; his house was a dozen miles distant, and half-way there, at the house of a friend, a dinner was awaiting him. With impatience, then, he commanded that she be brought to the chapel; and the dying woman was placed in a hammock and suspended between poles, and carried to the priest, over a mile of rough, steep road, patiently suffering, anxious only to receive extreme unction before she passed away.

The same Sabbath there was buried at the foot of the cross the oldest inhabitant of the nation, a very old Carib woman, whose death I lamented, as I was awaiting her recovery to secure from her a vocabulary of Carib words. My grief was only alleviated by the thought that an opportunity might occur for exhuming her skeleton, which would prove a valuable acquisition to the Smithsonian Museum.

Formerly, the Caribs buried their dead in a sitting posture, in order (as an old Indian told me) that they might be all ready to jump, when the Spirit came for them; and facing the sunrise, to see the light of morning. When the master of a house died, they buried him in the center of his hut, with his knees bent to his chin. They then left the hut and built another, some distance from it.

Eight days after the death of Madame Jim, the neighbors had a sort of wake, or 'praise'; until midnight, the girls sang hymns. After twelve o'clock, all the younger people formed themselves in groups and played games until morning, while the wicked Meyong and a few more of the ungodly—who had amused themselves by tickling the ears of the choristers with straws and palm-leaves, in vain attempt to upset their gravity—improved the hours so assiduously in imbibing the new rum furnished by the husband of the departed, that the morning light saw them thoroughly fuddled. The whole settlement attended, old men and women and children, even to babes at the breast. The expense of the bereaved husband must have been great; and his reflection upon this fact, coupled with the equally saddening one that the wife of his bosom would never again labor for him in the garden, or relieve him of the burden of domestic duties, must have caused him to regret her departure. [...]

Carib Country is that portion of the island of St Vincent lying between the central ridge of mountains and the Atlantic coast. It is the most fertile and level, spreading from the foot of the hills in gentle slopes and undulating plains. Formerly in possession of the Caribs, it early attracted the English by its fertility, and, by processes well known to the white man when he desires his red brother's land, it soon changed hands. Though one may lament this usurpation of the Indian's territory, and deprecate such deeds on general principles, one is soon reconciled to the change after he has been domiciled among the people in present possession.

It has never been my fortune to meet a Scotchman on his native heath, and whether he is improved by being transplanted to another clime, I cannot tell. One thing is indisputable, he could not be more generous, more hospitable, more companionable than are those rare Scotchmen in the West Indies, with especial reference to the managers of those estates in Carib country. As all the estates were owned by one firm, and that firm held that there were no managers so skillful and faithful as their own countrymen, this part of the island was often alluded to as New Caledonia.

From 'Happy Hill', accompanied by its manager and those of adjoining estates, I cantered, on a borrowed pony, down the coast to the Carib settlement. At Rabaca is the celebrated 'Dry River' of the eastern coast, which is very broad, and often swept by torrents from the mountains. My friends rode with me as far as Overland, a most interesting negro village of wattled huts, built in a thick wood of cocoa-palms and bread-fruits. Here they left me with friendly adieus, and I went on alone. The Soufrière rose grandly from out its surrounding forests, and the great rock, shaped like a lion couchant, near which my cave opened, was sharply cut against the bluest of skies.

The Carib settlement of Sandy Bay is the most secluded in the island; it is also the most picturesque; but, as rocks and wooded hills are the principal elements of a picturesque landscape, I fancy the Caribs isolated here would gladly exchange their portion for the more fertile fields near Rabaca.

An Indian named Rabaca, a pure Carib, one descended from an ancient family, met me and aided me in my search for a house, and I was comfortably fixed before night in a little house of reeds, wattled and thatched. It contained two rooms eight feet square, separated by a matting of tied wild-plantain ribs. The result of my observations here is incorporated in chapter nine, but there are some incidents of Indian life that have not been alluded to in that narrative.

My nearest neighbor was 'Captain George', an Indian descended from the 'Black Caribs'. That is, his father, or grandfather, was a negro, while his mother, or grandmother, was a Carib. From either paternal or maternal ancestor he had inherited a kinky wool and rather thick lips, but the Indian blood showed itself strongly. Captain George was intelligent beyond the average Carib, and possessed a good knowledge of the ancient language, which his grandmother, who had 'brung him up', had taught him; and as he was always ready to impart to me the words and idioms of the Indian tongue, I was a frequent visitor to his cabin, where I would sit for hours listening to the tales and traditions handed down from his ancestors. He had an interesting family; and, as he had married a 'Yellow Carib', a woman of uncontaminated Indian blood, his children did not resemble in complexion either him or his wife. Nothing can better show this difference than the photograph I took of the group one afternoon, as we returned from hunting in the hills. The children were blessed with abundant, black, straight hair, which was worn by the girls in long braids; it was a trifle coarser than that of the mother, but yet beautiful.

Sandy Bay takes its name from a beach of gray sand guarded by volcanic rocks, lined with tropical vegetation; at its northern end was a single cocoa palm leaning over a thatched hut used as a boat-house. Beneath this hut I encountered some of my Indian neighbors, dividing their spoils from the sea; there were fish of every color: 'parrot fish', 'butter fish', and 'silver fish', radiant with all the hues of the rainbow. To each man Captain George laid aside his portion, and from each little heap took a fish for the stranger sojourning among them. This done, he retired with me to a log beneath the thatch, and overhauled his store of traditional Indian lore. The seas came up with white crests, reaching far up the strand; the sun was down below the volcano, leaving a long, cool twilight, to which the leeward shore is a stranger. [. . .]

[Captain George] regaled me with numerous stories of the achievements of the Caribs during the war with the English in the last century. He firmly believed that his grandfather and other Caribs owed the preservation of their lives to certain charms obtained from an obeah man in Martinique.

'One time, six Carib kill um white gen'leman, but dey not see he serbant hide in de bush. When serbant get 'way he tell soldier, "Carib kill one buckra, my massa." Well, soldier go dah; bam! bam! de ball fall all 'bout; hit um leg, hit um heel, but drop right off, and no hurt Carib 'tall, 'tall, fo' dey hab obeah charm to keep um from make to dead.'

This allusion to the strife once carried on between Carib and English drew out the entire story of the war in which the Carib power was forever destroyed.

20. *The Island of Cocoa Palms.* From Frederick Ober, *Camps in the Caribbees: The Adventures of a Naturalist in the Lesser Antilles* (David Douglas: Edinburgh, 1880), frontispiece.

21. *Captain George and His Family.* From Frederick Ober, *Camps in the Caribbees: The Adventures of a Naturalist in the Lesser Antilles* (David Douglas: Edinburgh, 1880), 211.

In 1772, the best part of the Carib lands having been seized, the Indians commenced hostilities, but soon came to terms. By treaty, they were then secured in the best portion of their lands, and kept the peace until, six years later, instigated and aided by the French from Martinique, they revolted. Soon the entire island was in French possession, without much, if any, bloodshed. In 1784, the island was restored to Great Britain by the treaty of Versailles. Incited by the French republicans, in 1795, the Caribs again revolted, defeated the troops sent against them, and swarmed upon the heights above the town. By the opportune arrival of soldiers and marines from Barbados, they were driven back, but again assembled, and a great fight ensued, in which the English were at first beaten; but finally, by aid of large reinforcements, the Caribs were defeated.

Thus the war went on with varying fortune for a year and a half. The negroes were assembled, appraised at their full value, their owners to be reimbursed for any killed, and sent against the Caribs; but these 'forest rangers', as they were called, though they proved very active and useful in destroying the canoes of the enemy, and in bringing in women and children from the mountains after the warriors had surrendered, did little good service. Doubtless they were animated with the high resolve of saving the colony the expense of paying their owners.

At one time, having been driven from Owia, a point on the north-east side of the island, the Caribs executed a masterly retreat over the volcano, to the Caribbean coast, and committed great ravages; a party sent against them there was defeated. In all their battles they showed consummate skill and great bravery, seizing upon the most advantageous positions, fortifying them and holding them to the last. The English were at first unfortunate in their generals. One of them, 'Sir Paulus Æmilius Irving, Bart.', who was pursuing the Caribs with a large body of troops, became frightened by a six-pounder ball passing near him, and ordered a retreat. Subsequently the English were nearly cut off, and lost several hundred men under this gallant general.

The Indians understood and practiced the trick of posting their best shots in the tall trees, for the purpose of picking off the officers. At last there arrived the famous General Abercrombie, fresh from his capture of St Lucia, who pushed the French and Caribs so hard, with his army of four thousand men, that they were obliged to surrender. The French and colored, officers and soldiers, were released on parole, with the privilege of returning to their own island; but the poor Caribs, thus abandoned, were allowed only unconditional surrender. Refusing these terms, most of them fled to the mountains, and in the dense forests found shelter for a long time, defeating several detachments of troops sent against them.

Deprived of crops, and all provisions such as a successful foray could obtain, they were gradually gathered in, by use of force and by the necessities of their situation, until, of men, women, and children, nearly five thousand were captured. These were removed to the small island of Balliceaux, off the coast of St Vincent, deprived of canoes and arms, and kept there for months. Captain George declared that the English government aimed to destroy as many of them as possible, and caused lime to be mixed in their bread; but of course this was false, and probably arose from the fact that the water, being impregnated with lime, caused much sickness and death.

In February, 1797, they were all carried to the island of Ruatan, off the Honduras coast. When the vessels arrived there, it was found necessary to dislodge a party of Spaniards in possession, who had built a fort. After a hard fight it was taken, and the Caribs left to the mercy of whomsoever should appear against them. The Carib lands were thus left desolate; they were declared forfeited, surveyed and sold. In 1805, the few remaining Caribs were pardoned, and a tract of two hundred and fifty acres, near Morne Ronde, was granted them, this territory not being considered fertile nor available for sugar-land. Here the majority of the Indians have lived in peace ever since.

It appeared strange to me that this settlement at Morne Ronde was composed almost wholly of Black Caribs, the few families of pure Yellow Caribs living on the eastern shore and paying rent for land once in full possession of their ancestors. It may have been that the innate cowardice of the Black Caribs, born of their negro blood, prevented them from taking an active part in the war, and may have induced them to seek the protection of the English. The 'Rangers', also, who scoured the woods after the Caribs were subdued and scattered, and committed many murders, may have been moved to spare people so much resembling themselves.

How similar has been the fate of the Caribs to that of the Seminoles of the Southern States! At the beginning of the present century, the latter were peaceful and happy, cultivating their gardens with an intelligence that shows them to have been superior people. They, too, were driven to war, stripped of their property, and hunted by white troops. Their resistance lasted for seven years, but in the end, nearly all were captured and transported far from their homes. Of them a remnant lingers in the hunting-grounds of their fathers, engaged, like the present Carib, in agricultural pursuits. With them, too, the negro found a home, married with them, and to them communicated the curse of his race.

The memory of the war of his ancestors stirred Captain George to wild song, and his daughters danced in the moonlight while he made music on a drum hollowed from a log and covered with cow-skin, chanting the while a song, of which I can remember but two lines:

> *Neech-i-goo, bah-li, boó ni,*
> *Leh-bi chi, wei-i-ga-mah, ah'-wah-si.*

He attended me to my cabin, late in the evening, and as he had imbibed freely of distilled cane-juice (vulgarly known as rum) he was very confidential, and communicated to me the important secret that, in a cave on one of the islands to which the Caribs were transported, there was a treasure. Of the exact

22. *Carib House at St Vincent, British West Indies, with Group of Carib Making Baskets.* From J. Walter Fewkes, *The Aborigines of Porto Rico and Neighboring Islands*, Bureau of American Ethnology. 25th Annual Report (Smithsonian Institute: Washington, DC. 1907). pl. 8.

nature of this 'treasure' he did not inform me, but left me to infer that it might be gold, or might be of value only to the archæologist. To this latter opinion I was inclined when told that it belonged to the oldest Indian of the nation, who, rather than allow it to be taken by the English, buried it in the cave. I inferred from this that it must be of the nature of a charm or token, such as the Indians, when living in primitive simplicity, carried about them.

Nearly three months later I visited the island where the Caribs had been incarcerated previous to their transportation, and as my discovery there strongly verifies my Indian friend's story, it may be as well in this connection to relate my adventures during that short trip.

The island of Balliceaux, the scene of Carib captivity, is about twelve miles from St Vincent, and is one of the northernmost of the chain of islands and islets known as the Grenadines. It is about a mile in length and perhaps an eighth in breadth, rocky and dry, covered for the most part with a sparse growth of trees. It is owned entirely by one of the largest land proprietors in St Vincent, Mr Cheesman, who has stocked it with goats, guinea-fowl, and deer, intending it as a preserve, to which he occasionally resorts for sport with some friends.

As his guest, in company with a dozen more valiant Scotchmen and Creoles, I left the blue hills of St Vincent, one morning in February, for Balliceaux. We landed from the drogher on a sandy beach, above which drooped a solitary palm, and wended our way to the comfortable house, where we were met by the manager, and to which, later, our store of provender was transported. Our generous host understood well the art of entertaining guests, though it is almost superfluous to say this of any West Indian, either adopted or to the manor born, and as soon as our feet touched the soil of his preserve we felt the truth of his assurance, that all was ours as well as his.

I searched the shore for traces of the Caribs, but was unrewarded save by a few shards of pottery; however, I was promised a guide for the morrow, who could pilot me to a sepulchre of skulls. Alas! that morrow did not bring its promised pleasure, and those skulls may yet linger for some other explorer, for aught I know to the contrary.

Close in sight, about two miles distant, rose the islet of Battowia. It was little more than a huge rock several hundred feet in height, and clad with vegetation on its western slope. In the eastern cliffs was the cave which some of the Indians had occupied, and which we desired to explore. After early coffee the morning succeeding our arrival at Balliceaux, three of us embarked in a 'Moses-boat' for Battowia.

The Moses-boat is a peculiarly strong boat built for transporting sugar and other heavy freight through the heavy surf of the eastern shore. In shape it is something like the famous craft in which those 'three wise men of Gotham' departed on their sea-voyage. It is very buoyant, and owes its great strength to numerous knees and thick planking. Regarding its name, whether it was named for Moses the great 'lawgiver', or for the man who built the first of the kind, will forever remain a mystery.

In the Moses-boat we embarked: the sea was smooth, and we made the passage without mishap. There were four of us 'buckras', or white men, and an equal number of negroes. The negroes pulled the boat, and the whites encouraged the negroes, and withal we made a very satisfactory voyage. Having secured the boat a little way from shore, we marched up the slip toward the summit. Our host had provided a substantial breakfast, to be eaten at the cave, and the men staggered under divers kinds of nourishment contained in bottles with wired corks, a tub of ice and other necessaries.

Soon the bushes grew so thickly that we were obliged to 'cutlass' our way, and took turns in cutting out a path with the great, sword-like knives of the blacks. It was hot, weary work, and we made slow progress. C. started up a great iguana, quite five feet in length, which was basking on the rocks. Part of our party got lost in the thick growth, and this delayed us so that it was well toward noon when we arrived at the ridge and felt the cool breezes from the east.

After a light lunch, we scattered down the cliffs in search of the cave. A whoop from one of our attendants drew us half-way down the precipice, where we were introduced to a deep fissure-like hole in the rock, hidden by trees. Crawling carefully over the loose rock, three hundred feet above the surf beating at the base of the cliff, we entered the cave and prepared to explore it. A glance showed that it was not large nor deep, and we soon found that it led in only a hundred feet before the crevice grew so narrow that it could not be followed; but we were satisfied that it led down to the sea as we could distinctly hear the booming of the waves.

Along each side of the cavern were hollows, evidently artificial, begrimed with smoke, as though they had been used as fireplaces. We found no living things but bats and tarantulas; the former flew about in great numbers. While my companions were engaged in the farther end of the cave, I groped among the loose fragments of stone near the mouth, where, one of the men told me, an Indian chair had been found some fifteen years before. Carefully displacing the stone chippings, I at last found what seemed to be an image of stone; but scraping with a knife revealed that it was of wood. It was a tortoise, four inches long and two and one-half broad, curiously carved. Two holes, a quarter of an inch in diameter, are bored through back and breast; the back, upper part of the head, and the throat are covered with incised figures, and the eyes carefully carved hollows, as if for the reception of some foreign substance.

There is little doubt that this image once belonged to an Indian living many years ago. I choose to consider it a *zemi*, having as my authority the account given in Irving's 'Columbus', of the finding of similar objects by the Spaniards, among the natives of Haiti. Speaking of their religion, he says: 'They believed in one Supreme Being, who inhabited the sky, who was immortal, omnipotent, and invisible. They never addressed their worship directly to him, but to inferior deities, called *zemes*, a kind of messengers or mediators. Each cacique, each family and each individual, had a particular *zemi* as a tutelary deity, whose image, generally of a hideous form, was placed about their houses, carved on their furniture, and sometimes bound to their foreheads when they went to battle. They believed their zemes to be transferable with all their beneficial powers; they therefore often stole them from each other, and, when the Spaniards arrived, hid them away lest they should be taken by the strangers. They believed that these zemes presided over every object in nature. Some had sway over the elements, causing sterile or abundant years; some governed the seas and forests, the springs and fountains, like the nereids, the dryads, and satyrs of antiquity. Once a year each cacique held a feast in honour of his zemi, when his subjects formed a procession to the temple; the married men and women decorated with their most precious ornaments, the young females entirely naked, carrying baskets of flowers and cakes, and singing as they advanced.'

In the 'Smithsonian Report' for 1876 is an elaborate article describing, with many engravings, a collection of antiquities from Porto Rico, containing several Indian 'stools' of stone and wood. These stools are ornamented with a head-piece resembling this tortoise, and even the eye-sockets have the appearance of having been hollowed out for the reception of jewels or bright metal; as the author of the article mentioned above remarks: 'In the wooden objects, as in the stone one, the eyes excavated for precious stones are plainly visible, but the stones are wanting.'

The same author quotes Herrera's accounts of the visit of Columbus to Cuba, when a party, having penetrated to the interior, returned with glowing accounts of their reception by the Indians. They found a village where each house contained a whole generation. 'The prime men came out to meet them, led them by the arms, and lodged them in one of the new houses, causing them to sit down on seats made of a solid piece of wood in the shape of a beast with very short legs and the tail held up, the head before, with eyes and ears of gold.'

This relic of antiquity was undoubtedly taken by the Caribs from their enemies of Haiti, and brought here by the captor, or it may have belonged to a captive Arowak living among the Caribs. The same old negro who found the 'stool' was of our party, but he could not afford any further light except to say, 'Me tink him b'long to Injun seat.' [...]

22. *The Carib Reserve*
Henry Hesketh Bell (1902)

¶ *Sir Henry Hesketh Joudou Bell (1864–1952) has a key role in the modern history of Dominica. During his six years as Administrator of Dominica, right at the beginning of this century, he was responsible for many attempts at innovation, which laid the basis for the island's future development. In particular, his determination to create a proper road system, though not fully achieved even in his (very long) lifetime, began to make overland visits to the Carib quarter more feasible for relatively casual visitors. Bell himself made an official visit in 1902 to announce to the Caribs that he was recommending that the area of Dominica where they lived should become a recognized Carib Reserve (see Plate 24). An official account of this visit was published by the Colonial Office later that year, from which the first extract is taken. Drawing on this report but also on notes and letters from the time, Bell wrote another account in his autobiographical* Glimpses of a Governor's Life *(1946) from which comes the second extract.*

Bell was born in France but joined the British colonial service at an early age, working in Barbados, the Bahamas, and Grenada before becoming Administrator of Dominica in 1899. In 1905 he became Governor of Uganda, and later continued his colonial service in Nigeria and Mauritius. He retired to Cannes in 1924 but went to live in the Bahamas during the Second World War.

Bell, like many colonial officials of the time, was something of a writer and an amateur anthropologist. His early book, Obeah: Witchcraft in the West Indies, *contains an extraordinary scene in which the discovery of a Carib* zemi *prompts a romantic reverie full of beautiful native maidens and scenes of ghastly human sacrifice (1893: 87–92). His penchant for graphic descriptions is apparent even within the pages of the Colonial Report. The emphasis in his writings is always on the contrast between the glories of yesteryear and the tawdriness of present reality. During his tenure of office on Dominica, Bell took anthropometric measurements of Caribs and others, seeking instructions in the proper techniques from the Royal Anthropological Society in London. After his retirement he took extensive notes with a view to writing a book on the Caribs, but never did.*

23. *Administrator of Dominica: 1899, aged 34* (H. H. Bell).
From Henry Hesketh Bell, *Glimpses of a Governor's Life*
(Sampson Low, Marston & Co.: London, n.d. [1946]),
facing p. xi.

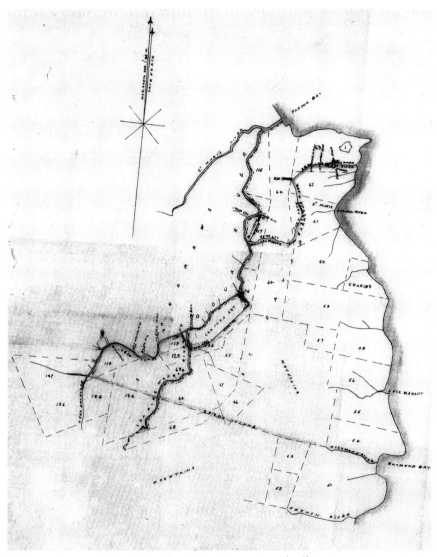

24. *Plan of proposed Boundaries of the Carib Reserve* (1901). Public Record Office, Kew: MFQ/890 188343. This plan was drawn up by the surveyor of Dominica, Arthur P. Skeat, and accompanied Hesketh Bell's letter to Joseph Chamberlain.

1. REPORT ON THE CARIBS OF DOMINICA

Government House,
Dominica,
29th July, 1902.

SIR,

On more than one occasion you have expressed a desire to be informed as to the present condition of the Caribs of Dominica, and I now venture to submit the following report upon the last surviving remnant of these West Indian aboriginals.

2. I trust I may not be considered to be overstepping the bounds of an official dispatch if I preface my description of the Caribs, as they are to-day, by a short sketch of such meagre items of their history as are still available.

3. Cuba, San Domingo, Jamaica, and the other larger islands in the West Indies, appear to have been inhabited, at the time of their discovery, by a mild and timid race, generally called Arouages by Labat, Du Tertre and other French historians of the 17th century. The smaller islands, stretching from St Thomas to Tobago, seem, on the contrary, to have been peopled, at that period, by a warlike and indomitable race of savages, collectively known as 'Charaibes' or 'Caribs', who heroically resisted every attempt at colonization on the part of European intruders, and preferred death to the withering slavery that became the fate of the natives of the larger islands. So stubborn was the resistance offered by these dauntless savages that permanent settlements in the places held by them were not effected until long after the other islands had become flourishing plantations and civilized communities. [. . .]

15. So hopeless appeared the prospect of any friendly arrangement with the Caribs that, by the treaty of Aix-la-Chapelle, in 1748, which purported to settle the ownership of all the Lesser Antilles, Dominica was apportioned to neither British nor French, but was especially set apart as a neutral island for the sole benefit of the Caribs. It was stipulated that no European nation should make settlements there, and a native chief was to be recognized as master of the island. For a considerable period subsequent to this arrangement, the Caribs appear to have remained more or less quiescent, and to have refrained from attacking the settlements in neighbouring islands. Later on, we find their alliance being sought by both French and English, and the Dominica Caribs were frequently to be seen fighting on the side of one or other of the contending nations.

16. Dominica, however, was much too fair and desirable a possession to remain effectively protected by the provisions of the Treaty of 1748, and the French soon unofficially commenced to resume their small trading stations and plantations on the leeward coast. These encroachments were usually made

while the French were 'allies' of the Caribs. Gradually, the savages awakened to the danger that menaced them from the increase of these small settlements. Friction arose, and the colonists were attacked. They defended themselves vigorously, repulsed the Caribs, and thanks to their foothold on the seaboard, drove the aborigines further and further from their settlements.

17. The progress of the French was, nevertheless, constantly hampered by the attacks of the small British parties. Under the pretence of enforcing the provisions of the Treaty and of protecting the rights of the Caribs, the English would land and burn the plantations of the French. If fortune favoured the interlopers, the rights of the Caribs were speedily lost sight of, and the British filibusters would retain possession of the French estates. The Caribs would find that the nationality of the trespassers was the only difference in the case, and that the English took up the aggressions where the French had left them off.

18. By the ninth article of the Peace of Paris, in 1763, the previous arrangement was set aside. Dominica was definitely assigned to the British, and a Lieutenant Governor was formally appointed. Though no vigorous steps were taken to develop the new possession, yet the plantations and villages of the settlers continued slowly to spread around the coasts of the island and to creep up the valleys towards the interior. The claims of the Caribs to any of the arable land were now systematically ignored. So long as they kept to their forests and roamed about the mountains of the interior, they were tacitly allowed to live, but the white settlers eagerly looked forward to the day when privation, disease, and violence would wipe them out with the same completeness as had been the case in the other West Indian islands.

19. So thoroughly were the aborigines considered to have lost all claim to their homes that, in 1764, when Commissioners were appointed by the King to survey the whole island, parcel it out into lots, and sell the same by auction, a paltry reservation of 232 acres, in one block, was alone set apart for the behoof of the unfortunate Caribs. They were probably looked upon much in the light of so many head of game roaming over the land, to be dealt with according to the pleasure of the purchaser. Those who acquired the lots, at the sale by auction in London, had, however, reckoned without their hosts. The Caribs, though much reduced in number, were found to have lost little of the indomitable spirit of their ancestors, and they resisted so strenuously all attempts at cultivation in any of the blocks that were out of the immediate reach of the seaboard, that the purchasers soon found their speculations anything but profitable. Assisted by the run-away slaves, who made common cause with them, the Caribs successfully defended their forests and mountains against all comers, while the constant expeditions despatched by the Government on the coastline, so frequently ended in disaster that all efforts to dislodge the Caribs and to cultivate the interior appear, for many years, to have been abandoned. To the stubborn defence made by the natives should be attributed the fact that, to-day, Dominica is the only island in the West Indies where

almost the whole of the interior still remains in primeval forest and entirely undeveloped.

20. At the latter end of the 18th century the Caribs, in their efforts to get away from the hated intruders, seem to have gradually found themselves congregated at a point on the north-east coast as far distant as possible from Roseau, the principal white settlement. Here, the land being of very poor description and little likely to tempt a colonist, they hoped they might be safe from further molestation and free to follow their own customs. Their numbers seem to have been much reduced by the constant warfare of the two preceding centuries, and, in 1791, the Caribs were reported to comprise not more than 20 or 30 families. It is probable that, by this time, their old passion for human flesh must have died out for lack of opportunity and, judging by the meagre references made in the local records to this unconquered remnant of their race, the Caribs appear, thenceforward, to have settled down peacably in their villages of Salybia and Bataca, and to have refrained from further opposition to the white settlers.

21. A century of peaceful avocations has completely metamorphosed the Carib. Instead of a bloodthirsty, man-eating savage, he is now as law-abiding and mild a subject as any the King has. He no longer paints crimson circles of *roucou* round his eyes and stripes of black and white over his body, but—and I state it with sorrow—on high days and holidays, he wears a tall hat and a black coat. His *Zemis* have been scattered among collections of curios, and instead of yelling round a sacrificial stone, the Carib of to-day goes to confession to the parish priest, and tells his beads with edifying fervour. The picturesque abode depicted by Peter Martyr, where faggots of human bones represented most of the furniture, and a bleeding head hung on a post like a picture, has been replaced by the less romantic, if more comfortable, shingled cabin. The Carib has even lost the debt of gratitude to his forebears. He sleeps on a bed, like everyone else, and he must be poor indeed if his little shanty contain not at least a couple of chairs and a table. The stone implements, with which in the old days he used to brain an adversary or hollow out his canoe, have long ago been replaced by the hoe and the axe from Birmingham, while the beautifully sharpened celts that once caused him so much labour to fashion are now only found hap-hazard under some inches of earth, and are greedily snapped up by the neighbouring negroes as 'thunderstones', accounted passing good for the concoction of 'medicine'.

22. The hundred years of peace and protection have arrested, almost at the last gasp, the extinction of this interesting remnant of one of the world's races. The 20 or 30 families reported at the beginning of the century are still with us to-day, if we count only the Caribs of pure breed, while at the last census, the returns showed, as the population of the Reserve, nearly 400, who 'claimed' to be Caribs. It is to be regretted, from an ethnological point of view, that the breed is suffering much from the admixture of negro blood. Out of the 400 who are settled on the reserve, I doubt whether more than 120 are full-blooded

Caribs, and those are undoubtedly the last survivors of their race in the West Indies. The so-called 'Caribs' of St Vincent are much more akin to negroes than to their original types, and so early did the fusion between the St Vincent natives and the negroes begin, that, even two centuries ago, they were known as the 'Black Caribs' in contradistinction to the 'Red' or pure-bred savages of Dominica and Guadeloupe. There were never two separate colours of Caribs in the lesser Antilles, as has been stated, and the negro admixture of the St Vincent people is proved in Southey's 'History of the West Indies' by the fact that when the French emissaries, in 1772, tried to rouse the St Vincent Caribs to an outbreak against the English, they told him that, 'as they were mostly descended from a cargo of slaves bound in an English ship to Barbados, but wrecked at St Vincent, the heir of the owner had obtained an order to sell them as his property'.

23. When I visited the Carib settlement a short time ago, I found 78 children in the school that had just been established there. Of these, I was able to pick out 26 who appeared to be of pure blood. These children all had extremely bright and intelligent expressions, and many of them, in spite of their oblique eyes, were very pretty. Their hair, though very straight and rather coarse, was of a beautiful blue-black. In complexion they varied from brown to a pinkish yellow, and judging by these specimens, the original Carib must have been a very handsome race. These little children showed remarkable intelligence. Though the school had only been opened a few weeks, some of the little ones, who could not have been more than five years old, already knew their letters. This was the more remarkable, as not one of them could speak a word of English. [...]

25. Two or three old dames were brought to me, in one of my visits to the Carib Reserve, who were supposed to retain some knowledge of the old language, but my faith in the accuracy of their illustrations was shaken by one of them assuring me in *patois* that the old Carib form of salutation was 'Goomorring'. Generally speaking, 'creole patois' is the only dialect used by the Caribs, and I found it to be French, of a rather less debased character than that spoken by the negro inhabitants of Dominica.

26. I judged, according to the pronunciation of their name by the aborigines themselves, that the accepted spelling is phonetically faulty. The early writers seem to have been much in doubt on the point, and we find the French authors calling the 'Indians' Charaïbes, Caraib, or Carribé, while the English travellers dubbed them sometimes Charrib, Carribee, Carribbee, or even Crab. In fact, we find even to-day among the Barbadian negroes, who have a high opinion of themselves, a jingle to the effect that they are 'neither Crab nor Creole, but true 'Badian born'. All the Caribs I have met have always pronounced the name as if it were spelt 'Cribe', rhyming with scribe.

27. The Dominica Caribs are still famous for their canoes and their waterproof baskets, and the manufacture of these comprise their only industries. The long dug-out which, in the old turbulent times, brought terror to the hearts of the

first settlers, remains, to-day, exactly the same in shape and character as it appeared to Columbus when he described it in his diary. The straight thick stem of the great gommier tree is always the one selected for the construction of a canoe. The bark is hacked off and the heart burnt into charcoal. Heavy stones are piled into the hollow, so as to widen the sides, the ends are both sharpened, and the craft is then ready for the water. In these cranky dug-outs, the Caribs venture far into the ocean on fishing expeditions, and though a turn-over may be a common occurrence, the crew, who swim like fish, speedily right their craft and take the incident as a matter of course.

28. Fish is the staple food of the Caribs. They catch enormous quantities, but make no attempt to cure or smoke the surplus. A few of them possess a head or two of cattle or sheep, and the usual skinny West Indian fowl is generally to be found around their cabins. In spite of the poverty of their land, they raise a sufficiency of plantains, yams, tannias, and other vegetables common to the tropics. They are excellent woodsmen, and earn such money as they require by cutting native timber and splitting shingles.

29. It is much to be regretted that, generally speaking, any cash received by them invariably finds its way to the rum shop. No licensed dealer in spirits has been allowed to run a business in the Reserve, but, when on liquor bent, a trudge of many miles will not deter a Carib. Drink is his besetting sin, and unlike the negro inhabitants of Dominica, a small quantity of spirits rapidly shows an effect upon him. At Christmas time they especially give way to their love for liquor. For several weeks before the festive season they set to work to manufacture the well-known 'Carib baskets' for which a ready sale is always found. A certain number of the tribe are deputed to journey to Roseau with the stock and charged to return with rum and gin. A general jollification follows the receipt of the liquor, and no work is done until the supply has disappeared. I do not, however, wish to give an impression that, like his cousin in the American 'Far West', the Dominica Carib is being wiped out by the curse of drink. On the contrary, circumstances over which he has no control prevent his getting hold of any abundance of intoxicating liquor, and while the inclination to excess is undoubtedly there, the opportunities for gratifying it are few and far between.

30. Politically, the Caribs are now of no account. With the exception that they are exempted from any direct taxation, they are treated exactly like other natives of the island and have the same privileges. In return for their freedom from taxation, they are required to keep in order the two miles of high road which traverse their Reserve. The Government, however, has always recognized a chief or headman of the Caribs, and though he has never received any stipend or other advantage he is supposed to settle petty disputes among his people and to adjust any differences that may arise as to the cultivation of the land held in common.

31. The present chief of the Caribs is called Auguste François, but generally known as 'Ogiste'. He claims to be of pure breed, but a marked tendency to a

curl in his long black hair has inspired me with suspicions on this score. The Chief's hut on the Reserve is neither better nor worse than the others. It is a little wooden shanty, with a thatched roof and is crowded round by mango trees and cocoanut palms. When I saw it last, a gorgeous 'flamboyant' tree, in full bloom, was shedding its scarlet blossoms all over the russet thatch, and many a greater potentate than Auguste might envy him the magnificent tints of his surroundings. The Chief's old wife is blind and their children seem to have all died. A little grand-child alone represents the continuance of the dynasty, but unfortunately, she is more negro than Carib, and moreover, the Salic Law prevails.

32. In spite of the peaceful air of the settlement, it is not without its 'burning questions', and the Caribs are much exercised respecting the 'Batards'. Under this uncompromising denomination, are comprised all those who are not full-blooded Caribs. They now number three-fourths of the whole population of the Reserve, and it is to be feared that in a few decades there will not be a single pure-bred specimen left to show the true type of this interesting people. [...]

33. I will now deal with one or two matters and suggestions connected with the Caribs, which I hope may have your favourable consideration.

34. Although, for over a century, the district now occupied by the Caribs has always been officially recognized as their 'Reserve', no proper grant of the land appears to have ever been made to either the Chief or to any other proper representatives of the tribe. Though the paltry allotment of 232 acres, in 1764, comprised in lot 60 in Byres' plan, seems never to have been seriously considered as the proper limits of the settlement, I can find no trace of any formal arrangement by which the Caribs were allowed to consider as their own the area now held by them. The very year after Byres had completed the survey of the island, delimiting all the blocks of land that had been sold in London, Dominica was captured by the French, and remained in their possession until 1783, when it was re-taken by the British. It is not impossible that the limits of the Carib Commonage were settled during the French occupation, but no record of the fact can be found in the local archives. It is, however, almost certain that no plan or survey ever appears to have been made of the area intended to be granted, and the present boundaries of the Reserve, though generally accepted, are open to considerable doubt. There is also reason to believe that neighbouring landowners have, in years past, encroached upon the area which was intended to be reserved for the Caribs, and since I have been in Dominica, I have been called upon to settle several disputes as to boundaries.

35. I have, in preceding pages, reported that most of the land in the Carib reserve is of the poorest description and practically worthless. To the poverty of the soil should, I think, be ascribed the fact that, generally speaking, these natives grow no produce save the commonest vegetables and foodstuffs, and whenever I have impressed upon them the advisability of planting cocoa, limes

and other profitable products, I have always been assured that the land in the Reserve was too arid to grow anything of the kind. Some months ago, however, it was brought to my notice that a good many of the Caribs were working plots of land in a valley that appeared to be outside the northern boundary of their reserve, and that they already possessed several flourishing patches of cocoa in that locality. The matter was brought to light through Mr Wm. Davies, the owner of the adjacent plantation 'Concord', who submitted an application for a block of what he described as 'Crown lands adjoining his estate'. Mr 'Government Officer' Robinson was sent to inspect the locality and he returned with the report that the land applied for by Mr Davies was in the actual occupation of the Caribs and was being well cultivated by them. The Caribs, moreover, claimed that the valley does form part of their original Reserve, and they would, I believe, strenuously resist eviction.

36. It appeared to me very desirable that the limits of the Reserve should be properly and finally delimited, and I commissioned Mr A. P. Skeat, a licensed surveyor, to survey the land held by them and to make a plan. He was instructed to follow the recognized boundaries of the Reserve and to adopt, wherever possible, streams, cliffs, and other natural landmarks. He was also authorized to include that part of the Hatton Garden Valley in which their cocoa and other plantations are situated. The land, moreover, was to march with the limits of the neighbouring estates, so as to leave no intervening narrow strips of unoccupied land.

37. Mr Robinson, an old Government official, long resident in the district, well acquainted with the Caribs and much respected by them, was associated with Mr Skeat in making the survey. The Carib Chief and the principal men of the tribe were also consulted, and the proposed boundaries were accepted by them as very satisfactory. They also expressed much gratitude for the proposed liberality of the Government.

38. I attach hereto the plan of the survey made by Mr Skeat. It will be seen that the Carib Reserve, within the boundaries now proposed will include 3,700 acres. The inclusion of the valley lands, whose ownership has hitherto been open to doubt, will probably add three or four hundred acres to the area heretofore held by the Caribs, but I hope that this suggested liberality will meet with your sanction. This surviving remnant of the race has been so badly treated in the past that a little kindness to them in the future may not be considered Quixotic. The proposed extension of the Reserve involves only the gift of Crown lands situated in a district which is not likely to attract settlers, and all proper precautions will be taken that the Crown's disposal of them is open to no counter claim.

39. I will conclude by recommending to your favourable consideration the advisability of granting to the Carib Chief a small stipend. The present headman, Auguste François, is very poor, and has not long to live. I doubt if his subjects contribute much to his support, and I believe that an allowance of £6 a year

would be gratefully received. The stipend might be paid out of Crown Land Funds.

I have, &.

H. HESKETH BELL,

Administrator.

2. GLIMPSES OF A GOVERNOR'S LIFE

December [1899].

Accompanied by a young prospective settler, I left Roseau, three days ago, on a tour of inspection round the island. The weather was perfect and the ride around the coast was delightful. The windward side of Dominica is nothing but a succession of steep hills and valleys running down to the seas; a regular switchback. The cliffs are so precipitous that the main road cannot be kept at sea level, and goes up and down constantly. Some of the ascents are extremely steep, and I had often to hang on to my horse's mane to keep in the saddle. In one place, which rejoices in the delightful *patois* name of *paix bouche ou*, the road must have a gradient of at least one in five. The name means 'hold your tongue', derived from the fact that a peasant, walking up and carrying on his head the usual load, has no breath left for talking.

We put up, on the way, at the house of various hospitable planters. Judge Pemberton, at his beautiful cocoa estate, Pointe Mulatre, treated us with especial generosity. About ten miles beyond Roseau we came, at last, to the Carib settlement, a visit to which was one of the chief objects of my tour.

NOTE.—At the time of Columbus's first visit to these islands (1493) he found all the smaller ones, which now form the Leeward and Windward groups, inhabited by a race of indomitable savages to whom the earliest writers on the West Indies gave the name of *Charaibe* or Carib. Unlike the mild and timid Arawaks, who peopled Cuba, San Domingo, Jamaica and other of the larger islands in the Caribbean Sea, these valiant people preferred death to slavery, and, for three centuries, waged an almost incessant war against the Spanish, French and British intruders.

Although the accounts of the West Indies, written during the seventeenth and eighteenth centuries by Oviedo, du Tertre, Labat, Peter Martyr and several other authors, contain numberless references to the Carib inhabitants of the Lesser Antilles and to the constant wars with them, nothing in the shape of a separate history of the Caribs has, I believe, ever been written. This is a strange thing, as the material is copious, and the exploits of this dauntless race, of which there is now only a dying remnant in Dominica, are full of instances of heroism and high adventure not only on the part of the British, French and Spaniards, but especially on the side of the dauntless savages who defended their islands.

Those who peopled Guadeloupe, Martinique, Dominica, St Vincent and St Lucia, being of light complexion, were known as Yellow or Red Caribs.

According to their traditions, they came originally from some part of the North American continent, a few centuries before the advent of Columbus. They exterminated the male aborigines and married the women. The Europeans, who tried to establish plantations and settlements in the Caribbean islands during the seventeenth and eighteenth centuries, found themselves energetically opposed by these virile savages. The extremely mountainous nature of the interior of Dominica, especially, gave such facilities for defence that it long remained the chief stronghold of the Caribs. Not only did they resist all encroachments on their own island, but, in association with the St Vincent and Guadeloupe Caribs, they made frequent descents on the settlements in Antigua and Porto Rico and were the terror of the colonies.

The characteristic of the Caribs which most keenly attracted the early historians was their remarkable passion for human flesh. It appears, however, that they rarely ate members of their own tribe, and that, in order to satisfy their craving, they would put to sea, in their frail dug-outs, and paddle hundreds of miles in quest of the gentle Arawak who still survived in the islands farther south and on the mainland. It is thought, in the West Indies, that Daniel Defoe placed the scene of his inimitable tale in Tobago, and that the mild Man Friday was one of a hapless lot of Arawaks whom a party of Caribs had captured on the Spanish Main and were carrying home for the delectation of their tribe.

Though white men, negroes or Arawaks were all meat to them, yet they seem to have shown a decided preference for certain nationalities. Davis, for instance, in his *History of the Caribby Islands*, written in the eighteenth century, tells us that 'the Caribbeans have tasted of all the nations that frequented them, and affirm that the French are the most delicate and the Spaniards are hardest of digestion'. Laborde, also in one of his jaunts in St Vincent, related how he had overtaken on the road a communicative Carib who was beguiling the tedium of his journey by gnawing at the remains of a boiled human foot. This gentleman only ate Arawaks. 'Christians', he said, 'gave him the belly-ache!'

In spite of their cannibalistic habits, these Yellow Caribs appear to have been a fine and rather noble race of savages. They fought like sportsmen, and numbers of instances of heroic fortitude, on their part, are recorded by the early writers on the West Indies. They fought openly and to the death, with spears and tomahawks, bows and arrows, and appear rarely to have descended to the use of poisoned weapons. When in full war-paint they must have presented a fearsome appearance, for they painted their bodies a bright red with the juice of the *roucou* (*annatto*), and their flashing eyes were encircled by broad rings of gleaming white pigment. Their long black hair was decorated by coronets of brilliant feathers, while necklaces of human teeth hung from their necks. French and Spanish missionaries, who wrote about them, describe these Caribs as of tall stature and handsome shape, and lay stress upon their pride and self-possession. Many of the characteristics of these people so closely resemble those of the North American Indians that one is inclined to conclude that the Yellow Caribs of the Leeward and Windward Islands must originally have been an offshoot from the brave and handsome race that peopled the broad prairies of North America.

One can imagine the terror which these dauntless savages created in the minds of the early settlers in the islands farther north. Without a sign of warning, the long black canoes, crowded with painted warriors, would, in the darkness of the night, suddenly round a headland and swarm into the little harbour of a peaceful settlement. Before the white men could fly to their arms or concert a plan for defence, the scarlet-hued savages, yelling like fiends, would be in their midst. In an instant the little town, with its brown thatched dwellings, would be in a blaze. Overpowered by numbers, the unfortunate traders and artisans, fighting as best they could in the glare of their burning homes, would fall under the stone hatchets and tomahawks of the Caribs, leaving the shrieking women and children at the mercy of their captors, doomed to a horrible fate in a distant land.

Maddened by rum and loaded with plunder, the savages would hasten back to their canoes, and long before the neighbouring planters could get together to repel the attack the swiftly paddled canoes would have vanished into the gloom of the sea, far beyond the reach of rescue or revenge.

It is probable that the Caribs of the various islands coalesced so as to make their descents in greater force. The Spanish settlements suffered especially from these attacks, and a writer, in the middle of the sixteenth century, reported that 'the cannibals have, in our time, violently taken out of the said island of Sancti Johannis (Porto Rico) more than 5,000 men to be eaten'.

When reading one of these early histories of the West Indies I came across a very interesting account of a visit paid by a party of Dominica Caribs to the island of Antigua, not long after that island had become an English settlement.

It was during one of the periods of peace which sometimes occurred between the Caribs and the white settlers, and, in answer to a cordial invitation from Colonel Carden, the Governor, the principal Carib Chief of Dominica, with a number of his warriors, came in their canoes to pay a visit to the town of St John's. The party were led up to the residence of the Governor and were invited to partake of a banquet that had been prepared for them. In honour of the occasion the Caribs were in 'full rig' of red paint, feathers and glistening beads. On entering the dining-room the visitors were invited to take their seats on a number of plush-covered stools that were disposed around the table. The Chief, who was a complete stranger to the refinements of civilization, was greatly puzzled by what he saw before him. Porcelain plates and dishes were a complete novelty and he wondered what could be their use. Then, looking at the beautiful plush covering of his stool and realizing that it would be spoilt by the greasy red pigment that decorated his anatomy, he promptly concluded that the best use to which he could put a plate was to insert it between his person and the beautiful chair. His example was immediately followed by all his companions.

This action caused much merriment to the white hosts, and the Governor is said to have laughed loud and long at the excellent joke. The Caribs, who were by nature extremely sensitive to ridicule, were intensely offended by the hilarity of their hosts, and the Chief declared that they would not eat a morsel in a house in which they had been so grievously insulted. They would accept no excuses or apologies, and, in high dudgeon, immediately left the house to return to their canoes.

The Governor, who had accompanied them down to the beach, did all in his power to placate his irate visitors, but they maintained a stony silence. The historian relates that the Caribs, 'more treacherous than the wild beasts that haunt the desert, had no sooner reached the place where their canoes were stationed than they suddenly fell upon their kind host, cruelly murdered him, and broiled his head, which they afterwards carried with them to Dominica'.

In a measure, as the British and French settlements increased in number the Caribs found their homes torn from them and their hunting-grounds disappearing under the cane-fields and coffee plantations of the intruders. One by one the northern islands were evacuated by them, until, by the beginning of the seventeenth century, we find the Caribs remaining masters only of Guadeloupe, Dominica and Martinique. Even in those islands small colonies began to be established at the mouths of rivers and at other places on the coasts where the configuration of the country admitted of an easy defence.

Owing, however, to the mountainous nature of Dominica and to its almost impenetrable forests, the Caribs of that island remained, for a long time, in sole possession of the greater part of the country, and, from their hidden strongholds, would constantly descend into the lowlands to pillage and burn the plantations of the outlying settlers. So hopeless appeared the prospect of any friendly arrangement with the Caribs that, by the Treaty of Aix-la-Chapelle, in 1748, which purported to settle the ownership of all the Lesser Antilles, Dominica was apportioned neither to the British nor to the French, but was specially set apart as a neutral island for the sole benefit of the remaining Caribs. For a considerable period subsequent to this arrangement they appear to have refrained from attacking the settlements in the neighbouring islands.

Dominica was, however, much too fair and desirable a possession to remain efficiently protected by the Treaty of 1748, and the French soon resumed their encroachments on the coast. The island was also coveted by the British, and in 1763, by the ninth article of the Peace of Paris, the claims of the Caribs were ruthlessly set aside and Dominica was definitely assigned to the British.

During most of the nineteenth century the Caribs, who by that time had been reduced to only a few hundreds, lived in peace with the local Government. They occupied remote parts in the interior of the islands on the windward coast, and kept themselves strictly apart from the negroid population. They lived mainly on fishing and the hunting of wild pigs, and apparently abandoned all their old cannibalistic customs. The majority of them gradually settled themselves in a locality on the east coast, known as Salybia, and, by a tacit agreement with the Government, the district was considered to be a Carib Reserve.

No definite allocation of this land had ever been arranged, and it seemed to me highly desirable that the small remnant of the people, who once owned the whole island, should be permanently guaranteed the possession of their last homes. I decided, therefore, that their Reserve should be properly delimitated and officially recognized. It was with the object of informing the Caribs of my decision that I was making my journey to their district.

At the entrance to the Reserve we were met by the old Chief of the Caribs, surrounded by about 150 of his people grouped around a small 'triumphal arch' made of coco-nut branches and decorated with flowers and fruit. I must say that their appearance was a considerable disappointment. After all I had read about the Caribs of the old days, their fine physique, their heroism in battle and their engaging cannibalistic habits, I had conjured up visions of splendid men of the Red Indian type, and half expected to see them covered with feathers and red paint.

The reality was far from my imagination. These last remnants of the magnificent savages that were once the terror of the Caribbean seas wore a distressingly dull and prosaic appearance. Auguste, the Chief, was clad in an old and dilapidated black morning-coat that shone green in the sunlight, with a pair of white cotton trousers, while, on his head, was precariously perched—as it was manifestly much too small for him—one of those flat-topped, hard felt hats beloved of churchwardens. His old wife, who was blind, stood beside him, was dressed in a clean, print gown, and on top of her white head-kerchief wore a man's black, soft felt hat, crushed flat. All the rest of the Caribs were similarly dressed in ordinary European clothing, and there was nothing but their faces to show any difference between them and the ordinary Creole inhabitants of the island.

Their village, composed of neat little shingled houses, was of the usual Dominican type with a little wooden Roman Catholic chapel in the centre of it. But afer the first feeling of disappointment I became much interested in these people and their physique. They seemed to me to be typical North American Indians. Straight, coarse, blue-black hair, copper complexion and high cheekbones. What especially struck me was the oblique tilt of their rather piercing black eyes, giving them a distinctly Mongolian expression. I was told that, some twenty years ago, a Chinaman who, haphazard, had found his way to Dominica, had drifted to the Carib quarter. He declared that they were his own people and married one of them. By her he had three daughters, and while they were, presumably, half Chinese and half Carib they showed no variation whatever from the pure-bred people in the Reserve.*

The old Chief and his people were, of course, very pleased to hear that the possession of their Reserve was to be definitely secured to them, and that they

---

* Some years later a medical man, when telling me about his work in China, said that many newly-born Chinese babies had a small round spot of dark-coloured skin at the extremity of the backbone, just over the coccyx. I then remembered that, when in the Carib Reserve, I had been told that newly-born Carib children also had the same curious characteristic, but that it soon faded away.

would thus be protected from the encroachments of the Dominican peasants who were constantly trespassing on their land. I was sorry to see, however, that a very large number of Caribs were evidently not of pure descent, and I was told that the younger generation unfortunately show but little pride of race. The men have been intermarrying with the negro women in the neighbouring districts, and a large number of the young children showed the mixture of the strains. I was pained to see that, out of the three or four hundred individuals, who are now the sole representatives of the dauntless race which occupied all these islands in the time of Columbus, not more than 120 are now of pure blood. I said what I could to make them realize that they are now the last remnant of a fine race and that they should try to keep their breed pure, but I fear that the claims of ethnology will not have much effect on them.

The Reserve, which I have apportioned to them, will amount to about 4,000 acres. I have also arranged that the old Chief, Auguste, is to be recognized as the head of the Caribs and will receive a small stipend. When I asked the old man whether he had any grievances he, at once, complained of the presence in the village of a half-breed who, he declared, was slowly killing him and his wife by witchcraft.

'*Li tini la main sale*', he assured me, meaning in the quaint old French *patois* that his enemy was a well-known sorcerer. He insisted that this individual, by his spells, had caused the blindness of his old wife, and that, in his own case, he had placed *des bourdons* (bumble-bees) inside his arm and head. He assured me that he could feel them constantly buzzing in his flesh and brain, and that he would infallibly die unless the spell were removed by the banishment of the man.

I was inclined to think that the old Chief really did have a 'bee in his bonnet' until I heard from the good padre who ministered to the Caribs that not only was Auguste a very intelligent man but that he was well known as being himself the most potent sorcerer in the island. Such a reputation he had for the power of his spells and potions that people even came from the neighbouring French islands to enlist his aid. That there is more in sorcery than what 'meets the eye' is incontestable, and it is certain that the 'Obeahmen' of the West Indies are as firm believers in their occult powers as were some of our own witches in the seventeenth and eighteenth centuries.

25 and 26. Early examples of photographs of Carib groups: they were produced as postcards during the 1930s.

27. *Wild Carib Indians of Pure Blood.* Photograph by Symington Grieve. From Symington Grieve, *Notes upon the Island of Dominica (British West Indies) Containing Information for Settlers, Investors, Tourists, Naturalists, and Others* (Adams & Charles Black: London, 1906), opp. 93. The Royal Commonwealth Society.

Grieve mentions his debt to the French priest René Suaudeau: 'Since I was interested in the remnant of this interesting race, he entertained me, took me to see the King and Queen, got the pure Caribs to send some of their children to be photographed and showed me such attention as I had no reason to expect. This young priest is held in great respect by the Caribs, and to them he acts as friend, preceptor, and guide, but, owing to his modesty, apparently almost without knowing it himself' (85).

28. (*left*) J.-B. Corriette. From M. Neveu-Lemaire, 'Les Caraïbes des Antilles', *La Géographie*, 35 (1921), 143. The Royal Commonwealth Society. Jules-Benjamin Corriette (1853–1933) was Carib chief from 1916 to 1926. During a short-lived and unsuccessful attempt to register Carib land-rights in 1918 (which gives a valuable insight into Carib agricultural practices in the early twentieth century), Corriette claimed 1,014 spice trees, 500 lime trees, 223 cocoa trees, 61 coconut trees, 20 coffee trees, and 4 breadfruit trees.

29. (*right*) Carib woman. From Ph. Schelfhaut, *Dominica: Het eiland der Caraiben* (Drukkerij Emiel Van Haver-Martens: Sint-Niklaas-Waas, 1908), 21. The Royal Commonwealth Society.

23. *Frederick Treves and Victorine* (*1908*)

¶ *Sir Frederick Treves (1853–1923) is best known as the foremost surgeon and anatomist of his day. Born in Dorset he was educated at William Barnes's school, where he met Thomas Hardy, a life-long friend. The text-books on surgery that Treves wrote in the 1880s and 1890s were standard works in their field until after the Second World War. He was appointed surgeon extraordinary to Queen Victoria in 1900 and gained world-wide fame by successfully conducting an appendectomy on King Edward V II two days before his coronation, a service which gained him his baronetcy. A later generation knows him better as the doctor who befriended Joseph Merrick, the Elephant Man. Treve's last book,* The Elephant Man and Other Reminiscences (*1923*), *is the source of all subsequent work on the topic.*

Shortly after his elevation to baronet, Treves retired from surgery. He had published an account of his experiences of the South African War, Tale of a Field Hospital (*1900*), *and the success of this book encouraged him to spend the next twenty-five years travelling and writing about his travels. 'Victorine and Her Forefathers' is just one chapter from a long and detailed book about his trip to the West Indies,* The Cradle of the Deep (*1908*). *He also wrote about Palestine, Italy, Uganda, and France.* The Other Side of the Lantern *is the outcome of a world tour.* Highways and Byways of Dorset (*1906*) *is still in print. There is a recent biography: Stephen Trombley,* Sir Frederick Treves: The Extra-Ordinary Edwardian (*1989*).

Treves's travel books offered a kind of 'report on Empire', a fairly leisurely survey written in a distinctly less anguished tone than that, say, of Froude, some twenty years earlier. It appears that Treves did not visit the Carib Territory itself. Dr Henry Nicholls, a not insignificant medical figure himself, who had taken an interest in the Caribs, clearly acted as a go-between, offering the figure of Victorine as an emblem of 'Caribness' for Treves to contemplate and around whom to weave his historical meditations. It is not uncommon for visitors to focus on an adolescent girl: Victorine, whose portrait forms Treves's frontispiece, is wearing more clothes than most.

The nursery rhyme that Treves refers to is probably the one that goes:

> Hokey, pokey, whisky, thum,
> How d'you like potatoes done?
> Boiled in whisky, boiled in rum,
> Says the King of the Cannibal Islands.

A special interest attaches to Dominica in that it is—as Dr Nicholls says—'the only island where pure-blooded descendants of the original inhabitants of the Antilles are to be found'. There is a remote spot on the north-east coast of the island a Carib Reservation provided by the Government. Here these ancient people live in peace and contentment. Although their numbers are diminishing, they can still muster about three hundred. 'They pay no taxes, but are required to keep open the main road through the Reserve, and their chief receives a small stipend from the Government. They are now quiet, peaceful, and well mannered ... They have lost all trace of their double language (for the men used to speak one language while the women spoke another), and occupy their days by fishing, making their celebrated waterproof baskets, and cultivating small plots of West Indian fruits and vegetables.'*

It would appear that the earliest-known inhabitants of the West Indian island were peoples of two types, the Arawaks and the Caribs. They both came from the South American mainland, the Arawaks from Northern Brazil, the Caribs from parts further south. Both are described as races of the Mongolic type, with yellow to olive-brown skin, long, lank, black hair, a broad skull, almond-shaped black eyes, slightly oblique, and bodies of moderate stature. The Arawaks were no doubt the earlier of the two to reach the islands, were savages of a low type, indolent, gentle and unprogressive. The Caribs, who gradually displaced these docile folk, were of greater average height, were fierce, warlike and intelligent, and frankly addicted to cannibalism. They could claim to be a race of fine people. Drake when he visited Dominica describes them as 'very personable and handsome strong men'.

At the time of the discovery of the New World by Columbus the greater Antilles and the Bahamas were inhabited by Arawaks, the Lesser Antilles by Caribs. It was a day of lamentation for the islander when he met with the enlightened white man, who came from the unknown East bringing with him the 'blessings of civilisations'.

The place of meeting of these two was at an island called by Columbus San Salvador, but now known as Watling's Island. It received its latter name from a sin-hardened old pirate, John Watling, who was shot in 1681 while attempting to plunder a city. It is a small island, some twelve miles in length, belonging to Great Britain, occupied mainly by salt-water lagoons and low wooded hills; yet it manages to support a population of 600 people, and to

* *Dominica*, by Dr H. A. Nicholls, C.M.G., Antigua.

merit a reputation for breeding excellent sheep and cattle. Watling's Island is the first land sighted by the mail steamer in her homeward journey from New York to the West Indies. It should therefore be familiar to many. If the ship passes in the night there is still the flash from the lighthouse to show where the island lies.

It was an ever-memorable morning, the morning of October 12, 1492, a day portentous and terrible. The naked savage of San Salvador, when he gazed from the sea-commanding hills, must have wondered where the great water that spread eastward came to an end. The West he knew: there were familiar islands, and that wide continent which figures in the traditions of his tribe. As to the East, the white beach at his feet marked the extremest limit of the known world. From behind the eastern sea rose at dawn the sun and at night the stars, while from out of the same mystic heaven blew the abiding wind; but nothing that had life had ever emerged from over the unchanging ocean rim. No canoe that had passed beyond that margin had ever returned to the land again.

Now, on this October morning, there came out of the unknown three fearsome things that moved upon the sea.* The islander would behold the faint image of a towering ship made ghostly by the uncertain haze, and so colossal that its masts reached to the clouds. As the dawn broke he would see the foam about the sullen bows, the bellying sails, the castle on the fore, the tower on the poop. Every wondrous rope and spar would be cut clear against the tender light; the rocking yards would stretch across the clearing sky; the figures of men and the gleam of arms would be seen along the rail. It was not for him to know that the banner at the mizzen was the standard of Castile, and that the great cross painted on the mainsail was the sign of the Redeemer. This ship from out of the unimaginable abyss would seem to the islander to have sailed from the sun. As it came on the sky around it would break into lilac and crimson and gold, light would radiate from it as rays from a planet, and encircled by the many coloured halo of the dawn, the majestic craft would roll towards the land.

Columbus, clad in armour and wearing a scarlet cloak, landed on the beach with profound solemnity, and in this wise the wild man and his destroyer met. The simple naked folk brought as presents balls of cotton, spears and parrots, and received in exchange scarlet caps, beads, and hawk's bells. The foremost and ever present desire of the adventurer from Castile was that 'the Lord in His mercy would direct him to find gold': after that came a yearning to see these poor untutored people 'free and converted to the Holy Faith'. To set them free; they who were as free as the sea-birds! To strive that they may be 'saved from the darkness of their happy innocence, and brought to the light of a religion that had just evolved the Inquisition'!†

---

* The three vessels of Columbus were the *Santa Maria*, 100 tons, the *Pinta*, 50 tons, and the *Nina*, 40 tons.
† *Christopher Columbus*, by Filson Young, vol. i. page 107: London, 1906.

It would have been happy if the bartering had ended with balls of cotton and hawk's bells; but it soon became a traffic in which the only island goods that were marketable were human lives.

The first settlement of the Castilians was on Haiti. The natives here— estimated at about a million in number—were childlike, unresisting Arawaks. They were soon wiped off the earth. They were made to work as slaves in the mines until they died of starvation and excessive toil. They were massacred wholesale with appropriate treachery, were hunted down as if they were rabbits, were decimated by imported diseases, or beaten to death for not attending Mass. The gentle Queen Isabel did what lay in her power to protect them. Slavery was by her forbidden, but the prohibition was easily evaded by ingenious forms of indentured labour. It was urged too, that it was good for the natives to work in mines, as idleness was demoralizing. The poor Indians could not look after themselves, the slave-driver said, and moreover if they remained in their villages 'it was impossible to instruct them in the principles of Christianity'. Even supposing that they were enslaved, murdered, or worked to death, at least in every instance they were baptized.

When Haiti became depopulated the pious Spaniards extended the field of their missionary labours to the Lesser Antilles; but in these islands the cause was not blessed, for they had to deal with the warlike Carib who was more than a match for them. Thus it was that these pioneers of civilization turned their attention to the Bahamas. Here they kidnapped the docile islanders without having to murder very many of them, baptized the survivors and sent them to the mines to rot.

It was never forgotten that the object of these man-hunting forays was to enable the Arawak to be instructed in the Holy Faith. 'It would be necessary', explained the Governor of Haiti, 'that they should be transported to Hispaniola (Haiti); as missionaries could not be spared to every place and there was no other way in which this abandoned people could be converted.'* It was by this energetic method of extending the blessings of religion to the abandoned natives of the Bahamas that those islands became as bare of human life as a desert.

The zeal with which the ministers of God from Spain kept the recently baptized savage from heresy and insured his attendance at Mass attracted the notice of such explorers as came to the New World. Samuel Champlain, for example, made a voyage into these waters between the years 1599 and 1602.†
He gives, in the book he wrote, a picture of seven Indians burning in one fire, while a couple of elaborately dressed Spaniards stand by to watch them roasting with unaffected boredom. The abandoned natives were probably being burned alive on account of inaccurate views as to the Real Presence, but as they were ignorant of the Spanish tongue the offence was small.

In another engraving Champlain shows how the savage, after he had been

* *History of the Buccaneers*, by Captain James Burney, R.N.: London, 1891.
† Hakluyt Society, 1859.

276

brought under religious influences, was induced to attend the service of his church. At the door of a house of prayer stands a priest with a book in his hand. The fingers of the other hand are raised as if he were about to pronounce a blessing. In the forecourt an Indian is being beaten with a club by a very powerful man. The ecchymosed savage is gazing at the priest with curiosity. It is explained that the club, which would fell an ox, is a means of Grace whereby the thoughtless were led to attend to their devotions. It is further explained that each convert who was absent from Mass received at the hands of the athletic missionary thirty to forty blows from the Gospel club in the precincts of the place of worship.

Champlain in his account of the natives remarks that 'they are of a very melancholy humour'. Those who were irregular in their church attendances and who survived their bruises and broken ribs had certainly reasons for depression.

The Caribs in the smaller islands, although they may have had the good fortune to escape the missionary, fell victims to the man with the musket and the man with the keg of brandy under his arm. They both came to him with lies on their lips and treachery in their hearts. The Carib had to fight for his life and for every foot of his native land. He had to fight in turn the Spaniards, the French, the English and the Dutch. It was the hopeless battle of arrow and spear against powder and ball; the war of the naked savage against the world. The brown man, however, held his own valiantly. In Dominica he defied all comers for some two centuries and a half. He had strength, sagacity and courage, and behind him the gorgeous arms of an impenetrable forest. He might have held his lands longer but for his taste for rum.

During my stay at Dominica I was able, through the kindness of Dr Nicholls, to make the acquaintance of a pure-blooded Carib from the Reservation. She was a girl of ten, whose name was Victorine. She was a picturesque little maid, with pretty manners and a singularly sweet voice. Her complexion was yellow-brown, her hair long, lank and black. She had the lacquer-black eyes of a Japanese doll, almond shaped and a little oblique, a fine mouth and lips, slightly prominent cheeks. The type of her face was distinctly Mongolian, without the least suggestion of the negro in her outlines. She was as erect as an arrow and walked as only an Indian can walk. Her dress was of pink stripes, and her head-dress a primrose-coloured turban or madras. [See Plate 30.]

Victorine was brought out to see the steamer. It was her first experience of a large ship. Everything delighted her except the engines. It was about the bath-rooms that she was most curious, for in a quiet imperious manner she signified that it was her pleasure to visit them a second time. She seemed to connect them somehow with religion. She was not as graceful in her mode of eating as in her walking. She was given tea, but declined the use of a saucer as superfluous. Whatever she ate was first dipped in the cup.

Victorine could claim at least an interesting ancestry. Her people roamed the

30. *Victorine*. From Sir Frederick Treves, *The Cradle of the Deep: An Account of a Voyage to the West Indies* (Smith, Elder. & Co.: London, 1910), frontispiece.

island for centuries before Columbus came. They saw the sailing hither of the first great ship the *Marie Galante*. They watched the landing of Drake and Hawkins when they came for 'refreshing', just as now they may gaze at blue jackets coming ashore from the modern ironclad. Victorine may not be 'the daughter of a hundred earls', but among her forefathers might have been that 'King of the Cannibal Islands' who is for ever famous in the English nursery song.

She might still have been attracted by a scarlet cap, a string of beads, or a hawk's bell. None of these being at hand, she was offered her choice of certain commonplace articles. With a remarkable precision and with more than mere instinct she selected a purse and two half-crowns, those being the largest of the coins laid out before her. It was impossible not to feel that the most fitting present for this little wild thing, with her brown skin and piercing eyes and her wilder ancestry, would still have been a hawk's bell.

PART   V

The 'Carib War' of 1930 can be taken to mark the beginning of the most recent period in the history of the Carib Territory in Dominica. The incidents of that war are still remembered by older Caribs, and the theft of the chief's copy of the map of the Reserve has contributed to the current disputes with the Dominican government over the exact extent of the Territory (No. 24).

The writings about the Caribs in this period become much more specialized. For the first time professional anthropologists make an appearance, doing their fieldwork in the Carib Territory and producing articles and monographs of a serious and valuable kind. Their work falls outside our frame of reference, but we have included a more popular piece by Douglas Taylor, the English linguist, who lived on Dominica for many years, married a Carib woman, and whose large body of writings is an indispensable starting-point for the study of Carib lifeways (No. 26).

This section also includes two exceptionally fine pieces of writing. Jean Rhys is the only Dominican writer represented in this anthology. Having left the island to go to school in England, she returned only once, in 1936, and made a single trip to the Carib Territory, a fictionalized account of which is included in her story 'Temps Perdi'. Then, soon after the Second World War, Dominica was visited by Patrick Leigh Fermor, widely recognized as the finest travel-writer of the last half-century. We include a piece on the Caribs that he wrote for a geographical magazine, and which appeared in extended form in his prize-winning book *The Traveller's Tree* (1950). (Nos. 25, 28.)

How the Caribs have been visualized has always been important: we have included in the anthology a selection of early engravings, and some of the many photographs taken over the last ninety years. On two recent occasions, though, the Caribs have appeared in moving pictures of some significance, and we have represented those two events here—the Gainsborough studios film of *Christopher Columbus*, some of which was shot on Dominica in 1948, with Caribs as extras, and the visit of the television traveller Alan Whicker during one of his early BBC series, made in 1964. (Nos. 27, 29.)

Fording streams and crossing swing-bridges, Whicker is in some ways the last of the classical travellers. The improvement in Dominica's road system in the 1960s means that it is now easy to visit the Carib Territory from the capital, Roseau. Anthony Weller's piece from 1983 is nevertheless cast in the same dramatic mould as its predecessors, though the final article, José Barreiro's from 1990, marks a recognition of the pan-Amerindian consciousness that has become a significant feature of the changes in contemporary Carib culture. (Nos. 30, 31.) These changes can be traced back to the strange story of Hillary Frederick, who was taken to be educated in the USA at his father's wish, by Arthur Einhorn, a social studies teacher with a long-standing interest in the Caribs. Frederick's time in the USA coincided with the growth of the American Indian Movement, and Frederick began to realize what the Dominican Caribs had in common with other Native American groups. He returned to Dominica in 1977, became Carib chief in 1979 and, later, political representative for the north-east of the island. At the Non-governmental Organization conference in Geneva in 1981, called to discuss The Rights of Indigenous People and Their Land, he gave a scholarly and hard-hitting paper, subsequently published as *The Caribs and Their Colonizers* (1982).

It was at Hillary Frederick's instigation that North American charities and other NGOs began to take an interest in the Caribs. Save the Children helped finance and build the Waitukubuli Karifuna Development Centre, a community house built in the form of a traditional Carbet (Plate 45). Contact-Plenty, CUSO, and the OAS have also worked on the Territory, as have a group from the Saskatchewan Indian Federated College. (For some relevant reports, see Mayer 1982; Duque Duque 1985; Mackenzie and Logan n.d.; Mondesire and Robinson 1987.)

Outside interest in the Caribs has quickened again with the approach of the quincentenary. Meanwhile the Carib Council was actively involved in the extraordinary '500 Years of Indian Resistance' gathering, which took place in Quito in July 1990, the first time that representatives from all the major Amerindian nations of the continent had met. The historic *Declaration of Quito* resolved to reject the attempts to celebrate the quincentenary, and promised to 'turn that date into an occasion to strengthen our process of continental unity and struggle towards our liberation'.

Just in case the reader is in any doubt, having been reading of their imminent desires for so many pages, the Caribs of Dominica and St Vincent survive. On Dominica, at least, their presence is recognized by the Carib Act of 1975, they are involved in documentation and heritage projects, and they form part of both Caribbean and American indigenous movements that are asserting the rights of the continent's native inhabitants, 500 years on.

Further Reading

Other recent works on the Dominican Caribs include Owen 1975, 1980; Layng 1979–80, 1983, 1985; Hamot-Pézeron 1983; Baker 1988; and Grégoire and Kanem 1989. On the Vincentian Caribs see Gullick 1985.

24. *The 'Carib War' of 1930*

¶ *On Friday 19 September 1930 five Dominican policemen entered the Carib Reserve before daylight with orders to search for smuggled goods. A hurricane had hit the island less than three weeks earlier and much repair work was still in process. Goods were found and confiscated and three people arrested, but in the yard belonging to Esther Frederick (Ma Titou) at Salybia an altercation developed. The police constables opened fire and several Caribs were shot, two fatally: Dudley John and Frederick Royer. The policemen, disarmed and beaten, were driven off the Reserve. Two were treated for minor injuries.*

The Administrator of Dominica, E. C. Eliot, acting on the advice of the head of the Leeward Islands Police Force—then visiting Dominica—requested a warship. The Governor, Reginald St Johnston, based in Antigua, telegraphed the H M S Delhi to steam from Trinidad. Over the next few days marines were landed at Portsmouth and trucked over to the Reserve, the Delhi set off flares and starshells to scare the Caribs into order, extra policemen were landed from Antigua in full battle gear, and marines escorted local police who searched the Reserve and took seven Caribs prisoner. The chief, Jolly John, came to Roseau of his own volition and was immediately arrested and held in detention. The local press was scornful of what it saw as overreaction on the part of an Administrator it disliked. By the time the story reached London, it had blown up out of all proportion: under the dramatic headline STARVING CARIBS' ATTACK ON ROSEAU, The Times *reported that local police had to be called out of barracks to defend Roseau from Caribs who were looting foodstores as they made their way across the island. No deaths were reported but four policemen were said to have been seriously injured.*

Jolly John and five other Caribs were charged with wounding policemen and rescuing goods seized by them. The trial lasted most of January 1931 and turned on two key questions: the nature of the warrant issued to the policemen (which had been signed in blank), and whether the police had been under attack when they opened fire. The police evidence collapsed under cross-examination and a jury acquitted the Caribs on all charges.

31. A Carib Documentation Project is now compiling oral histories of members of the Carib community. On 22 Nov. 1990, the 1930 'war' was recalled by these three older members, Myers Frederick (brother of one of the Caribs shot by the police), Kate Antoine, and Nesta Frederick, in a videotaped interview that now forms part of a Carib collective memory. Photograph by Neil Whitehead.

32. *Local Council of the Carib Reserve* (1939). Photograph by Lord Moyne. The Royal Geographical Society: 060916. 0914.

Eliot, clearly piqued, refused to reinstate Jolly John, whom he had suspended after the original incident. There were calls both locally and in the House of Commons in London for an inquiry which would clarify the legal standing of the Reserve as well as reporting on the recent incidents. The resulting Commission of Inquiry (undertaken by J. S. Rae and S. A. Armitage-Smith) completely ignored the verdict of the Dominican jury and, in effect, overturned its findings, judging the Caribs, and especially their chief, 'morally responsible' for the deaths that had occurred.

Conditions in the Carib Reserve, and the Disturbance of 19th September, 1930, Dominica: Report of a Commission Appointed by His Excellency the Governor of the Leeward Islands, July 1931 was published by His Majesty's Stationery Office in 1932. Sir James Stanley Rae (1881–1956) was a prominent West Indian lawyer who ended his career as Attorney-General for the Leeward Islands (1931–7). Sir Sydney Armitage Armitage-Smith (1876–1932) was an important British civil servant who dealt principally with matters of finance and currency. He had been Secretary-General of the Reparations Committee from 1924 to 1930. His early death, shortly after the publication of the Commission of Inquiry, attracted some comment in Dominica.

Antigua
30th July, 1931

TO HIS EXCELLENCY THE GOVERNOR, LEEWARD ISLANDS.

YOUR EXCELLENCY,

We, the Commissioners appointed by a Commission dated 6th May, 1931, under the Commissions of Inquiry Act (Cap. 116) 'to enquire into conditions generally in the Carib Reserve and into all circumstances connected with a disturbance there in September, 1930, with particular reference to any special privileges which the Caribs may possess; and having due regard to the requirements of good Government in Dominica generally' and 'to make recommendations for the future welfare of the Caribs', have the honour to submit to Your Excellency the following Report:—

Procedure of the Commission

At the outset of our Enquiry we met Counsel for the Caribs and for the Government in private session in order to settle the procedure to be followed. It was agreed that the evidence taken at the Inquest on two deceased Caribs, the depositions taken before the Magistrate on which the Caribs were charged before the Circuit Court, and the evidence before the Commission, with such other evidence as might be called by either side or by the Commissioners. The arguments of Counsel before any of these Courts, together with the notes of argument taken by the Magistrate and His Honour the Puisne Judge who presided at the trial, as submitted by them, should, it was agreed, also be admitted for the assistance of the Commissioners.

285

We also intimated our intention of visiting the Reserve, and requested Counsel to inform us of any particular matters to which they might desire to draw attention during this visit.

Further, we intimated to Counsel that we did not propose to limit the Caribs on any matter on which they desired to complain, as we wished the enquiry to be as full and complete as possible; that so far as Counsel were concerned the procedure would be for Counsel for the Caribs to open their case and to call their witnesses; Counsel for the Caribs then to address, the Attorney-General having the right to reply. As the Attorney-General did not fully open his case, Counsel for the Caribs was allowed to reply on certain fresh issues raised by the Attorney-General in his Reply.

We also decided to reserve to ourselves complete discretion to take evidence in private whenever and if we found it desirable to do so. We did not, however, find this necessary.

We sat in open session for nine days, and examined twenty-seven witnesses; twelve called by Counsel on behalf of the Caribs, six by the Attorney-General on behalf of the Government, and nine whom we called ourselves.

We visited the Carib Reserve between the 21st and 24th May. We returned to Roseau on the 24th May and continued our sittings until the 27th when the Chief Justice was compelled to return to Antigua for the Circuit Court. [...]

The incident of 19th September, 1930

The facts with respect to the Incident, which are undisputed, are as follows:—

(1) Early on Friday the 19th September, 1930, a party of five Leeward Islands Police under the command of a Corporal entered the Carib Reserve. Four of the five were armed with revolvers and carried six rounds of ammunition apiece.

(2) They did not know whether or not they would be joined by Inspector Branch, who had sent the party to the Reserve, but their orders were, whether or not he arrived, to carry out their instructions.

(3) These instructions were to search for smuggled goods in the Carib Reserve at a place or places to be indicated to them, to seize goods suspected of having been smuggled, and to arrest the persons suspected of smuggling or harbouring the smuggled goods.

(4) Before dawn on the day in question they arrived at Salybia, the principal village of the Caribs, which lies about the river of that name in the heart of the Reserve a few miles south of Marigot and north of Castle Bruce on the north-east (Atlantic) coast of Dominica.

(5) After sunrise they proceeded southwards across the Salybia river to the house of one named Licente. They searched his house without protest, found goods they suspected of having been smuggled, arrested him, handcuffed him, and seized the suspected goods.

(6) They then proceeded to the house of Madame Titroy where they rejoined

the rest of the party, searched the house of this woman and the compound, and found other goods which they suspected of having been smuggled, to wit, some rum in the house, found under the bed, and some rum and tobacco concealed in the bushes of the compound.

They arrested Madame Titroy, but soon afterwards on the arrival of her husband, they released the wife and arrested the husband and handcuffed him.

They remained at or about the premises continuing their search for about an hour but found no more goods.

At a certain point in time, after the search and arrest, but before any attempt to depart, and before the search was completed, there arrived Thomas Jolly John the 'Chief' of the Caribs.

Numerous other Caribs also arrived.

The 'Chief' requested (or commanded) the Corporal in charge to release his two prisoners, namely, Licente and Titroy, and to take their seizures and depart, and to proceed against the suspected smugglers or the suspected harbourers of smuggled goods by means of summons instead of arrest.

The Corporal complied with the first part of this request and released the two prisoners.

The crowd which had assembled in the compound was not satisfied with the release of the prisoners but insisted on the release of the seizures.

The Corporal in charge requested the 'Chief' to calm the people who had begun to assume a threatening attitude.

The Chief, however, withdrew into the shop in the compound—a very small wooden building near the house of the family Titroy.

A struggle then began between the police who attempted to remove the seizures and the crowd who attempted to resist the removal.

Missiles were hurled against the Police, one or more Police were wounded, shots were fired by the Police with revolvers, Caribs were wounded, and the Police attempted to depart with their seizures, viz., rum and tobacco.

They escaped from the compound with their seizures and proceeded towards the 'road' which crosses a little stream and then, after rising at right angles to the coast, runs parallel to the sea towards the northern boundary of the Reserve.

On the way to this boundary, but not beyond, the Police were pursued by Caribs, beaten and wounded by fists, sticks, missiles, and pellets of shot from a shot gun, compelled to abandon their seizures, and after severe handling escaped from the Reserve, at the boundary of which the assault and battery appear to have ceased.

The Police escaped with their lives, but beaten and battered, to Marigot, without either prisoners or seizures.

On the other hand four Caribs had been hit by bullets fired by the Police, of whom two succumbed to their wounds. [...]

Question of the propriety of the shooting by the police

We now approach the gravest part of the Incident of the 19th September, viz., the fact that the Police fired on the crowd with the result that two persons lost their lives.

On the circumstances which led to this fatality we find the evidence of the Caribs generally unreliable, and the evidence of the police often unreliable and nearly always conflicting.

We are therefore forced to attempt a reconstruction of the events in the light of such facts as are agreed and such inference as we can draw from evidence of this questionable nature.

The premises of Madame Titroy, where the police were conducting their second search for smuggled goods, are situate in a compound adjoining a public road or rather pathway now surrounded by hedges, trees, and plants, which have begun to grow and recover since the hurricane. A path about 4 feet wide leads from the public pathway to the 'yard' which contains (*a*) the dwelling-house, (*b*) the shop, and (*c*) an oven.

The 'shop' is a small wooden hut divided into two portions by a half screen of wood.

When the Police arrived at the house, Madame Titroy and her three daughters were there alone, though, according to one witness, there was also a man in the yard.

The Police searched the house and yard without protest, with the result that the following suspected articles were found, viz.:—

  (*a*) in the house, a demi-john, three parts full of rum (a demi-john is the equivalent of two gallons),
  (*b*) in the shop, an empty demi-john,
  (*c*) on opposite sides of the yard concealed in bushes and grass, two demi-johns of rum,
  (*d*) also in the yard, concealed in the bush, 40 lb. of tobacco in a box.

No satisfactory evidence has been submitted to us to rebut the charge that this rum and tobacco were smuggled goods.

With regard to the rum, it is true, evidence was submitted that a similar quantity had been purchased at a licensed shop in Roseau on 12th September, but (*a*) the sale notes were not produced, and (*b*) with regard to the shop-keeper's book, which was produced to us, we observed that the entry with respect to this alleged transaction had been inserted between two others disturbing the order of date, and that in the case of one date there had been an erasure.

Further, no one attempted to explain why, had the goods been purchased legitimately in Roseau, they should have been concealed in various parts of the yard, nor was the alleged owner at any time called as a witness to prove her innocence or the illegality of the seizure by the Police.

Whatever might have been the result of a case tried before the Magistrate, the Police were amply justified in believing these quantities of rum and tobacco concealed in the yard to be smuggled goods.

During the search it is admitted on both sides that people began to gather in the yard and that at some time after the arrest of Madame Titroy the Carib 'Chief' Thomas Jolly John arrived.

The 'Chief' demanded the release of the prisoners, and the Corporal acquiesced on account of the threatening attitude of the crowd.

The 'Chief' further told the Police that they could take the goods away, a view angrily disputed by some of the Caribs in the yard.

The 'Chief' then left the Police and went into the shop, sufficiently composed in mind to be able to read an account book which he picked up whilst passing to the inner division of the shop.

Before leaving he had been appealed to several times by the Corporal to speak to the people and calm them.

This he did not do, but left the Police with the crowd. The angry murmurs and shouts of the crowd, which he could not but hear in the shop, can have left him no doubt as to the attitude of the people towards the Police.

At this point, at any rate, if not before, the Police must have realized the difficulty and danger of their position.

They had been left by the only Carib whom they knew, and the only man to whom they could look for help in preserving peace amongst the people, and they were faced by a crowd which had now been swollen from ten to thirty or forty, or from fifty to two hundred according to the varying estimates of Caribs and Police.

The critical moment arrived when the Police prepared to remove their seizures.

Immediately there was a rush at the box of tobacco lying in the yard, and a struggle ensued between Lance-Corporal Greenaway and a Carib named Dudley John and Madame Titroy.

At the same time a piece of wood was thrown at the Corporal, striking him across the ridge of the nose and forehead and causing him to bleed from mouth and nose.

Another stick was hurled at Lance-Corporal Greenaway but he dodged it and it felled Madame Titroy to the ground. This fact shows clearly the violence of the crowd and supports the conclusion which we have formed that an attack had been launched against the Police before any shot was fired.

In our opinion this attack upon the Police was premeditated and prepared.

We accept the evidence that Caribs had been arming themselves with missiles, certainly sticks, perhaps stones also, and it is clear that they were determined to prevent by force the removal of the seizures.

The Caribs deny that there were any persons present with sticks and stones. We do not believe this statement and we accept the evidence of an eye-witness, the Government Schoolmaster, to the effect that some Caribs were armed with sticks, and that owing to the demeanour of the crowd and the fact that the

Police began to 'unbuckle' their revolvers, he thought it best to retreat for safety to the back of the shop. This witness also swears that he heard the first revolver shot before he reached the back of the shop, a distance of only a few yards.

It is contended on behalf of the Caribs that (1) there would have been no general assault on the Police if the Police had not fired first, (2) that they were not justified in firing when they did, and (3) that a Private (Joseph) shot in cold blood the Carib who was attempting to rescue the box of tobacco immediately after the wounding of Lance-Corporal Greenaway.

On the other hand the Police deny that any shot was fired in the yard, and assert that the first shots fired were fired into the air as a warning.

We reject both contentions and arrive at the following conclusions:—

(a) the first shot was fired by Private Joseph at the Carib Dudley John whilst he was in the yard,

(b) no warning shots were fired into the air,

(c) at the moment when the first shot was fired a serious attack had been launched against the Police, who had good reason to believe that the Caribs intended them grievous harm, and they were in fear of their lives.

The Police were surrounded in a remote and difficult country by an unfamiliar people, they had no arms except their revolvers, and they were faced with the following alternatives, viz:—

(a) to give up their seizures,

(b) to hold on to their seizures until they were overpowered,

(c) to use the only weapon they possessed to protect their seizures and their lives and to uphold the authority of the law.

As a matter of discipline it would of course have been more regular for the firing to have been done on an order from the Non-Commissioned Officer in charge, and it would have been better if warning had been given, neither of which, we find, was in fact done; but having regard to the circumstances set forth above and in particular to the fact that the resistance to the removal of the seizures was felonious, and to the fact that the attack on the Police was of a general nature and at close quarters, we find that the action of the Police, in using their revolvers was justified.

We are, however, of opinion that it was an error of judgment on the part of Inspector Branch to have sent this armed search party into the Reserve in command of a Non-Commissioned Officer, without the direction and moral support which would have been afforded by the presence of a Commissioned Officer.

Therefore the conclusions at which we arrive are the following:—

(1) The Police were legally in possession of goods reasonably suspected to be smuggled at Salybia on 19th September last.

(2) They arrested persons reasonably suspected of smuggling such goods.

(3) They were compelled by reason of fear of violence to release the persons

arrested.

(4) When they attempted to remove the suspected goods they were violently assaulted in the execution of this duty by Caribs, which violence constitutes a felony.

(5) They were exposed to violence from a crowd greatly out-numbering themselves and were in fear of their lives.

(6) They were attacked in the discharge of their duty without provocation on their part.

(7) They used the only weapons they possessed, viz., revolvers, in defence of their lives and in order to discharge their duty, viz., the removal of smuggled goods.

The action of the Inspector of Police in sending a search and arrest party into the Reserve where no search had been conducted before and without a Commissioned Officer being in charge constitutes a grave indiscretion.

The moral responsibility for the death of two persons and the wounding of three others rests primarily on the Caribs who feloniously resisted lawful action by the Police.

Secondarily the responsibility rests on the Carib Chief who made no attempt to control the mob.

Two other points raised before us may conveniently be noted here.

The first is the suggestion that the moment chosen for the raid, viz., very shortly after the hurricane and its resultant distress, was inopportune. Such a view we cannot accept.

Even before the hurricane the authorities had knowledge of an intended smuggling; the attempt to smuggle was in fact delayed by that event.

It is the duty of the authorities to protect the revenue, and the date of the misdemeanour (i.e. smuggling) necessarily determined the date of action. It is impossible to defend the lawless action of a few by reference to a disaster which caused distress to all.

Secondly it has been alleged that the conduct of the Police towards the 'Chief' on the occasion of his subsequent arrest was improper.

The 'Chief' of the Caribs complained that after his arrest, and before he was taken to the Police Court, the policeman 'undressed him and took away his collar and tie as also his shoes'. There was no denial on the part of the Police, who may have regarded this as a small matter, but we regard it as an instance of indiscipline, and one which discloses a spirit of vindictiveness which should not exist within the Force. In our opinion action of this kind should not be overlooked by the officer in charge. The powers of the Police are ministerial not punitive. [. . .]

Measures for the amelioration of the social and economic condition of the Caribs

Before we proceed to make our recommendations under this head, we venture to give a brief account of our visit to the Reserve in the hope that it may prove of general interest to those who have at heart the welfare of this people.

We left Roseau early on Thursday the 21st May by motor-launch for Portsmouth, whence we motored over a rough and inadequate road to Marigot and Hatton Garden, a house placed at our disposal by the courtesy of the Honourable Mr D. H. Shillingford, where we arrived about 6 p.m.

The next morning, about 7.30 a.m., we rode to the Reserve accompanied by two interpreters, for the Caribs, like most Dominicans, though they understand some English to a certain extent, prefer to speak 'patois'.

Shortly after crossing the boundary of the Reserve we were met by the 'Chief' Thomas Jolly John, at whose house we rested for a while, and then after visiting his 'office' a little further on the road reached Salybia about 10 a.m.

There is a Government School at Salybia to which we repaired, to find some 130 children in attendance, about 80 girls and 50 boys, of whom about 50 girls and 30 boys were alleged to be 'pure' Caribs.

At our request the Schoolmaster caused passages from the school manuals to be read to us, and we were happy to say that the girls who were selected for this demonstration gave evidence of marked intelligence and application.

The performance of the boys (like their attendance) was less satisfactory; we understand that they are more prone to the pursuits of an out-door life.

At the close of our visit the pupils rendered the National Anthem heartily and gave three cheers for His Majesty the King.

We then arranged the children in groups on the hill-side outside the School and photographed them and also groups of adults of 'pure' and 'mixed' blood. [. . .]

The women very readily responded to our invitation and showed obvious pleasure in displaying the long tresses of bluish-black hair which they regard with legitimate pride as a distinctive characteristic of their race.

We had requested the 'Chief' to assemble so many as possible of the people to meet us, and after luncheon this meeting took place in the School-house which was filled to overflowing.

We put questions to them designed to elicit an expression of their ideas and desires, and we permitted them at the end to question us, making it clear to them, however, that we had no power to take any action whatsoever save that of submitting our recommendations to the proper authority.

We do not think it necessary or desirable to reproduce the substance of these conversations; we allude to them to show that we have done what appeared possible in so short a time to understand their character and their aspirations, with some of which we sympathize, as will appear from the constructive suggestions which appear below.

After this interesting and suggestive conclave we visited the yard of Madame Titroy, the *locus* of the regrettable incident on the 19th September last, a visit which was of great value to us in the attempt to reconstruct in detail the events which we have described above.

Various suggestions have been submitted to us with a view to improving the social and economic conditions of the Carib community; for instance, that their right to occupy the Reserve should be guaranteed by a formal Ordinance; that they should be exempted from all direct taxation, also by Ordinance; that jurisdiction should be granted to their 'Chief' in respect, not only of disputes as to the occupation of land, but also in cases of larceny and minor assault; that steps should be taken to alleviate their poverty, and to afford them greater facilities in respect of education, communications, and agricultural development.

It has also been suggested that the area of the Reserve, already more than 3,700 acres, should be extended, and generally that every care should be taken to preserve and develop their individuality as the last remnant of an ill-used and heroic race.

We have weighed these and other suggestions, having due regard on the one hand to the well-being of the Carib people, and on the other to the good Government and welfare of the Presidency as a whole.

In formulating our proposals we have tried constantly to bear in mind the size and nature of the problem, and to view the Carib question in due perspective.

In the first place it must be remembered that the persons now residing in the Reserve number less than five hundred souls, and that of this number, on the best estimate that we can make, not more than one-third are of 'pure' Carib blood, this term being used with the necessary reserve to which we have earlier alluded.

Further, that the 'pure' Caribs have almost entirely lost the qualities and characteristics which distinguished their ancestors.

It is true that the men still possess their ancestral skill in making and handling canoes and in following the pursuit of fishing.

One other hereditary trait should be mentioned, viz., their addiction to strong liquor and their peculiar susceptibility to its potency.[*]

The people of 'purer' blood of both sexes display features of a pronounced mongolian character which differentiate them without the possibility of error from their neighbours.

Sixty years ago a scientific traveller[†] who spent some weeks amongst them found relics of their customs and of their ancient languages.

At the present time one searches in vain for any trace of primitive customs or traditions. Not even the oldest inhabitant claims to remember a word of the Carib language (or languages).

They have no folk-lore, no songs or music, no dances or customs, no costume or ornament to distinguish them from other inhabitants of Dominica.

No inscriptions, carvings, or relics could be pointed out to us in the Reserve. They have become part of the Roman Catholic community.

---

[*] Cf. le R. P. Labat. Nouveau voyage aux Isles de l'Amérique, Paris 1932 (Collection Ailleurs), page 132:—'Ils ont une passion effrénée pour l'eau-de-vie et les autres liqueurs fortes; ils donnent tout ce qu'ils ont pour en avoir, et en boivent jusqu'à l'excès.'

[†] Ober. 'Camps in the Carribees': Boston 1880.

For the once famous Carribean race the past is lost, forgotten, never to be recovered.

Under these circumstances the sentimental desire expressed in some quarters to conserve the racial individuality of the people commands a less ready sympathy than would otherwise be the case, and gives to the most impartial observer a sense of unreality and pretence.

Closely connected with the question of race-identity is that of the occupation of the Reserve.

We think that the Reserve should be maintained, at any rate for the immediate future, and subject to satisfactory conduct on the part of the Caribs; it should certainly not be extended beyond the generous limits fixed in 1903. But the question arises—who should be recognized as entitled to profit by it?

On this question we consulted so many of the Carib people as we were able to get together to meet us at Salybia.

The demands expressed by these people (about half, we imagine, of the community) were to the effect that only the existing inhabitants of the Reserve (of whom about two-thirds are of mixed Carib and negro blood) should be entitled to enjoy the privileges in question, and that inter-marriage with persons outside should involve expulsion and exclusion.

Such a principle, it was freely admitted, would involve a reversal of the immemorial custom of the tribe which is as follows:—

A Carib man is free to marry a non-Carib woman and bring her into the Reserve, their offspring being entitled to remain in the Reserve and to be regarded as Caribs; a Carib woman who marries a non-Carib man to be removed from the Reserve and the offspring of such a union to be excluded together with their parents from the privileges of residence therein.

This rule, we may observe in passing, is the expression of the Carib unconscious race philosophy, illustrated from the earliest traces of their history which have come down to us in books of explorer and missionary, which attaches supreme importance to paternity, less or none to maternity, a view which has encouraged them to recruit the mothers of their people from the most diverse races.

We are strongly of opinion that it would be most unwise to modify the existing custom in the sense suggested to us by these people.

The custom must represent the wishes of most of those heretofore interested or else it would not exist.

We consider that a Carib, whether pure or mixed, should be free to decide for himself whether or not he will maintain the purity of the race and should not be penalized for the exercise of his undoubted right to choose his mate from within or from without the circle of the Reserve.

A Carib is a human being, not a specimen in a somewhat inaccessible ethnological museum, and the domestic affections have more title to respect than academic curiosity.

If the 'pure' Caribs wish to and are able to preserve the continuance of their race they will do so. If they are unable or unwilling to do so they will gradually become merged in the surrounding population.

The Carib Reserve is neither the sole nor the most important territory where aboriginal inhabitants continue to exist within the British Empire.

Naturally we have turned for guidance to the experience of other Colonies where a similar problem exists on a larger scale, notably to that of British Guiana.

We recommend that the Government should appoint an officer charged specifically with the care of the Carib people.

His duties would be to guard the Reserve against the invasion of unauthorized persons (and incidentally to prevent unauthorized incursions of Caribs into land outside the Reserve); to safeguard the application of the tribal rule as to the results of intermarriage as set forth above; to settle disputes about the occupation of land within the Reserve, i.e., the sole category of disputes which by their nature are not susceptible of submission to the Courts; and generally, with the collaboration of the competent departments (usually those of Education and Agriculture), to develop the prosperity and improve the standard of life in the Reserve.

In the exercise of these duties, particularly with respect to land disputes, the Government officer should listen to the advice of a Chief or Head Man who should be elected by the inhabitants of the Reserve, but subject always to the approval of the Government by whom he would be appointed.

No power, authority, or jurisdiction whatever should be given to the Chief, whose functions would be purely advisory and who would be remunerated in such a manner as the Government think fit.

It is of course evident that nothing contained in our recommendations can be interpreted as limiting the freedom of the Caribs to entrust to the Chief or indeed to anyone else authority to act as arbitrator in their disputes, whether with respect to the occupation of land or otherwise. Indeed, such arbitration is to be welcomed, subject always to the condition that Government cannot properly provide a sanction for the arbitrator's awards.

If and so far as any Carib possesses sufficient moral authority or influence to discharge this useful service he should be encouraged to do so.

It is obvious that to grant any jurisdiction or power to the Chief would imply the necessity of supplying him with the force necessary to implement his decisions, a course not only difficult but most undesirable. Further, we are not satisfied that there is in the Reserve anyone possessed of the character and intelligence required to occupy a position of primacy over his fellows.

Amongst this primitive people there has never been anything resembling an hereditary monarchy or ruling cast; leaders have been chosen for the most part *ad hoc*, for their qualities of courage and leadership. Such a choice would now be difficult or impossible.

The present Head Man or 'Chief' under suspension is wholly unfitted for the discharge even of such limited duties as those which we have suggested above.

His conduct both before and during the Incident show that he has no real influence with the people, and that he is either unable or unwilling to collaborate with the Government in the preservation of peace and order.

With regard to the extension which has been advocated of Carib privileges, especially fiscal privileges, the claim advanced before us shows both confusion of thought and lack of principle.

Some years ago (1894) when Sir R. Hamilton came as Royal Commissioner to the Island, the Caribs asked for educational and medical facilities which they did not then enjoy. To us they urged the need for road construction in order to enable them to evacuate their produce. It is only since 1894 they have a school at Salybia where they may and ought to send their children.

The hospitals of Roseau and Portsmouth are open to Caribs as to non-Caribs and before long we hope to see completed a serviceable road from Marigot near the confines of the Reserve to Portsmouth.

It appears not to be generally realized that the demands put forward for isolated and exceptional treatment together with fiscal immunities and a greater share in the enjoyment of facilities in respect of medical service, communication, education, etc., provided by Government and financed by taxation, are mutually repugnant. It cannot reasonably be claimed at one and the same moment that Caribs should be excused from paying taxes and should enjoy the services rendered possible by taxation alone.

For ourselves we have no hesitation in thinking that isolation is not in the true interest of this small community and that the more they take part in the common life of the Presidency the better for them.

The truest service which can at the present time be rendered to the Carib community is to help them to understand that they owe obedience to the law.

They have been encouraged in the erroneous belief that in some respects they are outside or above the law. This illusion should be dispelled and they should be taught to understand the nature of their citizenship.

In other words the choice lies between two alternative policies. The first, which we think unwise, is to encourage the Caribs in their squalid isolation, by permitting them to regard themselves as outside the ordinary law, criminal and civil, and to restrict the privileges of the Reserve to the existing occupants and the offspring of marriage between such occupants alone. Such a policy makes an appeal to the sentimental in proportion as they are lacking in vision or principle.

The second policy, which we recommend, is, whilst conserving for the Caribs those advantages which have indisputably been accorded to them in the past, viz., the usufruct of the Reserve and exemption from boat tax, to bring them into closer contact with their neighbours and to give them in increasing measure, as circumstances permit, the advantages offered by the Administration and financed from its resources.

If, but only if, the second policy is adopted we submit the following specific proposals which represent the result of careful and sympathetic study of the nature and of the conditions of this interesting remnant of a primitive race, viz.:—

(a) Vocational training should be given to pupils who desire it at the Salybia school, in school hours.

This will tend to interest the boys, especially, in school work, and may in the end result in making the people of the Reserve less dependent on the purchase of necessary supplies in Roseau and Portsmouth.

(b) One or two selected pupils of superior intelligence and the right disposition should be taught in Roseau by the Agricultural Department the sort of agricultural knowledge that would be most fruitful in the Reserve. To this end a subsistence allowance (for which there is precedent in this Colony) should be given to them during their period of residence, at the end of which they should return and pass on to the others the practical knowledge which they have acquired as to planting and gardening.

In view of the superior intelligence and application of the girls, we think that there might be advantage in selecting these agricultural missionaries from the female rather than from the male scholars, and the demeanour of the two sexes at the meeting which we held with the people at Salybia encourages the belief that, at least in present times, that portion of the Carib community is not unable to make its voice heard, and to take due part in the affairs of the community.

(c) Without waiting for the results of such missionary enterprise we re-commend that the Department of Agriculture should again offer its services with a view to advising on immediate steps to increase the production of the soil in the Reserve.

The most promising direction would appear to be the cultivation of an improved variety of bay-trees ('Canelle') with a view to the sale of bay-leaves to be treated in the immediate vicinity of the Reserve, and the plantation of coconuts and coffee.

When circumstances permit the amelioration of the road system, especially the section between Marigot and Portsmouth, the Caribs will profit from such improved communication when they are in a position to produce for sale.

We cannot, under existing circumstances, recommend the expenditure, which would be large in respect of maintenance, required for a road to connect the Reserve via the Imperial Road and Roseau, as such a road, however desirable, would be less fruitful economically to the community as a whole than some others serving more productive areas, and especially as the Caribs are accustomed to go to Roseau by canoe.

The measures which could be taken to improve the economic position of the Caribs form the subject of a special report made at our request by the Agri-cultural Department to the Administrator, and the proposals outlined above are based upon information contained in this report, as well as upon the impressions which we received from personal observations with the Caribs at Salybia.

(Signed) J. STANLEY RAE, CHAIRMAN
(Signed) SYDNEY A. ARMITAGE-SMITH

25. *Visiting the Carib Quarter*
Jean Rhys (1936)

¶ *Jean Rhys (1890–1979) was born on Dominica and lived there for the first seventeen years of her life. After her departure for Europe in 1907, she returned only once, for a month in 1936. Her novels and stories are shot through with memories of the Caribbean, but only the following extract, taken from the story 'Temps Perdi', draws directly on that brief return to Dominica, most of which she and her second husband Leslie Tilden Smith spent on the north-east coast of the island at an estate called Hampstead.*

Rhys probably never went to the north-east coast of Dominica during her childhood: the overland journey was arduous, and her family connections were with the south coast, the Geneva plantation at Grand Bay. However, her father was a prominent doctor in Roseau and the family was therefore acquainted with Henry Hesketh Bell, initiator of the Carib Reserve.

The fictionalized visit to the Carib Territory was based on a visit she and her husband actually made. Rhys's memories of stories about the Caribs had appeared in her earlier novels, especially Voyage in the Dark *(1934), and had obviously been revived by the special number of the Paris magazine* L'Illustration, *which featured various articles about the Caribs and an illustration which Rhys remembered from her childhood. The story itself is of special interest in the present context because of its brief but damning comment on the 'Carib War' of 1930, and its determined refusal to romanticize the Caribs.*

'Temps Perdi' was started shortly after Rhys's return to England from the Caribbean, but not published until 1969. What follows is the last third of a complex story which begins in England and moves, through memory, to Vienna and Dominica.

Nicholas was the overseer of Temps Perdi, an estate near the Carib Quarter. Temps Perdi is Creole patois and does not mean, poetically, lost or forgotten time, but, matter-of-factly, wasted time, lost labour. There are places which are supposed to be hostile to human beings and to know how to defend themselves. When I was a child it used to be said that this island was one of them. You are getting along fine and then a hurricane comes, or a disease of the crops that nobody can cure, and there you are—more West Indian ruins and labour lost. It has been going on for more than three hundred years—yes, it's more than three hundred years ago that somebody carved 'Temps Perdi' on a tree near by, they say.

The estate house had been empty for so long that a centipede fell out of a book when I opened it. Everything had run wild, but there was still hibiscus growing by the stone garden walls and butterflies made love over the thorny bougainvillea. Every morning Myra, Nicholas's daughter, put little earthenware bowls of fresh flowers along the low partition which separated the veranda from the sitting-room. From the veranda we could see Guadeloupe, the Saints and Marie Galante; sun on dark trees . . .

But the white-cedars at the end of the garden—the lowest about eighty feet high—had dropped their leaves and were covered with flowers, white flowers very faintly tinged with pink, so light and fragile that they fell with the first high wind and were blown away as soon as they fell. There used to be a famous Creole song about the white-cedar flowers but I can't remember it. 'Here today and gone tomorrow'—something like that, it must be.

'There is nothing to see in the Carib Quarter,' Nicholas insisted. He had a handsome Negro face, a big chest, a deep, booming voice.

'These people', he said, 'don't even live near together. Their houses are each far away from the other, and all hidden in the bush. There is nothing to see in Salybia. Besides, the new road only goes as far as the river. After that you'll have to ride. It will take a couple of hours or so.'

'But can't it be arranged? Can't we get the horses?'

'Oh yes, it can be arranged,' Nicholas said disapprovingly.

But I wasn't so easily put off. All my life I had been curious about these people because of a book I once read, pictures I once saw.

Whenever the Caribs are talked about, which is not often, the adjective is 'decadent', though nobody knows much about them, one way or the other or ever will now. There are a few hundreds left in the West Indies, or in the world, and they live in the part of this island called Salybia. They had not intermarried much with the Negroes and still have smooth, black hair, small, slanting eyes, high cheekbones, copper-coloured skins. They make baskets, beautifully plaited, light and waterproof, dyed red and brown or black and white. The largest is the island's substitute for a trunk, the smallest would just hold a baby's shoe. Sometimes the baskets are made to fit one inside the other, like Chinese boxes.

Nobody else seemed to want to visit the Carib Quarter, nobody seemed at all anxious to take a long ride in the sun with nothing much to see at the end of it.

'They are supposed to have two languages. The women have a language that the men don't know. So they say.'

'They say so, do they?'

'Well, we'll ask Nicholas ... Nicholas, isn't it true that the Carib women have a secret language?'

Nicholas said, grinning, that he thought he had heard something of the sort. Yes, he fancied he had.

Tormented with the fear that I had imagined the closely-printed book, the gaudy illustrations pored over as a child, I produced the special number of *L'Illustration*, 23 November 1935, for the *Tricentenaire des Antilles Françaises* and exhibited '*Homme Caraibe Dessiné d'après nature par le Père Plumier*'. Early eighteenth century, probably. Bow and arrows in his right hand, a club in his left, a huge, muscular body and a strange, small, womanish face. His long, black hair was carefully parted in the middle and hung smoothly to his shoulders. But his slanting eyes, starting from their sockets, looked wild and terrified. He was more the frightened than the frightening savage.

'We had a print very like this—perhaps it was the same one—in the dining-room at home.'

'He isn't very attractive.'

'Everybody used to say that.'

And he always used to look so sad, I thought, when they laughed at him. With his wild, strained eyes and his useless bows and arrows.

'The original West Indian, is he?'

'Oh no, that's a Carib. The original West Indians were killed by the Spaniards or deported to Hispaniola—Haiti. Well, most of the men were. The Spaniards told them they were going to Heaven. So they went. Weren't they suckers? Then the Caribs, the cannibals, came from the mainland of South America and killed off the few men who were left.'

But that book, written by an Englishman in the 1880s, said that some of the women, who had survived both Spaniards and Caribs—people were not so thorough as they are now—had carried on the old language and traditions, handing them down from mother to daughter. This language was kept a secret from their conquerors, but the writer of the book claimed to have learned it. He said that it definitely established the fact that there was communication between China and what is known as the New World. But he had a lot of imagination, that man. Wasn't there a chapter about the buried Carib treasure in La Soufrière, St Lucia—one of the mouths of Hell, they say—and another about Atlantis? Oh yes, he had a lot of imagination.

The day we went to the Carib Quarter the wind was blowing heavy luminous clouds across the sky, tormenting the thin crooked coconut-palms on the slope of the hill opposite the verandah, so different from the straight, healthy, glossy-green coconuts just around the corner of the road—tame trees, planted in rows to make copra. We arrived punctually at the place where the horses were to wait for us, but it was a long wait before they turned up, so young Charlie,

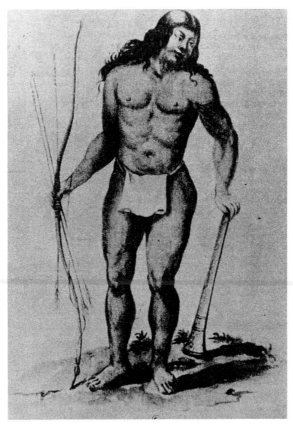

33. *Homme caraïbe des Isles Antilles avec son arc et ses flèches dans la main droite et son boutou dans la gauche*, by P. Ch. Plumier. From *L'Illustration*, 4838 (23 Nov. 1935), 'Le Tricentaire des Antilles' (supplement), p. vi.

aged sixteen, who was our guide, went on ahead. He was beautifully got up in white shirt, shorts and socks, but hideous, heavy black boots that squeaked with every step he took. There were stepping-stones across the shallowest part of the broad river. On one of these Charlie's horrible boots betrayed him and I thought he had fallen into the water, but he managed to save himself. When he got to the other side it was a relief to see him sit down, take off his boots and socks and hang them round his neck before he walked on.

The horses came at last. They were so thin that every bone showed in their bodies and they had the morose, obstinate expression which is the price of survival in hostile surroundings. Negroes like to be in the movement and hate anything old-fashioned, and horses are now definitely old-fashioned.

However, when we mounted they jerked their necks strongly and clip-clopped without hesitation into the clear, shallow river. I had forgotten the lovely sound of horses' hooves in water, that I hadn't heard for so many damnable years.

Then they heaved and strained us on to a wide, grassy road. There was a flamboyant tree with a few flowers out. Next month, I thought, it will be covered; next month all the flamboyant trees—the flame trees—will be covered, and the immortelles will flower, but I shan't be here to see them. I'll be on my way back to England then, I thought, and felt giddy and sick. There were a lot of iguanas along that road. I shut my eyes and saw one of the illustrations in the book about the Caribs, vivid, complete in every detail. A brown girl, crowned with flowers, a parrot on her shoulder, welcoming the Spaniards, the long-prophesied gods. Behind her the rest of the population crowded, carrying presents of fruit and flowers, but some of them very scowling and suspicious— and how right they were!

In the midst of this dream, riding through a desolate, arid, lizard-ridden country, different and set apart from the island I knew, I was still sensitive to the opinion of strangers and dreaded hostile criticism. But no, it was approved of, more or less. 'Beautiful, open, park-like country. But what an *extreme* green!'

The road had been gradually rising and, as we came round the shoulder of a hill, smiling Charlie met us, accompanied by a Negro policeman. An official welcome to Salybia? . . . Below us we saw small clearings among the low trees— low for that part of the world—and the bush riddled with narrow paths. But not a human being. ('These people live all separated from each other, and all hidden in the bush. These people hide when they see anybody.')

'That's the king's house,' the policeman announced, and I thought 'So, there's still a king, is there?'

Round another bend in the road we saw below us the big clearing where the police-station stood with five or six other houses, one of them a Catholic church.

In the station the rifles were stacked in a row, bayonets and all. The room was large, almost cool. Everything looked new and clean, and there was a circular seat round the palm tree outside.

'We had trouble here,' our policeman told us. 'They burnt the last station, and they burnt twenty feet off this one while it was being built.'

'Why?'

'Well, it seems they thought they were going to have a hospital. They had asked the Government for a hospital. A petition, you know. And when they found out that the Government was giving them a police-station and not a hospital, there was trouble.'

'Serious trouble?'

'Pretty serious. They burnt the first one down, and they burnt twenty feet off this one.'

'Yes, but I mean was anybody hurt?'

'Oh no, only two or three Caribs,' he said. 'Two-three Caribs were killed.' It might have been an Englishman talking.

'There is a beautiful Carib girl', the policeman said, 'in the house over there— the one with the red roof. Everybody goes to see her and photographs her. She and her mother will be vexed if you don't go. Give her a little present, of course. She is very beautiful but she can't walk. It's a pity, that.'

When you went in it was like all their houses. A small room, clean, the walls covered with pictures cut from the newspapers and coloured cards of Virgins, saints and angels, Star of the Sea, Refuge of the Distressed, Hope of the Afflicted, Star of the Sea again, Jesus, Mary and Joseph . . .

The girl appeared in the doorway of the dark little bedroom, posed for a moment dramatically, then dragged herself across the floor into the sun outside to be photographed, managing her useless legs with a desperate, courageous grace; she had white lovely teeth. There she sat in the sun, brown eyes fixed on us, the long brown eyes of the Creole, not the small, black, slanting eyes of the pure Carib. And her hair, which hung to her waist and went through every shade from dark brown to copper and back again, was not a Carib's hair, either. She sat there smiling, and an assortment of brightly-coloured Virgins and saints looked down at her from the walls, smiling too. She had aquiline features, proud features. Her skin in the sun was a lovely colour.

We took a few photographs, then Charlie asked if he might take the rest. We heard his condescending voice: 'Will you turn your side face? will you please turn your full face? *Don't* smile for this one.' ('These people are quite savage people—quite uncivilized.')

Her mother, who looked like an old Chinese woman, told us that in her youth she had lived in Martinique in service with a French family and then had been taken to Paris.

'I come back here,' she said, 'because I want to see my mother before she die. I loved my mother. Now I must stay because I am old, I am old and who will take me away?'

'She like that since she four,' she said, pointing to her daughter.

'*Hélas!*' she said, gesticulating. She had thin, lovely hands. '*Hélas, hélas!*'

But the girl, sitting in the sun to be photographed, smiled contentedly at us, pushed a strand of hair from her shoulder to her back, smiled again. And all the Virgins and saints on the walls smiled at us too.

The night in Temps Perdi is full of things chirping and fluttering. The fireflies are out—they call them labelles. It is at night, lying caged under a mosquito-net, that you think, 'Now I am home, where the earth is sometimes red and sometimes black. Round about here is ochre—a Carib skin. In some lights like blood, in others just pretty, like a picture postcard coloured by somebody with a child's paintbox and no imagination.'

It is at night that you know old fears, old hopes, that you know unhappiness, turning from side to side under the mosquito-net, like a prisoner in a cell full of small peepholes. Then you think of that plant with thick, fleshy leaves edged with thorns, on which some-up-to-the-minute Negro has written over and over again 'Girls muck, girls muck', and other monosyllabic and elementary truths. When I was a child we used to draw hearts pierced with arrows on leaves like that and 'Z loves A'. It all comes to the same thing, probably.

But when you have drunk a good tot of rum nothing dismays you; you know the password and the Open Sesame. You drink a second; then you understand everything—the sun, the flamboyance, the girl crawling (because she could not walk) across the floor to be photographed. And the song about the white-cedar trees. '*Ma belle ka di maman-li—*' (A lot of their songs begin like that—'My lovely girl said to her mother'.) 'Why do the flowers last only a day?' the girl says. 'It's very sad. Why?' The mother says 'One day and a thousand years are the same for the *Bon Dieu*.' I wish I could remember it all but it is useless trying to find out because nobody sings these old songs any more.

26. *Anthropologist of the Caribs*
Douglas Taylor (1941)

¶ *Douglas Taylor (1901–81) spent most of his life studying the Caribs of Dominica.*
A linguist by training, he is author of the important Languages of the West Indies
(1977) and of numerous articles on Carib language, folklore, and culture, of which
the piece that follows, 'Columbus Saw Them First' (1941), is one of the most
popular and accessible.

Taylor first went to Dominica in 1930 (and was thought by the island's
Administrator to be responsible for fomenting the 1930 'disturbances'), eventually
settling there in 1938. That same year the Smithsonian Institute in Washington
published a long essay of Taylor's which is recognized as the seminal work of
anthropology on the modern Caribs of Dominica. Here, at the start of his career,
Taylor wrote about the Caribs' 'unique historical and sentimental interest' as the
last survivors of the indigenous population of the Caribbean: 'Of their story little is
known and less written; and it is with the purpose of recording, before it becomes
too late, something of this vestige of a once virile and powerful people, that my own
attempt at knowing them has been made' (1938: 109). Taylor's reconstructive
exercise in the present essay—'Had we arrived in the evening . . .'—is marked by
an outsider's knowledge of Carib lifeways and language unmatched since the French
missionaries in the eighteenth century.

Until recently, understanding of native Caribbean cultures has been dominated by
the archaeologically based hypotheses of Irving Rouse, enshrined in his articles on
'The Arawak' and 'The Carib' in the Handbook of South American Indians *(Rouse*
1948a and 1948b). Taylor's intimate knowledge of the twentieth-century Caribs,
based on his investigations of their oral traditions and language, led him to present
data that are now seen as undermining such stereotypes, as even Rouse himself
appears to acknowledge (1986).

On Sunday, November 3, 1493, Columbus and his followers made the first
landfall, after leaving the Canaries, in their second voyage to the New World.

Almost simultaneously, four islands hove into sight. The loftiest he called Dominica, in honor of the day; the others were named for his ship, the *Marie Galante*, for the Spanish monastery, Our Lady of Guadeloupe, and, to mark the attainment of their desired goal, la Desirada.

On the following days, he and his crew made contact with some of the inhabitants—the second group of 'American Indians' to become known to history. Those encountered on the first voyage, the Taino of Haiti, had already told Columbus about these warring 'Cariphúna' (from which our words Carib and cannibal have been derived), who by advancing through the Lesser Antilles had at that time occupied the most easterly part of their island.

Again it is Sunday, November 3, and now, from the only spot where a single native 'Indian' may yet be found in the entire island chain from Florida to the delta of the Orinoco, I am looking out across the timeless Atlantic where Spanish ships were spied just 447 years ago by some long-forgotten ancestor of the men and women around me here today. For there are still Caribs on Dominica,—though they and their Taino foes have long been extinct in the other islands. Here, in the last Carib Reserve, the records of bygone days are enhanced by many living traits. It is not hard to retrace the centuries in imagination and reconstruct a scene we might well have witnessed, had we, as unobtrusive strangers, visited this coastal strip in the days before the Conquest.

Then as now, we might have followed a tortuous path worn in the red volcanic clay of a hillside or in the rich black loam of decayed vegetation. On either hand great hardwood trees, whose gnarled roots provide steppingstones in the dank mire or a stairway on steep declivities, rise 100 feet into the moisture-laden air, their evergreen foliage forming a dense screen from the blazing noonday sky. Far overhead in an ungainly flight, parrots whir and scream their Carib name, '*cooriwhek, cooriwhek!*' While from some hidden branch or dark gully the mournful, reiterating notes of a mountain whistler (*Myiadestes*, sp.) or the unearthly coo of a native dove put the lone traveler in mind of the spirits of the forest.

There is little else to break the heavy silence. The island's only two native mammals are not in evidence: the *manicou* (a native opossum) is asleep in his nest in the treetops, and the agouti (*Dasyprocta aguti*) is hidden safely from all but a dog's nose. True, we might meet with a hunter advancing stealthily between his curious mute dogs (*áuli*), bow in hand, his naked body of the same color as the dead leaves beneath his feet. And from him, had he unexpectedly chosen to be communicative, we might have learned much of what the forest meant to the men of his race. He might have spoken of bird calls and snares, of the manner of catching young parrots alive by stupefying them with the fumes of burning pimentos, of 'honey-trees' where the tiny stingless native bees deposit their aromatic syrup in pockets of black wax. But more likely that native hunter would have sought to instruct us by telling of strange

307

34. Jolly John, Douglas Taylor, and Jimmy Benjamin. Photograph by H. M. & E. L. Ayers. From Douglas Taylor, 'Columbus Saw Them First', *Natural History*, 48 (June 1941), 43. This is one of the first sets of photographs of Caribs to name its subjects as a matter of course.

35. Mimi Etienne. Photograph by H. M. & E. L. Ayers. From Douglas Taylor, 'Columbus Saw Them First', *Natural History*, 48 (June 1941), 45.

'precautions'—charms practiced on man and dogs and restrictions to be observed before, during, and after the hunt—rules a man must know before he can hope to become a successful hunter.

The Carib has always preferred the danger of the sea or the mystery of the forest to the monotonous labor of planting, weeding, and gathering. Most of such work he has left to the women.

Here and there in our walk we may chance upon the stout bole of a centenarian *gommier* (*Dacroyodes hexandra* Gr.) lying hewn in the graceful form of a dugout canoe between its fired stump and severed head, waiting, amid a heap of chips, to be hauled with gaiety and song to the coast, there to be further shaped and fitted for a new and roving life.

We would find clearings, too, where charred stumps and rotting logs stood out blackly in the yellow sunlight amid a purply green field of manioc. To such clearings, felled and burned by the men, the women came to plant or weed. They trudged back to the coast in the evening, their loads of manioc or sweet potatoes, pumpkin or corn, slung from their foreheads in long, narrow knapsacks of woven palm roots.

Thus the Carib's life was, and largely still is, patterned by three elements: the 'high woods', in which game is becoming scarce and difficult to get as the tall trees retreat before the woodsman's ax; the 'gardens', which are still cultivated by the primitive system of burning the soil and which must follow the forest inland, leaving behind an impenetrable waste of tangled weeds; and lastly, the sea, which bore the Caribs, like others before and after them, to these shores.

On the last mountain ridge the trade wind hits us full in the face with a refreshing tang of salt and ozone. Two thousand feet below, the Atlantic spreads glittering eastward, and toward the northeast the shadowy trapezoid form of Marie-Galante bars the horizon. In deeply wooded valleys and ravines between the headlands, run clear, crayfish-filled brooks that may, after heavy rain, 'come down' as raging and impassable torrents.

Two essential considerations have ever governed the Carib's choice of a site for their dwellings: the proximity of running water for bathing and drinking; and a view of the sea, their only highway. The Caribs are sailors by tradition as well as by taste, and it is interesting to note that we get our word 'canoe' not from the birchbark craft of the Indian but from the Carib *kanawa*, a dugout, whose length—believe it or not—was upward of 60 feet. Its sides were raised by the addition of planks, and it was about eight feet wide in the middle. This 60-foot 'canoe' carried two masts, each supporting one sail, and could accommodate 50 or 60 men at the paddles. The other type of dugout used by the old Caribs was, and still is, a smaller craft of similar construction. This *ukuni* or *kuriala* was used for fishing and short journeys. The ones made today vary in length from fifteen to 30 feet, 20 feet being the most usual size.

In the old Carib settlement a central long house, or *tabwi*, built near the mouth of a valley, formed the nucleus of what was usually no more than an extended family group. This building, which attained upward of 24 by 60 feet, served as armory, men's club, and bachelor's residence, and was usually supplemented by a guesthouse of similar construction but smaller. Two stout forked posts stuck in the ground supported the ridgepole. On either side of these came a row of smaller forks supporting a wall plate that ran the length of the house. Upon the latter rested a series of tiebeams from which the hammocks were slung. Over this framework came the long rafters, which went into the ground and crossed above the ridgepole, where they were held in place by a slighter pole resting above the crossing.

The individual houses, or *mwinâ*, rarely measured more than fifteen feet by twelve feet and were of simpler construction. They were dispersed, at the owners' fancy, at various heights on either side of the valley. Each had a courtyard of beaten mud and a surrounding fringe of vegetation where such domestic plants as cotton, calabash, annatto, and herbs of medicinal or magical virtue formed a screen that hid the house and its occupants from the gaze of the indiscreet stranger.

Had we arrived in the evening, when men and women were home from their various occupations, we should have been welcomed by the one whose duty it was to receive strangers. We should have been led to the guesthouse and served with cassava-bread, *túmali* (pepper and manioc-water sauce), *sákuti* (a manioc beer), and whatever meat or fish, fresh or barbecued, was on hand, set before us on little basketwork tables. We should have drunk out of a half calabash that might have been lacquered and decorated with such designs as cross-hatching, Greek key, diamonds or crosses. We should have sat on long low stools carved out of a single piece of wood. Only when we had finished eating would the Chief and elders come to greet us individually, and in order of precedence. Their greeting would have been a pat on the shoulder and a '*mabwika!*' which has about as much significance as our 'how do you do?'

If we ourselves had arrived from the Guayanas, our hosts' appearance and manners would cause us no surprise. The islanders, like their kindred on the mainland, were mostly sturdy men of rather short, stocky build, with Mongoloid features, straight black hair cut in a fringe across the forehead, and light reddish-tan complexion. Used only to a climate where clothes serve more as adornment than any useful purpose, the Caribs' principal covering consisted of a coat of vermilion paint composed of crabwood oil and annatto, and reputed to prevent sunburn and insect bites.

Two languages in each family

What perhaps would have struck us first was that the men and women did not speak the same language. We would have been told, had we inquired, that the Caribs' forefathers were a branch of the mainland Galibi. Driven from their lands, they had set sail under the leadership of a small though indomitable chief. They had landed in these islands where, after killing the native warriors, they had taken their women to wife. Since that time, their daughters had preserved something of their mothers' tongue.

The Caribs believe that a mother endows her child with its body, while the father's contribution is its spirit. This belief may explain two ancient and widespread American-Indian practices, known as the 'couvade' and 'cross-cousin marriage'. When a man got his first-born son, he took to his hammock, abstained from all food for five days, and thereafter fasted partially for a further period. Even today the young Carib observes certain restrictions intended to safeguard the welfare of his newborn child.

Unless he were a chief, the newly married man went to live in the home of his bride's parents, who, because of the custom known as cross-cousin marriage, were often his own paternal aunt and her husband. Here he passed a sort of probationary period of one or two years, hunting, fishing, and clearing gardens for his father-in-law. His wife followed the usual household routine of fetching wood and water, baking cassava and brewing manioc beer, weaving hammocks, bands and loincloths, and going to the beach to carry home her husband's catch.

After this period, if all went well, they usually made a home of their own. If they should not agree, the man returned to his father's home, while any children remained with their mother.

Although there was a chief in each settlement and one, or sometimes two, supreme chiefs for the island as a whole, their authority was not conspicuous. These chiefs used neither titles nor insignia. They were chosen from among the elders to play the role of paternal arbiter because of superior knowledge or endurance rather than for wealth or family. In wartime, special leaders were chosen to command forces and fleets, and these had to be obeyed throughout the expedition. But in peace, within the family, as within the tribe, commands were practically unknown, and the only sanctions were those of personal or family vendettas.

Usually a quiet, gentle, and easy-going people, the Caribs are given to nursing their wrongs in fits of melancholy and to unreasonable caprice, which under the influence of drink may develop into violent rage. In the old days such was often the origin of murder or even a war raid. Luckily, these fits were quickly spent. We are told that those prisoners who escaped the first violence of the Caribs' anger were brought home and treated by their captors as their own people. The first missionary fathers to come to Dominica in the seventeenth and eighteenth centuries also relate that the Negro slaves acquired by the Dominica Caribs were much more gently treated than by the run of white masters. In fact, these French fathers—Du Tertre, Rochefort, Breton, Labat—despite their almost total failure to make proselytes, gave the islands a very good name. Although they deplored their laziness and indifference in matters of religion and acculturation, Breton, who spent 20 years among the Caribs in Dominica (first settled by whites in 1760) declared them to be hospitable, polite, honest, and truthful, adding that 'be it said to their glory and to the confusion of Christians, they never behave publicly in an immodest manner'.

Few legends have withstood misplaced missionary zeal and the general breaking up of Island Carib culture. What little survives points to a common origin with that of the Guayana tribes. Several tales current in Dominica mention a giant snake that can crow like a cock and in whose head a stone of dazzling brilliance is set. The old Caribs relate how this creature would appear in human shape to their wise men, helping, advising, endowing them with charms, and even on occasion begetting the early progenitors of their nation. One of the latter, Bakámô by name, had, they say, the body of a snake with a man's head; he was carried out to sea where he became the constellation of that name (our Scorpio). Other stories identify other constellations and heavenly bodies with early culture heroes, but never as objects of worship.

Medicine men

There existed a class of men called *bwayé*, or *piayé*, who, in order to become 'wise', submitted to a severe and often painful apprenticeship, which enabled them to fulfill the role of doctor, priest and sorcerer. They acquired from their masters one or more familiar spirits, which they evoked by incantations and offerings whenever the need for consultation arose. I have spoken to old Caribs who remember such séances. They tell me that offerings of cassave and rum* were placed on tables on one end of the *mwinâ*, which was completely darkened. The *bwayé* would sing and mutter, until the spirit 'fell in' with a thump. The spirits spoke in strange voices, and 'you could not tell what they were saying, but you could hear the "glou-glou" sound as they drank the rum'. When the house was re-opened, the offerings appeared to be intact and were consumed 'early in the morning before eating' by those who so desired. The spirits, I was told, consumed 'only the soul of the offerings'.

Like their kindred in Guayana, the Island Carib still believes that the woods, rivers, and sea are the homes of particular kinds of spirits. On occasion, these may show themselves in a benevolent light, but their appearance is more often of evil omen to man.

Trade

No doubt even before the coming of white men a barter went on between the islands. Crescent-shaped ornaments of a gold alloy called *carácuri*, green stone charms, and no doubt certain raw materials and products made of them must have been acquired from the mainland either by war or in exchange for something, perhaps canoes, that the islands made with greater facility. But all in all, each island and even each settlement in the island was independent of others for their everyday needs. Hardwood was varied and abundant for all purposes, but iron and bronze were unknown, and stone-cutting implements such as axes, adzes, and knives were tedious both to make and to use. For

---

* Introduced by white men. In earlier years native beers were used.

that reason fire was often used to fell a big tree. Nevertheless the Caribs, or their Taino predecessors, used to manufacture by primitive means and through months of labor not only weapons and tools, but also pierced cylindrical beads and carved figures of stone. Whenever possible, the Carib made use of natural objects: thus, his fishhooks were usually a kind of thorn, his arrow points of wood or reed hardened by fire, his scalpel, the pointed tooth of an agouti set in a leg bone of the same animal. Fishbones provided him with needles, necklaces and boring instruments. The women made some pottery when suitable clay was at hand, and calabashes of all shapes and sizes provided the kitchen with a varied array of buckets, pans and dishes, boxes and bottles.

Meat and fish are roasted directly in the fire, or smoke-dried on a wooden grill over it. The basis of the Carib diet is manioc. Because the tuber of this plant contains a cyanic poison, it has to be rendered harmless by fire before it can be eaten. Without necessarily crediting the Carib with the original discovery, we must marvel that a plant which is poisonous to eat should have been made edible by a process so complex. The tubers are peeled, washed, and then grated into a vessel rather like a small, six-foot dug-out canoe. The resulting pulp is next squeezed in a long stocking-like contraption of close-woven basketry, called *matapi*. Then it is sifted through a basketwork sieve, or *hebichet*, and finally baked on a stone slab either into thick, round cakes of cassava-bread, or by constant stirring, into a coarse meal. The water squeezed out of it soon deposits a fine starch, which may be added to the meal or used separately. As for the remaining manioc water, it can be boiled together with pimento and other seasoning to form what is known to the present-day Creole as pepper pot or cassareep, and to the Carib as *túmali* or *syúti*. After being sufficiently boiled, the manioc water is reduced to a thick brown sauce, which has the quality of preserving any meat cooked in it. For drink, certain thick cassava cakes were formerly chewed by the maidens and spat into a vessel containing water. After a few days' fermentation, this mess was strained and drunk under the name of *ouíku* or *sákuti*.

Apart from their household duties, the women looked after the gardens, collected fruits and berries, made crabwood oil and paint, decorated pots and calabashes, painted the men, spun cotton, and wove hammocks. The hammocks sometimes attained twelve or fourteen feet in width and were closely woven on a simple frame without—according to Breton—either heddles or shed-stick!

Besides hunting, fishing, and clearing land for gardens, the men made dugout canoes, paddles, sails, and fishing line from a species of bromelia, together with the axes and adzes used in their making. They carved war clubs, stools, bowls, and cassava troughs out of red or yellow hardwoods. The same sort of war clubs are used nowadays for killing fish, and are called by the same name, *bútu*. Besides this the men made most of the basketry and other utensils used by the women. It is small wonder that they had but little conception of the passage of time and the value of strange articles.

A NATIVE weaving the outer layer of a waterproof basket

A CLOSE-UP of the weaving shows artistic workmanship

All photos by H. M. and E. L. Ayers

A BANANA LEAF lining goes between the inner and outer basket covering

THE COMPLETED BASKET, fitted with handles, is a useful object of trade

36. Basket-making. Photograph by H. M. & E. L. Ayers. From Douglas Taylor, 'Columbus Saw Them First', *Natural History*, 48 (June 1941), 48.

Outside influences on the Carib

Although contacts between Carib and European or Carib and Negro must have been few and far between at first, acculturation began at an early date, as is shown by the 'Caribized' words of Spanish origin included in Father Breton's dictionary of 1665. There were at that date Caribized words for horses, cows, pigs, goats, and rats, guns, knives, nails, needles, plates, iron and silver. The words for clothes, hats, shoes and smallpox had also been adopted into the Carib's idiom, and it seems probable that the things they stood for, despite inborn conservatism, had influenced his culture to some extent.

As long as the Carib had to depend upon his own efforts to produce not only food and housing, but also his tools and weapons, utensils and ornaments, he maintained through tradition and invention a relatively high standard, which doubtless would have improved as time went on. But when he was confronted with the products of a technique far beyond his comprehension and ability, a technique which included guns and steel axes, he naturally abandoned his native crafts, to devote himself more and more to the production of articles for exchange or sale. Unfortunately, most of his products had little value to the Europeans except as curiosities; and so the more he produced, the less he received in exchange. When he was unable to improve his technique,—and this usually was the case—, the Carib could only lower the quality of his work. Moreover, not all of the European products that appealed to the Carib were as useful to him as guns and steel axes. The labor expended for the purchase of clothes, hats, shoes, rum and so on was simply lost, because these things replaced nothing in his old economy. Time hitherto devoted either directly or indirectly to the production of food or comfort was henceforth used, for example, in cutting timber and building canoes to sell to the white man. This process, which is not yet complete, has led on the one hand to a lamentable defor-estation, paucity of game, and impoverishment of the soil; and on the other hand, it has led to frequent visits to the town, from which the Carib returns without anything to show for selling his canoe except a sick headache, or at best, some gimcrack and useless product of 'the export trade'. I had almost reversed the order, and said 'at best a sick headache', for the Indian thoroughly enjoys getting drunk, while the more solid goods foisted upon him merely delude his misguided vanity.

The retreat before civilization

Innate shyness and conservatism as much as European musketry drove the Carib to the more rugged isles, and in them to the least accessible parts of the windward coast. After the last of their number in St Vincent had perished in the volcanic eruption of 1902, Dominica remained the red man's sole island of refuge.

By that time, bows, arrows, hammocks, and native pottery were forgotten, and had been replaced (among those who could afford them!) by guns, beds, and cheap crockery; but the Caribs' voluntary isolation, coupled with their paltry commercial value and hard-dying reputation as 'dangerous savages', ensured them a relative independence that since then is slowly being broken down by the incursion of Negroes.

It is in the past 40 years that this small group has suffered what is perhaps its greatest loss of integrity—its language, or languages. Doubtless to some extent mutually corrupted, these two idioms subsisted side by side until about the end of the first decade of this century. Both succumbed before the French Creole patois of the West Indian Negro and 'coloured man'. Even today, when their memories of what they laconically term 'the language' are jogged, old men and old women of the Reserve still often give different words for the same concept. But with the last Carib speakers there doubtless disappeared many cultural links with the past that never can be replaced. The use of a common idiom leads inevitably to a community of notions and mental attitudes. And so it is that the Island Carib of today knows little of his own culture and nothing about our culture except, as it were, through Negro eyes.

Intermarriage

Although the older Caribs sometimes declare that '*mékeru k'hinsi kasi kámukuru*' (Negroes stink like grass gourds), the younger generation feels no compunction at interbreeding. Out of 400 inhabitants of the Reserve today, 300 are at best, as they themselves admit, '*bâtards Caraïbes*' (half-breed Caribs).

The girls no longer take easily to the old ways, and demand, like their coloured sisters, hats, shoes, and sewing machines. The boys learn just enough at school to lose interest in the old pursuits, and far too little to have a chance of success at the new ones. Few are those who still take readily to fishing, and fewer still are those who have any skill or liking for the hunt.

Basket making and canoe building of an inferior quality, together with sawing boards and scantlings, continue chiefly because they are usually the only available means of obtaining the money to buy the products of the colored trader. Many still yearn for a roving life, but it is to the plantations and sugar mills of Guadeloupe, Santo Domingo, and Cuba, or to the oil refineries of Curaçao that they aspire, rather than to the rivers and forests of their Guayana forebears.

27. History in the Movie-Making
Elma Napier (1949)

¶ *The 1948 film* Christopher Columbus *was a disaster. The producers tried to pull out when they saw the script, the leading actor, Fredric March, would not go to the West Indies for the filming, one of the replicas of the ships was burned out in Barbados. The critics were unanimous in their dislike for the overblown epic; it failed at the box-office.*

The making of the film completely disrupted the economy of the north-east coast of Dominica and affected the lives of all its inhabitants, from the local member of the legislature, Elma Napier, who wrote this account, to the Caribs themselves, willing extras—at European rates of pay—in a film with little or no claim to historical accuracy. In one of his essays about Dominica, Alec Waugh recalls a conversation with one of the film's historical advisers in which it became clear that the only point to be insisted upon was that breadfruit should not appear in the film: everyone had seen Charles Laughton in Mutiny on the Bounty *and therefore knew that breadfruit had been taken from Tahiti to the Caribbean in 1789 (1958: 306). So the Caribs played Arawaks, and the beach at Woodford Hill Bay, surrounded by cliffs and mountains, doubled for the flat beaches of the Bahamas. Carib involvement is not credited in the film itself or in any of the publicity material.*

Elma Napier (1892–1973), writer and politician, went to Dominica with her second husband, Lennox, in 1934. She wrote a novel and several books of memoirs, and contributed articles to English newspapers and magazines during the 1930s and 1940s. She was the first woman elected to a West Indian legislature.

The longboats in the channel toss and sway to the sea's moving. Surf breaks heavily over streaky sand, leaving a jagged stain. Noonday sun blazes on to sweating, bearded sailors in grey and yellow and red serge tunics. Standing in the prow of the centre boat, an understudy Christopher Columbus, clean shaven, wearing chain armour and a scarlet cloak, holds himself upright by means of a rope.

At a given signal, furious activity of oars propels the boats into the surf, where at the last moment waves take charge, bearing them forward with a great sweep of water, into which Columbus leaps to make his first landing in the New World. The sailors, throwing their oars to the sea, jump after him into the swirling foam and run their boats on to the sand.

'O.K.' shouts the director. 'That's a take.'

Johnny Wardrobe, emerging from under the seagrape trees, wrings the hem of the cloak, spreads it over a branch to dry. Columbus, stripped of armour, of grey hose, of black suède riding-boots, flings himself into the kindly cooling ocean. Even the Great God Camera, with its attendant High Priests, relaxes. Carib Indians, laying down their property bows and arrows, put on the shirts and trousers, the cotton dresses, they had left folded in their canoes.

No one had supposed that our Catholic Caribs would so readily undress. To tease the directors we have visualised Reverend Fathers rushing into the picture waving Mother Hubbards. Now, unselfconscious as a Folies Bergère chorus, the women wearing brassières for American audiences, their breasts veiled by long black hair for the English version, they move about the beach in especially dyed loin cloths, or climb among the seagrape trees which the camera-man insists on calling dingleberries.

'Taffy,' he yells to a man with a saw, 'rid me of these dingleberries.' Or sometimes 'Bring me dingleberries'—to be a frame, to make a shadow. And Taffy, thankful to break his idleness, hurries obsequiously with a branch of round, glossy leaves and green, pinhead-size fruit—fruit we shall never see again without thinking of the giant camera under its green umbrella; reflectors swathed in mosquito netting; waves of shimmering sand-heat dowsed by buckets of sea-water, and the small brown bodies, checkered by sun and leaf patterns, of obedient Indians, indifferent to their nakedness, indifferent to everything except five dollars a day. Few Caribs have ever been to a cinema; none knew what the sequences mean. But they know what five dollars mean in terms of rum and cloth.

This business of entertainment demands curious twists in the décor. For Columbus landed originally in what we now called the Bahamas, where there are no mountains ('but we'll take poet's licence on that one,' said the director, pointing to Morne au Diable, 'because scenic effects are expected of the West Indies')—and found Arawaks on San Salvador, not Caribs. The gentle Arawaks, however, having long since vanished from this planet, and Dominica being the only island where the next-best-thing in Indians is still to be found, Dominica was chosen in which to make certain shots of the Columbus film, although Columbus never in fact set foot there. He made it his landfall on the second voyage and, finding the natives hostile, went over to Marie Galante, which he named after his ship. Now our church-going, rum-smuggling, basket-making Caribs are earning one pound and tenpence a day (a normal wage is two shillings) by pretending to be the Arawaks whose ancestors, with the co-operation of the Spaniards, they effectually exterminated.

37. Columbus (Fredric March) discovers the hammock. Still from *Christopher Columbus* (1948: dir. David MacDonald. J. Arthur Rank, Universal-International). By courtesy of The Rank Organisation plc.

38. Columbus (Fredric March) has caught Pedro (Edward Rigby) bartering broken crockery for pieces of gold: he reckons a small bell constitutes a fairer exchange. Still from *Christopher Columbus* (1948: dir. David MacDonald. J. Arthur Rank, Universal-International). By courtesy of The Rank Organisation plc.

Strange words echo, for a fortnight, from our lonely cliffs; are repeated by the slow-moving river; whispered by palm-trees. Strange things are seen.

'Stand by for rehearsal. Stand by for a take. O.K., Cyril? O.K., Reg?'

A sulky boy holds a blackboard with the number of the sequence in front of the camera. Before every take, the beach must be cleared of anachronisms. The sailors of Columbus drank coconuts no more than Coca-Cola. We take poet's licence, if we must, on a mountain, but not on grapefruit and bananas, on bathing-suits and sneakers. Nor, for the matter of that, on Negroes. Actors, doubles, extras, rid themselves of straw hats and watches. At the last moment a cigarette is snatched from a Carib, dark glasses from a bearded warrior.

'Are we all set? Do we turn? Are we rolling? Action!'

Follow a few breathless seconds when even the sea seems to keep silence, the very birds hold their flight, till the assistant director throws up his arms and cries: 'Cut.' Then, 'Let's repeat right away. Repeat without cloak.' And again, 'Hold it, please, for colour stills.'

Over and over, for many days, seamen have rowed and Columbus leapt. Sometimes the ocean takes charge and boats come broadside on, wallowing in confusion. Sometimes the actor lurches or stumbles, sinking too deep in sand and sea. Sometimes sailors are slow in their reactions, or waves unduly buffet them. When artists and oarsmen, boats and surf and sand, have collaborated towards perfection, so that the O.K. is bestowed like an accolade, every scene must still be repeated without the red cloak of Columbus; for the star in the London studio has not yet made up his mind whether or not he will use it. And on some days the surf is less heavy than on others. Paddy, the continuity girl, slumped in a deck chair behind a jug of limejuice and two pineapples, cannot control the beat of the waves or the cloud formation in the sky.

Bursts of feverish activity resulting in at best a thirty-second take (on a good day there may be as many as two minutes showing-time in the can), alternate with periods of aching boredom, wherein directors and camera-men go into conference, artists sleep, extras play with the sea, and disgruntled seamen, hired not to be actors but to man the still unfinished galleons, put about the story that all work done has been wasted because the star has after all decided to wear a beard. Which rumour spreads like the stain of the sea over the beach; is whispered by sandpipers to the river; and—so fantastic the film legend—is by nearly everybody believed.

The American nightclub proprietor from Barbados, who came to Dominica to watch the filming of Columbus and found himself pushed into a beard and yellow serge garments, condemned to stand barefoot on hot sand holding a crossbow, said: 'Never tell me Britain is bankrupt.' Which he amended with: 'If she ain't bankrupt now she will be when this picture is finished.'

Danger money. Lunch money. Protective clothing. A transport bill of three hundred pounds a week—expenditure fantastically out of proportion to our tiny island economy. Two hundred people of a dozen different nationalities

320

have taken possession of a beach which normally is trodden only by an occasional fisherman, shuffling crabs, herons. Now Greeks, Italians, Pan-amanians, crew of the yacht which brought the Unit from Marseilles, have been pressed into service as extra seamen. English actors, Scottish directors, Welsh property-men; an Irish doctor turned artist; our own Polish medical officer; his French wife; American visitors; Negroes; Carib Indians. Of all dialects spoken the strangest to hear in this place is Cockney; and of all the odd phrases the oddest is 'danger money'.

Lunch money means five shillings a day for Union members whose contract provides for a knife-and-fork meal at mid-day. Here in the old works—where once limes were crushed and (longer ago) sugar, there are served only sand-wiches and 'cokes'. (Three hundred bottles of Coca-Cola per day and no opener, so that bottles are jerked against trees and rocks and reflectors, even on the very legs of the camera; and I think that bottle caps will lie forever and forever in this sand, till the day when the New World is rediscovered by some new Christopher Columbus after the next Dark Ages.) But danger money is drawn by those going to sea in heavy armour who cannot swim.

Every car and truck in the Northern District is under contract to the Unit. I—Member of the Legislature—have to say 'Please', before using a taxi; must listen to ignorant strangers, telling me that *this* should be done for the island and *that* grown, until with a cry of pain I protest: 'Not once in a fortnight have I told you how to turn your camera.' Hucksters, vendors of hard-boiled eggs and fruit and drinking coconuts, throng the road beside the sinister mang-trees, the fever-haunted stream; and money—money for goods, money for wages—oozes, percolates, here a little and there a little, like rain after drought, into the villages and the deep valleys.

On the second day of 'shooting' a swing bridge broke (a series of planks sustained by wire) and thirty Carib women and children fell into the river, and twenty-three broken limbs were set by a Pole and an Irishman in our four-bed hospital. Why no one was killed I cannot imagine; but I think not even death could have kept the Caribs off the location, for a hundred of them, and more, are earning five dollars a day.

The rest of the Unit, such of it as has not found private hospitality, is based on the yacht, fifteen miles away. Every morning at half-past seven the convoy passes my gap. Mine is the problem of waking Columbus to meet it. The prod with the tennis-racket; the douche of cold water; the solemn promise followed by the instant relapse into slumber. An enquiry of the telephone exchange. 'Yes, the buses have left.'

'No, you can't have aspirin and brandy for breakfast. Here's your orange juice; your egg.'

This is worse than getting children ready for school. I am right back in the bib-and-highchair period. One spoonful for Daddy, one for Mummy, one for the cat. 'You know, they won't send back a car for a double. Only yesterday the director said you were giving yourself the airs of a prima donna.' Hurry,

321

hurry, down the drive; sleep again for two minutes under the mang-tree; sleep in the imperturbable lorry, carrying artists and technicians back to the sun and the hot sand; to cloak and armour and longboats; to landing in the New World and taking it for Spain.

Scenes are enacted on the beach which a few of us—this year, next year, some-time—may see on the screen. Most of us—never. The Landing. The Tea-party; fraternisation of Caribs and Spaniards; parrots, red peppers, and pineapples; a frightened child. The Prayer Meeting, Columbus kneeling in the sand to give thanks to Almighty God; and I groping back into history for something, someone, who is not Columbus. Sir Galahad? Cœur de Lion? I have gone back too far in time. This is Sybil Thorndike's St Joan. And the Taking Possession scene, whereat irreverent laymen remind each other of the long-ago *Punch* series of 'entertainments-at-which-we-have-never-assisted' when, having heard Columbus proclaim that 'this soil shall be forever Spanish', Caribs come forth from among the seagrape trees and, throwing down their weapons, cry 'Hooray', and 'Hooray'.

Other scenes, painted on memory only, the screen will never show. The cliché of the beach is: 'What I want to see is the picture of filming the picture.' Varied by: 'This isn't what Columbus discovered the New World *for*.'

The director, susceptible to sunburn, with blue scarf draped Arab-fashion about his head; the assistant director, straw-hatted, khaki-suited, his trousers soaked to the knee; the assistant-assistant director, trying to look as though he had something to do. A sailor in a buff tunic and red stocking-cap, trousers made ragged by Joan Wardrobe's little scissors, lying asleep in a canoe. The sandbank in the river become a dressing-room, whereon Robbie Hairdresser combs and re-combs wigs. A naked seaman on a rock, drinking from a bottle, making prototype for Soglow's pepsicola advertisements; while another, whose pike has crumpled under him, listens to the director's scathing: 'What the something do you suppose properties are for? To lean on?'

Most unforgettable of all is Ernie, Camera or Props, I have never discovered which, Ernie—where bathing trunks are *de rigueur* for those not actually in fancy dress—wears grey trousers with braces, a white shirt, a grey cloth cap. 'Aren't you ever going to sunbathe, Ernie? Get into the sea?' But Ernie doesn't 'old with foreign 'abits; is modest; is adamant. 'Lily-white I left my old woman,' he says, 'and lily-white I'll go back to 'er.'

28. *The Hittites of the Caribbean*
Patrick Leigh Fermor (1950)

¶ *Patrick Leigh Fermor (b. 1915) was one of the first travellers to make an extensive tour of the Caribbean after the Second World War. He had already spent eighteen months walking to Constantinople and fought for several years in Greece and Crete, but it was the book that resulted from his Caribbean travels,* The Traveller's Tree *(1950), which established his reputation as a writer, winning critical acclaim and two literary prizes.*

In The Traveller's Tree *Fermor acknowledges Elma Napier's assistance, and it was from her house, Pointe Baptiste, that he and two travelling companions set out to visit the Caribs, travelling south on horseback through Marigot into what Fermor calls 'the upper marches of the Carib domain'. Although their visit was brief, Fermor had prepared himself well—Labat was his constant companion—and his descriptions are valuably precise. He sees the Caribs, dramatically, as a 'doomed race', but is impressed by their dignity and their remarkable skills. The company they keep in his prose is telling: Etruscans, Hittites, Manchus. As with many of the twentieth-century travellers, a sharp contrast is made with the Afro-Dominican majority, here characterized as the 'black tide' which is likely to sweep the Caribs into oblivion.*

The following self-contained piece was published in the Geographical Magazine *in 1950 and, in the same year but in a slightly longer form, in* The Traveller's Tree.

Our preparation to visit the last surviving Caribs—the lonely handful of forest-dwellers in the precipitous British West Indian island of Dominica that are the only representatives of the former *Herrenvolk* of the Caribbean—was a small adventure in itself. The horses, however, were found at last, the negro porters assembled, the guide engaged. Leaving the only road of northern Dominica, we crossed the river, and found ourselves in the upper marches of the Carib domain.

The trees soon closed over the steep bridle path, dappling the soft, red clay with ragged stripes of sunlight. The road twisted as it climbed, and the thickness of the sodden leaves turned it into a dense and tortuous cavern. Each convolution hoisted our little procession higher into the foot-hills of Morne Diablotin, whose leafy cone pierced the sky miles away. The path grew level at last, and through a gap in the trees we could gaze from our lofty headland into a deep gorge downy with tree-tops; the sea reached inland between the steep sides of the canyon to meet the emerging river.

All day long our path followed this long climb and fall. The island is so rich in rivers that it is rumoured to possess one for each day of the year. The road suddenly widened into a clearing, where a group of shingle huts lay back under the trees, and by the edge of the path a group of men were standing, as though they were expecting us. So sharp was the contrast of their complexion and bearing with those of the islanders, that I thought for a moment that they were white men. But they were Caribs.

We dismounted and walked towards them, and, as we met, hats were raised on either side with some solemnity. We all shook hands. This meeting with the last survivors of this almost extinct race of conquerors was as stirring and impressive in its way as if the encounter had been with Etruscans or Hittites.

We were now able to see that they were either ivory-coloured in complexion or a deep bronze, with features that were, except for the well-defined noses, almost Mongolian or Esquimaux. Their straight black hair was cut across their foreheads in a fringe. They had a dignity of presence that even their hideous European rags could not stifle. A tall man in the middle, smoking a pipe and equipped with an elaborate walking-stick, took charge of us with a diffident, almost Manchu solemnity. This was George Frederick, the king or chief of the Caribs, and the elders that surrounded him were members of the Carib Council. He led us up a steep path, through the leaves to a little green glade in front of his own shingle hut, where we sat down under a mango tree, and leaned our backs against a half-excavated canoe.

An old man in a doorway was weaving a basket. These are remarkable things, accomplished with great intricacy and finish. Different coloured rushes and leaves are shredded into fine strands, and woven into complex angular patterns that give the effect of mosaic. The basket is composed of two deep oblongs, open on one side, which fit into each other as smoothly as the halves of a Revelation suitcase and grip each other so tightly that no other fastening is needed. The fineness of the mesh makes them completely water-tight. As we watched the strands overlap in the skilful fingers, a dozen coconuts came thundering from a palm tree, and a young Carib slid down the trunk with his bare cutlass in his hand. The king opened them deftly, and offered us the milk.

The presence of these men sends the mind winging into the vague centuries before the November Sunday in 1493 when, with a volley of poisoned arrows,

39. Author's party on bridge. Photograph by A. Costa. From Patrick Leigh Fermor, 'The Caribs of Dominica', *Geographical Magazine*, 26/6 (1950), 257. Reproduced with permission.

40. *George Frederick, the King or Chief of the Caribs, outside a Hut in His Little Forest Capital on the Eastern Coast of Dominica.* Photograph by A. Costa. From Patrick Leigh Fermor, *The Traveller's Tree* (John Murray, London: 1950). Reproduced with permission.

the ancestors of these Caribs drove the sailors of Columbus back to their boats, forcing the Admiral to set sail again in the direction of Guadeloupe. How many centuries earlier, nobody knows, for the only traces of that dim pre-Columbian age are half-a-dozen lumps of stone scattered among the islands, incised with a few barbaric golliwogs, and all the rest is surmise. It is now generally agreed, however, that, like their peaceful predecessors in the Caribbean chain, the Arawaks, their origins can be traced to the South American hinterland between the basins of the Orinoco and the Amazon, where both Arawaks and Caribs still survive.

When the Spaniards came to the Windwards and Leewards in 1493, Columbus dropped anchor at each of the islands, went ashore on some of them, and symbolically claimed them for his king. In nearly every case he was greeted by a fierce resistance; in Guadeloupe the men were reinforced by an army of Amazons who came down to the shore to loose off their poisoned shafts. He sailed away again, and on paper Hewanorra became St Lucia, Madanino became Martinique, Karoukera Guadeloupe, Wytoukoubouli Dominica, and so on, and that, for over a century, was all. There were brighter lures for the Spaniards in Mexico and Peru, and a long war with these savages for a handful of green tufted rocks was an unprofitable thought. Dominican monks landed occasionally to convert the Caribs and were massacred. The Conquistadors Ponce de Leon and Jerrando, and even Sir Francis Drake, failed to dislodge the savages. The Caribs remained unchallenged masters of the Lesser Antilles. In the first decades of the 17th century, France and England started to settle in these languidly held possessions of Spain, and their wearisome two centuries of wars began. But the prolonged and ferocious resistance of the Caribs in some of the islands and the impossibility of subduing them prompted the English and French to agree, at the treaty of Aix-la-Chapelle in 1748, that Dominica, St Vincent, St Lucia and Tobago should remain neutral, with the Caribs in undisturbed possession. De Rochefort and Fathers Du Tertre and Breton (who wrote a Carib dictionary, and translated parts of the liturgy into Carib), give us a clear idea of how these savages lived, but it is the pen of Father Labat that suddenly transforms these aboriginal phantoms into real and vivid people. It is he who tells us of their customs and superstitions, their methods of warfare and domestic life, and how they conquered the wild Arawaks, exterminating and devouring the men, and marrying the women. The Arawak tongue, he says, survived as a squaws' language; and, apart from their vernacular Carib, they also possessed a secret language of religion and council.

The neighbourhood of two elements as irreconcilable as the Caribs and the white colonists could only end in the extinction of one of them, and by the end of the 18th century the Caribs had virtually vanished as a race from all the islands except Dominica and St Vincent. They were removed from the latter island after a revolt, at the time of the French Revolution, to British Honduras. Their descendants are now as black as their West Indian neighbours.

The Caribs of Dominica remained the only authentic pocket of them but it was not large. Father Labat, at the beginning of the 18th century, reckoned that there could not be many more than two thousand in the island, though this number was certainly increased by countrymen fleeing from extermination in the other Antilles. In spite of the island's neutrality, many French planters settled there and imported slaves. It was finally assigned to the English in 1763, and, with short interregna of French invasion and occupation, it has remained in their possession ever since. Roseau and Portsmouth were suddenly full of Union Jacks and redcoats and powdered wigs. As the colony became organized and the population of slaves increased, the number of Caribs shrank. Bit by bit, all three of their languages disappeared to be replaced by Creole and, during the first decades of the 19th century, a more plausible and, at any rate in appearance, more deep-rooted conversion to the Catholic faith took place. Cannibalism had died out long ago, and many other customs, including their war paint and their dress, vanished one by one. Lost in the overwhelming Negro world, they had ceased to be dangerous. In 1903 the British Government, disturbed at their decline in numbers through miscegenation and in prosperity through their inadaptability to alien ways, created by decree the Carib reserve where they now live. There, in these few miles of mountains and forests, scarcely five hundred remain, and of these many have a small amount of African blood. In the whole world there are now only about a hundred pure-blooded Caribs left, and the little rearguard is growing smaller every year. They are a doomed race lingering on the shores of extinction, and in a genera-tion or two, unless some miracle of regeneration and fecundity intervenes, the black tide will have risen and swept them off the face of the earth for ever.

They are all, Caribs and mestizo-Caribs, consumingly proud of their race, and, whatever their internal feuds may be, they are a stubborn and compact community in their attitude to the outside world. For the last few decades they have been presided over by a sort of elective voivode with the style of king, though the title is legally in abeyance at the moment owing to certain difficulties with the authorities in Roseau. The present king or chieftain, George Frederick, whose office entails a civil list of ten shillings monthly from British Government funds, is the head of the Carib Council, which is responsible for the conduct of Carib home affairs. George Frederick owes his present position to his ability to read and write English as well as Creole. Most of the other elders spoke it imperfectly and all talked Creole among themselves. The only responsibility of the Caribs is to keep open the bridle path which runs through their territory by cutting back the creepers and undergrowth.

The king and his council accompanied us from hut to hut of their little forest capital of Battaka. Most of the houses were built of shingle or bamboo and palm trash, and scattered about singly in the woods. The women were pounding cassava in wooden mortars, sorting jute or cocoa-beans on cloths spread out on the ground, or weaving baskets. Many of these Carib women were fine

327

looking, with smooth blank faces of pale copper colour, and long gleaming black hair. In one clearing an elderly Carib lay smoking in a hammock stretched between the door-post and a calabash tree that suspended above his restful figure half-a-dozen heavy green balloons.

It is considered an indignity for the men to bear anything on their heads in the manner of their women and the Negroes. They carry their loads lashed on to a shelf which is supported at the sides by ovals of basketwork, the whole being slung on their backs in the fashion of a haversack. Their little society is still a tangle of feuds and jealousies and they frequently resort to their own sorcerers, who practise a survival of their aboriginal magic known as *piai*. Belief in dreams and their interpretation plays a great part in their lives. One of the strangest customs is that of adopting a pseudonym, which they rigorously maintain whenever they undertake a long journey, so that any actions or gestures during their absences are considered to have been done by an unknown stranger. Death and burial are accompanied by elaborate wakes and fumigations which are often the occasion of celebration and dancing and the swallowing of enormous quantities of rum. The pleasures of drink are still as important to them as ever they were in the past. When legally obtained supplies are too dear, shebeens are sometimes erected in secret.

Indifference to money, inaptitude or scorn for trade, and a total lack of ambition render them, for many of their fellow-islanders, a perplexing community. They have a marked distrust and contempt for laws and taxations imposed from without. Their purpose is to keep their own way of life in the woods and on the sea unchanged, and with the minimum of interference from outside: a wish that seems, in spite of their many grumbles, to be fairly liberally indulged. Their food is mainly fish, and often, still, crabs, and, above all, yam and dasheen. They fish in the rivers at night by torchlight, and catch crayfish with cassava bait. Fish are also killed by poisoning the mountain streams with *larouma*, a vegetable whose venom is innocuous to humans. Lobsters are captured by divers, and elaborate wicker pots are woven to entice and imprison turtles. Iguanas, which are one of their great delicacies, are hunted with a technique as strange as their ancient mode of parrot-catching. The hunter steals under the leafy haunt of one of these reptiles, and whistles to it gently for hours, until it is hypnotized into a sort of aesthetic trance. The little prehistoric dragon is gently lassoed, and then, bound hand and foot, carried joyfully home. They cultivate vegetable gardens in the high woods, which they clear by felling the trees and burning the bush. When they have exhausted the soil they move on and repeat the same process elsewhere. Little parties of them, laden with their garden produce and with Carib baskets for sale, climb the footpaths over the watersheds and ravines to the market in Roseau.

Many of them were hacking with adzes and cutlasses at the inside of canoes. When a Carib purposes to make one of these *gommiers*, he chooses a tall *dacroyoda hexandra* in the high woods and fells it at the time of the new moon. The shape is roughed out where it lies, and the centre excavated. The maker

THE HITTITES OF THE CARIBBEAN

then summons his friends and the hull is dragged to the rhythm of special songs down to the foothills with ropes made of liana. There, under a tree near his hut, he trusses the ends and splays it open by filling it with water and then stones and, keeping the sides wide, like an alligator's mouth, with sticks, finally expands it amidships over a slow fire. The inside of the hull is ribbed and cross braces are inserted. The sides of the craft are heightened with planks which converge at one end in a high blade; the seams in the planks are caulked, and when its two masts and a mizzen and lugsail have been prepared, the vessel is ready for launching.

Travel by sea is still a passion among the Caribs; for trade, for smuggling, and sometimes purely for fun. They have been known to sail their canoes far beyond their little archipelago, sometimes as far as Cuba, the Guianas, and the Spanish Main. They have cronies in all the neighbouring islands and frequently they return from their expeditions in a condition of ancestral tipsiness, harmlessly capsizing several times along the way. They are accomplished smugglers, and load their pirogues with pigs and chickens and turkeys, which they exchange for the cheap untaxed liquor in Marie Galante or the Saints or even Guadeloupe, and then slip back to their creeks without paying the excise duty. The Government send motor boats to patrol the island waters and catch them red-handed, but as the Caribs work by night and have known every cove and rock and current since centuries before the Europeans arrived in the Antilles, it is usually a vain task. A serious smuggling incident occurred in the thirties. Five policemen penetrated the Carib territory and seized a quantity of contraband rum and tobacco. A battle with sticks began and a riot ensued, with two Caribs killed and two injured, while some of the police suffered injuries. It was only quelled by the Navy dispatching a ship to the Carib waters which fired into the high woods with its heavy guns. It was then that, as a punishment, the kingship was abolished and the royal mace carried away to Government House in Roseau.

It is a problem to know what course the authorities should take if a Carib commits a capital offence. For, being the last specimens of a race that is almost extinct, each pure Carib has a world-wide importance that transcends by far all legal considerations.

When the time came to leave the Carib capital, we sent the porters and ponies ahead to Salybia, and the king and his council accompanied us on foot. George Frederick is a dignified, rather melancholy grandee.

During a rest on the mountainside, we produced a bottle of whisky which we had bought at the Syrian shop. It did one good to see the way their eyes lit up. We drank in turns, and the enormous swigs of the Caribs brought the whisky-level down two inches at a time. I brought out Mr Douglas Taylor's treatise on the Caribs, which gives a vocabulary of the few dozen Carib and Arawak words that have survived the deluge of Creole. None of them had ever seen it, and they were flattered and excited when they heard us clumsily pronouncing the words of their ancient tongue: *Ahahoua* or *Twahleiba*, a snake;

Aotou, a fish; *Canoa, Couriala, Oucouni*, a boat; *Calleenago*, men; *Careepfouna*, women ... An impish elder, who seemed the brightest of the council, pronounced a word that doubled them all up with laughter. The king archly whispered the meaning. This was followed by other words that sent them all into paroxysms of hilarity. It is clear that the improper terms of the ancient language will be the last to die.

Our three Negro porters looked substantial and normal after the Caribs, who, even after such a short time, began to seem as curious and unfamiliar as Martians. As we rode southwards we saw one or two more in the woods, a shade darker each time, but still straight-haired and Mongoloid, and the children, gathering sticks by the road, were as pretty as Japanese dolls. Finally the miscegenate fringe petered out and we were again in the heart of the Negro world.

Every few miles the porters sat down for a rest, and we dismounted and smoked cigarettes until it was time to move on. One of them was a good-looking young man, who sang Creole songs in a soft voice or whistled without ceasing. I asked him what he thought of the Caribs. 'De're maad people,' he answered, 'but dey got lovely, lovely hair.' His mouth opened in a large smile as he passed his palm over his own scalp: 'Not like me.'

41. *The Last Family of True Caribs on St Vincent.* From Harry Luke, *Caribbean Circuit* (Nicholson & Watson: London, 1950), pl. 18. Despite the melodramatic title of Luke's photograph, the Vincentian Caribs still survive in the north-east of the island. Although not as clearly defined a community as their Dominican counterparts, they are fully involved in the organization for Caribbean Indigenous Revival, which met in St Vincent in Aug. 1987.

42. *Author with Carib Women and Children, Salybia, Carib Reserve, Dominica.* From Harry Luke, *Caribbean Circuit* (Nicholson & Watson: London, 1950), pl. 19. This picture was taken during three years Luke spent as chief representative of the British Council in the Caribbean at the end of the Second World War. His book also describes the festival of Santa Rosa in Arima, Trinidad, with its 'Carib queen'.

29. *Whicker's Caribs*
Alan Whicker (1964)

¶ *Alan Whicker's pioneering documentary programmes for the BBC's* Tonight *programme in the 1960s included a series on the Caribbean, one ten-minute segment of which recorded Whicker's visit to the Carib Territory in Dominica. What follows is a transcript of that segment.*

Many of the tropes will by now be recognizable. The difficulty of the journey is emphasized—'expedition into the remote territory . . . almost inaccessible'— although the traditional horses have now been replaced by a Land Rover. The Caribs are seen as living out a 'tragic destiny . . . doomed to extinction'. This last, and other phrases such as the comparison with the Martians, make it clear that The Traveller's Tree was Whicker's most important source.

This text has been transcribed by us from the original BBC recording. It was first transmitted on BBC1 on the evening of 10 April 1964, and then formed part of Whicker's World: A Caribbean Compilation, *broadcast on BBC2 on 5 February 1966, just as Queen Elizabeth II began an extensive tour of the area.*

One of the most beautiful of the Caribbean islands, Dominica is poor, almost forgotten, and still not completely explored. Three hundred years of British rule has meant that they've got an airstrip but have only just started to build roads across the island.

Today an expedition into the remote territory of a great and warlike people who gave their name to this whole part of the world—and to cannibalism. Today in this wild island which has still not been completely explored, they are living through the final chapter of what is perhaps the most lonely and tragic destiny in the world, for they are the last of their race, the rearguard growing smaller in numbers each year of a doomed people, listlessly awaiting extinction. So today, if we can reach them, we are off to see this dying race, the Caribs.

43 and 44. As with Patrick Leigh Fermor (Plate 39), Alan Whicker crossing one of Dominica's swing-bridges can be taken as symptomatic of the traveller's transitions to a different world, although the horses and Shanks's pony have now been replaced by a Land Rover (Plate 43). Germandois Francis was probably the first Carib chief to be interviewed on television (Plate 44). *Whicker's World*, BBC TV, 1964.

They are not easy to reach in their final resting-place, an almost inaccessible reservation created for them just sixty years ago by an anxious British government, mindful no doubt that for several centuries we, along with the French and the Spanish, did our very best to exterminate the Caribs. But when, at the beginning of this century, the plight of this disappearing race came to official attention, the Caribs were given back an isolated fifty square miles of Dominica, most beautiful island of the West Indies. Here the Caribs await the pathetic close of their epic, for once they ruled the islands of this, their sea. They had come here in fleets of war-canoes from the regions of the Amazon in South America, attacked and conquered the gentle Arawak Indians, who in their millions occupied all the islands from Trinidad north to Cuba. The Caribs dealt with this unwarlike enemy by the direct method of killing and often eating the men, marrying the women, adopting the children. Some remained here, some moved on, marrying and eating their way through the Windward and Virgin Islands. In 1493 the ancestors of these men drove the sailors of Columbus back to their boats and forced the admiral to set sail, for the resistance of the Caribs was too fierce, their poisoned arrows too thick to make the capture of this island worth-while. So the Spaniards, after naming the island Dominica, because they had arrived here on a Sunday morning, the Spaniards sailed away towards the easier conquest of Mexico and Guatemala and Peru, to deal with the rather more tractable Maya and Aztec and Quiche.

Despite their reputation as cannibals, the Caribs devoured their victims as a war-ceremony or in a rage but never out of sheer gluttony. The historian de Rochefort, writing three centuries ago, said that the Caribs of his day had very decided and very discriminating views about meals of this kind. By far the best and most tasty of the Europeans, they had decided, were the French, and they were considered absolutely delicious. Next in flavour came the English. The Dutch were rather dull and tasteless, while the Spaniards were so stringy and full of gristle as to be practically uneatable. The taste of the Arawaks had, by then, evidently been forgotten, while their own was too commonplace to mention in this gruesome catalogue of taste sensations.

Watching these placid people today it is hard to recall that back in those hungry, cannibal days Carib women would paint their menfolk bright red, from their long black hair, anointed with palm-oil and piled in a crown upon their heads, down to their feet. The men wore loin-cloths and long knives but nothing else. Ornaments hung suspended from their ear-lobes and nostrils and lower lips. The women, who still spoke Arawak among themselves, were an inferior caste, five or six of them often sisters as wives of the same man.

In the eighteenth century they finally dropped their unpopular man-eating customs, and since then they've lived mainly on an inadequate diet of fish, cassava, yam, and a sort of turnip. The few remaining pure-blooded Caribs today look like tropical Eskimoes. The men have small, square-shouldered bodies and sleek, straight black hair that sets them apart from their African neighbours. With wide cheekbones, low foreheads, and with small slanting eyes, shiny as black beads, they are almost Mongolian. Their womenfolk are often fine-looking, with long, gleaming black hair, smooth, blank faces of pale, yellowy copper colour.

On this reservation, rum breaks down reserve. And rum has done perhaps more than anything else to destroy the Carib race. Their language is dying with them. Most speak the creole patois of the Dominican negroes. Only a few phrases of Carib remain, and a few songs, remembered hazily by the older men. These remnants of a conquering race are ruled by a king or chieftain, elected every three years to head the Carib Council, usually for his ability to speak some English. The office entails a civil list of £10.8s.4d. a year, from government funds. The present chief is Germandois Francis, aged 28, an occasional barber, who is not too optimistic about the future of his people.

'Well, I don't think as the women are doing now, I don't think the race will last for long.'

'What are the women doing now?'

'Well, they are mixing the blood too much with people from outside.'

'Now you are a pure Carib?'

'Yes, I'm a pure Carib. My mother's a pure Carib, my father's a pure Carib.'

'But you're not married?'

'No sir, not married as yet.'

'Well, what are you doing about the perpetuation of the race?'

'Well, sir, I'm trying to see, taking my time. I'm only looking, but then I don't know what time I'll get married, but I have to choose one, besides, the same thing with my future.'

'Are you looking for a pure Carib girl or would you marry a negro girl?'

'No, sir.'

'You wouldn't?'

'No, sir, it is not my intention of doing such.'

'Why not?'

'I prefer to marry the Carib woman, Carib likewise myself.'

'Now, of course, your language is dying with the race; it seems there aren't many people who can speak even a few phrases of it.'

'Yes, sir, but not so many. My father can speak a good bit, and a lady from Bataka by the name of Sullivan Viville know a lot of the Carib language.'

'You're a pure-blooded Carib?'

'Yes, sir.'

'Can you speak any?'

'Well, I can tell you "howdy" in the Carib language: *Mabríka, mabríka Karifóona ... cúmanáténu nákaroo ... mulatú*, that is, when you are saying "howdy" to a Carib you're saying *mabríka, mabríka Karifóona cúmanáléenu na Karifóona*. I mean to say "What about you? Good morning or good afternoon", anyhow it may be; "and what about you?" To take a little drink, now you're saying *al ácoüacoutóu, eree caímalené coíake*. Are you having a drink?'

'What does that mean?'
'Saying, "we are having a drink, good luck and prosperity".'
'For good luck and prosperity is what the Caribs have not had.'
'Yes.'

Staunch Catholics today and, on their turnip diet, anaemic and often sickly, they have no hospital on the reservation and there's one visiting nurse who charges them about a pound to deliver a baby, if they can afford it, and most of them can't. Their bananas must take the track we've just covered to get to market which makes them uneconomic; there's a recurring suggestion that the government wants to take back their Reserve, which may be tribal property or may be Crown land; and, through all their trials, the Caribs, not perhaps without some historical justification, feel injured, feel that the rest of the world owes them a living. And the rest of the world is about as familiar with Caribs as with Martians.

Soon these bewildered descendants of the warriors who defied Columbus will have retreated from their wretched and pathetic today, and faded away to join their forebears in the valhalla reserved for them in the history books, leaving only their sea, the Caribbean.

30. *Still Conquering the Caribbean*
Anthony Weller (1983)

¶ *Visitors to the Caribs seem drawn to historical speculation: here Anthony Weller confidently finds the Caribs' 'last' home, and notes that they will vanish within a century—a prediction that has been frequently made over the last 200 years. An observed game of cricket is bizarrely noted as 'as good an occupation as any for a dying race on a sunlit morning'. The road system has by this time effectively ended the isolation of the Carib Territory: Weller and his companion can hop on a lorry in Roseau and be in Salybia within a couple of hours. Nevertheless, a strong sense of mystery is maintained through the style of writing—especially the arrival at twilight in a seemingly deserted village. Weller and his unspecified companion visit the Territory only briefly, but long enough to feel confident about contradicting almost every statement made to them by the chief, Hillary Frederick: they only hesitate over whether he is giving out 'deliberate mis-information' or 'wishful thinking'.*

Like visitors before him Weller is deeply concerned with the Carib language and has a valuable interview with Dupigny, widely regarded as the one living Carib with a reasonable knowledge of the old language. For the rest the old stories are given another airing: Caribs eating and marrying their way up the Antilles, the men and women's languages, the devouring of missionaries, the differential edibility of the various European nationalities, the inevitable reference to Labat.

Anthony Weller is a New York-based journalist. The piece appeared under the title 'Conquerors of the Caribbean' in the Colorado journal Geo in April 1983.

On a wild island of legendary beauty, along a steep coast of palms facing the Atlantic, the last indigenous race of the West Indies has made its final home. Once conquerors and roving seamen, now farmers, the Caribs will vanish within a century, doomed by intermarriage. Yet here on Dominica, the last dim echoes of their past may be heard, a past of war canoes sailing up the islands, of a population that once numbered in the millions, of annihilation by the Europeans—and eventual shelter on these eight miles of rough coast.

Dominica rises suddenly from the Caribbean Sea between Guadeloupe and Martinique, dense with rain forests and converging mountain valleys. Mists drift among the peaks, which at 3,000 feet and higher are the summits of submerged, long-extinct volcanoes. The few roads are rugged and empty save for an occasional rattling truck or a solitary figure trudging through the fervent landscape, a machete dangling from one hand. Columbus christened the island on his second voyage, in 1493, and sailed on without ever setting foot on it, deterred by the apparent absence of natural harbours. Nowadays, the few villages that pepper the coast, and even Roseau, the small, innocent capital, contribute paradoxically to the impression that little has changed here in 500 years.

The sense of isolation and secret grandeur is overwhelming. The hurricane of 1979, the frequent landslides due to heavy rains, the ever encroaching foliage, all have wrought havoc on the poor roads that attempt these green mountains. The Carib reserve—3,700 acres that have not legally belonged to the Caribs since Dominica achieved independence from Great Britain in 1978— lies on the eastern coast of the island. To get there from where we were staying, we hitched a ride in the back of a truck passing along the road that winds like twine among the Carib hills. A breeze rushed upon us as the truck jolted along through the gathering evening. A blue twilight spilled across the profuse palms to the sea on our right. On our left were hillsides thick with the giant, lackadaisical leaves of banana trees. No one was about, and the twilight was failing.

Then, abruptly, the road curved once again, and small houses began to appear on the hillsides in clusters or set along the road. Behind each house, a smaller structure issued smoke. The scents of cooking reached us, and we realized that we were among the Caribs at last, but as our truck hurried on, we saw no one. And then behind us a man stood diminishing in the road, barely visible in the twilight, waving and smiling curiously at us. He looked oddly dignified, barefoot and bare chested, wearing only long trousers: his skin was copper, and he had the blackest hair imaginable. Then he was gone as the road descended, and the truck stopped to let us clamber out. We were in Salybia, the main Carib village.

Night was falling, and in the moonlight we saw a stream coursing over rocks down a hillside thick with palms. An old man, who we learned was a coffin maker, adjusted his scarlet-ribboned straw hat when he saw us coming. We were looking for the chief, we said. He serenely pointed toward a clay path that ran alongside the stream.

At the head of the path, shrouded in darkness, was the house of the Carib chief, Hillary Frederick. He is 25 and received his high-school education near Watertown, New York, under a judge's sponsorship. Not long ago, the 800 voting adult Caribs elected him chief for a five-year term over seven other candidates.

45. Waitukubuli Karifuna Development Centre, Salybia, Dominica. Photograph by Peter Hulme. 'Waitukubuli Karifuna' means 'Dominican Caribs' in their original language, and expresses a new-found pride in their cultural history.

In the tradition of Carib chiefs since Jolly John, who led the 'Carib War'—a violent confrontation with several British policemen over smuggling in 1930—the present chief is more spokesman than leader. He lit a candle and invited us into his house. He was glad to see us, he said, if we would tell the truth about the Caribs. The Caribs had never been cannibals, he insisted; whoever had made up that story, centuries ago, was a cannibal himself. No, the Caribs had never kept slaves. His mission, he argued, was to bring back the old Carib ways, especially the language, which had been replaced at the turn of the century by French patois and English.

How many pure Caribs remained? we asked. He shrugged. Perhaps 20 or 30, no more. He did not look at us as he spoke, except when he smiled, and we were never able to determine how much of his false history was deliberate mis-information and how much was wishful thinking.

As we left Salybia that night, stumbling down the clay path in the darkness, the Carib reserve seemed deserted, and it was difficult to believe that the continuous belt of six villages contained some 2,500 inhabitants, including children. But Caribs tend to go to sleep soon after nightfall and to rise with the sun, and the next morning Salybia hummed with activity. Some Carib girls were bathing nude in the stream: they were not particularly shy and eventually emerged in simple dresses. They wandered down the road with huge plastic containers filled with water balanced on their heads, confidently chatting and turning as they walked. Lean dogs roamed about but never barked. Chickens scurried about the houses unmolested by cats, and a few piglets nosed around.

Today was the weekly banana boxing day, and a huge open warehouse was filled with Caribs. Like most Dominicans, the Caribs subsist mainly through agriculture, and though there is no private property on the Carib reserve (perhaps the strongest remaining Carib tradition), a person may live on any land he or she works. Bunches of bananas were piled all around the warehouse. They were being weighed and passed to a huge tank of water to be washed; they were then brought to tables to be boxed for trucks that would carry them to Roseau. Each box contained 33 pounds of bananas. Caribs of all ages worked at weighing and washing and boxing, and it was the week's main communal event besides Sunday mass. Two thousand boxes are sent to Roseau every boxing day.

Beneath several palms, a handful of men waited to have their bananas weighed. A boy with a machete lopped off the ends of fallen coconuts—the Caribs' other main source of income—and handed the coconuts to people to drink from. One Carib man lay stretched out on a branch a few feet above us like a sleeping lion; everything we said to him made him laugh. The features of these men were distinctly Carib, though some of them had skin that was quite dark; thus, long after there are no more pure Caribs, the features will persist. The dark skin of some of the men could no doubt be traced back as far as the seventeenth century, when the Caribs kept black slaves who had been

340

captured from Europeans. We were to find that the chief's estimate of the number of pure Caribs was inexplicably low. There are certainly more than 100 left, and they are by no means all old.

One middle-aged woman in a blue smock came over to talk to us; she was followed by her teenage son, who remained strangely silent, his gaze fixed on the middle distance. He had fits, she explained, and could not take care of himself, so he followed her around and kept her company. He was her fifteenth child. After a time, she introduced herself: we could call her Mistress Thomas. We asked what she thought of the chief's idea of bringing back the old Carib language. Was it possible?

She shrugged. Her voice was rather plaintive: 'I don't think so. Some of the older Caribs remember a few of the words. We had a language book, but we lost it. If you want to meet any of the pure Caribs, go to Bataka and Sineku, two of the older villages.' Then she put the problem of intermarriage very simply: 'You see, many of the Carib girls have to leave the Carib reserve to get work. And what do they bring back for husbands? It's not a white, it's a black. And if you have a mango and you graft it with some other plant, it doesn't give you a pure mango.'

The Caribs settled Dominica perhaps as many as a thousand years ago. They were a tall race, and they came from the banks of the Orinoco River in South America and conquered the docile, smaller and lighter-skinned Arawaks, who had populated the West Indies in vast numbers for centuries. The Caribs had great oceangoing skill—they used canoes up to 60 feet long that were equipped with sails—and they were tremendous warriors, as European accounts are quick to point out. The defeated Arawak men were eaten—not as a means of torture but so that an enemy's spirit could no longer do harm yet could give strength from within—and the women and children who were not eaten were taken into the tribe. Thus the people we speak of as pure Caribs are the result of intermarriage between the Caribs and the Arawaks. The Caribs ate and married their way up the Antilles, but the Arawaks flourished in the Bahamas until the European conquest. Today, the only Arawaks in the West Indies are on the Jamaican coat of arms.

Eventually this intermarriage resulted in two languages, one spoken by the women (Arawak), one by the men (Carib): the two languages merged as the race dwindled. By the time the language was abandoned, around the turn of the century, it was proportionally more Arawak than Carib, which was indicative not only of the power of the women's tongues within Carib society but of the influence the Arawak culture had on that of the Caribs.

Throughout the sixteenth and seventeenth centuries, with Spain's power in the New World waning, it was the British and the French whom the Caribs resisted, devouring any hopeful monks who visited their islands and carrying off Negro slaves and European women in raids. It was a struggle the Caribs could not possibly win, and both Britain and France ordered their destruction. By 1700, the Caribs on most of the other islands had been virtually wiped out, and only 400 survived on Dominica. During this time, the Caribs resisted European attempts to enslave them; a captured Carib simply ate dirt until he died. The slaves owned by Caribs were invariably well treated.

The Caribs devoured the first Spanish priests, whose colleagues quickly came to the conclusion that the Caribs were not worth the trouble, a conclusion that had already been reached by the Spanish Navy. Thus it is to the journals of the French monks of the mid-seventeenth century that we owe our knowledge of the early Caribs. Though light trade had by this time made the Caribs more amenable to Europeans, they were poor subjects for conversion. Cannibalism was still practiced: according to a seventeenth-century French historian, the French, followed by the English, were considered the most delicious Europeans, while the Dutch were dull and the Spaniards so tough as to be practically inedible.

The Caribs were tremendously adept weavers of reeds, a skill that persists to this day, and they slept in hammocks. Their main weapon was the bow and arrow, which was also used for sport, and in 1700, Père Labat reported with incredulity seeing small Carib children bring down birds from far away without missing. The arrowheads were made from fish bone and smeared with poison sap from the manchineel tree. Parrots were captured as pets either with blunted arrows or by setting fire to pimentos placed under trees so that the fumes rose and stunned the birds. The Carib name for Dominica was *Waitukubuli*—'tall her body'.

Justice among the Caribs was simple. The wronged party might choose to take revenge on the offender, and if the wronged party did not survive, his family might choose to take up the feud. The Carib practice of adopting a pseudonym while on a journey—one that all concerned apparently accepted, so that any actions performed by that person were treated as if they had been done by another person—derived from the Carib's dislike of the indiscriminate use of his given name by strangers. We found that the Caribs are still reluctant to divulge their name until they are deep in a conversation.

The traditional love of journey has been diminished over the years by the violence of the Atlantic, though Caribs still think nothing of walking over the mountains to Roseau in order to sell their woven baskets. Several fishermen told us they had made a rare voyage to Guadeloupe for the fun of it, traveling in small canoes (the word comes from the Carib *canoua*) as their forefathers had done.

One morning we met at dawn on the shore below Salybia with a fisherman named Joseph. The previous afternoon we had watched Joseph's canoe, with its square red sail, heave through the high waves to where the other fishermen's canoes were drawn up on the shore. Everyone had returned empty-handed that day. Dolphin and flying fish are frequently caught, but there are also shark, kingfish and swordfish in the Atlantic, and the Caribs catch them with a harpoon as long as a man's forearm. They can throw accurately at a distance of 35 feet.

Joseph rowed us out through the wild surf and then raised the sail. Walls of gray water rose around us, and the canoe seemed ready to turn over at any moment. 'Of course, I would prefer to fish the Caribbean; it is always calm,' said Joseph. 'But what can we do? We are here. It is disappointing to go out in this rough sea and get nothing. There are not so many fish as there used to be. Years ago, we caught sharks so big that several boats would have to help bring them in.' That day the sea proved too rough even to try, and we turned back.

Walking up from the shore, we passed the tiny cemetery of Sainte-Marie and the Carib Catholic church, a stone building with green doors flung open like big shutters and an upside-down canoe as an altar. Lizards were everywhere, and the high palms blotted Salybia, above us, from view. Several laughing girls came down the rough road of stones to greet us. Their names—Miranda, Felicia, Theresa, Andrea—suited their caroling voices. The girls led us up the hill, past the long pale-blue wooden school. Did one learn about Carib history in class? we asked. Nothing at all. Because the teachers were from outside? No, the teachers were Caribs themselves. The ignorance of their own history came about because there was no syllabus, no Carib textbook, the girls said. It was the fault of the generation that lost the language, the parents of the oldest living Caribs. They were told by the priests to give up their Carib ways, that the Carib language and all the old stories were jokes. Now it was too late.

We made our way past Salybia, up several steep clay paths to Bataka, hoping to find someone who remembered even a phrase of the old language. The young girls had not even known the Carib name for Dominica. In Bataka the houses were larger, more permanent, and we stopped before a large, extraordinarily well tended vegetable garden. Beside it, a canoe half full of water was held off the ground by two Y-shaped sticks. There were two dams of fist-size rocks in the canoe to make it expand. In a few weeks a fire would be lit under it to boil the water and cause the wood to expand further.

A pure Carib man in his fifties greeted us. Yes, he was Juan Louis du Pigny. He laughed when we asked if he spoke any of the old tongue. 'A little. My father-in-law spoke some. But there was no need, with the patois and the English. Two languages are enough.' His wife, small son and two daughters surveyed us from the house. 'It would be good to go back to the old language, but difficult. We need more land. Anyone from outside can marry a Carib girl and move here. It was once not that way. And much of our land is not good for farming.' He made a helpless gesture with one hand.

But there were still quite a few pure Caribs left, he said. 'My parents were both pure Carib, and there were ten children. My wife is pure Carib also, and we have six children. We are proud to be different, but the ways are gone. Fish are scarce. Once, if you didn't have money you could still get enough to eat. Not now. Now the Caribs die young, fifty, sixty, seventy. We are not as healthy a people as we used to be. My mother-in-law was ninety-four when she died. My grandmother, one hundred fourteen. No longer.'

Du Pigny told of an elderly woman in Bataka who some said was a witch. He would not say if he thought she was, but he would not give her name either. She could fly up in the night and change her skin; she could hurt us if she wanted to, or heal us if we were sick. The Caribs still believe the legend of the great snake—the *téte-chien*—whose passage carved a long staircase of rock to the sea. And they believe the reeds of a thatched roof should be cut during the new moon because a worm will get into the thatch if there is moonlight.

We wandered down from Bataka, back toward the sea. Near the church and school, several men were playing a furious game of cricket. It seemed as good an occupation as any for a dying race on a sunlit morning. We passed the tiny cemetery, with wooden crosses the color of driftwood, and skirted a ridge above the narrow beach. The waves were deafening. A few hundred feet from shore lay two islets of rock that the Caribs used to believe turned into great canoes at night, bearing the spirits of ancient Caribs out to sea.

Then we heard a strange, measured sound over the sea's booming. We peered over the ridge. Below us a naked man stood on the sand wielding an ax with great determination. A fallen gommier tree lay at his feet; he was beginning a canoe. In the thunderous sunlight of the coast, this tireless Carib seemed a shape out of time.

It began to rain torrentially, even though the sun was out, and when we reached the road, Salybia looked deserted. Then we heard giggling and saw three little Carib girls running up the hill, green banana leaves flopped over their heads. They squealed with delight and ran past us. The rain stopped as suddenly as it had begun. A truck rattled by with a red motto painted on the side: *God save us or we perish.*

We hopped in the back. Old friends were there already: Mistress Thomas and her fifteenth child, the boy who had fits, the boy who could say nothing. The truck picked up speed going down the hill, and the boy's face was transfigured with joy from the rush of air, the billowing palms, the dancing light on the sea.

Then Mistress Thomas rapped on the back window of the truck, which jolted to a stop. She threw her legs over the side—she did not need our help—and watched her son slowly clamber out, as though he were doing it for the first time. His face was still shining with wonder. The truck started up again, and we waved; they waved back and turned away. The road dipped, and we never saw them again.

31. *Carib Gallery*
José Barreiro (1990)

¶ *Despite the frequent predictions of their imminent demise, the Caribs survive and prosper in Dominica. The last twenty-five years have seen major changes on the Territory: good roads have made contact with the rest of Dominica much easier, and visitors from outside much more common. However, far from diminishing Carib culture, these changes have been associated with a renewed sense of Carib difference and, for the first time in perhaps 200 years, with political contacts with other indigenous groups on the mainland of Central and South America.*

José Barreiro's 'Carib Gallery' reflects a new kind of writing about the Caribs, no longer an elegy to a dying way of life, but a celebration of survival through adaptation. The traditional craft of the boat-builder is traced through a named individual, Napoleon Sanford, and the writer's personal reflections are given second place to the voices of the Caribs, especially that of current chief Irvince Auguiste.

Labat is quoted, from the popular résumé made in the 1930s (Labat 1931) but the passage selected highlights, unusually, the bravery and resourcefulness of the Caribs, rather than their supposed cannibalism or their 'ferocious' or 'melancholy' bearing.

Napoleon walked deftly through the tall succulent trees. A Carib Indian and master boat-builder, he knows the bush like his mother's face. The rainforest, one of the few in the Caribbean, covers most of this small island in a dense canopy. 'Here,' Napoleon said, palming a tall one. 'Gommier.'

Gommier is the tree from which he makes a canoe, a traditional trade he learned from his father. The Caribs, some 3,000 strong, have a reserve, known as the Carib Territory, in the northeast corner of Dominica. They make the best dugout canoe on the island that they share with an 80,000 population African-Dominican majority. Fishermen from all over the island come to Napoleon to buy his boats.

46. Napoleon Sanford. Photograph by Tim Johnson. From José Barreiro, 'Carib Gallery',
Northeast Indian Quarterly, 7/3 (1990), 47.

47. Boat-building. Photograph by Tim Johnson. From José Barreiro, 'Carib Gallery',
Northeast Indian Quarterly, 7/3 (1990), 49.

Napoleon posed next to a gommier tree he would choose to carve. 'You want a straight tree, of course, no cracks and deep root.'

Napoleon Sanford is a fisherman. Like many Caribs, he goes to sea in a canoe, sometimes paddling or sailing as far as Marie Galante island, some forty miles away. Carib fishermen work a rough windward sea and have many stories of encounters with large sharks, storms and other perils. Yet, 500 years after Columbus, they still make their dugout canoe and they still go out to sea.

On his second voyage, Columbus first sighted land at Dominica, precisely in the area of the Carib Reserve. The Caribs and the Arawak-Taino shared a common material culture.

Napoleon learned canoe-making from his father. Now he teaches other young Caribs, working a method thousands of years old. Carving out the tree trunk is only the beginning. The process involves a period of weathering, during which large stones are used to widen the hull and ribs are carved by machete. At a carefully chosen moment, when after months of weathering, the carved trunk suddenly starts to open, the canoe is 'fired'. The firing sets the carved-out opening, so it won't curve in on itself and crack. Nowadays a second plank is added to the side, glued with resin from the same gommier tree and nailed.

Like many Indians, Napoleon wants his people to improve their lives but not lose their traditions. 'Carib is a very independent people,' he said. 'Like our old canoe. It is real simple, not fancy like some of the fishing boats at Roseau area. But out to sea, even if it flips over and fills with water, we just take one end, turn it and jump back in. Bail the water out and we're on our way. Fancy boats go down easy, but our canoe never sinks.'

Both Ferdinand Columbus (Christopher's son) and Hernandez de Oviedo, an early chronicler, detailed the making of Caribbean Indian canoes. Wrote Columbus: 'these canoes are so nimble and built with so much artifice, that if they turn over, they straighten them out while swimming, flipping them to dislodge the water ... then bailing out the rest with dried out calabashes, cut in half.'

On top of a hill looking out on the Atlantic, Napoleon had four boats in the making.

'I learned from my father,' Napoleon said. 'Four is a lot of boats to do at once. With my father, he may not make boat for three, four years. Then one day, he'd say, "I make a boat this year." Then he'd go out in the bush and take the uncles and me with him. He would select a good tree of the gommier. There are rules to follow in that. Then he would cut it and we would all drag it out, up and down, out of the bush.'

Two old Carib men stopped by to see the boats. One told the story of the 'riot of 1930'. That fight broke out when Dominica officials attempted to 'tax' items brought home by Carib pilots from nearby Marie Galante island. The old man had been shot in the arm. 'We fought hard that time,' he said. 'We are tough sailors.'

The other told stories of going out to sea, traveling from island to island. 'It takes a big man to go out to sea like that,' he said. 'Our men still do that. In the old days, we were even bigger men. Tough. Our people were tough. We took on the weather. Canoe tip over, we right it, bail it out, keep going. We meet big shark, we take him on. No problem.' He laughed. 'That big shark, the White, he is really smart and he has a lot of teeth. Rows of them. He will grab your boat and shake it, try to dump you out. Yes sir, God Save the Queen, our Indian men have big hearts.'

Reading about Carib history, one encounters 'The Memoirs of Pere Labat, 1693–1705'. Pere Labat, a French priest who sailed the Caribbean for the church and had occasion to meet Dominica's Caribs 200 years after Columbus, recorded a most interesting encounter between a young Carib and a twenty foot great hammerhead shark.

The priest wrote in his memoirs that 'after a hammerhead shark had bitten off an Indian child's leg, when he was bathing in the harbor, a Carib volunteered to kill the fish ... The Carib armed himself with two well-sharpened bayonets, and after raising his courage by drinking a couple of glasses of rum, he dived into the sea.

The hammerhead, which had now gotten a taste of human flesh, attacked the Indian as soon as it saw him. The Carib allowed it to approach without doing anything until the moment he thought it was on the point of making its rush. But at the instant it charged, he dived underneath it and stabbed it in the belly with both bayonets ... This scene was enacted seven or eight times, and at the end of half an hour the hammerhead turned belly up and died.

After the Carib came ashore, some people went out in a canoe and tied a rope to the shark's tail, which was then towed to the beach. It proved to be a monster twenty feet long, and its girth was as large as that of a horse. The child's leg was found whole in its stomach.'

Napoleon remembered once a Great White followed him almost all the way home but he had good luck; although it bumped his dugout a couple of times, the shark did not attack.

On a hill overlooking the rock beach where the Carib fishermen launched their boats is a small Catholic church. Inside the church, at the altar, is a full Carib Gommier boat, polished in offering to the deity.

A Carib Indian group that included several councilors and their chief, Irvince Auguiste, had gathered to discuss strategy. We had met with the Carib leaders over the years and given advice on several projects on their reservation. The first topic this evening was the upcoming quincentenary of Columbus, set for 1992. It was an appropriate setting for the discussion.

Among the toughest and most fiercely independent Indian peoples, the Caribs were also the most maligned in the early conquest. They were accused of

48. Irvince Auguiste. Photograph by Tim Johnson. From José Barreiro, 'Carib Gallery', *Northeast Indian Quarterly*, 7/3 (1990), 55.

cannibalism by a couple of early chroniclers and the charge stuck through the writing of many histories. The early chroniclers based their accusations on two letters reporting Columbus's second trip. The letter writers, one an admitted rapist, were both compromised by their relationships to Columbus, who was actively justifying slavery and needed good reasons to enslave the Indians. The Caribs laugh about it now. 'They even claimed that we had a preference for French meat,' says the Chief, 'that we ranked French, British, Spanish and so forth. I think maybe the Dutch were supposed to be the worst tasting.'

Earlier, at the Carib Culture Building, we entered a small library where Chief Auguiste looked through three shelves of books. He pulled out a history book and opened it to a Columbus-era chapter. His finger pointed to a description of Carib Indians that used the words 'fierce' and 'cannibals'. The chief smiled. 'See. No communication then either.'

About the accusation that his people were cannibals, Chief Auguiste said, 'It is a very wicked lie.' He said he hoped the Carib people would get a chance to tell more about their real culture and history at the 1992 Quincentenary of the first Columbus voyage. Not that they cared to 'celebrate' Columbus, he said, but to reanalyse what happened.

'This cannibal lie,' he said. 'It goes back to the Spaniards, to the English. Columbus came to the new world looking for gold ... he met the people inhabiting these islands and tried to enslave them. And the Carib people had enjoyed centuries of freedom, making their cassava bread and catching fish. Naturally they would retaliate against anyone trying to enslave them.'

The Chief allowed that in war, within their ancient warrior tradition, a slain enemy might be cut and parts of him might be eaten, a practice documented to warrior/soldiers in many wars. Although it is depicted in early European paintings of Caribs they did not use human meat as a staple, Chief Auguiste said. He smiled, 'We have too many good things to eat.'

He continued: 'Then, when they first brought in Black slaves, the English told them we Caribs ate Black people, so that the maroons would not seek to join us when they ran away, and would fight us when they did. Like that they kept our two peoples divided a long time.'

In one island, St Vincent, in order to control their slaves, the British plantation owners went as far as to import poisonous snakes into the more remote swamps. As a result, it is today the only Caribbean island with that dangerous non-indigenous nuisance.

At the evening meeting, Chief Auguiste, a young man but already seasoned in community leadership, quickly stated the second reason for the discussion.

'In 1992 comes not only the anniversary of Columbus's 500 years,' the chief said, 'that is also the year when our tariff relationship with the British Commonwealth ends. Dominica's main export crop, bananas, now on a special status with that market, will have to compete with the larger banana producers. Dominica, including our own Carib farmers, will suffer very much. It could be a horrible time economically for our country.'

Chief Auguiste's comments began a discussion about the future economic potentials of the Carib people and the country of Dominica. A council member, Raphael, framed the question thus: 'We know what Columbus did to us, and yet we survived. But what I wonder is: how do we face, as Caribs and Dominicans, this economic crisis that threatens us?'

Chief Auguiste recalled an earlier strategy meeting in 1988, when eight elder women and two men had gathered to discuss projects. This circle of elders has a consistent membership and is highly respected by the younger leaders. Chief Auguiste had gathered the elders at that time to solicit their opinions about a proposal to privatize reservation lands. The elders were adamantly against the proposal, reaffirming the principle of holding reserved lands in common. The elders reasoned that the Carib identity is rooted in the land, which would be dispersed over the generations if individuals were allowed to own parcels of it. One woman said: 'We have to think of the next generation, and the next, so they have something too.'

This sentiment, typically expressed by Indigenous elders, is an understood pillar of the Carib development philosophy. Chief Auguiste referred to the meeting with the elders. 'It is understood we will not divide the land,' he said. 'This is basic to our thinking.' Other principles are seek and value the elders' advice, sustain indigenous culture and plan for the future generations.

As the evening's conversation continued, these principles provided a framework and stimulated the planning for a strategic exercise. With the Carib leadership, an indigenous development group recently surveyed various necessary activities to conduct adequate planning, such as a reasonably stable political framework and a way to create information resources to survey development possibilities.

The Carib community is in a state of flux, the councilors said. Many changes are coming into their reservation these days, some good and some bad. They are a poor community that for many years has maintained a traditional farming and fishing economy at the margin of Dominican national life but is now modernizing rapidly.

They stressed that their Carib tradition is experiencing the effects of rapid change and many of their young people are growing up with little Indian identity. Although they still have elders who know the Carib history and much of the culture, the Carib history taught in the schools is full of stereotypes that hurt their children. Chief Auguiste emphasized the lack of adequate technical and professional training for the community's young adults, especially in the health and nutrition fields.

The community leaders were interested in more specific information about possible solutions to pressing problems. These included: strategies of reforestation and protection of present forests; strategies of evironmental impact assessment; strategies of human and natural resource assessment; strategies to harness the small but steady trickle of tourism that tours through the reserve daily; strategies to project Carib and other Dominican products to new international markets. 'We have good farmers, good basketmakers, some keen businessmen, but we need better organization,' said the chief. 'This is what I want to get out of a strategy session.'

Strategic planning in Dominica, and particularly for the five-by-seven kilometer Carib Reservation, necessarily imposes a scaled-down sense of development. The whole island's population and geographic dimensions are smaller than the average American or Canadian town. This can be a problem, as the small scale creates difficulty for producers looking for international markets, which are set out on mega-numbers and large supply flows. On the other hand, the small scale focus makes problems manageable and solutions are achievable. As Dominica's Prime Minister Eugenia Charles has said: 'If the United States would buy just one in every thousand oranges it imports from Dominica, it would go a long way toward building prosperity on the island.'

The Caribs have a drama and dance troupe called Karifuna, which is the name of their language. In the large community building next to the library, Prosper Paris, a young man with flowing black hair, leads the group. With fourteen members, the group has been together for ten years and has 'graduated' dozens of community youngsters.

'Most of our music and dance, it was almost gone, just as our Carib language is now mostly gone,' Prosper said, with an eye on the stage, where the dancers were rehearsing. 'We started the culture group first to bring back our identity as Indian people. We still fish, make dugout canoe, we can live off of nature— but we still are losing our identity.'

Garnett, a Karifuna founder, stopped by. He said his biggest concern now is to videotape the elders who know skills. 'Just since my childhood, many things you used to see are now gone. Old people die and nobody learns their skills. I want to do something about that.'

Garnett and Prosper, surrounded by the other members, told about their Karifuna tours of Europe and North America. They saw that work as an attempt to cultivate international friendships for their Carib people and for Dominica in general. 'We have a right to fight for our Indian culture. We have the right to recover even the things we have lost. Even our language. In our region and all over the Americas, we should seek each other as Indian peoples, just like the Jewish people do, or the Irish or the Italians or the Galicians or the Arabs.'

They point out that there are several other Carib communities where the traditional Indian culture is more alive—in Belize, in British Guyana, Trinidad and at the Sandy Bay Carib community of nearby St Vincent island. Carib delegates from the various communities have visited each other in recent years and have formed a Caribbean Organization of Indigenous Peoples, with headquarters in Belize. They plan to seek out all Caribbean Indian communities and recognize each other.

In the late afternoon, Napoleon took a couple of us to the 'l'Escallier Tete Chien', or snake's staircase at an ancient place called Sineku, where a lava rock extension in the form of a snake juts out into the deep ocean. A trail through rich woods ends on top of the snake stairs. According to his old people, Napoleon told us, it was here that the Master Snake came out of the ocean and onto the land. 'The old people would come and smoke a pipe, a little white pipe, here. Then they would sleep and the master snake would come out to answer their questions in dreams,' he said.

'When the Caribs disappear, the old people said, the Master Snake has vowed to return to the underbelly of the ocean. And the world will end.'

A Note on Some Native Caribbean Words

Comparatively little is known about the native languages of the Caribbean islands. Europeans encountered a number of related, and probably mutually comprehensible, languages, all of which belonged to what linguists now call the Arawakan family. Certain specialized jargons were also developed, some based on Cariban languages, and used for trade or political contact with the mainland. The major misconception that the inhabitants of the Lesser Antilles spoke 'Carib' was not clarified until relatively recently: 'Island Carib', as their language was called, is an Arawakan language. It survives, inevitably altered, as Garifuna, spoken by the descendants of the Black Caribs transported from St Vincent to Central America in 1797.

From Columbus's first voyage onwards, native words were noted that gradually passed into the European languages: the English words *canoe, hammock, barbecue, hurricane, cannibal, cacique, roucou, cassava* (formerly *cassado* or *cassada* or *cassain*) are all examples of such adoptions. Later travellers sometimes took as native words European terms such as *ananas* (pineapple), *variola* (smallpox), *vins* (feast), and *carbet* (meeting house).

Cannibal is an especially complex term, because it belongs to a whole series of ways in which Columbus and other Spanish travellers transcribed the name of some of the native inhabitants, or the place where they lived. *Cannibal* was eventually hived off in Spanish and English as a general word replacing anthropophagite, leaving *caribe* and its variants to describe the native inhabitants themselves. The long-standing confusion over the nature, language, and provenance of 'the Caribs' is mirrored by the multifarious terms used to describe them. Even within the confines of this anthology there are more than twenty different transcriptions, including *canima, canibal, canybal, caraïbe, caraib, caraibe, carebie, carib, caribb, caribe, caribbee, carribbee, caribbian, carribé, carribee, charaib, charaibe, craib,* and *cribe*. In Raymond Breton's original Latin manuscript (see No. 9), the form *karaib* is also found. A modern variant is the new Kweyol (Creole) spelling *kwaib*. Also used are modern variants on the self-referential term recorded in the seventeenth century by Breton, *callíponam, careepfouna, cariphúna, karifuna.* Carib terms recorded for other groups include *allouague* (for the Lokono of the mainland coast), *balanaéle* (spirits from the sea, meaning the Europeans), and *tamon* (for black slaves).

Columbus records many of the native place-names (see Plate 1). Some Islands, like *Cuba, Haiti,* and *Jamaica,* resisted attempts to rename them. Thousands of native toponyms still survive.

The term *cemi* (also *zemi, zemeen, chemeen*), meaning spirit, is usually associated only with the so-called Taino, but was widely recorded amongst the Caribs as well. Associated terms for the spirit world include *mabouya* (also *mapoia, maboya, maboia*) and *eocheri*. The human mediators with this spirit world were referred to as *boyé* (also *boiyako, bwayé),* and *piaye* (also *piai*).

The persistent interest of the Europeans in the sources of precious metals led to the recording of several native terms such as *tuob, caona, goanin, caracoli, noçay*. However, their referents were not simply 'gold' alone, but more generally reflected the place of 'brilliant metals' in native cosmology. Hence, for example, the terms *goanin* and *caracoli* referred not only to special gold-copper alloys, but also to the mythical sources of these objects. As a result, elements of these words were sometimes incorporated into the honorific titles of powerful chiefs.

References

This list contains details of the books referred to by date only in our introductory sections and captions. For more detailed information see the bibliographies by Sued Badillo 1978*a* and Myers 1981 and 1987.

ALEGRÍA, RICARDO E. (1980), 'Las experiencias de Luisa de Nabarrete, puertorriqueña, entre los indios caribes de La Dominica (1576–1580)', *Revista del Museo de Antropología, Historia y Arte de la Universidad de Puerto Rico*, 2: 39–44.

Archives Nationales, Paris (= ANP).

Archivo General de Indias, Seville (= AGI).

ATWOOD, THOMAS (1791), *The History of the Island of Dominica*, London.

BAKER, PATRICK L. (1988), 'Ethnogenesis: The Case of the Dominica Caribs', *América indígena*, 48/2: 377–401.

BEAUMONT, PHILIPPE DE (1668), *Lettre du Révérend Père Phillippe de Beaumont ... où il est parlé des grands services rendus aux François habitans des Isles Antilles, par les sauvages, Caraibes & insulaires de la Dominique*, Poitiers.

BELL, [HENRY] HESKETH J. (1893), *Obeah: Witchcraft in the West Indies*, 2nd edn., London.

BOROMÉ, JOSEPH A. (1966), 'Spain and Dominica 1493–1647', *Caribbean Quarterly*, 12/4: 30–46.

—— (1967), 'The French and Dominica, 1699–1763', *Jamaican Historical Review*, 7/1–2: 9–39.

BRETON, P. RAYMOND (1665), *Dictionnaire caraïbe–françois*, Auxerre.

BULLEN, RIPLEY (1966), 'The First English Settlement on St Lucia', *Caribbean Quarterly*, 13/2: 29–35.

Calendar of State Papers (1860–1969), *Colonial Series, America and West Indies*, 36 vols., London, HMSO (= CSP).

CÁRDENAS RUÍZ, MANUEL (1981) (ed.), *Crónicas francesas de los indios caribes*, Río Piedras.

CLODORÉ, J. (1671), *Relation de ce qui s'est passé dans les isles & terre firme de l'Amérique, pendant la dernière guerre avec l'Angleterre & depuis en exécution du Traitté de Breda*, 2 vols., Paris.

COKE, THOMAS (1808–11), *A History of the West Indies, Containing the Natural, Civil, and Ecclesiastical History of Each Island*, 3 vols., Liverpool.

CRATON, MICHAEL (1982), *Testing the Chains: Resistance to Slavery in the British West*

Indies, Ithaca, NY.

CRATON, MICHAEL (1986), 'From Caribs to Black Caribs: The Amerindian Roots of Servile Resistance in the Caribbean', in Gary Y. Okihiro (ed.), *In Resistance: Studies in African, Caribbean, and Afro-American History*, Amherst: 96–116.

CROUSE, NELLIS (1940), *French Pioneers in the West Indies, 1624–1664*, New York.

—— (1943), *The French Struggle for the West Indies, 1665–1713*, New York.

DAVIDSON, GEORGE (1787), *The Case of the Caribbs in St Vincent*, ed. Thomas Coke, London.

DUQUE DUQUE, CECILIA (1985), *Consultant Report on the Cultural Revitalization Project in Dominica*, Bogotá.

FERMOR, PATRICK LEIGH (1950), *The Traveller's Tree: A Journey through the Caribbean Islands*, London.

FREDERICK, HILLARY (1982), *The Caribs and Their Colonizers*, London.

FROUDE, JAMES ANTHONY (1887), *The English in the West Indies; or The Bow of Ulysses*, London.

GONZALEZ, NANCIE L. (1988), *Sojourners of the Caribbean: Ethnogenesis and Ethnohistory of the Garifuna*, Urbana, Ill.

GRÉGOIRE, CRISPIN, and KANEM, NATALIA (1989), 'The Caribs of Dominica: Land Rights and Ethnic Consciousness', *Cultural Survival Quarterly*, 13/3: 52–5.

GULLICK, C. J. M. R. (1976), 'The Black Caribs in St Vincent: The Carib War and Its Aftermath', *Actes du XLIIe Congrès international des américanistes*, Paris: vi. 451–65.

—— (1978a), 'The Ecological Background to the Carib Wars', *Journal of Belizean Affairs*, 6: 51–60.

—— (1978b), 'Black Carib Origins and Early Society', in Jean Benoist and Francine-M. Mayer (eds.), *Proceedings of the Seventh International Congress for the Study of the Pre-Columbian Culture of the Lesser Antilles*, Montreal: 283–90.

—— (1985), *Myths of a Minority: The Changing Traditions of the Vincentian Caribs*, Assen.

HAMOT-PÉZERON, SIMONE (1983), 'The Caribs of Dominica, Island in the West Indies', dissertation, Université de la Sorbonne-Nouvelle, Paris III.

HONYCHURCH, LENNOX (1984), *The Dominica Story: A History of the Island*, 2nd edn., Roseau.

HULME, PETER (1986), *Colonial Encounters: Europe and the Native Caribbean 1492–1797*, London.

HUTH, HANS (1962), 'Agostino Brunias, Romano: Robert Adam's "Bred Painter"', *Connoisseur*, 151: 264–9.

KIRBY, I. EARLE, and MARTIN, C. I. (1986), *The Rise and Fall of the Black Caribs*, 2nd edn., Kingstown, St Vincent.

LABAT, JEAN BAPTISTE (1724), *Nouveau Voyage aux isles de l'Amérique*, 2 vols., The Hague.

—— (1931), *The Memoirs of Père Labat 1693–1705*, trans. and abridged by John Eaden, London.

LAYNG, ANTHONY (1979–80), 'Ethnic Identity on a West Indian Reservation', *Revista/Review interamericana*, 9/4: 577–84.

—— (1983), *The Carib Reserve: Identity and Security in the West Indies*, Washington, DC.

—— (1985), 'The Caribs of Dominica', *Ethnic Groups*, 6/2–3: 209–21.

MACKENZIE, Chief TOM, and LOGAN, BILL (n.d.), *Caribbean Report: Recommendations for Training and Education for Indigenous Communities and Organizations in the Countries of Dominica, St Vincent and Belize*, Regina, Saskatchewan [1985].

MARSHALL, BERNARD (1973), 'The Black Caribs: Native Resistance to British Penetration into the Windward Side of St Vincent 1763–1773', *Caribbean Quarterly*, 19: 4–19.

MAYER, ENRIQUE (1982), *The Carib Reserve in Dominica: Integrated Rural Development Project Supplementary Report*, OAS, Department of Social Affairs, Washington, DC.

MONDESIRE, ALICIA, and ROBINSON, NELCIA (1987) (eds.), *Report on Conference of Indigenous Peoples: Caribbean Indigenous Revival*, Kingstown, St Vincent.

MYERS, ROBERT (1981), *Amerindians of the Lesser Antilles: A Bibliography*, Human Relations Area Files, New Haven, Conn.

—— (1984), 'Island Carib Cannibalism', *Nieuwe West-Indische Gids*, 58: 147–84.

—— (1987), *Dominica*, World Bibliographica Series vol. 82, Oxford.

NAGY, ADAM S. (1982–3), 'Las rutas del comercio prehispánico de las metales', *Cuadernos prehispánicos*, 10: 5–132.

OBER, FREDERICK A. (1893), *In the Wake of Columbus: Adventures of a Special Commissioner Sent by World's Columbian Exposition to the West Indies*, Boston.

—— (1904), *Our West Indian Neighbours*, New York.

—— (1908), *Guide to the West Indies*, New York.

OWEN, NANCY H. (1975), 'Land, Politics, and Ethnicity in a Carib Indian Community', *Ethnology*, 14: 385–93.

—— (1980), 'Conflict and Ethnic Boundaries: A Study of Carib/Black Relations', *Social and Economic Studies*, 29/2–3: 264–74.

RAT, JOSEPH NUMA (1897), 'The Carib Language, as now Spoken in Dominica, West Indies', *Journal of the Anthropological Institute*, 27: 293–315.

RENNARD, P. JOSEPH (1929), *Les Caraïbes: La Guadeloupe 1635–1656: Histoire des vingt premières années de la colonisation de la Guadeloupe d'après les relations du R.P. Breton*, Paris.

—— (1954), *Histoire religieuse des Antilles françaises des origines à 1914*, Paris.

ROUSE, IRVING (1948a), 'The Arawak', in J. H. Steward (ed.), *Handbook of South American Indians*, Washington, DC: iv. 507–46.

—— (1948b), 'The Carib', in J. H. Steward (ed.), *Handbook of South American Indians*, Washington, DC: iv. 547–65.

—— (1986), 'The Tainos', in his *Migrations in Prehistory: Inferring Population Movement from Cultural Remains*, New Haven, Conn. 106–56.

ROUSSEAU, JEAN-JACQUES (1973), *The Social Contract and Discourses*, trans. G. D. H. Cole, rev. J. H. Brumfitt and John C. Hall, London.

SAUER, CARL ORTWIN (1966), *The Early Spanish Main*, Berkeley, Calif.

SOUTHEY, THOMAS (1827), *A Chronological History of the West Indies*, 3 vols., London.

SUED BADILLO, JALIL (1978a), *Bibliografía antropológica para el estudio de las culturas indígenas del Caribe*, Santo Domingo.

—— (1978b), *Los Caribes: Realidad o fábula?*, Río Piedras.

TAYLOR, DOUGLAS (1938), 'The Caribs of Dominica', *Bureau of American Ethnology, Bulletin 119*, Anthropological Papers No. 3, Washington, DC.

—— (1954), 'Diachronic Note on the Carib Contribution to Island Carib', *International Journal of American Linguistics*, 20: 28–33.

—— (1977), *Languages of the West Indies*, Baltimore.

TROLLOPE, ANTHONY (1860), *The West Indies and the Spanish Main*, London.

TYLER, S. LYMAN (1988) (ed.), *Two Worlds: The Indian Encounter with the European, 1492–1509*, Salt Lake City.

REFERENCES

WARNER, AUCHER (1973), *Sir Thomas Warner: Pioneer of the West Indies: A Chronicle of His Family*, London.

WAUGH, ALEC (1958), *The Sugar Islands*, London.

WHITEHEAD, NEIL L. (1988), *Lords of the Tiger Spirit: A History of the Caribs in Colonial Venezuela and Guyana 1498–1820*, Dordrecht.

—— (1990*a*), 'Carib Ethnic Soldiering in Venezuela, the Guianas, and the Antilles, 1492–1820', *Ethnohistory*, 37: 357–85.

—— (1990*b*), 'The Mazaruni Pectoral: A Golden Artefact discovered in Guyana and the Historical Sources Concerning Native Metallurgy in the Caribbean, Orinoco and Northern Amazonia', *Journal of Archaeology and Anthropology*, 7: 19–38.

YOUNG, EVERILD, and HELWEG-LARSEN, KJELD (1965), *The Pirate's Priest: The Life of Père Labat in the West Indies, 1693–1705*, London.

Sources of Extracts

1. Columbus's *Letter* first appeared in Seville in March 1493 in Spanish, and was then translated and published throughout Europe. There are many editions and translations. Our translation is based on the transcription in Cristóbal Colón, *Textos y documentos completos*, ed. Consuelo Varela (Alianza: Madrid, 1984).

2. Columbus's *Journal* (in Las Casas's abstract) was first published in Madrid in 1867. There is a good full transcription and English translation of the *Journal: The* Diario *of Christopher Columbus's First Voyage to America*, ed. Oliver Dunn and James E. Kelley, Jr. (University of Oklahoma Press: Norman, Okla., (1989). Our translation is based on their transcription.

3. A copy of Dr Chanca's report was discovered in a monastery and is now in the library of the Royal Academy of History in Madrid. The best recent edition in Spanish is in *Cartas de particulares a Colón y relaciones coetáneos*, ed. Juan Gil and Consuelo Varela (Alianza: Madrid, 1984).

4. The testimonies of Luisa de Navarrete and Pedro the 'caribe' are in the Archivo General de Indias (Seville), Patronato 179, ramo 1, No. 4, fos. 9–11, 28–9.

5. The 1564 Hawkins extracts are taken from Richard Hakluyt, *The Principal Navigations, Voyages, Traffiques, & Discoveries of the English Nation* (1598–1600), 10 vols. (J. M. Dent: London, 1927–8), vii. 20, 23–4, 29; Laudonnière ibid. x. 42–4; the two Drake pieces ibid. vii. 87–8, and Mary Frear Keeler, *Sir Francis Drake's West Indian Voyage 1585–6* (Hakluyt Society, 2nd ser. 148: London, 1981), 191–3 (reproduced by permission of the Hakluyt Society); White from Hakluyt, *Principal Navigations*, vi. 214–15; Preston ibid. vii. 174; the 1595 Hawkins piece ibid. vii. 185; Keymis ibid. vii. 383–4; Cumberland from Samuel Purchas, *Purchas His Pilgrimes* (1625), 20 vols. (James MacLehose: Glasgow, 1905–7), xvi. 52–6.

6. William Turner's account was excerpted by Samuel Purchas, *Purchas His Pilgrimes* (1625), 20 vols. (James MacLehose: Glasgow, 1905–7), xvi. 352–4. John Nicholl's account is from his *An Houre Glasse of Indian Newes, or A True and Tragicall Discourse, Shewing the most Lamentable Miseries, and Distressed Calamities Indured by 67 Englishmen, which were Sent for a Supply to the Planting in Guiana in the Yeare. 1605* (Nathaniell Butter: London, 1607), pp. B^r–D3^v.

7. From Thomas Gage, *A New Survey of the West Indies* (1648), 2nd edn. (J. Sweeting, London: 1655), 16–19.

8. The first extract about Indian Warner is taken from William Dampier, *A New Voyage*

361

Round the World, 4th edn., 4 vols. (James Knapton: London, 1699–1709), ii. 5–6; the second and third from Jean Baptiste du Tertre, *Histoire générale des Antilles habitées par les François*, 4 vols. (Thomas Jolly: Paris, 1667–71), i. 82–5 and iv. 66–9; and the fourth, the 1676 'Remonstrance' of the Antiguan colonists, is reprinted from *Calendar of State Papers*, Colonial Series: America and West Indies, for the years 1675–6, 325. The remaining extracts, bar the last, are drawn from two volumes of the same series of the *Calendar of State Papers*, for the years 1661–8 and 1669–74: the originals which they summarize are in the Public Record Office, Kew, under CO 1/22, CO 1/31, CO 1/34, CO 324/110, CO 1/35, and CO 1/37. The final extract is taken from Jean Baptiste Labat, *Nouveau Voyage aux isles de l'Amérique*, 2 vols. (P. Husson *et al.*: The Hague, 1724), ii. 100–1.

9. The Breton piece is translated from P. Joseph Rennard, *Les Caraïbes: La Guadeloupe 1635–1656: Histoire des vingt premières années de la colonisation de la Guadeloupe d'après les relations du R.P. Breton* (G. Ficker: Paris, 1929), 46–9, 57–61, 71–4.

10. From Charles de Rochefort, *Histoire naturelle et morale des Îles Antilles de l'Amérique* (1658), 2nd edn. (Arnour Leers: Rotterdam, 1665), in the translation published as John Davies of Kidwelly, *The History of the Caribby-Islands* (O.M. for T. Dring and J. Starkey: London, 1666), 259–65, 313–17.

11. From Jean Baptiste du Tertre, *Histoire générale des Antilles habitées par les François*, 4 vols. (Thomas Jolly: Paris, 1667–71), ii. 356–9, 383–6, 413–19.

12. Jean Baptiste Labat, *Nouveau Voyage aux isles de l'Amérique*, 2 vols. (P. Husson *et al.*: The Hague, 1724), i. 27–32, ii. 105–11.

13. From Sieur de la Borde, *Relation des Caraïbes sauvages des Isles Antilles de l'Amérique* (Louis Billaine: Paris, 1674), 3–15, 26–32, 39–40.

14. The first two extracts are translated from documents in the Archives Nationales, Paris: Colonies C8–a, 12: fos. 102–5 and Colonies C10–a, 1, No. 98, 3 Sept. 1705; the third is from Nathaniel Uring, *A History of the Voyages and Travels of Nathaniel Uring* (J. Peele: London, 1726), 104–9.

15. From the Joseph Senhouse papers in the Cumbria Record Office (Carlisle). Reproduced from the *Journal of the Barbados Museum and Historical Society*, 37 (1985), 279–85, with the permission of the Cumbria Record Office, James C. Brandow, and the Barbados Museum and Historical Society.

16. From Thomas Coke, *Some Accounts of the Late Missionaries to the West Indies in Two Letters from the Rev. Dr. Coke, to the Rev. J. Wesley* (n.p.: London, 1789) 8–12.

17. From [Sir William Young], *An Account of the Black Charaibs in the Island of St Vincent's* (J. Sewell and Knight & Triphook: London, 1795), *passim*.

18. From Sir William Young, *A Tour through the Several Islands of Barbadoes, St Vincent, Antigua, Tobago, and Grenada, in the Years 1791, and 1792* (1792), vol. iii of Bryan Edwards's *History of the British Colonies in the West Indies* (John Stockdale: London, 1801), 260–301 *passim*.

19. From Alexander Anderson, *Geography and History of St Vincent*, ed. and transcribed by Richard A. and Elizabeth S. Howard (The Arnold Arboretum: Cambridge, Mass., 1983), 57–61, 78–84, 86–98. Reproduced with the permission of the publishers and of The Linnean Society of London.

20. (1) From Father du Lettré, 'Rapport adressé à Monseigneur l'Évêque de Roseau sur l'état de la religion dans le quartier méthodiste de la paroisse de Saint-André, Dominique' [1856], 2–3. Archive of the Bishop's House, Roseau, Dominica. Reproduced in the editors' translation with the permission of the bishop of Roseau. (2)

Father Clément-Désiré Ardois, Letter to the Father Superior of the Eudist Order, 23 March 1864, Archive of the Eudistes, Paris (ref. N86). (3) From [Robert G. C. Hamilton], *Report of the Commission (Appointed in September 1893) to Inquire into the Condition and Affairs of the Island of Dominica* (HMSO: London, 1894), 91 and 117. (4) From Father René Suaudeau, *Au pays des Caraïbes: Lettres d'un missionnaire pendant son séjour dans l'île de la Dominique (Antilles anglaises)* (Des Presses de l'Imprimerie Fontenaisienne: Fontenay-le-Comte, 1927), 51–3.

21. From Frederick A. Ober, *Camps in the Caribbees: The Adventures of a Naturalist in the Lesser Antilles* (David Douglas: Edinburgh, 1880), 73–83, 95–9, 208–24.

22. (1) From [Henry Hesketh Bell], *Report on the Caribs of Dominica*, Colonial Reports: Miscellaneous, No. 21 (HMSO: London, 1902), 3–4, 6, 8–11, 12–16. (2) From Henry Hesketh Bell, *Glimpses of a Governor's Life: From Diaries, Letters and Memoranda* (Sampson Low, Marston & Co.: London, n.d. [1946]), 14–21.

23. From Sir Frederick Treves, *The Cradle of the Deep: An Account of a Voyage to the West Indies* (Smith, Elder, & Co.: London, 1910), 168–74.

24. From [J. Stanley Rae and Sydney A. Armitage-Smith], *Conditions in the Carib Reserve, and the Disturbance of 19th September, 1930, Dominica*, Colonial Office Report (HMSO: London, 1932), 2–3, 8–10, 13–17, 22–9.

25. From Jean Rhys, 'Temps Perdi', © Jean Rhys 1969. Reproduced with the permission of the Jean Rhys Estate. The full story is available in Jean Rhys, *The Collected Short Stories* (W. W. Norton & Co.: New York 1987).

26. Douglas Taylor, 'Columbus Saw Them First', *Natural History*, 48 (June 1941), 40–9. Reproduced with permission from *Natural History*, June 1941; © the American Museum of Natural History, 1941.

27. Elma Napier, 'History in the Movie-Making', *Strand Magazine*, 117 (July 1949), 40–4. Reproduced with the permission of the author's literary executors.

28. Patrick Leigh Fermor, 'The Caribs of Dominica', *Geographical Magazine*, 26/6 (1950), 256–64. Reproduced with the permission of the author.

29. Alan Whicker, *Whicker's World*, BBC Television 1964. Reproduced with permission of Alan Whicker and of the BBC.

30. Anthony Weller, 'Conquerors of the Caribbean', *Geo*, 5 (Apr. 1983), 68–76, 102, 105–6. (Efforts to trace Anthony Weller and the publishers of *Geo* have not been successful.)

31. José Barreiro, 'Carib Gallery', *Northeast Indian Quarterly*, 7/3 (1990), 47–55. Reproduced with the permission of the author.

Index

Topographical references are gathered under the modern name for island or country except in cases where identification is unclear.

DATE DUE